Computer Networks
and
Their Protocols

WILEY SERIES IN COMPUTING

Consulting Editor
Professor D. W. Barron, *Department of Mathematics, Southampton University*

Numerical Control—Mathematics and Applications
P. Bézier

Communication Networks for Computers
D. W. Davies and D. L. A. Barber

Macro Processors and Techniques for Portable Software
P. J. Brown

A Practical Guide to Algol 68
Frank G. Pagan

Programs and Machines
Richard Bird

The Codasyl Approach to Data Base Management
T. William Olle

Computer Networks and their Protocols
D. W. Davies, D. L. A. Barber, W. L. Price and C. M. Solomonides

Algorithms: Their Complexity and Efficiency
Lydia Kronsjö

Data Structures and Operating Systems
Teodor Rus

Computer Networks
and
Their Protocols

D.W. Davies

National Physical Laboratory, Teddington

D.L.A. Barber

Director, European Informatics Network

W.L. Price and C.M. Solomonides

National Physical Laboratory, Teddington

A Wiley–Interscience Publication

JOHN WILEY & SONS
Chichester · New York · Brisbane · Toronto

Library of Congress Cataloging in Publication Data:

Main entry under title:

Computer networks and their protocols.

'A Wiley–Interscience publication.'
Includes bibliographical references and index.
1. Computer networks. I. Davies, Donald Watts.
TK5105.5.C6492   001.6.44.04   78-21973

ISBN 0 471 99750 1

Contents

Preface

Computer networks are derived from a combination of computers and telecommunications—two technologies with very different histories and traditions. Before computers, machines of very great organisational complexity had been produced for automatic telephone switching. Then in the mid-twentieth century, there were two rapid changes. Organisational complexity leaped ahead with the concepts of the stored program and of programming languages while solid-state electronics set in motion a rapid improvement in the speed and cost of digital processing which still continues. The concepts and the techniques which the computer stimulated were found to apply just as effectively to telecommunications.

We now have a *technological* convergence of computers and telecommunications, both sharing the same kind of logic, storage, switching and transmission. Convergence has another meaning, because information handling systems now employ telecommunications and information-processing in such an intimate mixture that we find it difficult to say what is processing and what is communication. This convergence of *systems* is the theme of our book. The new network concept, which takes us beyond programming languages, is that of a formalised protocol governing the interaction of systems.

The rapid growth of the technology is remarkable enough—its potential for changing human society is even more significant. There is a general belief that in the advanced countries we are leaving the era of the industrial society and entering the age of the 'information society' in which manufacture, though still vital, is no longer the central feature of the economy. This is like the way that manufacture itself overtook farming, though the production of food remains essential.

The railways came with the industrial revolution to move fuel and goods, and later to carry people. Computer networks have arrived early in the second 'revolution' to move information and to reduce the effect of distance. Networks may have begun as extensions of computers but perhaps, like the railways, a large part of their use will be to serve human communication. They are part of the essential infrastructure of the post-industrial world.

xiii

Information technology is not new. It began with natural language, so far back in time that a mechanism for handling the syntax of natural language seems to be 'hardwired' in the human brain. Writing and printing were the first elaborate forms of information storage and replication. The pace of development has been increasing with the telegraph, the telephone, facsimile transmission and xerography adding to our range of information handling tools. Modern information technology is coming to terms with natural language in the forms of writing, printing, and speech. In this way the computer network can be seen as one recent step in a long process of evolution of man's ability to use information.

Computer networks are part of a general trend towards distributed computing which can be seen in multicomputer systems, in distributed data bases and in the use of intelligent terminals. The rapidly decreasing cost of processors removed the need to concentrate computing power and gave the economic incentive for distributed computing. This new flexibility in system design enables the functions of a complex system to be divided physically as well as logically. A computer network connects terminals, computers, databases etc. at a distance one from another. The communication function has inherent limitations, such as delay, throughput restriction, errors and breakdowns. We are therefore concerned, in this book, with multicomputer systems which can operate satisfactorily in this harsh environment.

Chapter 1 gives a general introduction to computer networks. This is followed by the two main sections of the book dealing respectively with the communication subsystem and the protocols by which computers and terminals interact through this subsystem. Packet switching is the subject of Chapter 2 and the following two chapters treat the routing of packets to their destinations and the methods by which flow is controlled and congestion avoided. This section of the book is completed by Chapter 5 on packet broadcast systems, which are growing in importance, from local to global networks.

The concept which has dominated the later development of networks is that of a protocol—a formal procedure for interaction. This is the theme of the second section, comprising three chapters. Chapter 6 takes the subject of communication protocols up to the 'high-level data link control procedures' and the X25 interface, both of which are international standards. In Chapter 7, protocols from the transport service upwards are described, while Chapter 8 deals with the complex matter of terminal procedures and standards.

The final two chapters address the security of data in networks and the optimisation of network design. There follows a glossary giving brief definitions of some 150 technical terms used in the book.

Network research in our Laboratory began in 1966. Some of the ideas we describe originated in this early work and we owe a great debt to our friends in the team. A similar debt is owed to the international community in which all the ideas have been cast around, thus acquiring some polish and precision.

Particularly we want to mention our close interaction with the ARPA network project, the Cyclades project and the European Informatics Network. We could not mention by name all the people in this lively community and it seems better not to single out a few. The references in the text give some idea of the contributors and the community gets larger all the time. We shall have achieved our aim if this book introduces many more people to the fascinating subject of computer networks and their protocols.

Chapter 1

Computer Networks

1.1 COMPUTER NETWORKS AND THEIR SUBSYSTEMS

When the cost of a processor dominated the thinking of system designers it was natural to regard a computer as the centre of a system, to which all data and all requests would come. At first this meant the physical transport of data on cards or tape to the computer room from the outside world, whence the information came and to which the results went in voluminous tabulations. This approach to computing can still be seen in operation. Its faults were the remoteness of the system from the user and the concentration of system design into one unit. The remoteness, for example, meant that dealing with errors and exceptions accounted for a large part of the system. They had to be handled without any recourse to the absent user. The concentration meant that all the parts of the system could interact without an overall discipline and the system could easily become untidy and unmanageable.

Remoteness was the first problem to be overcome and the first steps, leading to the first computer network, seemed easy. Some computer terminals were teleprinters and these could be moved to distant locations and connected, by telex lines or modems and telephone lines. This began to happen as soon as multi-access or 'time-sharing'—the dividing of the power of one processor between many almost independent users—had been achieved. It formed the earliest kind of network and gave remote access to a central computer. The simplest view of a computer network is still that it provides remote access.

Such a network is centred around one computer and in the early networks the computer provided a single function, such as accounting for banks or seat reservation for airlines. Since all the communication lines came to the centre they were connected like a star. These centralised systems were found to be inflexible when their owners tried to add new functions or operate more than one central computer to provide the services. Centralisation had the unfortunate effect of combining all the various functions in the system. Transaction processing and communication tasks were mixed and the details of design obscured the boundary between these functions.

The computer networks which are the subject of this book are not merely 'access networks' nor do they serve one central computer system. A typical network now provides many different functions. A request from a user can trigger off a chain of messages through the network. For example, the user might be interacting with a computer-aided design system which, for some of its calculations, requests data from a distant data bank. Examples of interaction between computers in a network are not yet commonplace but become more important as networks enter into commercial and business life.

Modern networks tend to be heterogeneous, using computers and terminals from many manufacturers. Unfortunately, no single standard governs their interfaces, formats and procedures. By itself, this would prevent any useful interaction in a network, so a large part of network design is concerned with formalising the ways in which its various active components will interact.

In any complex system design problem the first and critical step is to break down the system into subsystems which can be designed separately. Success depends on the right choice of functions for these subsystems in order to minimise the complexity of the interface. In computer networks, one major division is recognised, and this is the separation of the various computer services and terminals that have a well-defined communication subsystem.

The Communication Subsystem

Figure 1.1 shows how a computer network can be subdivided into a number of separate units all joined together by a common communications subsystem.

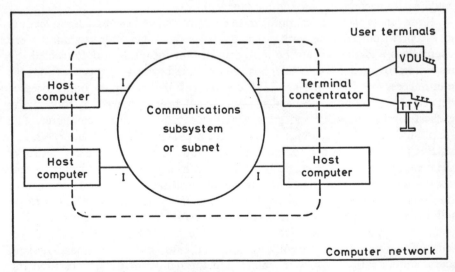

Figure 1.1   Separation of the communication subnet

The network includes computers which provide the services (computing, information, transactions, storage of data) as well as terminals for the users of the network and concentrators to join a group of users' terminals into the communication subsystem.

Because of their origin in the fusion of computer and communication technologies, when we talk about computer networks there are some words which can have different meanings according to whether one's viewpoint is computer or communications oriented. The first word to give trouble is *network* itself. We shall regard a computer network as containing all that is needed to provide a complex of different services to many different terminals. Within this we have a communication network and, when a distinction is needed, we shall refer to this as a communication subsystem or *subnet*.

From the communications point of view, everything attached to the subnet is a 'terminal'. Computer people usually reserve the word 'terminal' for those peripherals, such as display units and teletypes, which form the human interface to the system. Where there is any doubt we may refer to things connected to the subnet as *subscribers* by analogy with the customers of the telephone service. We may also use the word *terminal* when the meaning is clear.

Computers attached to the subnet are often called *host computers* or *hosts* which is a word derived from the ARPA network. The word probably derived from the idea that the main computer on a site acted as a 'host' to the communications network also installed there. The term 'host' has stuck and is in wide use. A host usually provides a service to the rest of the network but it can also use services from other hosts.

The design of the subnet could be greatly simplified by providing it with only one kind of standard interface to its terminals or subscribers and this would be, in the case of a host computer, a multiplexed interface allowing a number of conversations to take place at once. Networks like Cyclades and the European Informatics Network have been designed on this principle. Figure 1.1 shows a subnet with one standard kind of interface, labelled I. It is very different from the interface of a teletype or a visual display unit (VDU) without any built-in processor. Such terminals simply send and receive a stream of octets. Since they cannot use the subnet's standard interface a group of these simple terminals can be provided with a 'terminal concentrator', an intelligent device that can manage the standard interface. But some subnets, particularly public data networks, have a variety of interfaces, not only for hosts but also for many types of simple terminal. These subnets can be regarded as including their own terminal concentrators.

The separation of a network into a subnet and its subscribers depends on defining precisely the functions of the subnet. In practice, there is no single answer to the question 'what is a communication function and should therefore be in the subnet?'. These differing views have been the cause of most of the controversies in network design. For example, if the subnet handles messages, should it be able to replicate a message and send copies to several destinations or should this message replication be handled outside the subnet?

It is therefore an oversimplification to say that all communication functions must be in the subnet. Nevertheless the subnet should contain all those communication functions which are essential, such as overcoming line errors by retransmission or bypassing failed parts of the network by rerouting traffic. We shall later find that some communication functions inside the host computers can improve the reliability. Then we have a further 'standard communication interface' defined inside the host computers, as Figure 1.1 shows by the broken line.

Before public data networks existed, private networks using leased circuits derived from a public network were the general rule. These gave us many versions of the subnet functions. Public networks have introduced standards but computer manufacturers at the same time produced proprietary systems which were designed to differ.

1.2 NETWORK PROTOCOLS

All communication is governed by rules of procedure. The most useful kind of communication, whether between people or machines, is a two-way interaction rather·than a monologue, yet programming languages chiefly serve for monologues. Conversation cannot avoid having procedural rules to determine when the listener may speak again, what to do if the message is not understood, and so forth. Between people these rules are informal, but subtle and complex. Between computers they are formal, and probably relatively simple and crude. Because of the need for precision and formality, very difficult problems arise in designing, testing and verifying the correctness of protocols for use in computer networks. These are the subject of later chapters in this book.

A formal protocol is involved in the interaction between a person and an information handling system (such as a computer or network). It is a formal protocol because it must be fully designed on the machine side of the interface. If it is well designed it will be easy for the person to understand. As the functions of networks become more complex the need for a better understanding of the human interface is increasing. In this book we shall mainly be concerned with the protocols in networks which govern the way in which users' terminals interact with host computers and host computers interact with each other.

Protocols and Interfaces

Protocols are related to an earlier concept, the interface. When systems became so complex that it was necessary to break them down into subsystems, the interaction between the subsystems had to be defined very carefully. The boundary across which the interaction took place was the 'interface'. The designers operating on either side of the interface needed to know precisely what interaction was expected, so a formal interface definition was produced. Note that an interface is not a piece of equipment but a boundary across which the interaction is defined.

Its definition is rather like that of a language. First we must know what kinds of signals can pass across the boundary. The form of the connector and the levels and significance of the signals are defined. They might, for example, consist of a stream of binary digits in either direction. Then we need to know more about the meaning of these signals and this can require several levels of definition. For example, a convention may be established which breaks the strings of digits into blocks so that each block has some significance as a message. The format of the blocks is defined and the meaning of certain messages laid down. Then a procedure defines the responses which are expected to the various messages or stimuli which pass across the boundary. If the responses were defined in full for every circumstance, once the interface was established its behaviour would be fixed and it would perform no useful function, so there is always a degree of flexible behaviour and usually a class of messages for which the meaning is undefined. These are the messages which really carry information across the boundary.

The protocols which are important in networks operate between distant parts of the system, making use of the network's ability to carry messages. We have seen that an interface can have similar procedural rules based on a means of communication which is part of the interface definition. The essential difference is that an interface is defined locally but a typical protocol defines an interaction between non-adjacent subsystems.

Hierarchies of Protocols

Figure 1.2 shows schematically how the protocols operating in a network are related. Below the subscriber interface is the communications subsystem and attached to it above the line are two host computers. Taking the subsystem first, protocols exist here to carry messages over the transmission lines between switching centres and there may also be end-to-end protocols inside the subnet. Across the subscriber interface there will usually be a link protocol which is designed to carry messages across this interface without error. There may be a further protocol across this interface for interaction between the host computers and the network itself, such as setting up a call.

The purpose of these protocols in the subnet and across the subscriber interface is to provide the means to carry messages reliably between host computers. In order to organise this message-carrying facility in a standard way it is convenient to have a 'basic transport protocol' established between the hosts. This is shown in the figure as though it took place between two boxes, each forming part of a host. The boxes represent 'protocol mechanisms' which are built into the software of the hosts. The earliest of these basic protocols was the ARPA network's 'host-to-host' protocol.

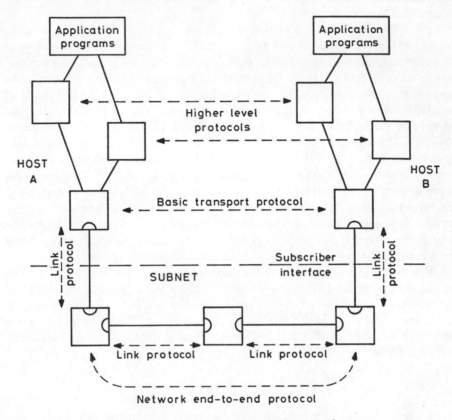

Figure 1.2   Inter-related network protocols

From one point of view, the communication subsystem includes the basic protocol and enables the upper part of the figure to base all its operations on an identical and convenient interface to the basic protocol mechanism. Using the transport facility which this protocol provides, higher-level protocols can be established and these are shown as operating between the parts of the host software which implement them, though, of course, they actually operate by sending messages down through all the mechanisms shown below.

At the top of the figure are application programs written by the users of the network and employing facilities which are provided by the higher-level protocols. Users anywhere in the network, with different kinds of computer, all employ these same higher-level protocols and basic transport protocol.

Some of these protocols are described in later chapters. We shall return, later in this chapter, to the subject of the user's view of the computer network. In the next section we look at some of the forms which the communication subsystem can take.

1.3 FORMS OF SUBNETWORK

The communication subnet is treated in the following four chapters of this book, with an emphasis on packet-switched networks. Let us briefly consider some of the alternative forms of subnet, first their geography, then their data transmission technology and finally the alternative switching and multiplexing methods.

The most obvious way in which the subnets can differ is in their geographical aspect—the way in which the terminals or switching centres are joined together by communication links. This is usually called the topology of the network. Some representative topologies are shown in Figure 1.3 using for the example a set of six points which represent terminal locations.

The first form shown is the *star* in which a centre is chosen and connected to each of the terminals. In this case the centre has been placed roughly at the 'centre of mass' of the network. The total length of transmission path scaled for our figure is 116 mm. With the same centre, the *tree* network allows lines to merge at intermediate terminals and this gives a transmission path length of 83

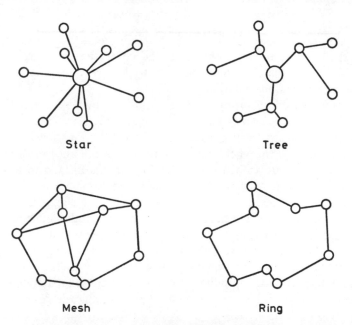

Star

Tree

Mesh

Ring

Figure 1.3   Forms of network connection

mm which is the smallest total for any of the layouts. Indeed, there is a 'minimum spanning tree' for any given set of points which reduces the total path length to its smallest possible value.

The third example is a *mesh* and this is the form most often found in public data communication networks and also in some modern private networks. The path length is much greater, 168 mm, but it provides alternative paths between the points. The fourth of our examples is a *ring* network. With a line length of 98 mm it is, of course, less economic than the tree but it proves better than the star network and, with appropriate methods for routing data either way round the ring, it can have better availability. In practice, the ring configuration is more often found in a local network.

Each of these topologies assumes that the nodes or terminals are connected by point-to-point links. Radio systems, on the other hand, can operate in a 'broadcast' mode and this enables networks to be designed without fixed topologies. With mobile terminals the connections available between radio stations could change at any time. Some radio systems employ a central station which communicates with all terminals and so have a kind of star topology. Others use a satellite relay station to provide links between any two ground stations. These broadcast systems are the subject of Chapter 5.

We return to the subject of network topology in Chapter 3 in connection with routing of packets and in Chapter 10, where the optimisation of topology is described.

Transmission Technology

We shall not attempt, in this book, to cover the very large subject of transmission technology, but some pointers to the direction of development are useful as background information.

The traditional forms of telephone transmission by wire, coaxial cable and radio employ analogue channels in which the amplifiers are made as linear and the circuits are as noisefree as possible. The difficulty is that noise and distortion accumulates through the whole path of a telephone call and very strict control is needed so that switches can connect many circuits in tandem to connect a call. This is one of the reasons that telephone transmission is gradually moving towards digital methods, even though the data rate of a single voice channel is 64 kbit/s. This rate is made necessary by the bandwidth of telephone speech which is 4 kHz and the sampling theorem which requires that the waveform be sampled at 8000 times per second in order to reconstruct it unambiguously. Each sample has 8 bits of information to represent the analogue waveform (in logarithmic form) and this produces the digital channel capacity of 64 kbit/s. This representation of a voice signal by digital samples is called *pulse code modulation* or PCM.

To carry digital signals through the analogue telephone network they must be transformed into a waveform suitable for the transmission channel. At the receiving end the waveform must be interpreted back to digital form. These are the tasks of the *modems* at each end of the line. The operation of the modems must be designed to withstand the accumulated noise and distortion of the analogue telephone line.

In the design of a *digital* transmission system this constraint can be removed because the distorted signal is *regenerated* at many points on the transmission path. By regeneration we mean restoring the waveform to a satisfactory shape, both in time and amplitude. The regenerators are placed so that the recognition of 0 and 1 signals is almost error-free, with an error rate in the region of 10^{-7} or 10^{-8}. Regenerators remove noise and distortion completely at the cost of this small error rate. With the ability to place regenerators wherever necessary, digital transmission can operate at the speed needed to carry voice in coded form.

Digital transmission is a feature of nearly all the recently developed transmission media. Even the traditional forms of transmission path which are wire pairs, coaxial cables and microwave radio are being modified and adapted for digital transmission. In this way, advanced countries have already installed a large amount of digital transmission equipment and can build transmission networks for data based entirely on this mode of operation.

The newer transmission technologies are satellite relay, waveguide and glass fibres. Each of these has been designed for digital transmission almost from the start.

Because the majority of communication traffic consists of telephone signals, the economics of installing new transmission facilities is governed by telephone costs. Digital transmission is therefore installed when it proves economic for carrying the 64 kbit/s streams in competition with analogue voice channels. For data transmission this should mean that the wider use of digital methods greatly reduces the cost of lines, as well as improving their reliability and error characteristics. This is very welcome, but unfortunately the economic dominance of the telephone system operates against the interests of data users in some countries. We can hope for a time when transmission costs in well-designed data networks are very low indeed but in many countries this will be several years in the future.

Analogue transmission over long distances employs high bandwidth lines with channels formed by frequency division multiplexing a large number of telephone channels. In a similar way the long-distance digital transmissions operate at a high digit rate and the signals are formed by time division multiplexing of large numbers of telephone channels. The starting point is a multiplexed group of either 24 or 30 PCM telephone channels.

There are two multiplexing schemes in wide use which can be called, from their place of origin, the 'North American' and the 'European' schemes. Figure 1.4 shows the digit rates which are used in these multiplexing schemes. Each channel contains slightly more than the total digit rates of the channels which it combines because of the need for extra pulses for framing and alarms. The European scheme shows a constant multiplexing factor of 4, starting from the primary group. The US multiplexing scheme has the factors 4, 7 and 6. In addition to multiplexed PCM channels the digital channels will carry data and, in pulse-coded form, picturephone, television channels and higher levels of the analogue hierarchy. None of these other uses of the hierarchy are yet fully standardised because of continuing development.

Switching and Multiplexing by Circuits and Packets

The communication subsystems of computer networks are either packet-switched or circuit-switched. This book treats the packet-switched subnet in detail but in this section we refer to both.

Circuit switching is familiar in the telephone network. A circuit is a two-way path for carrying information and it has no storage associated with it except that which is implied by the inherent transit delay. Therefore, the stream of bits passing into a circuit emerges from the other end with the same time pattern delayed by a constant interval. This is analogous to the way that an incompressible fluid passes through a pipe. There is no built-in control of the flow, therefore, if the receiver cannot handle the incoming bits, they are lost. This trouble can be avoided by the procedures operating between the two ends of a circuit but the circuit itself takes no part in such flow control.

Although circuits may be handled in a multiplexed form within the network, to the user of the communication system they are individual circuits and operate quite independently.

Levels of the hierarchy

	1		2		3		4	
Telephone PCM Channels	24	30	96	120	480	672	1920	4032
Europe (CCITT) Mbit/s	2·048		8·448		39·368		139·264	
North America Mbit/s	1·544		6·312			44·736		274·176

| Wire pairs |
| Coaxial 2·8mm |
| Coaxial 4·4mm |
| Coaxial 9·5mm |

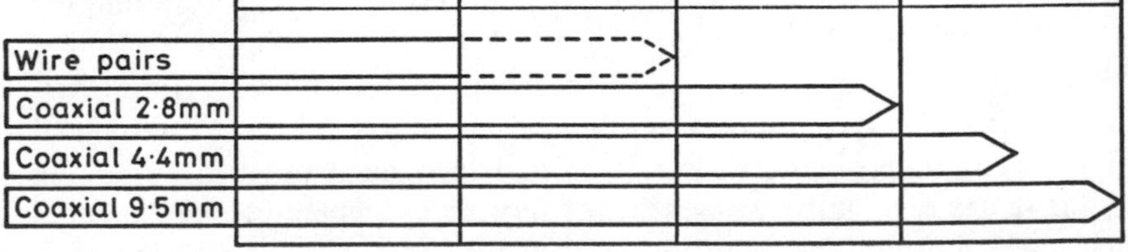

Figure 1.4   The digital transmission multiplexing hierarchies

A communication network has to share its transmission capacity among all its users who, in general, do not want to use and pay for a transmission circuit at all times. Therefore, it establishes circuits when they are requested and disconnects them later. This circuit, held for a period, is known as a *call*. In designing a circuit switched system it is the statistics of calls that defines the traffic: the calling rate, average call duration and distribution of call lengths.

Establishing a call through a circuit-switched network requires a path to be found along which there are available circuits that can be connected, end to end, to make the required path. Therefore, associated with each switch is a control system which receives requests for setting up calls, both from the subscribers it serves and also, through the network, from neighbouring switches. The communication between these controllers consists of short messages known as *control signals*.

The switched circuit has a constant bit rate throughout its length. To meet the needs of data users a circuit-switched system must offer a variety of data rates. From a functional point of view, these operate as though there were separate networks but the multiplexing schemes can handle different rates together.

Figure 1.5 shows schematically that a circuit-switched network is made from three types of component: switches, controllers and a network for control signals. In practice, traditional design of telephone networks carried the control signals through the same path as the telephone circuits, but modern designs, particularly those intended for fast call set-up and release, increasingly separate the control signals in their own store-and-forward network.

In the figure, a call originated by the telephone first sends control signals (such as dial pulses) to the local control (1) which issues orders (2) to the switch enabling it to connect the call to a free line to the next switch. Control signals (1') pass also to the next switch to indicate the route or destination required. These give orders (2') to switch the call further and more control signals (1'') to the next switch. In earlier forms of telephone network the control signals pass over the newly established telephone circuits (3 and 3'). When the call reaches

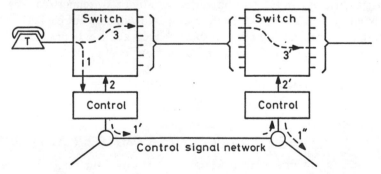

Figure 1.5   Schematic of a circuit-switched network

its destination a control signal can be returned, via either the control signal network or the telephone circuit, to let the originator know and give the ringing tone. Eventually the completion of the circuit when the called subscriber answers is signalled in the same way.

For the telephone network, circuit switching is very appropriate because of the uniform bandwidth of 4 kHz and the duration of calls, which justifies the cost of establishing the switched circuit. This is not so certain for data traffic with its wide range of data signalling rates and different traffic pattern.

The information handled between computers and terminals is not primarily a synchronous stream of binary digits and is better regarded as a sequence of messages. This is the reason for the development of *packet switching* in which short messages called *packets* are handled individually by the network mechanism. In its simplest form, switching consists merely of directing the packets on their way to their destinations while multiplexing consists of interleaving packets from various data streams. Because packets are stored at each intermediate node which switches them this is known as a 'store-and-forward' method. Packets can be entered into or removed from the network at the speed which suits the terminal, so the network acts as a speed changer.

Packet switching is described in more detail in Chapter 2 and for the present we need only list some of the differences between packet and circuit switching.

Circuit switching deals with information as binary streams at a prescribed speed while packet switching deals with information as short messages at any convenient speed. The standard which unites the source and destination of a circuit is its rate in bits per second while the standard which unites the source and destination of a packet is the maximum number of bits it can contain. Multiplexing of circuits can use frequency or time division but this is irrelevant to the needs of the network user who has to deal with each circuit individually.

Multiplexing in packet switching is by interleaving packets and it is easy for a programmed device to handle more than one packet stream at a time, simply by recognising the packets according to a channel number contained in their format. Circuit switching produces a small and constant transmission delay but packet transit delay is greater and variable. Circuit switching requires a path to be found through the network before any data can pass but packet switching, in its simplest form, can begin to transport packets at once. In practice, however, packet switching has been elaborated to take on some of the characteristics of circuits and this will be described in Chapter 2.

For the remainder of this chapter we look at networks from the point of view of their users.

1.4 THE USER'S VIEW OF THE COMPUTER NETWORK

The user is not interested in computer networks but in the services they offer. In the extreme case, a communication network is entirely transparent and the user interacts with a distant service in any way that service happens to require. This viewpoint makes a network no more than a collection of miscellaneous services, each having its own terminal type and access conventions. There are other viewpoints; for example it has been suggested that a computer network could share its work between the mainframes attached to it and appear to each user as though it was a single computer.

Neither viewpoint is realistic though each can be valid in a particular circumstance. The difficulty of treating computer network design in general is the number of different ways in which the users view the services which it can offer.

The computer system designer may think of a computer in terms of its job control language, its file system and the languages in which it can accept programs. From his standpoint this is a complete view of a computer but it is only one view and therefore does not tell the whole story. This kind of specialist would expect a network to be used through the medium of a 'network job control language' and for the network to give the appearance of having a unified file system, even though the files were not always located in the same machine. We shall examine this viewpoint later on.

A far greater number of users will expect their service to engage in specific transactions. They may use it to book travel and hotel reservations or transfer money to and from banks. The services they use must be carefully tailored to the requirements of the particular transactions.

A third type of user, also numerous, looks to computer services for information. He may be searching for financial or market information, for legal precedents or for engineering data.

All these different viewpoints, and others, are valid. Furthermore, a user will not, in future, be interested in only one kind of service but sometimes in information, sometimes transactions and sometimes computing. If computer networks are to do more than provide communication paths to services that could otherwise stand on their own, they must take account of the varying viewpoints of the user.

Incompatibility

The basic problem is one of incompatibility and this is due to the rapid growth of the technology which has led to many independent developments running far ahead of the growth of standards. The incompatibilities are such that it may be physically impossible for a given terminal to be used with a particular service. The keys available on the keyboard, the behaviour of the display (whether it scrolls the text like a teleprinter or moves a cursor on the screen) and such questions as locking a keyboard until a response is needed or echoing characters from the remote computer—all these variable factors can impede or actually prevent useful interaction. The techniques used in networks to overcome terminal incompatibilities are part of the subject of Chapter 8.

Assuming that interaction is possible, the user may be confused by varying styles of interaction. The three main possibilities are question and answer, menus and form-filling. Question and answer is possible where the range of answers is either obvious or known to the trained operator. For example, some operating systems indicate that they expect a command in the hope that the user knows the full range of commands. Often, they provide a list of the possibilities if the user knows the appropriate way to access such a list. In other cases, the user is provided on each occasion with a short list of possibilities from which he chooses, a list which is known as a *menu*. A more complex type of interaction, but one which is familiar by analogy with paperwork, is filling a form on the display.

When the response from the service will take a long time, it may or may not be possible for the user to start another line of interaction and be reminded when his earlier one is completed. None of these details in the 'style of interaction' is obvious without training and their variations form one range of stumbling blocks to the user who needs to access a number of services. In the realm of information retrieval Marcus and Reintjes[1] recount that where librarians have been trained as information specialists to assist users in searching on-line data bases they found that several weeks of training and continued practice at the terminal were needed by the specialists to get a high level of proficiency and maintain that level. A significant part of the learning difficulty was caused by the differences among data base systems. Even specialists found it desirable to specialise in a small number of data bases and sometimes in only one or two systems, at least partly for the reason of the heterogeneity of data bases and systems.

The language of the interaction forms another stumbling block. Each of the words, 'list, print, summarise, output', has been used with the same meaning as another word in that list in another computer system. Although well-designed systems provide the necessary prompts to teach a new user the language being used, there are occasions when the user becomes trapped, unable to escape from a particular interaction because he does not know the magic word. These incompatibilities frustrate the user, waste time and often lead to a deliberate decision not to employ the full range of services.

Some of the incompatibilities are a result of basic differences in the facilities provided, and could not be circumvented by any new feature which a computer network could provide. For example, information systems may be searched by keyword, by a subject classification, by a text string and no doubt in many other ways. Two services that, at first appearance, do the same thing may be basically incompatible. Nevertheless, with a well-developed uniform access language, the user can make a request which both he and the network understand and be told, politely, that the service cannot meet that request. The value of network-wide standards is not diminished by the fact that computer services do many and various things.

The following sections describe some of the ways, above the level of the terminal, in which network designers are attempting to overcome incompatibility problems and provide the user with a satisfactory view of the computer network.

Network Information Service

As one of the first large-scale networks the ARPA network faced the problem of telling the users what was available to them. The network information centre provided a resource notebook.[2] The information in the notebook was provided by each of the host computers which gave access to its services. In addition to the printed form, the text was stored and made accessible through the network. Ideally, such a directory should function as a kind of 'yellow pages' for the network services which would be listed and cross-referenced under a number of subject headings. The on-line version of the directory could search under keywords and, in principle, this listing of network services could be comprehensive and relatively easy to access.

A second requirement, which would create a much greater volume of text, is the basic information for the new user to begin with an unfamiliar computer service. In the long run, standardisation will make the testing out of a new service easier. It would be reasonable to expect any service which operates on a commercial basis to offer help to new users in learning about what it has to offer by means of an on-line interaction before the user has yet subscribed. Enquiries about subscription, bookings and payment should be possible within the communication system. Printed directories should offer only a first introduction, both to save page space and to utilise the superior possibilities of the on-line system.

The service on the ARPA network called REX (Network Resource Manager) not only helped to find the service that the user wanted but also made the connection at his request.[3] The resources which were listed in the REX system included particular software and hardware, computer types (such as IBM 370, PDP10), editors, host names and help facilities. The various resources were classified in categories and a command called FIND searched the lists for particular resources. An example of a FIND command is:

FIND (FORTRAN OR WATFOR) AND (MIT-DMCG OR USC-ISI)

This determines which of the hosts listed in the final bracket have either Fortran or Watfor.

The REX system also had a DESCRIBE command which would spell out the contents of all the lists of resources meeting the specification, with useful information such as means of access, help facility and cost. The following is a DESCRIBE command which would list the languages and their attributes at all sites that do not have the TENEX operating system:

DESCRIBE LANGUAGES AT NO TENEX

The third feature of REX was the ACQUIRE command, giving the ability to make a connection to the system which had been found, though, in its initial form, it made access only to tutorials. When REX is interposed between the user and the tutorial it shields the user from some of the peculiarities of the host system, taking action on error messages as far as practicable, for example. The authors of the REX system decided that complete success in providing the user with the network as a coherent entity could not be obtained without more standardisation in operating systems and hardware architecture.

In small networks it is possible for the network authority to hold and maintain comprehensive information about all the services offered. In practice this is rarely done well. As networks grow in size and networks are interconnected to form a very big market in services, this centralisation of service information becomes impracticable. Then service information must be held by each service centre, with a number of indexes or compendia of data source information to guide the user. Lack of standards in the interaction with these service information facilities would (perhaps will) be a serious disadvantage of future networks. Therefore the move towards a more consistent network image should begin with the way that information about the services is presented.

Network Job Control Language

Early operating systems were responsible for running individual jobs in sequence as they were presented. The job usually came complete with data or asked for particular magnetic tapes to be loaded when they were required. In order to specify the way that the job should be run, the program was preceded by job control instructions, usually in the form of cards, which formed a primitive kind of job control language.

Though batch processing had, by this time, developed a little, the advent of time-sharing systems was mainly responsible for establishing the file system as the central feature of a computer's operations. This development went along with the greatly increased storage capacity given by disc stores so that dependence on magnetic tapes was reduced. In time-sharing systems the job control language became interactive but the connection between this and the languages used in batch processing was not, at first, apparent. In BASIC, job control functions such as LIST and RUN are integrated with the programming language so that the average user is unaware of the distinction. Someone who wants to make the fullest use of a time-sharing system and employ all the resources of a large computer needs something more elaborate. The result has been that job control came to be seen as a language problem and that the languages devised are suitable for interactive use and batch processing. These are job control languages or JCLs.

These job control languages are necessarily complex and unfortunately diverse. Each manufacturer regards his job control language as a feature of his special offering to the computer buyer.

From the unsatisfactory state of job control languages which once existed there were several hopeful developments leading to high level languages, machine-independent languages and, eventually, to languages designed for job control in a network environment. Several high level languages were developed, some by manufacturers, such as Burroughs's 'Workflow language' and ICL's 'System control language'.

The first step towards job control in a network is to use a common language for all the machines in use, even if this gives no more facilities than the individual, single-machine language. Three successful examples of machine-independent JCLs have been reviewed by Rayner[4] who states that they tend to cope with 80–95 per cent of users' jobs without recourse to the target machine JCL. These languages are compiled onto the target JCL. They each have been demonstrated with a number of different machine types and operating systems.

The setting of parameters is a complex part of the commands in these languages. The less experienced and less ambitious user can ignore the existence of most of these parameters and take standard values which are provided for him. By having a comprehensive set of such 'default values' the language, in effect, gives a different appearance to users with less ambitious tasks to perform. The setting of only some of the parameters is assisted by the 'keyword' method of setting in which the name of the parameter goes along with its value. The alternative of associating parameters with positions in a fixed format is much less convenient.

Users have their own habits in the way they employ the language features and these can be incorporated in a 'user profile' which sets default values for a user's requirement.

A lot more has to be done before the concept of a network job control language is sufficiently well understood that standards can be attempted for wide use in networks generally. The experimental systems have shown that the attempt is worthwhile.

A network job control language should do more than provide a uniform user interface to the existing features of standard operating systems. It should allow the user's work to be split between more than one computer in a network, to use data from the files of any of the computers to which he has access and to file the results in any of these machines and use their peripheral equipment. This is the next stage towards the concept of the network as a single machine.

Practical experience in this area began with homogeneous networks comprising a number of similar computer systems. In the ARPA network there were a number of PDP10 computers connected as hosts and all employing the TENEX operating system. For these a resource-sharing executive called RSEXEC[5] was developed. This system provided for managing file directories in several hosts and for interactions between these hosts such as the moving of files and their use in various jobs running simultaneously. The RSEXEC program was present in each of the hosts which took part in the work. The user employed one embodiment of the RSEXEC program as his command language interpreter.

A network job control language for inhomogeneous networks must have all the properties of a machine-independent JCL and more. It must provide access to all the file systems on the network in a uniform way, giving the user the impression of a single file system for the whole network. It should enable the user to run different aspects of his job on different machines without requiring him to supply redundant information or manage the synchronisation of tasks explicitly. It should also provide a simple interface for the user who does not want to know about the network and prefers to think of it as one machine. Such an ideal NJCL does not yet exist.

A network job control language would provide the means for controlling a distributed computing job in an inhomogeneous network. Even with the aid of an NJCL such a job would be difficult to manage. The concept of 'network job management' goes further and tries to provide all the administrative help it can. A network user will need to keep track of the location and state of all his files. He may need to keep accounts at several centres to pay for his work and have to keep it within a budget. A management system which helps the user in all these aspects will probably be run on a processor close to the user for most of its tasks.

There is a different approach to this problem in which a specially provided computer works on behalf of a local user or group of users—a network access machine.

The Network Access Machine

The consistent human interface is most difficult to achieve in an open network. The open network is typically a public data communication system to which any services and user terminals can be attached. Even if we look into the future when terminal incompatibilities may have been overcome, the possibility of obtaining a uniform and convenient human interface to many services in an open network is remote.

In these circumstances the user's problems can sometimes be eased by associating intelligence with his terminal. The trends of computing economics could make this a commonplace in the near future. Where terminals are clustered, with a cluster controller containing processing power, each of the terminals can become an intelligent terminal. One of the first functions of terminal intelligence is to handle the problems of terminal incompatibilities by providing an agreed virtual terminal interface to the network. Beyond this there are many possibilities for helping the user with compatibility problems.

A general term for the computer associated with the user which helps in accessing network facilities is the *network access machine* (NAM). This is the name of a particular implementation[6] based on a minicomputer at the National Bureau of Standards. Figure 1.6 shows how a network access machine can help a network user by calling several services on his behalf and initiating transfers between them.

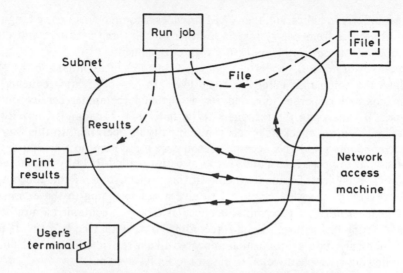

Figure 1.6   The network access machine

The system at NBS runs on a PDP10 under the UNIX operating system, and can thus serve many users at a time. It contains three parts (1) the command interpreter, which interacts with the user in the 'common language', (2) the macro expander which expands the users commands into a series of commands to the distant machine, using macros defined earlier for sub-tasks and (3) the response analyser which reacts to responses from the distant machine, including various kinds of faults and retries.

The NAM can be 'programmed' for a variety of network services by a specialist who writes the macros. It then becomes a useful tool for the non-specialist network user. It can call services on any of three networks, the local network, the telephone network and the ARPA network, but the user does not concern himself with these details. At the same time (and partly as a diagnostic aid) it can make a full transcript of the interactions with distant machines. It can, if requested, present all this chat to the user in a verbose mode.

The system has been used to access five different bibliographic retrieval services with a common command language including such commands as

connect to system ....

display file names

display terms related to ....

display n citations

access file ....

find ....

stop session

In a different application, the NAM provides a common command language for shifting files from one system to another on the three networks and keeps control of file names in this multi-network environment.

A survey of network access techniques was made by Rosenthal.[7] In the NBS machine the commands entered by the user are expanded into sequences of commands and responses intended for a particular computer service on the network. By analysing the responses to its individual commands the network access machine can check its progress and modify its operation. In this way the same commands could give access to resources on different host computers.

A similar project at the Rand Corporation was called RITA[8] which signifies the Rand Intelligent Terminal Agent. In this project some of the concepts of artificial intelligence were employed to give a new meaning to the expression 'intelligent terminal'. The terminal behaved as though it contained a number of 'agents' acting on the user's behalf according to rules that he had set. It used production rules in a syntax which appeared like a restricted form of English. The following is an example of a rule in the RITA system.

IF: the latest-command of this user is 'show action items' and the state of the system is 'command unfulfilled'

THEN: send the action-items of the user to the user and set the state of the system to 'command fulfilled'.

A monitor continually tests the IF conditions for each rule of the set and executes the THEN actions of any rule whose conditions are all true.

The data base of RITA contained files, network sites and persons known to the system. With the aid of the rules it could carry out a realistic conversation with the user about all the items of these types and their many attributes contained in the data base. The objects, attributes, and their values, were created and deleted dynamically by the actions of various rules. The designers of RITA expressed understandable doubts about its usefulness to the less expert user and the effect it would have on security.

A network access machine could operate much more effectively among computer services that had adopted a uniform network job control language. It should then be possible for the average user to initiate tasks involving more than one of the network's computer services. Typically, the network access machine would make the necessary connections to the other machines, using passwords which it stored on the user's behalf, and send the necessary commands in the full network language. It could establish its instructions from the user interactively but would carry them out non-interactively.

In a second mode of operation the user would talk through the network access machine directly to an interactive service. Having all the chores associated with the communication system taken care of, the user could give his attention to the commands he gives to a number of services, causing them to transfer files, process the data and present the results. This stage of development can be reached only when a collection of high level network protocols has been agreed and these protocols are the subject of Chapter 7.

1.5 THE PUBLIC DATA COMMUNICATION NETWORK

Data communication was necessarily carried at first only by the public telephone network. When early computer networks developed their communication subnets these became, in effect, private data communication systems. In the mid-1960s when packet switching came on the scene the view was strongly held, particularly among the established telecommunication carriers, that adaptation of the telephone network was quite sufficient for all future data needs. Though the argument for a specialised data network now seems conclusive it is perhaps necessary to review the reasons for this change of opinion.

The main reason for doubting the need for a specialised network was the low estimate of data communication requirements, both their quantity and their economic importance. It was argued that only the telephone network could justify the capital spending needed for a public communication system.

Those who favoured a specialised data network were influenced by the poor performance of the telephone network in this role. Since those times the design of modems has improved but it still remains true that circuits established by calls through the public network are of uneven quality and, when a good circuit has been obtained, it can sometimes deteriorate because of traffic building up on other lines. National networks vary in the extent to which they can be adapted satisfactorily to data. The presence of much outdated carrier equipment and step-by-step electromechanical switching centres is particularly damaging.

Private networks built from leased telephone lines suffered less from the unevenness of line performance but were affected by line failure and by the relative slowness with which, in some countries, the telecommunications carrier responded to calls for the restoration of failed lines. In retrospect it is difficult to imagine that telephone customers should accept this situation which made line failure largely their own problem. The data network user, even more than the telephone user, requires a highly reliable and consistent network.

In 1965 it was already clear that the future of telephone as well as data transmission lay with digital systems and the application of PCM transmission for the shorter-length trunks had already begun. Digital transmission could offer much better error performance but its value to data users, both in performance and economy, could only be obtained if the digital bearer was offered directly as a data carrier. It made nonsense to offer a digitally transmitted speech path to data users by means of modems, yet this was often done. Only a specialised data network can use digital transmission properly.

The other arguments for a specialised data network revolved around the extra facilities which it could offer by virtue of its switching system. Among these were the speed conversion which is characteristic of packet-switched networks and the 'closed user group' which could effectively isolate a group of users from the remainder of the network and give them the illusion that they were operating their own private system.

CCITT Recommendations for Public Data Networks

The International Consultative Committee for Telephones and Telegraphs (CCITT) is the official body at which telecommunications carriers decide how they will interwork. It is part of the International Telecommunications Union (UIT) in Geneva and that body is an organ of the United Nations. CCITT publishes recommendations which guide all the carriers. They do not have the force of standards because in many cases several different recommendations are adopted to suit different countries or groups of countries. Nevertheless, most carriers will wait for a CCITT recommendation before starting a major project to avoid the expense of a later change. It is the need to interwork internationally

Asynchronous, start–stop terminals

Class of service	Data signalling rate bit/s	Units per character	Address selection and call program signals
1	300	11	300 bit/s 11 unit International Alphabet No. 5
2	50	7.5	all at 200 bit/s 11 unit International Alphabet No. 5
	100	7.5	
	110	11	
	134.5	9	
	200	11	

Synchronous terminals		Packet-mode terminals	
Class of service	Data signalling rate bit/s	Class of service	Data signalling rate bit/s
3	600	—	—
4	2400	8	2400
5	4800	9	4800
6	9600	10	9600
7	48000	11	48000

Address selection and call progress signals at the same rates using International Alphabet No. 5.

Address selection and call progress signals as specified in recommendation X25 packet formats.

Figure 1.7   Summary of CCITT recommendation X1 for user classes of service

that gives them the will to arrive at common recommendations. CCITT also takes into account, though to a lesser extent, the needs of various groups of users and equipment manufacturers. In particular it works with the International Standards Organisation to arrive at agreed user interfaces, intended to give manufacturers wider international markets.

In 1968 CCITT established a study group for new data networks and in the course of the next few years this group formulated recommendations[9] which, with a number of gradual changes, have formed the basis for the present-day public data networks. The basic recommendation X1 sets out the classes of service which will be provided and does so under three headings shown in Figure 1.7. The first of these is 'start–stop' and it replaced an earlier intention to define a class of service for completely anisochronous signals. User class 1 has a specific envelope format and class 2 gathers together a number of formats which can be used in an anisochronous transmission facility. It is up to the users to ensure that the terminals connected together are employing the same speed and format.

The synchronous classes of service were generally agreed to be more important for the future and for these a customer interface was defined in recommendation X21. This interface provides for establishing and releasing calls in a switched network. For the benefit of existing users an alternative interface X21 bis was added, based on the present modem interface.

The third category comprises the packet classes of service and these serve the kind of access line which would join a computer or intelligent terminal to the network. Because of the speed-changing properties of the packet network it would interwork with terminals of the other seven classes.

The study group went on to define the inherent properties of the new services and the details of their customer interfaces. Customer interfaces are also a concern of the International Standards Organisation which works with CCITT in this area. A packet-switched interface X25 is the most important of these recommendations for packet networks and it is described below in Chapter 6.

The Virtues of a Public Data Network

A public data network can take one of two forms according to whether it includes switching or not. A leased circuit network should provide a means for transmitting digital information from point to point with high reliability and low error rate. Digital data services of this kind have proved their worth in North America. Using these leased line services private networks can be built and the higher quality of the lines makes the task of the private network easier. At first sight it appears that a leased circuit network should be a simpler system to build and operate than a switched service. This is not necessarily so and the reason for building leased circuit services before embarking on a switched network is that the service requirements are more easily defined and the market is better known. Leased circuit services must cover a range of data rates including, one supposes, those in CCITT recommendation X1. The procedure for adding new lines to a leased circuit system, updating the multiplexing system to get the best economy and keeping records of all the existing lines in each multiplexer and transmission system requires a complex organisation. It is likely that, in the long run, leased circuits are best handled by permanently switched calls in a future comprehensive data network.

A switched public data network can offer circuit switching, packet switching or both. In this book our main interest is in packet switching and in the next chapter we return to the subject of public packet-switched networks. Let us now consider the advantages which apply to any public data network.

For the established telecommunication carrier the switched data network is a new business opportunity. Public authorities which have a monopoly of telecommunications regard with apprehension the proliferation of private networks and the widening range of uses to which they are put. The defence of their monopoly requires complex regulations about the interconnection between private networks and between these networks and the switched telephone system. When the carriers operate a switched data system of their own there is more possibility for liberalising the interconnection rules without losing the monopoly position.

For the user, the public system gives a wider range of access to other users than any private network, but at first there is no incentive to employ this ability. To use it for business correspondence and formal transactions such as ordering, invoicing and payment we will need format and procedural standards. After a while, the wide access of the public network will become essential.

The other advantages of the public data network are engineering economies. Multiplexing and switching both enable information to be packed more closely on the available transmission lines. Private networks are, by comparison, often under-used. By assembling data traffic into larger groups for transmisson the greater economy of higher-speed lines is exploited. Only on the scale of public networks can redundancy in the form of highly reliable switches and alternative routing paths be fully provided.

Public data networks enforce standards in a way that would be undesirable in private networks where special tailoring is often counted a virtue. The enforcement of standards might seem to be a disadvantage but it leads to a bigger market for equipment manufactured to attach to the network. Standard interfaces with the users mean that manufacturers can compete for a large international market in terminals and this eventually benefits the network users.

Standards for common terminal types are a great need. To a limited extent the concept of a virtual terminal may help, but in the long run standards covering every aspect, from screen size to keyboard layout and communication interface are required. Public data networks help to bring about the last of these. In the same way, standard protocols and interfaces for computers and intelligent terminals are needed. The carriers, by their decisions at CCITT, help to fix at least the communication standards.

In some countries a public data network has been an instrument of public policy, bringing business and employment to regions that formerly were less developed. The needs of small network users, who could not afford a private network, are met by a public one. The introduction of a new public data network is expensive and profitability comes after several years. In some countries the initial cost has been justified as a public service, for regional development and to help the small user.

In the longer term, as more terminals are connected and traffic grows, public data networks will become very profitable. A further incentive to build them is the threat to the established telecommunication carriers of having many private networks. It is surprising that those established carriers not prevented by regulation did not seize the chance earlier. Lack of standards and the normal caution of many established bodies are two reasons but the retarding factor in most cases was the large and uncertain investment. The economy of public networks hardly works until they are large, and their utility to big user organisations depends on at least nationwide coverage. The earliest specialised public data networks were new bodies such as Telenet and Tymnet. National public networks and international connections are rapidly coming into use, so that international data communications have become a reality.

The Vices of a Public Data Network

Though the longer-term arguments seem strongly in favour of a public data network we cannot ignore the views of those who operate and expect to continue operating private data networks. Perhaps the strongest argument for a private system is that it can respond to an individual type of service requirement and offer a facility tailored to this requirement. A public network design is a compromise between the needs of many kinds of user. Some advantages of public and private systems can be had by using the switched data network for communication and adding the special facilities as services, operating in computers attached to the network. For example, a private network may provide, at its switching centre, for the logging of all messages and their storage and retrieval on request. Such a centre can continue to operate and give these special services without needing to provide any of the communication equipment, thus the communication subnet is part of the public system and all the other things which the former private network did are provided in a service centre. The need for these augmented communication services must be recognised by telecommunication monopolies.

Some of the worries of the operators of private networks result from a lack of confidence in telecommunications authorities. They fear that the existence

of a monopoly may lead to increasing charges though the network is fundamentally more economic than a smaller private network. In fact, the tariffs of
public data networks have been devised to be competitive with private systems
employing leased lines. The snag is that the same monopoly decides the tariff
for the leased lines.

A second factor which worries some private network operators is that they
doubt the ability of the public network authority to expand the data network
rapidly enough for all the demands. A private network must be able to take on
new terminals quickly, but the experience of the telephone network shows that
in some countries data services are difficult to obtain quickly. This is a question
of users' confidence in the ability of public network authorities. It can only be
resolved with time and experience.

The one apparently incontrovertible argument for public networks is their
wide coverage and even this may worry those users who feel it could compromise
the security of their data. This feeling is based on the mistaken belief that
private networks offer some kind of communications security. Since the leased
lines which they use are carried by multiplexing with other circuits and calls in
the public network any such security is illusory. In fact, because the leased
circuits follow fixed paths through the telecommunication system once their
security is compromised it remains so. Only the techniques of cryptography can
provide any real secrecy in communication and they apply equally well to private
and public systems.

In summary, a switched public data network can offer almost everything
that a private network offers and potentially at lower cost and with better
performance. Any remaining doubts about the virtues of a public data network
are questions of confidence in the network authority. Even if public networks
live up to the best that is hoped for, the change from existing private to the use
of public systems will take time and should not be enforced by a rapid withdrawal
of operating licences.

1.6 SOURCES OF NETWORK TRAFFIC

That computer networks will grow in extent and generate more and more
data communication traffic must be clear to anyone who has observed the first
decade of their development. Nevertheless the question is often asked 'Where
will all the data traffic for these future networks come from?'. The difficulty of
obtaining a good answer to this question can be imagined by trying to understand
how the same question would be answered at the inception of the telephone
network. Human imagination fails in such an exercise. We fail to see oppor-
tunities which seem obvious after the event. On the other hand we may imagine
possibilities which fail to take off. When telephony was begun there were two
ways it might have been used. One was for individual conversations and the
other was for broadcasting concerts and plays. Companies were formed to

exploit the new telephone as a broadcast medium but they failed and broadcasting had to wait for a radio system.

Forecasting is needed for the forward planning of large and expensive telecommunications systems. Fortunately, the traffic actually carried by present-day networks—largely private ones—gives some guide to the future traffic. Some European PTTs, operating through their joint organisation CEPT, have placed several contracts for the study of future data communication requirements in Europe. These surveys are broken down by type of user (branch of industry, commerce, etc.) and by countries and their main sub-regions. Such surveys extrapolate present-day uses and the rapid technological advance in computing; the changes in economics this brings and the rapid growth of new markets can invalidate such predictions.

We shall take two areas as examples of the type of new development we can expect and then discuss in the final part of this chapter how these developments may be related to the whole of our economic development.

Funds Transfer

Under the name 'electronic funds transfer systems' (EFTS) a whole range of new mechanisms have been proposed for the use of data communication as a method of making payments. Some examples of EFTS exist and a considerable expansion is very likely though, as we shall see, the precise direction of the development is still unclear.

The principal payment mechanism operated by banks has been the cheque. The cheque is an instruction to your own bank to make a payment to a third person and it finds its way to your bank by a lengthy route, as Figure 1.8

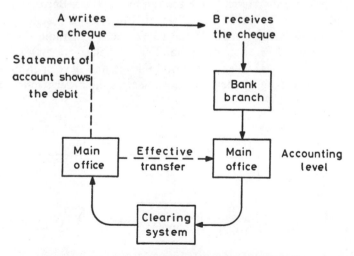

Figure 1.8 The mechanism of payment by cheque

illustrates for the case in which two banks are involved. In most countries the cheque document has to travel back to the bank on which it is drawn, but now that bank's accounting is centralised it need not, in many cases, go back to the drawer's branch of the bank. The cheque is handled by the bank of B, the payee, before the instruction reaches the paying bank. They make the credit to B's account after a delay sufficient for bank A to reply if there are insufficient funds. All the delays in the system provide interest for the banks because the drawer A is bound to keep funds available to meet the cheque.

This is a strange and cumbersome method of payment and, even with the best that automation can do, it is expensive to operate. Many banks, including the major banks of the United Kingdom, have automated their customers' accounts on centralised computers or in some cases two or three centres connected in a network. The feeding of data into this network is carried out by a multidrop centralised network and enquiries about the state of accounts use the same network. This covers the immediate requirements for data handling but the law in the United Kingdom still demands that the cheque itself returns to the bank for which it forms the instruction to pay, not necessarily to the bank branch. Further automation and greater economy in the cheque system seems unlikely.

An alternative and neater method of making payments between bank accounts is to instruct one's bank directly to make the payment. Then the document or information which moves through the system is a credit and not, as it was in the cheque system, a debit. Banking systems based entirely on this principle have been in use in Europe for a long time under the name of the Giro. Figure 1.9 shows this method. A Giro system is best centralised so that the transfers between accounts take place in one location and this has been achieved in those European Giro systems which are run by the state. Because accounting is centralised most of the traffic in traditional Giro systems is sent by mail and they are known as 'postal Giros'. If the payee needs to handle the payments document, for example a shopkeeper handing over the goods, the alternative route is used. In countries where the postal Giro is well developed many small purchases are made using the transfer document as the order itself, the details

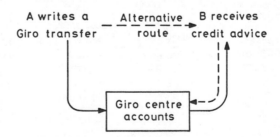

Figure 1.9   Payment by Giro transfer

written in a message space on the back. This is a highly economical method of combining ordering, invoicing and payment but it requires trust in the payee to deliver the goods. The development of the postal Giro by the United Kingdom Post Office came rather late and has not developed in the same way as its European counterparts. A Giro or credit transfer system could be fully automated more easily than a cheque system because the instruction document goes straight to the place where it is effective.

The next system which came into wide use was the credit card. A shop which accepts a credit card for payment is transferring the customer's debt to the card company. An accumulation of such debts is then settled by one payment from a bank (or Giro) account. It has been a very effective and efficient payment mechanism, particularly since credit card companies have become worldwide in their operation. The credit aspect, which means delaying payment of the final bill and obtaining extended credit, is not an essential feature and is not present in all card systems. Even where credit can be extended this does not always prove to be the feature that the customers of the system want to exploit. Therefore the credit card system can be regarded primarily as a payment mechanism.

Of all payments that take place the greatest number are by cash and this seems likely to remain so, but because the pre-electronic mechanisms (cheque, Giro, card) carry so few payments the scope for new methods that offer greater convenience is enormous.

One aspect of EFTS is the 'automated teller'. The teller is the bank employee who deals with its customers over the counter. The automated teller is a complex customer-operated terminal attached to the bank's accounting network and thus able to access the centralised accounting system. Banks introduce automated tellers to reduce their staff costs but retain some tellers to suit those customers who dislike the automated system.

Most of a customer's interactions with banks can take place at an automated teller. He can withdraw cash from his account, pay in cash or cheques and enquire about the state of his account. There is a formal difference when money is deposited because the receipt which the machine gives cannot be specific about the amount, having only the depositor's word for the amount. The depositor therefore takes the bank more on trust than he does in a manual operation.

For cash withdrawals and enquiries the depositor must make his identity known. We return to this question of personal identification in Chapter 9. In bank systems a magnetic card identifies the customer and a personal identification number (which he remembers and keys on a keyboard) authenticates him. There are other kinds of authentication but the identification number is the one most commonly employed.

One of the services of the automated teller has been in operation as a separate entity for a long time. This is the cash dispenser. The problem of identifying and authenticating the customer was first tested out in the context of the cash dispenser and this was perhaps the first widespread application of cryptography in a commercial network. Signals passing between the cash dispenser and the computing centre must be protected against tampering because anyone who could simulate the normal conversation on this line would be able to persuade the cash dispenser to dispense cash on an invalid card or personal identification.

It is worth considering, for a moment, the way that a cash dispenser interacts with the customer and the accounting centre, because it may be typical of the communication traffic generated by these complex but specialised terminals. The customer's magnetic card is read and he enters his personal identification number on a keyboard, then the amount of cash he requests. Only then need a message go to the centre. The card identifies him, the number authenticates him and the amount specifies the transaction. If the account is good and there is no adverse information on the card's identity the centre returns a message authorising payment. The terminal then returns the magnetic card and, when it is taken from the machine, dispenses the cash. Finally the terminal reports to the centre that the transaction is complete. In this transaction of three short messages a recovery scheme must be provided for each kind of message loss. Transactions are numbered and perhaps time-stamped to avoid any confusion from duplication of messages, either by accident or with fraudulent intent. All the messages must be enciphered. The same scheme can be used for vending machines which could use the same card, authenticator and account.

The development of EFTS which has been most widely heralded by the manufacturers is the one which integrates payments with the point-of-sale device. The cash register, which began as a local till and accounting device, has, in its electronic form, been connected within a large store or even a network of stores into a centralised system. With the aid of product identifiers encoded on the goods this same system can serve for stock control as well as accounting. Having now connected the point of sale to a network it becomes possible to make payments directly between accounts by means of signals from the same terminals. This, in its simplest form, is a credit transfer initiated by the customer's magnetic card and personal identification number. In the same way as with the cash dispenser the signals on the line between the point-of-sale device and the accounting centre must be enciphered. EFTS in this form has the same security requirements as the cash dispenser which preceded it.

The payment mechanism used at the point-of-sale device could equally well be a credit card transaction and perhaps the customer would prefer this, making the payment for a number of items by means of one cheque, or transfer, at a later date. The preference of the customer will determine whether his account is directly debited or he later receives a statement of purchases for a month and authorises payment. The shops will favour this point of sale EFTS if it is quicker to operate, so reducing the effort of sales staff. Rapid response from the accounting system and high availability is vital. In this respect the experience of cash dispenser systems is encouraging.

The banks engage in large payments between themselves and for this purpose they operate their own electronic funds transfer systems. The prime example is the SWIFT network, an acronym for the Society for Worldwide Interbank Financial Telecommunications. The SWIFT network carries messages internationally between more than 50 banks in 18 countries. For most messages the format is prescribed and there are many available formats. The type of message used for a given function such as 'customer cheque transactions' form a group, of which there are 25, classified into nine categories. The instructions contained in the message can be complex and can sometimes specify four different bank accounts. The transaction between particular accounts in the two banks concerned may be made on the instruction of a third bank and be in favour of an account in yet another bank. Such is the complexity of these transactions that one useful effect of the SWIFT network has been to formalise their statement and eliminate many errors.

The SWIFT messages contain an authenticator using a key which is known only to the two banks concerned. The presence of the authenticator makes it impossible, without knowledge of the key, to change the message contents. The SWIFT network is a message switching system which puts great emphasis on reliability and accountability. It stores messages for 10 days after delivery and can retrieve them quickly. Rapid delivery was less important and messages may be held for a long time if a terminal is off-line. The specification required normal messages to be delivered within 20 minutes and those of priority 'urgent' within 5 minutes. In practice most messages pass through in seconds. Though most messages go to a single destination, messages with up to 10 destinations are possible.

The accounting which follows up and reconciles the SWIFT payments is done with special accounts operated by the Foreign Department of the banks called *nostro* accounts. Statements of these accounts are carried as messages over the network, enabling errors to be found and referred to bank officials promptly. The transactions are complex and SWIFT has greatly improved their speed and accuracy.

Within the financial communities of New York and London large sums of money are transferred between banks and the speed and accuracy of these transfers is vital because the money attracts large sums in interest. Relocating money for overnight earning of interest is an important function of these transfers. Formerly, in the City of London, the transfers were carried by picturesquely attired messengers, but in both financial centres an interbank network on the same lines as SWIFT now carries these messages.

The quantity of traffic that will come from electronics funds transfer of all kinds is difficult to predict. It is critically dependent on the success or otherwise of capturing payment data at the point of sale. Taking into account all the many possibilities it seems highly probable that payments carried through data networks will be greater than the previous volume of cheque and credit card transactions and on this basis they will be one of the largest sources of traffic in the new data networks.

The Extension of Word Processing

The familiar concept of word processing is the generation, editing and printing of natural language text by a small processing system. These simple word processors chiefly take the place of the typewriter. But in every office which uses word processors, the texts they handle form part of a much larger communication system. The office filing system and the internal and external mail services are the other main components. The extension of word processing integrates the production of documents, their filing and transmission to other people and other organisations.

The user of the system can retrieve and read documents from the local file system. Subject to access controls he can alter them, so that several people can contribute to a document or progressively update a file. The generation and editing of documents is a purely local word processing function carried out within the terminal. For those transactions which need formal rules a questionnaire, a message or an interactive program are provided by the processor which handles the service. Sending a letter is such a service and it requires an address, date, reference number or subject reference and so forth. Many transactions, which would otherwise employ a data preparation operator, can go through the local office terminal, with its primary economic value derived from the word processing function.

The reason that this development is happening in the late 1970s and early 1980s is that information technology has just reached the right stage. The microcomputer was a principal component stimulating the development. Storage of text on floppy discs, bubble stores and large exchangeable discs gave almost all that was needed. The very large stores needed for some file systems are less well developed, but digital holographic storage seems likely to achieve the performance and economy required. Communications technology—in particular packet switching—is ready for the volume of traffic. Finally, the system design ideas and the human interface seem able to move on from word processing to the integrated system. The chief unknown is whether the simplicity of the human interface found in the best word processing can be maintained.

Electronic mail is one aspect of the new development. Rapid electronic message transport will be of little use unless these messages are integrated with the word processing function. The preparation, filing, transmission, logging, delivery and reply must follow rapidly without unnecessary key-punching. Used in this way, electronic mail will be a large part of future network traffic.

Messages can do much more than carry text. They can provide the means for an interaction to take place at a distant point. They can move in sequence to various people who require to read and approve them. By means of authenticated additions to the message the evidence of approval and the appended comments can be as effective as a circulated message on paper; in fact they can be more secure.

The cost of this mode of communication is now very favourable since packet switching charges are already very small compared with mail costs, even when the manual operation of handling the conventional mail is discounted. The complexity of the systems that will be required will, to some extent, delay their full development but the economics of communications and storage are clearly pointing this way. The result, when it comes, will be a vast increase in the traffic handled by future data networks.

Properly developed and free from restrictions, these integrated systems for handling the storage and communication of texts will impact the older methods, telex and mail services in particular. The need to keep an economic mail service and the proper roles of the various kinds of telecommunication need careful thought and planning so that we do not simply react to crises. Because there are new communication services which offer more than message transport we need to think before extending further the traditional ideas of regulation or monopoly. These are just a few of the problems raised by the interaction of network services with society but this has a larger aspect—how will society be affected by information technology as a whole?

The Information Society

Sociologists and economists have recently given much attention to the way in which information handling has grown in importance until, according to one view, it dominates our economy.

Fritz Machlup's book *The Production and Distribution of Knowledge in the United States*[10] identified the information sector as a major part of the economy which had a growth rate in the region of 10 per cent per year. Daniel Bell in *The Coming of Post-Industrial Society*[11] saw the emphasis moving from industry to services and information handling. More recently, Marc Porat in his thesis entitled 'The information economy'[12] extended Leontieff's input–output technique to include the information sector. The input–output matrix shows how the product of one sector of the economy provides the material for another. By expressing the relationships in a linear form the effect of a hypothetical change to the economy can be traced in all its indirect results. Marc Porat's work produced such a model in which, for the first time, the activity of information handling was given its proper place.

One of the figures of Porat's thesis is reproduced as Figure 1.10 and shows, for the US, the workforce (as a percentage of the total) for four sectors, information, service, industry and agriculture. For the US, industry had overtaken agriculture in 1906 to be replaced in 1954 by information handling as the major activity of the workforce. According to this criterion we are well into the post-industrial society which Porat has called 'the information economy'. The figure shows the size of the workforce, not the value of the product (and it relates only to USA). While the agricultural workforce declined its production of food for consumption and export was maintained. The industrial output continued to increase when its labour force fell.

Some have conjectured that the size of the information sector cannot increase because of 'limits to growth' like those for material and energy products. Until now, the workforce it employed did seem such a limit. But the scope for productivity in the information sector is apparently unlimited. Information handling and storage has no practical limitation due to energy or material shortage. The future development in semiconductors, glass fibres and holographic stores can reduce the material and energy cost by several factors of ten.

The exact definition of the 'information handling sector' is important and it contains two elements. The *primary* information sector handles information as its main objective and includes radio, television, printing, advertising, computing and telecommunications. The *secondary* information sector includes those workers in other fields such as industry, medicine, etc. whose main task is handling information. The primary and secondary information sectors are approximately equal. If we consider, for example, a doctor as contributing to the secondary information sector, the choice of the proportion to allocate to information at first seems subjective. Making use of surveys of a doctor's activities Porat concludes that 50 per cent of his time should be allocated to the information sector. Other choices, made with less detailed study, might lead to arguable factors in the definition of 'information worker', but the effect of

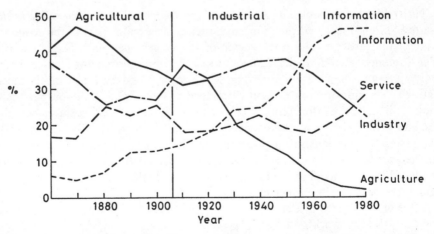

Figure 1.10   Four sectors of the US workforce (reproduced by permission of M. Porat)

		Agricultural Society	Industrial Society	Information Society
Production Power Structure	Production Power Form	(1) Land Production Power (Farmland) (2) Material Productivity	(1) Production Power of Motive Power (Steam Engine) (2) Material Productivity	(1) Information Production Power (Computer) (2) Knowledge Productivity
	Character of Production Power	(1) Effective Reproduction of Natural Phenomenon (2) Increase of Plant Reproduction	(1) Effective Change of Natural Phenomenon and Amplification (2) Substitution and Amplification for Physical Labor	(1) Systemization of Various Natural and Social Function (2) Substitution of Brain Labor
	Product Form	(1) Increase of Agricultural Product and Handiwork (2) Agriculture and Handicraft	(1) Industrial Goods, Transportation and Energy (2) Manufacturing and Service Industry	(1) Information, Function and System (2) Information Industry, Knowledge Industry and Systems Industry
Social Structure	Production and Human Relations	(1) Tying Humans to Land (2) Compulsory Labor	(1) Restricting Man to Production Place (2) Hired Labor	(1) Restricting Man to Social System (2) Contract Labor
	Special Character of Social Form	(1) Closed Village Society (2) Permanent and Traditional Society (3) Paternalistic Status Society	(1) Concentrated Urbanized Society (2) Dynamic and Free Competitive Society (3) Social Welfare Type Controlled Society	(1) Dispersed Network Society (2) Creative and Optimum Society (3) Social Development Type Multi Functional Society

Figure 1.11 One view of the information society (reproduced by permission of Y. Masuda)

Figure 1.10 is nevertheless striking and it raises the interesting question of what follows the information society. Perhaps the rising curve of the service sector shows the trend.

The industrial revolution changed society in very many ways—the growth of cities was one of them—and it is interesting to speculate on the effect of the technology now being built up so rapidly. Masuda[13] makes some interesting predictions. He believes that contract labour will replace hired labour, that people will disperse from cities and that knowledge creation will become a 'value' to replace material things. Part of a table from this paper is shown in Figure 1.11. His vision of the future shows little of the apprehension which journalists and other writers express. Elsewhere[14] Masuda estimates that the technology development which accompanies the information society is moving at 4.8 times the rate at which sources of power developed in the industrial revolution, from Newcomen onwards. The period of time during which the number of information workers exceeds the rest may be short-lived because of the rapid automation of information handling, particularly in offices. The future of employment may be better characterised by the increase of the service sector. Computer networks will retain their importance as part of the infrastructure of the economy in the same way that freight transport serves the production of material wealth.

References

1. Marcus, R. S., and Reintjes, J. F.,
   Computer interfaces for user access to information retrieval systems,
   Report ESL-R-739, Electronic Systems Laboratory, MIT, Cambridge, Mass. (April 1977).
2. *ARPA Network resource notebook,*
   NIC 23200, ARPA Network Information Centre, Stanford Research Institute, Menlo Park, California (1975).
3. Benoit, J. W., and Graf-Webster, E.,
   'The evolution of network user services—the network resource manager',
   Computer networks: trends and applications, IEEE, New York, 21 (May 1974).
4. Rayner, D.,
   'Recent developments in machine-independent job control languages',
   Software practice and experience, **5**, No. 4, 375 (1975).
5. Thomas, R. H.,
   'A resource sharing executive for the ARPANET',
   Proc. 1973 Nat. Computer Conf., 155 (June 1973).
6. Blanc, R. P.,
   'Assisting network users with a network access machine',
   Proc. ACM, 74 (November 1974).
7. Rosenthal, R.,
   'Network access techniques—a review',
   Proc. 1976 Nat. Computer Conf., 495 (1976).

8. Anderson, R. H., and Gillogly, J. J.,
   'The Rand intelligent terminal agent (RITA) as a network access aid',
   Proc. 1976 Nat. Computer Conf., 501 (1976).
9. 'Series X recommendations',
   The Orange Book, **VIII. 2**, Part II,
   International Telecommunications Union, Geneva (1977).
10. Machlup, F.,
    The production and distribution of knowledge in the United States,
    Princeton University Press, Princeton (1962).
11. Bell, D.,
    The coming of Post-Industrial society,
    Basic Books, New York (1973).
12. Porat, M.,
    'The information economy', Report No. 27,
    Institute for communication research, Stanford University (1976).
13. Masuda, Y.,
    'Social impact of computerisation',
    Proc. International Research Conf., Kyoto,
    Kodansha Ltd., Tokyo (1970).
14. Masuda. Y.,
    'Conceptual framework of information economics',
    IEEE Trans. on Communications, **COM-23**, No. 10, 1028 (October 1975).

Chapter 2

Packet Switching

2.1 INTRODUCTION

Packet switching was developed specially for the task of communication between computers. With computers we include intelligent terminals and terminal concentrators. It is more than just a switching method because it defines the method of carrying data on the trunk lines of a network as well as the multiplexing at the user interface. Many packet switching designs have been made that differ in detail. What we shall describe here are the principles that apply to nearly all of these designs.

The purpose of a communication subnet can be stated very simply. It is to transport data, quickly and unchanged, to any part of the computer network. With such a simple function it is perhaps surprising that there is so much complex detail in the communication subnet. There are two related reasons for this complexity. Firstly, communication is not cheap and the network design must economise in the use of its transmission paths by sharing them between many computer conversations at the same time. Secondly, transmission paths are unavoidably subject to noise, interference and the occasional breakdown. One of the purposes of communication network design is to make the system as it appears to the users much more reliable than its components.

We have to guard against the tendency to make the communication system even more complex by adding special features and services to it. If we can produce a basically simple communication system many of the added services can be provided by computers attached to it just as though they were subscribers to the network, or host computers.

In this book we are emphasising packet switching because it has been widely used in computer networks and it seems particularly well fitted for the task.

2.2 SWITCHING, CONCENTRATION AND MULTIPLEXING

A communication subsystem uses switching and transmission techniques to achieve its purpose of transporting data. Associated with these are the two related concepts of concentration and multiplexing. They can work in several different ways and are not always clearly distinguished.

The primary function of switching is easily understood—it is that of giving one network subscriber access to all the others. This kind of switching is controlled by the user when he specifies the destination of a message. Switching is the means by which the message or call is routed to its destination.

Switching has an equally important secondary function which is concentration. It is easiest to describe this in the first place for a circuit-switched communication network like the telephone system.

Figure 2.1 shows networks without switching and then with switching alone and with both switching and concentration. Figure 2.1(a) has eight subscribers and each subscriber sees seven separate lines leading to the others. In effect, the subscriber does his own switching by choosing on which pair of wires he will communicate. Clearly this is impracticable when it goes beyond a very few

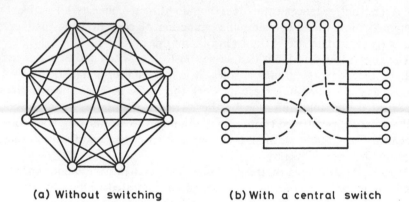

(a) Without switching   (b) With a central switch

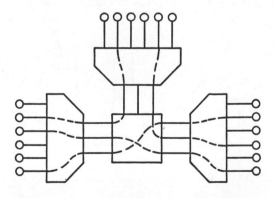

(c) A central switch with concentrators

Figure 2.1   Switching and concentration of circuits

subscribers. The centralised switch shown in Figure 2.1(b) brings all the lines from subscribers to one switching machine. The central switch has to deal with all the lines, yet the activity on them may be low. A switch that could potentially connect nearly all the lines at once may be unnecessarily large. It is more economic to use only enough lines for the traffic that is being handled.

We normally find that subscribers are not spread uniformly over a large area but grouped into clusters. Depending on the geographical scale we are talking about these clusters might be an office building, a business area, a town or an industrial region. When a group of connections is carried some distance towards the switch as in part (b) of the figure, the use of lines is wasteful because only a small proportion (such as 10 per cent) of lines is active at the same time. It becomes more economic to build a subsidiary switching function close to the cluster which will reduce the number of lines going to the central switch as in Figure 2.1(c). These subsidiary switches are referred to as *concentrators*. If they were true switches they would complete calls between their own group of subscribers, but a concentrator does not do this; it connects all active lines through to the switch. The simplified function of concentrating justifies the apparently redundant use of the transmission lines.

The concentrated traffic which passes on to the switch makes better use of the lines and, for large groups of lines, it is more uniform statistically. When switches are connected in a mesh network the traffic between them is already concentrated and the utilisation of the switches themselves is improved by handling only concentrated traffic. At the moment we are talking about circuit concentration and later we shall find that a form of concentration also occurs in packet-switched networks.

Most of the switching centres in a telephone system handle both unconcentrated traffic directly from subscribers and concentrated traffic over trunks to other switches. An efficient form of design is to separate the concentration and switching functions in the way illustrated in Figure 2.2 so that subscribers' lines

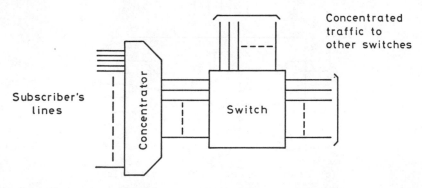

Figure 2.2   Separation of switching and concentration

entering the exchange are first concentrated and the main switching function applied only to concentrated traffic.

Circuit concentration implies a knowledge of the proportion of lines which is likely to be occupied by a call, but this number fluctuates. Suppose that in 100 subscriber lines we expect on average only 10 to be occupied at the busiest time of any day. If we choose to provide 15 lines for concentrated traffic there will be a certain probability that a caller at a busy time will find all the lines occupied. This limitation is measured by the 'grade of service'. In practice, perhaps, 20 lines would be provided to get an adequate grade of service at the busiest time. This illustrates that concentration always implies a risk of congestion and we shall return to this problem of congestion, in particular in Chapter 4.

The value of concentration improves as the size of the group of lines increases. With better averaging of traffic the proportion of extra circuits needed to keep congestion at bay is reduced. On each line, also, the traffic is more uniform as well as more concentrated; when we deal with a big group of lines the usage of the lines is better.

Multiplexing

Multiplexing is superficially similar to concentration, but there is an important difference. It replaces a group of lines with one transmission path of greater capacity. The high-capacity line is more expensive than each individual line but the cost per line is reduced, sometimes by a very large factor. A multiplexed transmission path provides exactly the same service as the bundle of lines it replaces. In that sense it is 'transparent', though in practice multiplexing techniques do not always completely achieve this transparency. There are very different multiplexing methods for analogue telephone signals and digital data streams.[1]

In the analogue telephone network the signal being carried is a voice waveform with a bandwidth which can be fitted into a 4 kHz space in the spectrum. By modulating the 4 kHz signal it can be shifted in frequency and a number of modulated speech waveforms can be carried together over a single channel. A standard method is to take 12 speech channels modulated at 4 kHz spacing and fit them into a 48 kHz band lying between 60 and 108 kHz. This is called a *primary group*. Frequency division multiplexing can be extended to larger bandwidths by multiplexing primary groups into a super-group and super-groups into a master group and so forth. The high bandwidth signals require special transmission paths such as microwave radio or coaxial cable. One of the larger systems in use is a coaxial cable carrying 10 800 telephone channels.

Voice channels are increasingly being carried digitally by pulse code modulation employing 64 kbit/s for each voice channel. To convert an analogue signal into a stream of digits it is sampled at 8000 times a second and each analogue sample is coded (almost logarithmically) into 7 or 8 bits according to the system. The result would be a stream of 56 or 64 kbit/s. In practice, the stream is always much faster and carries many telephone channels with their 7- or 8-bit samples interleaved. With each 7-bit sample is an extra bit used for control signals, so the samples to be interleaved are always 8 bits long.

To be specific, consider a group of 32 channels of speech each one represented by an 8-bit sample occurring each 125 μs. They are interleaved without any spaces between them in a frame of length 256 bits which exactly fills one sample period of 125 μs. The data rate is therefore 256 $\times$ 8000 bit/s which is 2.048 Mbit/s. This is the standard which is common in Europe. The scheme used in North America has 24 channels at 1.544 Mbit/s and a frame of 193 bits. In the 'European' system only 30 channels are used for speech, the other two being used for control signals.

This interleaving of digits (or samples) in a regular time frame is, of course, time division multiplexing, the digital equivalent to the analogue techniques of frequency division. It shares the property of 'transparency' and, as in the analogue case, not all practical systems fully achieve it.

Multiplexing differs from concentration by having no risk whatever of congestion. A multiplexed telephone channel gives to each telephone circuit the full bandwidth it would experience if it had a line of its own. Multiplexing is a technique associated only with transmission which, from a strict point of view, need have no relationship with the switching system.

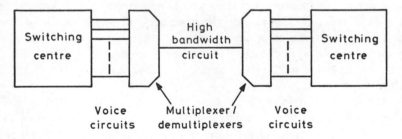

Figure 2.3   Frequency division multiplexing

Frequency division multiplexing in the telephone network is unrelated to the switching system. The switch operates on the 4 kHz voice waveform and as Figure 2.3 illustrates a bundle of such circuits leaves the switch and enters a multiplexer for transmission to a distant switch where it is demultiplexed again to individual circuits. One of the big economic advantages of time division multiplexing is that it can be integrated with time division switching. Time division switches can operate on the multiplexed stream, certainly at the level of the primary group if not higher, so that most of the multiplexing and demultiplexing functions are no longer necessary.

Demand Multiplexing

We have made a distinction between concentration, in which there is a certain probability of congestion, and multiplexing, in which each channel has full access to the necessary transmission capacity so that congestion is impossible. The distinction is blurred by the concept of 'demand multiplexing'.

In the classical time division multiplexing method each channel has its own slot in a frame which repeats regularly so that a constant and guaranteed transmission capacity is available for each of the subchannels. If we looked at the use being made of these subchannels we might find that most of the time they were not carrying data at all because there was no demand for their use. Demand multiplexing allocates the available time according to the demands of the various channels so that no slot is employed when there is no data to send.

In Figure 2.4 five incoming channels are shown which deliver blocks of data at random intervals to the demand multiplexer. Since they are contesting for use of the outgoing channel these blocks must be stored at their point of entry. A switch (shown schematically in the figure) can connect any of the buffers to the outgoing line and will always try to find a full buffer. Therefore the control device must have an indication of the occupancy of each of these stores.

If this multiplexer were to be operating in the classical or fixed time division mode the switch would rotate constantly and regularly so that the mere sequence of blocks on the outgoing line would indicate to which channel they belonged. In the case of demand multiplexing each block must be defined by an address attached to it as a short 'header' which is provided by the control device. Now the data stream comprises addressed blocks. In a sense, the name 'demand multiplexing' is a misnomer because this is clearly a form of concentration with all the dangers of congestion that that implies. There is also a variable delay due to the storage and the way that the switch responds to demands.

Demand multiplexing is a step in the direction of modern data communication. It associates storage with transmission as an integral part of the switching

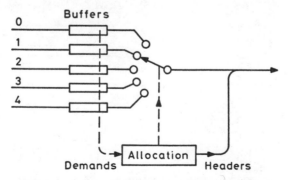

Figure 2.4   Schematic of demand multiplexing

and concentration function. The availability of cheap and fast stores and stored program control opened up vast possibilities in the design of communication networks. The first uses of such storage were in handling telegraph messages, *message switching*, which attempted to imitate an existing manual system and do it better. More recently packet switching exploited the new technology for the purpose of computer networks. Both are examples of the 'store and forward' idea.

2.3   STORE-AND-FORWARD APPLIED TO MESSAGES

In modern terminology the telephone network is a real-time system in which the user interaction requires that there be very small time delays. When a call has been made and the two-way transmission of speech has been established the network takes no further interest in the pattern of messages which pass between the subscribers.

We use the telegraph network in a different way by requiring it to deliver an individual message to a subscriber whose address we specify. Delay in transmission is not of such vital importance but, because we have no immediate feedback from the other end, we rely heavily on the integrity of the network to which we entrust our messages. Because of the different function of the message communication network a form of 'message switched' system was evolved in which the emphasis was on reliable delivery of each message, even at the cost of a possible delay.

The essence of this method is to store the message at each intermediate switching point and check its integrity before sending it on to the next stage of its journey. Then if lines are congested or unavailable for any reason the message can either be held for transmission later or sent round by a different route. Figure 2.5 illustrates the principles of a message switch.

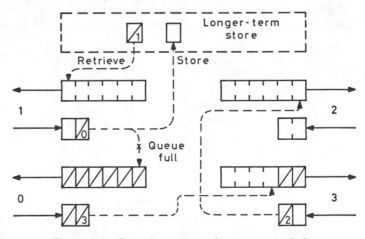

Figure 2.5   Queueing system of a message switch

Four circuits are shown in the figure with the two directions of transmission illustrated separately. Inside the switch there are buffers and queues as well as an area for longer-term message storage. A message switch typically serves a large number of low-speed lines. The traffic arriving for delivery on one of the outgoing lines fluctuates because it comes from many sources and can exceed the instantaneous line capacity. Therefore a queue is established for each outgoing line and one of these queues is shown as full in the figure.

Switching in this message switch consists of moving the addressed messages from the input buffers to the correct output queue. A computer system is responsible for this activity and presumably it could become overloaded so that an input buffer was not cleared before another message arrived. Adding to the number of input buffers would not solve the problem because traffic could still arrive faster than it can be handled. The figure illustrates by broken lines the movement between input buffers and the next free place in an output queue. In one case, the output queue is full and the message is moved to the longer-term store. A message is also shown leaving the longer-term store to enter a queue for an output line which has just become available.

Because of the responsibility of the message switching system for safe delivery of messages, each part of the system is subject to checking and provides for recovery from faults. Incoming messages are not only held in immediate access store but also immediately transferred to magnetic memory as a back-up. A log is kept of all the messages passing through the system so that problems of non-delivery can be investigated later. Most important, the transmission between one message switch and another is provided with error control.

Error Control

We shall return many times to the technique of error control on a communication link and in Chapter 6 there is a detailed description of a modern procedure. For the present it is only necessary to describe the basic principle.

The first essential is to detect any errors in transmission. A form of redundancy check can be calculated using all the bits of the message and this check field is added to the message before transmission. At the receiving end the redundancy check is calculated in the same way, giving a result which should agree with the received check field. Errors on the line are very likely to cause redundancy check failures so that the receiving end knows of the error. A procedure is established so that messages in error are retransmitted. There is also a possibility of completely losing messages which is covered by having the sender add serial numbers to the messages and checking the serial numbers at the receiving end.

The retransmission of a message could be triggered by an error message from the receiving end, but this would fail if the error message itself was damaged. It is better to use a positive acknowledgement for each message sent.

The sender then will not continue to transmit if the received acknowledgements have fallen behind schedule. This justifies the use of a limited amount of buffer space at the receiving end because any congestion in the message switch would delay the acknowledgements and stop the incoming stream of messages. This property of the link control procedure is an example of *flow control*.

Message switching networks give great attention to error control and this is not only because of the desire to preserve the customer's messages unaltered. It is equally vital to protect the header which carries the information about the message's destination and other administrative data such as its source, priority, etc. Obviously a message should not continue its journey if it fails the sum check. This is the reason that the entire message is stored before onward transmission.

Delay in Message Switching

When the system is heavily loaded the queues are in effect extended into the longer-term storage and the delay introduced by storage may increase indefinitely. In practice, the daily fluctuation of traffic provides a means of getting through the backlog. If the switch is very lightly loaded each incoming message will get immediate attention, but there will nevertheless be a delay due to storage equal to the transmission time of the message at the transmission speed employed. For the whole network, delays are in the range from a few seconds to a few hours. The network will hold a message for later delivery if the subscriber's terminal has not been activated for receiving. This is a form of delay due to the receiver.

The store-and-forward technique employed in message switching is well matched to the requirement. Because end-to-end interaction is not expected the network undertakes ultimate responsibility for message delivery. For this reason it employs longer-term storage and the logging of all traffic. These systems also operate in conditions where communication is expensive and line capacity cannot always be provided to deal with traffic peaks. The delays which result would not be satisfactory in interactive systems but serve the purpose of reliable message transport.

2.4 THE ORIGINS OF PACKET SWITCHING

The way in which people communicate with each other is strongly influenced by the communication system. When we write letters we use long statements and try to anticipate what the reader wants to know. The same exchange on the telephone uses short statements and rapid interaction. Generally the rapid interaction achieves what we want more quickly and uses less of our time. In the same way with computers the constraint of batch operating meant that people spent much more time preparing a task for the computer to eliminate errors and ambiguities, but the result was often a disappointment and the job had to be run again. The rapid spread of time-sharing in the early 1960s was a great relief to the computer user because it provided 'conversations' on a human timescale. In this way one of the major constraints of computer services was overcome and people could obtain answers or information from computers when they required it and not after a considerable and frustrating delay.

It was this exciting new ability which gave impetus in the early 1960s to the attempt to break down the other barrier—that of distance. Off-line data transmission had been practised for some time. Early time-sharing systems used teleprinters as their terminal devices, so the first and obvious extension to a network was to make these teleprinters remote and thus give access to the computer service from distant points. In this way early networks came to be computer-centred with the distant terminals permanently connected to one central service. The introduction of low-speed modems attached to the public telephone network then gave the possibility of making a telephone call from one terminal to a number of alternative services so that communication switching could be added to these early networks.

Two observations led to the suggestion that a different kind of communication service might be needed. The first was that the messages passing between the terminals and time-sharing services were predominantly very short and the communication line was much under-used. Jackson and Stubbs[2] and Fuchs and Jackson[3] made measurements on time-sharing systems and characterised this kind of traffic. The second observation was that time-sharing systems frequently employed a front end computer to assemble messages from the low-speed lines and present the message as a whole when the computer was ready to receive it. Correspondingly, the front end machines took a message which had been produced rapidly by the computer and spelt it out, character by character, at the speed that a transmission line could take it to the distant terminal.

These observations strongly suggested that a communication network which handled messages would make better use of lines and eliminate some of the functions of the front end computer. Figure 2.6 shows a histogram of message lengths for data coming into a typical interactive service and emphasises the predominantly short message length.

The Rand Corporation Reports

The first full description of a system which resembles today's packet-switched networks came from a study of a military communication network by Baran and his co-workers. This network was designed to carry speech and data with full cryptographic protection and have high resilience to the destruction of individual network components. A series of reports was published[4] together with a summary in the open literature.[5]

These reports 'On distributed communications' described a store-and-for-

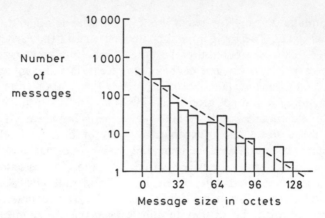

Figure 2.6   Message size distribution for an interactive service

ward system with a message unit of 1024 bits employing high-speed lines. Speech information was digitally encoded by delta modulation so that almost all the network equipment was digital. Low-cost microwave systems were described which could easily be transported and set up.

Because the topology of the network might change as its units moved about and the effect of destruction would also alter the topology in an uncontrolled way, the study laid great emphasis on automatic methods for routing message units towards their destination in a way which adapted itself to network changes.

This work of Paul Baran and his collaborators anticipated in a remarkable way the later developments which sprang from the desire to serve interactive computer systems.

The First Packet-Switched Systems

Starting from a different viewpoint a group at the UK National Physical Laboratory (NPL) proposed[6] that a store-and-forward system using short message units called 'packets' would be best able to serve interactive computers since they naturally generated and received short messages. The delays which are inherent in store-and-forward methods would be reduced by restricting the length of packets and using high-speed lines between switches. A particular feature of this proposal concerned the interface between the network and the computers and terminals attached to it.[7] The computers would be capable of handling data on a single communication path, interleaving packets from a number of terminals, and in this way the front end computer's functions would be largely eliminated. Terminals presented the more difficult problem which was to be solved by 'interface computers'. Messages coming in from terminals on a slow line would be assembled into packets for onward transmission and packets coming through the network from computers would be spelt out at the speed required by the terminals. In today's terminology this function would be described as 'packet assembly and disassembly'. Figure 2.7 shows the kind of system proposed.

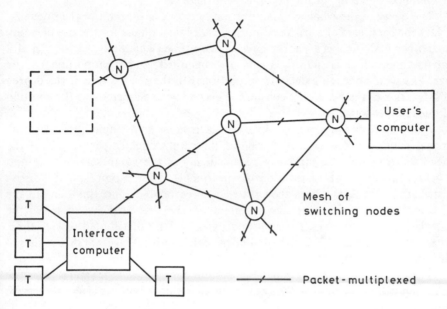

Figure 2.7   Structure of the network proposal

The practical outcome of the NPL work was a local packet-switched communication network[8] which grew, in a number of years, to serve about 200 VDU terminals and give them access to a dozen or so computer services.[9]

The Rand Corporation work was not aimed primarily at computer communication, but it led to the same kind of network design that later was proposed for packet switching. The new features of packet switching were the packet-interleaved interface and the packet assembly–disassembly function. The next important step was to combine these ideas for communication subsystems, which had been developing in several places in 1965–7, with a concept for a complete computer network. The concept was provided in the form of 'resource sharing'. The US Department of Defense 'Advanced Research Projects Agency' supplied the financial backing and the ARPA network began to be developed.[10] The first design of the ARPA network did not include the 'Interface Computer' of Figure 2.7 and thus required terminals to connect through a users' computer on the network (which was called a *host computer*). Later, the Terminal Interface Processor or TIP re-introduced the 'Interface Computer' in a different form, associated with a switching node.

The Packet Concept

The short message unit or *packet* was introduced to keep the transmission delay under control. A rough idea of the effect of packet length on delay can be obtained by an application of queueing theory.

The delay in the whole communication network is the sum of the queueing delays for each part of a packet's journey. A typical queue for the use of a link to another node delays a packet by a *waiting* time, which may be zero, and a *service* time, which is the time taken to transmit it, and is proportional to its size. The whole queueing delay is proportional to the service time if the degree of saturation of the network is constant. This can be explained using the notation of queueing theory.

A simple approximation is to regard each node as a single queue with its arrivals having a Poisson distribution at the rate λ packets per second. If the mean service rate is μ packets per second, μ^{-1} is the mean service time and $\rho = \lambda/\mu$ the degree of saturation of the queue. The assumption of Poisson distributed arrivals has been shown to give a reasonable approximation but the distribution of service time has an effect on the result. We shall make the calculation for two cases, constant and exponentially distributed service time. These correspond to the distribution of packet lengths. The extra delays due to time of flight or inter-packet gap are neglected.

The theory of the $M/G/1$ queueing system covers both cases and it gives the following values for *time in the system* which includes both waiting and service times:

$$\text{constant: } \frac{1}{\mu} \cdot \frac{2-\rho}{2-2\rho} \qquad \text{exponential } \frac{1}{\mu} \cdot \frac{1}{1-\rho}$$

The value for actual packet length distributions lies somewhere between the two values. It depends on ρ and practical systems cannot afford to operate with nearly saturated queues because the queueing delay would then be very sensitive to traffic fluctuations. The following table shows the time in the system as a multiple of μ^{-1} for the two cases at three levels of saturation.

ρ	constant	exponential
0.1	1.05	1.11
0.5	1.5	2.0
0.8	3.0	5.0

In practical networks the delay is unlikely to exceed twice the service time at each node visited. The important point is that mean packet length divided by line speed is the unit in which total delay is measured.

In a system handling messages of variable length we find that it needs only a small proportion of long messages to influence the average delay considerably.

Because the messages in queues are handled in sequence, one long message imposes extra delay on all those, including short ones, that get behind it. It is for this reason that a strict maximum size is imposed on packets. This is only a maximum size and there is no reason to pad out short packets to 'full size'. When packets are stored in switching nodes, since the packet store is not a large part of the total, it will generally be convenient to give up the space sufficient for the maximum packet. Transmission facilities are relatively expensive and therefore packets should occupy the smallest amount of time and not be padded out.

Messages longer than a packet must be sent by breaking them into packets at the sending end and reassembling them at their destination. The distinction between packets and messages is very similar to the distinction between *pages* and *files* in storage management. It is easier to allocate storage space in pages of constant length while allowing the user to define files of almost any length. The system splits files into pages, enabling the user, if he wishes, to ignore the existence of the paging mechanism. In a similar way a protocol can be introduced for the user who wants to send messages of arbitrary length, allowing him to ignore the packet switching feature. Because the great majority of messages will be less than one packet long splitting and reassembly will not affect most of them.

Early studies were based on transmission speeds of 1.5 Mbit/s and maximum packet lengths of 1024 bits. Delays of a few milliseconds per switching node could be expected. Experimental packet-switched networks, beginning with the ARPA net, employed line rates of 48 kbit/s which results in an average packet delay per node in the region of 80 ms at 0.8 of saturation. Queueing calculations like these were the basis on which the principle of packet switching was expected to succeed because they allowed networks of reasonable size to be built with expected delays from end to end which were short enough not to interfere with human interaction times.

Packets, Circuits and Messages

When we compare the three methods of switching, packet, circuit and message, we find advantages and disadvantages which vary according to the kind of traffic and the needs of the users. All three are likely to be needed in future networks.

There is a difference of kind between these three techniques. Packet switching implies the interleaving of packets on lines—a kind of multiplexing linked to the switching method. It is similar for message switching. Circuit switching has not in practice been integrated with frequency division multiplexing and so multiplexing has been treated in the past as a separate problem. Time division switching and multiplexing can form an integrated system but the multiplexing is not in a form which suits a multi-access computer.

Three aspects of packet switching seem to be disadvantages and all three are related. They are the delay due to storage, the variability of the delay (with its consequence of loss of packet sequence) and the processing overhead. In fact, the delay can be kept within suitable bounds such as 100 ms for today's networks and 10 ms or 1 ms as the speed of transmission increases with increased traffic. The loss of sequence can be avoided by suitable protocols and is prevented in many recent networks. The processing overhead might be significant in very long messages or data streams but is not important for short interactions. Rather, the cost of setting up and releasing a circuit may work in the other direction.

Packet switching can be more economical than circuit switching in its use of transmission lines because it interleaves packets from different streams according to their demand for channel capacity. This economy is offset by the overhead of packet headers and control packets of various kinds. It produces an economy where the use of a circuit would be intermittent or sparse—the case with much computer communication and most kinds of terminal interaction.

For very short interactions, circuit switching carries a significant overhead of processing, transmission and delay in setting up a circuit and releasing it. Approximately, we can estimate that this overhead equals four packet transmissions throughout the path taken by the circuit. In terms of delay it can be greater because the control signals of circuit systems use only a small part of the bandwidth. There will be many short interactions of three–four packets which would operate wastefully in a circuit-switched network.

The dynamically-interleaved, packet-carrying transmission line is used between switching nodes and also between the network and its 'intelligent' subscribers. Not only is this efficient on the user interface line, it also suits the mode of interaction of multi-access computer systems. Therefore in computer communication, the packet-interleaved interface is one of the attractions of the method. This principle of interleaving packets is illustrated in Figure 2.8. Packets from many sources interleave in a pattern dependent on their rates of production and are transferred across a single line at the subscriber interface to terminal D. Therefore D can be engaged in interaction with A, B and C at the same time.

Packet switching is associated with such aspects of data communication as flow control and error control, of which we shall say more later. These are not usually mentioned in connection with a circuit network. Nevertheless they are essential in both cases and they are added to a circuit connection in the form of an end-to-end data link procedure, such as HDLC. It is perhaps an advantage (though it is arguable) that packet switching combines these features into the network service. At least it makes the communication network responsible for error control, though it does not take the responsibility entirely away from the network's users.

The comparison of packet switching with message switching is also interesting because they are superficially similar. The difference lies in the interactive nature of packet communication compared with one-at-a-time message transport. The longer-term storage used in message switching is essential for the high integrity of messages, yet it can lead to long delays and certainly would prohibit interactive use of this type of communication system. On the other hand, packet-switched systems are optimised for short delay so that the users can employ interactive working. If there is any residual doubt about the arrival of a packet this can be covered by an end-to-end protocol.

In practice, most interactive computer services are self-checking in this respect. They have their own procedures which enable a user to determine whether something has gone wrong and take the necessary recovery action. If this is not sufficient a formal, computer-oriented, end-to-end protocol can be added, so that the user of the combined system (network plus protocol) sees a highly reliable communication system. In practice, packet-switched networks are reliable and would tend rather to duplicate a packet than lose it. The difference between them and message-switched systems lies more in the ultimate responsibility which on the one hand is reliable delivery and on the other high-speed delivery. It is a fortunate consequence of the way that packet-switched systems are designed that they prove to be simpler than message-switched systems, chiefly because they eliminate the longer-term storage and message logging.

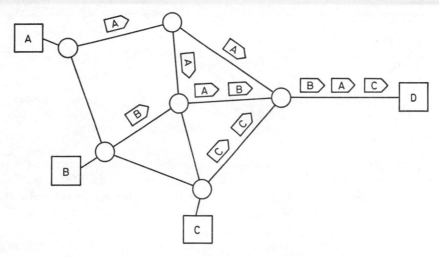

Figure 2.8 Packet switched network as a demand multiplexer

2.5 THE PACKET-SWITCHED COMMUNICATION SUBSYSTEM

The basic principle adopted from the start was that a communication subsystem should be a single entity with a well-defined and simple interface to its users or subscribers. The users need have no knowledge of the internal construction. All they require is the rapid and reliable delivery of packets. In this chapter we shall briefly introduce some of the design features that will be taken up in more detail later.

Packet-switched networks usually have a mesh structure with sufficient connectivity that the failure of one or two links is unlikely to disconnect one part of the network from another. The topological design of networks for this kind of reliability is described in Chapter 10. The extra lines needed for a mesh structure are justified by the likelihood of line failure and the magnitude of the problem if a network becomes disconnected. The failure of a single node in a well-designed mesh network should affect only the subscribers dependent on that node. Nevertheless, as we all become more dependent on computer networks, reliable design of the switching nodes themselves will become imperative.

The loss of a node need not disconnect all the lines which come in to it because a cross-connection can be made by standby equipment so that the connectivity of the remaining network is maintained. Figure 2.9 illustrates the

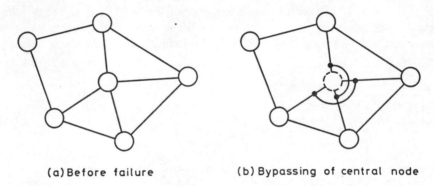

(a) Before failure   (b) Bypassing of central node

Figure 2.9   Reconnection of links after node failure

principle. The node at the middle of the figure has four lines connecting it to the rest of the network. If it fails, standby equipment connects these in pairs so as to improve as much as possible the connectivity of the remaining network. The subscribers connected to the failed node lose the network service but the unfailed lines are still being useful to the majority of subscribers.

Further improvements in reliability can be made by separating the switching node into smaller components and so minimising the number of subscribers affected by any single failure. For example, suppose that we replace a single switching node by 10 smaller nodes connected in the manner of Figure 2.10. The particular topology chosen is three-connected and each 'subnode' is connected to the others with at most one intermediate subnode. In the figure we assume that five links go to other switching nodes and each of these is duplicated.

If each of the subnodes handles a proportion of local subscriber connections the amount at risk with a single failure can be minimised. Methods like this become economic when the cost of switching equipment is sufficiently low.

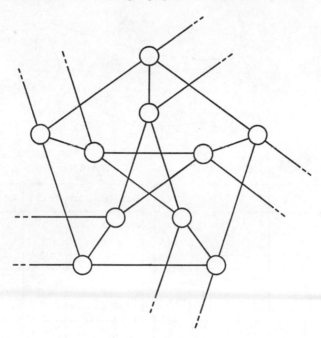

Figure 2.10   Internal structure of a multiple node

Addressing and Routing

A packet enters the network with an address in its header that specifies its ultimate destination. In principle this address could be converted at the first node into a complete specification of the packet's route through the network and the specification could take into account the latest information about line or node failures. In practice, the routing decisions are taken sequentially at each node the packet passes through. When the routing decisions are made individually each node must contain a routing table showing, for each ultimate destination, the direction in which the packet should be sent.

Figure 2.11 illustrates the routing tables for two nodes in a complex network and also shows a single alternative route in case the first one is either congested or broken. For example a packet arriving at node A and destined for D will have as its preferred choice the link 1 which takes it next to node B and as its second choice the link 2 which (the figure shows) leads directly to node J. It is often the identity of the next node that is used to label the outgoing link, but the ultimate and the immediate destination nodes must be distinguished. This form

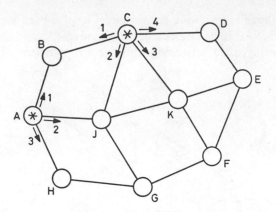

Routing table at A			Routing table at C		
Destination	Route	Alternative	Destination	Route	Alternative
B	1	2	A	1	2
C	1	2	B	1	2
D	2	1	D	4	3
E	2	1	E	4	3
F	3	2	F	3	4
G	3	2	G	2	3
H	3	2	H	2	1
J	2	3	J	2	3
K	2	3	K	3	2

Figure 2.11   Examples of routing tables

of routing table takes no account of the earlier history of the packet; whether, for example, it originated at A or, if not, where it came from. The details of routing schemes are described in Chapter 3.

Whenever a failure occurs or when one is repaired the routing tables must change. A node failure, for example, will call for changes in local nodes and in some nodes further away. Viewed from a great distance it may not be significant and, in general, routing changes due to any failures or local point of congestion do not propagate indefinitely. It is one of the advantages of a 'regionalised' scheme of routing that the propagation of changes can be contained.

In small networks it is possible to store in each node a collection of alternative routing tables to cope with most of the likely patterns of failure and this approach was employed in the SITA network.[11] More generally, an adaptive method of recalculating routing tables on a continuing basis is employed. One of these adaptive schemes was proposed in the Rand Corporation reports on distributed communications but proved to be unstable in practice. The method adopted in the ARPA network has formed the basis for many later developments which are described in the next chapter.

The Need for Flow Control

The communication lines between nodes and the subscribers' lines into the network can operate at different data rates. Because packets are stored at each switch there is no reason why line speeds should all be the same. In particular, subscribers' connections are generally of different speeds and the network operates for them as a speed changer. For example, a display unit operating at 4800 bit/s can communicate with a computer that has an access line to the network operating at 56 kbit/s. In the stream of data entering the computer the display unit's packets will generally be interleaved with those from other terminals. The true rate at which data is sent depends on how frequently packets are formed up and transmitted. This can vary from zero to the maximum of which the access line is capable.

The freedom to vary the flow of data carries a penalty because the sender can create packets faster than the receiver is able to take them. This implies a need for flow control which means that the receiver, in some way, controls the rate of the sender. An associated problem is the possibility of congestion in the communication subsystem.

Any communication system is capable of being overloaded and the overload manifests itself to the users in different ways. In the telephone network it will be impossible to make a connection so the whole purpose of the network is lost to some users for a while. In some kinds of data network, packets will flow but the delay will increase so that each user experiences a slower interaction than he would like. Given that the communication capacity is limited it is clearly very important to use it to its fullest extent but, in badly designed networks, congestion might lead to a state in which the total transmission capacity is greatly reduced. We need principles of design which avoid this wasteful phenomenon.

Message Reassembly

Messages longer than the packet must be divided into packets for transmission and then reassembled at the receiving end. Figure 2.12 shows how this process appears when plotted against time. It is theoretically possible for the splitting into packets to begin before the complete message is loaded at the source and for delivery at the destination to begin before all the packets have arrived. Taking these short cuts the total delay is much less than it would have been if the message had been stored and forwarded as a whole through the network.

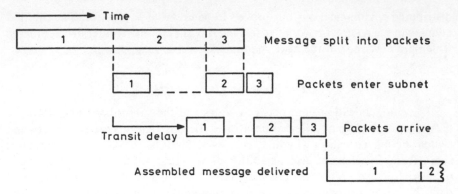

Figure 2.12   Message splitting and reassembly

Most packet networks and in particular the public networks that are now coming into operation do not offer to carry out the splitting and reassembling of messages. One notable exception was the ARPA network.[12] The packet maximum size in the ARPA network was 1024 bits and the network would accept a message of up to eight packets in length, break it into packets for transmission and reassemble them at the destination. One of the reasons for this design feature, in the first place, was to provide a form of flow control by allowing only one message in transit between a source and destination. Applied to individual packets this would have meant unacceptable throughput restriction. This flow control was based on the 'request for next message' or RFNM. The RFNM travelled as a packet through the network back to the source of the message. It originated at the switch next to the destination at the moment when the complete message had been completed ready for onward transmission. The host was constrained not to send a second message until an RFNM had been received.

An alternative philosophy used in most other networks has been to regard message splitting and reassembly as a task for the users, who could devise a protocol suitable for their own situation. In the ARPA network the reassembly defines, in effect, a larger packet of size 8192 bits. Messages of greater size than this still have to be split and reassembled by the users which is a function of the so-called 'host-to-host protocol'. It is therefore questionable how much was achieved by the reassembly function. Further problems[13] caused by the reassembly mechanism and the way they were overcome are described in Chapter 4.

Packet Sequence

When packets travel independently through the network they may arrive out of their true sequence. The extent of this problem must be understood. Many interactive communications take place by the alternate exchange of single-packet messages. If each party waits until it has received a packet from the other before replying there can be no loss of sequence. The sequence problem arises when one party sends more than a single packet without needing a reply to each. It is then important to have a means of restoring the correct sequence. In practice, this mechanism may not often need to be used when the transmission rate is low enough, but it must be there.

If the users are operating a protocol for message reassembly they can easily take account of packet sequence by serially numbering the packets which make up a message. The message reassembly will then happen rather in the manner of the ARPA network's internal mechanism but will be carried out by the subscribers of the communication system.

Most of the private and experimental packet networks operate on the principle that message sequence can be handled by the users as part of the reassembly protocol which they had to provide. When it was proposed that public packet-switched networks should be built the future users of these networks expressed a preference for a packet-switched system which would preserve packet sequence. The outcome of this discussion was the introduction of the 'virtual circuit', a concept which had been present in the early Rand Corporation studies.

2.6 THE VIRTUAL CIRCUIT

In its simplest form, packet switching provides for the transport of individual packets from their source to their destination independently. The packets form part of a conversation for which the conversing users or devices are responsible and this responsibility includes the question of packet sequence. Loss of sequence by one packet overtaking another in the network is not a probable occurrence but since it is possible the end-to-end procedures must take care of it. When public networks began as commercial ventures their designers started discussions with big potential users and packet sequence was found to be an important issue. A network service which carried packets individually required a new mode of operation which, even though it had been demonstrated in experimental networks, was unfamiliar. A service which preserved the order of packets would be closer to the properties of a data communication circuit and it would be expected to need less adaptation to existing teleprocessing software. To introduce a new kind of service and make it a commercial success is difficult. Something which approximates the properties of data circuits yet can offer attractive tariff rates and the speed changing and multiplexing features of packet switching is the obvious choice. This leads to the use of the 'virtual circuit', a concept that the Rand Corporation reports had already described.

A virtual circuit has one of the notable characteristics of a real communication circuit in that it preserves the sequence of information. A *real* circuit does not require the concept of a packet and its delay is constant for every bit that it carries so there is no question of loss of sequence. A packet-switched virtual circuit retains the packet switching advantages of speed change and the interleaving of packets which we described as demand multiplexing. So the virtual circuit has some of the characteristics of packet switching and adds a useful feature of a real circuit by retaining the sequence of the packets.

The virtual circuit changes the meaning of flow control. If a packet is not accepted at the destination none of those following it can be delivered. As soon as the network has absorbed as many packets as it can allocate buffers for this particular flow it must stop the input. A close coupling of flows from destination back to source is implied and this must be imposed by the network, which therefore must have a record in its storage at both ends that the virtual circuit exists. Whereas the transport of individual packets can be started very informally (from the communication subsystem viewpoint), a virtual circuit needs a procedure to establish it and when necessary to dissolve or clear it.

The Virtual Call

The circuits we employ in the telephone network are established for us when we make a telephone call. By dialling we tell the network the number or address we want to connect to, it establishes a switched circuit and we use this until the end of the call. The network then disconnects the circuit into its separate components so that they can be re-used as part of other switched circuits. The need for a virtual circuit is often short-term and the circuit is established by a calling procedure much like that of the telephone network. Thus a switched virtual circuit is established when the user makes a virtual call. Like the telephone circuit it is bi-directional or 'full-duplex'.

Since the network is basically just a packet network each virtual call involves it in setting up an internal procedure or structure which keeps the packets in sequence. This represents a cost to the network operator so he establishes the sequencing mechanism for each call when it is made and dismantles the mechanism when the call is disconnected. The way in which the call is set up and carried is different for different networks and some examples will be given shortly.

Those planning public networks, when they adopted the virtual call and decided that the main form of service would be of this kind, needed a name to distinguish the earlier and simpler version of packet switching. They described this as a *datagram service*. The datagram is, of course, no more than the familiar packet and a datagram service is nothing more than simple packet transport. It needs no new name except to distinguish it in the context of the virtual call facility.

The Need for a Datagram Service

The concept of the virtual call having been widely accepted the further question arose of the need for a datagram service. There is no difficulty of principle in providing both datagram and virtual call services in the same network. Indeed the customer interface for public packet-switched networks which is known as X25 can easily be extended to accommodate datagram service as an alternative—mixing virtual calls and datagrams at the same interface if necessary.

Interactive communication is, almost by definition, the alternate exchange of messages between the two parties to a conversation. If these messages contain many packets it is at least possible that they will be delivered in a changed sequence by the datagram service. Some of the important uses of future networks will be in simple, stylised transactions employing no more than one packetful of information in each direction for each 'utterance'. Perhaps the simplest examples are the cash dispenser, credit validation or electronic funds transfer transactions which must form a big part of a future network's traffic. Their messages fall easily within the compass of one packet. For such an exchange it becomes doubtful whether the overhead involved in setting up a virtual call is justified. Because of the half-duplex, single-packet nature of the conversation the virtual call mechanism adds nothing of value to the communication service. Whether a datagram service can be economically justified will depend on the eventual volume of such datagram conversations in relation to total network traffic.

Implementation of the Virtual Call

Conceptually the easiest way to build a virtual call network is to start by building a network that offers simple packet transport and add sequencing as an extra feature. Figure 2.13 illustrates the principle. In the centre is a packet network able to transport packets between the subscribers A and B. The packets which this carries are of two kinds. Some are the data packets passing between A and B, others are special packets to set up, control and clear the call. To distinguish them the procedures used at the two ends recognise a number of special packet formats. The usual locations for these procedures or protocols are the two switching nodes serving A and B. The stages of setting up and clearing a call are shown in the figure, showing only one possible sequence among many that include call rejection or clearing from the other end. The steps are numbered in sequence, but the responses 5a and 6a are local so their relative sequence is unknown—and immaterial.

The procedure begins with a call request packet from subscriber A specifying the destination B. This call request packet is received and noted by the local switch and the corresponding call request is passed through the packet network to the switch at the destination end. A call request then goes to the subscriber B containing, incidentally, the address of the caller. If subscriber B accepts the call (by means of a call accept packet) this is signalled back through the network and a call accept packet reaches subscriber A. In all these exchanges the setting

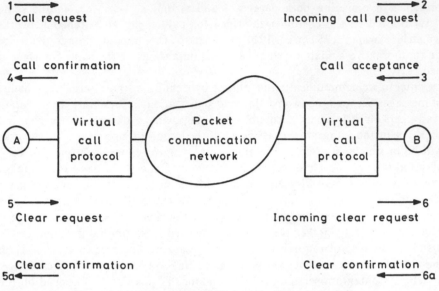

Figure 2.13   First method of virtual call implementation

up of the call has been monitored by the two switching centres at the ends of the call and they will have established the necessary computer processes, storage for packets and serial numbers to implement the virtual circuit. The main part of the call now begins, with the exchange of packets maintained strictly in sequence by the virtual call protocol mechanisms. Details of this type of mechanism will appear in Chapter 6. At the end of the conversation, a clear request packet from either subscriber is immediately confirmed and a packet sent through the network informs the other end which clears the call. Any processes and storage allocated to this call can then be released for other purposes.

Implementation of a virtual call in this way has the advantages that it leaves the basic packet network very simple and allows its alternative routing ability to be used to the maximum.

An alternative implementation is illustrated in Figure 2.14. The main network no longer simply transports packets but is able to maintain records of the path through the network for each of the virtual calls which it is sustaining. For each call which is established a path is found through the network and a record of it is maintained at each of the intermediate switching nodes so that succeeding packets of the same call can follow the same path. In this sense it becomes a real circuit through the network but the individual lines still maintain the demand multiplexing aspects of packet switching. It has been called *virtual channel switching*.

The call request packet comes from the calling subscriber and a special packet is generated which finds a path through the network to the called subscriber using a routing procedure which can be very much like the one used in a packet transport (datagram) network. Unlike a simple packet, this route-finding packet leaves a record of its path in each switching node it visits until it reaches the destination. The call accept packet returns by the same path and all subsequent packets of the conversation use this fixed route. If a failure happened among the switches or lines along the path this would cause the call to be released. Of course, duplication in the switches and duplication of lines can overcome this problem but it is a problem that is handled more naturally in the first method of implementation.

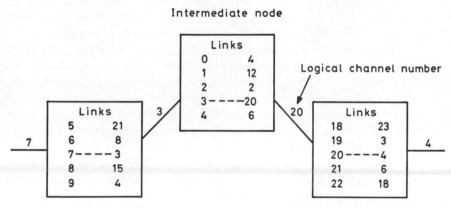

Figure 2.14   Second method of virtual call implementation

The second method of implementation has a compensating advantage. Packets passing through the network individually must carry with them the full address of their destination. When they pass along a fixed route the full destination is not necessary because the route forms a connected path. Each link between nodes identifies (by its own numbering scheme) all the virtual calls it is carrying. Within a switching node a pattern of virtual call connections is represented by a table showing which of these link numbers is connected to which others. Therefore the packet carries only a link address which is significant only for the link on which it is passing. The figure shows how this address is referred to the connection table, which determines the identity of the outgoing link and its new address on that link.

The address economy applies to the packets carried during the conversation, but the call request packet must carry the full addresses of source and destination because the linkages are not yet established. The second method of virtual call implementation lends itself to building special equipment for the rapid switching of packets after the call has been set up. The overhead for call set-up is perhaps greater than in the first method, but the switching mechanism can be simpler.

The Permanent Virtual Circuit

Those who use the telephone network for data transmission can employ either switched telephone calls or a leased line. Generally if they have sufficient· traffic to occupy a line for more than a few hours per day it will be cheaper for them to lease a line. This tariff advantage comes from the saving on switching equipment and the fact that lines are not fully used by switched calls, particularly outside the busy hours.

A corresponding facility has been devised for the virtual circuit network and is called the *permanent virtual circuit*. In this case a virtual circuit is established for the duration of an agreement between the subscriber and the network authority and is available to send packets in either direction at any time. It has all the features of a virtual call without the call set-up and release procedures. If we look at the methods of implementation we see that a permanent virtual circuit will occupy the same tables and procedure mechanisms that a call would require. It may also be necessary to retain the call set-up and clearing procedures and make them automatically restore the circuit from its controlling end if it happens to be broken. On cost grounds it can be predicted that the tariff advantage of a permanent virtual circuit will not be as good as that of the leased line facility. The earliest announced tariffs for public packet-switched networks confirm this supposition. The service which is offered exceeds that of a switched call in only one respect which concerns the possibility of congestion. If the network is overloaded it may have to refuse new calls but the permanent virtual circuits will remain established and be able to carry traffic, assuming that the flow control is good and that flow congestion is avoided.

2.7   SPECIAL FEATURES IN PACKET NETWORKS

The main purpose of a packet-switched communication network is to transport packets to their destination and, in the case of a virtual call network, to establish and release calls. There are a few additional functions which are commonly found in these networks and which are properly part of the communications subsystem. We shall describe these under the headings of delivery confirmation, trace, echo, drop, statistics, fault diagnosis and charging. Figure 2.15 illustrates their operation.

In addition there are services which the users find very helpful but are not strictly part of the subnet. For example a list of subscribers and their addresses—a network directory—can be presented as an on-line information service accessible to anyone with a suitable terminal. Not only the names and addresses of subscribers but also the services which they can offer are provided by a directory—a kind of data network 'yellow pages'. Because these are presented as on-line services much of the tedium of cross-referencing to find what is wanted can be done by the machine if the design of the system and the handling of its data is good. Because of the unlimited and comparatively uncharted nature of network-provided services the value of a public network may depend on the quality of its directory information.

By using the network it should be possible for the directory service itself to call up more detailed information and save the enquirer from making his own

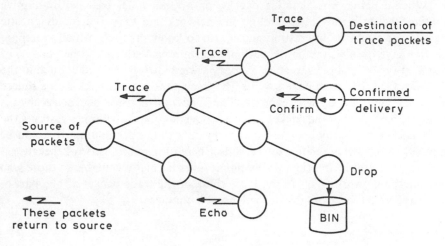

Figure 2.15   Special network features

calls to the services which interest him. Operators of services should be willing to provide this extra information without charge because it constitutes advertising material. The low cost of communication in these networks should remove the need for making an extra charge for directory service when it uses information from a third party.

Delivery Confirmation

In all telecommunications the ultimate confirmation that a message has reached the destination is the appropriate reply. If this comes all the way from the computer service at which the packet was aimed it verifies every part of the procedure. Some packet networks offer a special service of delivery confirmation, but this can only verify that the packet left the network over the interface to the destination subscriber and knows nothing about the fate of the information within the computer system. Nevertheless delivery confirmation is sometimes useful and it is requested by setting a bit in a special field in the packet header called the 'facilities field'. At the switch serving the destination this bit is recognised and, since the source of the packet is known, a special confirmation of packet delivery can be returned. In order to relate the packet to the one sent out it is sometimes arranged to repeat back the first few octets of the data content of the packet. The user can then, if he wishes, put a serial number in this position to ensure that delivery confirmations relate uniquely to the outgoing packets.

Trace Packets

When a network is handling packets on an individual basis with adaptive routing, the path they take through the network can vary and for diagnostic purposes it might be interesting and useful to know precisely which switching centres have been visited on the path of a certain packet. This is the purpose of a special type of packet known as a *trace packet* which is marked as such in the facilities field. For each node it visits, the trace packet sends back to the source a special report of its whereabouts. The sender of a trace packet receives a string of reports until the packet reaches its destination. In all other respects the trace packet is a normal one and can carry data to the destination. It would be unusual to offer this facility to the subscribers of a public network because it creates extra traffic and the information it gives is chiefly valuable to those who operate the network. We can therefore think of the trace packet as one part of the diagnostic tools available to the network engineer.

Echo

A software or protocol designer engaged in building network procedures must test these out in realistic conditions in the actual network. For this purpose he needs a cooperating destination and the network echo facility provides it. A switching node can be provided with a special echo destination such that a packet sent there is turned back to its origin with source and destination addresses interchanged. In this way a procedure involving two-way communication can be looped back to the originator. Echoed packets are marked as such by the echo source value. By using the echo facility at different nodes, varying path lengths can be tried in case they affect the procedure which is being tested. This echo facility is a useful one for the subscribers themselves. Strictly it need not be a special subnetwork feature because the echo destination can operate as though it were a terminal with special properties.

Drop

A different kind of test that the software designer might wish to perform uses the ability of its procedures to send packets but, for the time at least, he does not want to receive echoed copies. He therefore needs to find a destination which will accept packets at the rate he wishes to send them and simply throw them away. This is provided by a special 'drop' destination. A number of drop destinations could be provided but for the users a drop destination within reasonable distance is sufficient. Like echo it need not be a subnetwork feature but can operate on a special kind of terminal.

Network Statistics

Those who operate and maintain the communication subnet need to know how it is dealing with the traffic and what problems are appearing. For this purpose each node contains software that monitors the state of the network and collects reports and statistics. There is restricted access to this data. The kinds of data that can be collected are:

Traffic levels for each link in both directions,

occupancy of queues, including peak values,

use of the buffer space available in the node,

error rates and repeated transmissions on each link,

availability of links, short- and long-term closures,

in nodes with redundancy, the use of standby equipment.

Tables of values collected at regular intervals, together with accumulated figures, are transferred by messages to privileged destinations, usually at the request of the control centre. A related task is to report failures immediately to the centre.

When a network is first constructed its behaviour is uncertain so the statistics gathering is elaborate. The nodes and lines are typically under-used and the load of statistics is no problem. Later, when economy matters, just enough is collected to give advanced warning of impending overloads and help in the planning of extensions to the network. To enable the statistics gathering software to change according to current needs it should be modular and have provision for new modules to obtain variables which might prove worthy of attention in the future.

The Network Diagnostic Centre

When there is a fault in the communication network the symptoms may not be entirely straightforward. Because faults are, by definition, uncontrolled they can produce the appearance of faults elsewhere. To understand fully what is happening an overview of the apparent troubles in the whole of a network is required. The raw information for this overview comes from the statistics gathering in each of the switching nodes. Further diagnostic work to trace the cause of trouble involves looping back lines, disconnecting supposedly marginal or faulty lines and so forth. This is also best coordinated from one centre. Following the terminology of the ARPA network[14] this has come to be known as the *network control centre*, but the term is misleading because these networks are not centrally controlled and operate with distributed control. We propose to use the term *network diagnostic centre* which describes more accurately what is the main function of this centre.

The diagnostic centre has privileged access to all the nodes enabling it to request them to close down or attempt to reopen their communication lines. It can also call for reports of any of the statistics and fault information recorded at the nodes. In this way it is able to build up a comprehensive picture of the network situation.

The organisation of the diagnostic centre software can be at several levels. At the lowest level it carries out simple procedures to discover (by looking at both ends) whether a line is operational or not and to test whether it can be put back into operation. At the next level it makes regular routine checks of the state of the network and presents the information in a synoptic form to the network operators. It also undertakes the collection and presentation of statistics of queues and packet rates. At a higher level a general maintenance scheme can be written which carries out these functions at prescribed intervals and maintains a general log and display of the state of the system.

For most purposes the diagnostic centre operates as a host on the network but it has special privileges not enjoyed by subscribers to the network.

The diagnostic centre is not essential to the network's moment by moment operation but it is a valuable tool to assure the long-term health of the system. Depending on the reliability objectives it might be necessary to maintain two or more diagnostic centres at different switching nodes, well separated, to guard against the worst patterns of failure that will ever appear.

Private networks usually work with one operational diagnostic centre from which all maintenance operations are coordinated. Public networks, working on a larger scale, require greater specialisation in their diagnostic set-up. A central diagnostic facility such as we have described deals with the overall performance of the system. Local centres examine the performance and fault situation in subscribers' lines, since there are many of these and repair is a local matter.

Charging for Network Use

Private networks which operate for a single organisation can charge their cost as an overhead, for example by adding a fixed proportion to the charges for the services of computers in the network. When a communication system operates for a larger community such as a group of airlines or banks the cost must be spread over the organisations in an equitable fashion. It is not usual to establish a detailed tariff based on actual usage. A simpler basis is used for apportioning the cost.

Only in a public data communication network is the full mechanism of measuring network use and charging according to a stated tariff necessarily implemented. The information which has to be collected for each subscriber is the time for which calls have been established and the number of packets exchanged. Each node must collect these data. They can then be sent through the network to a central accounting facility on a regular basis.

The Closed User Group

One of the virtues of a private network is that it restricts access to those who have legitimate business with it. Operators of private networks, when contemplating the possibility of moving to using a public system, may be worried about the access this gives to switched calls from any other subscriber. Strict security can be provided only by proper cryptographic measures but nevertheless some users would like to see restricted access as an additional facility of public networks. This is the purpose of the *closed user group*. When they arrange to connect to the network a group of subscribers will request to be treated as a closed user group. This means that other users of the public network cannot call their terminals and they cannot call others. A variant can be provided which protects the members of the closed user group from outside calls but gives them 'outgoing access' to subscribers not in the group.

To operate the closed user group facility, call set-up packets or datagrams have a special field for numbers designating the individual groups. At the source of a call or datagram, the calling terminal claims the use of the group's facilities. Its membership is checked and if it is valid the packet is sent out with the group's designation attached. A closed user group terminal will not receive a call or datagram unless the incoming packet has the right group designation.

The implication of providing a closed user group facility is that the network authority will do its best to prevent any illegal outside access to the group from non-group terminals. Anyone who could generate traffic directly on the internode lines of a network could break into a closed user group if the group designation is carried in a clear form. This threat could be met by cryptography. Since the purpose of the closed user group is to discourage fraudulent or illegal operations it would be reasonable to expect the network authority to take security neasures which match the degree of threat.

2.8 WHY PACKET SWITCHING?

When packet switching was first proposed for computer communication, one of the purposes was to improve the utilisation of transmission paths. It was noticed that the short messages and sporadic traffic created by terminals left a large part of the communication capacity unused. Packet switching certainly makes better use of lines by multiplexing. On the other hand, with these relatively short messages the headers take up space. On the whole the advantage is with packet switching but it is not a strong one. In any case, the cost of communication lines is not a large part of the total cost of any dense network—in particular a public network in a medium-sized developed country.

A more tangible and positive advantage of packet switching is the facility for speed changing. In a digital communication path, the data rate of the line is strictly irrelevant to the information it carries. With packet switching. any terminal is able to choose the data rate appropriate to its traffic and its method of operation. In a circuit-switched network, on the other hand, the communicating devices fall into speed categories which are mutually exclusive.

Perhaps the most significant feature of packet switching is its interface with a multi-accessed computer. By multi-access we mean that the computer can engage in more than one conversation with other computers or terminals at the same time. The interface need employ only one transmission path on which packets for the various conversations are interleaved according to their current traffic demands. Not only does this provide better use of the communication channel (and these access channels have a significant cost) but it is also an interface which better suits the way that a computer works. Unfortunately, decades of software development based on direct 'transparent' links to terminals have generated complex telecommunication packages which are difficult to dismantle or adapt to the new circumstances. If we are able to start again, as we can in most specialised network applications, the software to handle a packet-interleaved interface is much simpler. This advantage of packet switching in the multileaved interface is one which will only gradually be realised as computer software is adapted.

The Virtues of Circuit Switching

Circuit switching is familiar because we use it every day in the telephone network. The software written for all established major ranges of computers to handle data communication by means of the telephone network gives it a big initial advantage, except perhaps for the complexity and size of that software. Some of the complexity is due to circuit switching's chief problem which is the variety of services at different speeds which cannot readily interwork.

Packet switching necessarily involves processing functions applied to each packet, but in a circuit network, after the call has been established, the data passes through in a 'transparent' manner. Therefore, circuit switching comes into its own with the transport of data in large quantities. The link protocol which is employed can be optimised for the particular communications problem using a block size and an error control scheme which makes best use of the link. The corresponding use of a packet-switched network has extra overheads because of the fixed maximum size of the packet.

There are some kinds of digital transmission in which the bits are truly isochronous, that is, tied absolutely to a timescale. The largest in bulk of traffic will be digital speech transmission, to be joined later by an increasing amount of digital facsimile and possibly video traffic. These bulky transmissions gain nothing from packet switching and their time-related demands are difficult for a packet network. In the military context it is probable that packet networks on the lines of the Rand Corporation studies are needed and will be built. For other purposes circuit switching is best for this traffic.

If this same speech or facsimile data is transformed to remove some of its high level of redundancy the situation changes. The rate of the source is then variable. For example, a speech channel could first eliminate silent periods. Then it could reduce channel requirements by linear predicted coding or simply by using the similarity of one larynx period to the next. These measures make a rapidly varying source rate. Storage to smooth out the rate introduces delay. The less redundant information could well be carried economically by a packet-switched service.

Integrated Networks

One of the stated aims of public network authorities is to achieve an 'integrated network' able to carry by a single kind of transmission and switching mechanism all kinds of telecommunication traffic. The conversion of all kinds of signal to digital streams in modern transmission equipment makes this feasible. Integration in transmission is inevitable but this is not the same as an integrated network.

One of the ideas behind this integrated network is that time division switching and multiplexing in the telephone network should be adaptable for data purposes. Unfortunately the economics of telephone switching do not lead to a suitable data service. For example, it has been suggested that fast circuit switching can provide the interleaving of short messages from many terminals and in this way provide one of the advantages of packet switching. A switch which was able to set up and release calls at this higher rate would be a poor match for telephone traffic. There is a real danger that a fully integrated network would treat data with lower priority as a factor in network design. The dominance of telephone traffic and the smaller revenues from data make this almost inevitable. If the two kinds of traffic have to be separated because of different calling rates, line occupancy and so forth, it is better to recognise the wide difference and meet the data communication needs in the best possible way.

If this dominating effect of the telephone network needs illustration, there is an example in the choice of envelope that has already been made for future circuit-switched networks. One of the most well-established features of computers has been the 8-bit byte or octet. It appears in character codes, word lengths and packet formats. Future standards may not need to be limited to an 8-bit structure but they should adapt to it when they can. A synchronous time division channel handles a small unit of data and the choice had to be made between 6 bits, which would suit the established pattern of the telephone network, and 8 bits, which would suit data communication. The 6-bit unit was chosen, though it complicated the network's data user interface greatly. A fully integrated network would in practice be a telephone network adapted to data use.

The telephone and telex networks have existed side by side without a strong argument for their integration although their traffic characteristics are much closer than those of speech and data. The switching costs for data can probably be made lower than those for speech and the transmission costs are likely to be very small so a non-integrated solution would improve the data network tariff.

Where integration is most needed is in the local network. The application of modern technology to most of the telephone network is under way but the kilometre or two of twisted copper wire between the local switch and the telephone set remains. Advances in switching and transmission, particularly for data, will have the effect of making this local distribution cost dominant.

Introduction of digital transmission into the local telephone network will take place very slowly because of the large capital investment and the size of the changeover task. When it does take place it is imperative that the system design employed should take full account of data. In general, most business and many domestic telephone connections will in future need to be accompanied by an independent data path—independent because the telephone and data connection will be used simultaneously. A telephone call will give rise to a data enquiry and vice versa. The technical means for this local network transmission are not difficult to find but their optimisation and practical realisation will take time.

One of the complicating issues has been the proposal that wideband services should also be incorporated, for television, facsimile and viewphone. It is here that national policies vary and we must beware of standards which favour one type of solution.

To summarise the situation, network integration between data and speech makes sense in two contexts. Transmission will always be integrated because of the cost saving. The local network is expensive and must be made to carry data, speech and other traffic. A strong attack on the redesign of the local network would yield great economies, leaving the two kinds of switching system to develop independently. Integration at the level of high-speed digital transmission is already a fact.

2.9 PACKET-SWITCHED NETWORKS IN PRACTICE

The proving of packet switching in a practical sense went through three phases. Firstly it had to be shown that it was feasible at all, secondly that it could handle the requirements of computer networks conveniently and thirdly that it could be elaborated into public networks with many more terminals and high reliability and availability.

The feasibility was not accepted at first. Those who had struggled with real-time software for stored program control of telephone systems believed that the ideas, simple as they seemed in practice, would run into similar problems. The complexity of telegraph message switching tended to reinforce the pessimistic view. Software design has improved in the meantime but it was still remarkable how little difficulty early packet-switched systems presented. The principle, and the way the system was modularised, seemed to lend itself to effective software design. The early examples were a local network at the UK National Physical Laboratory,[9] the famous ARPA network[10] and the SITA network.[11] Each one had complexity that might, in retrospect, have been separated out from the subnetwork. The NPL network controlled an elaborate byte-multiplexed terminal distribution system, the ARPA network had its reassembly feature creating a 'big packet' and the SITA network combined packet and message switching. In spite of these complications they each came into operation without many problems, considering the degree of innovation they represented. Subsequent networks of generally more 'streamlined' design such as Cyclades[15] and the European Informatics Network[16] reinforced the experience that packet switching is a designable technique.

The ARPA and SITA networks gave the earliest experience of widespread networks handling the traffic of many diverse users. In particular the early development of protocols in the ARPA network pointed the direction for the next step forward.

Packet switching was found to fit very well with the requirements of network protocols. First of all, network protocols demand their own formats for messages with specially devised headers for each level of protocol development. Packet transport (or any kind of block transmission) provides fixed points from which the format of messages can be defined. It is therefore very important that packet networks should retain the structure of each packet and not attempt to merge packets or split them in an arbitrary way. Where merging or splitting is done a larger definition of 'message' is employed and the message should be identified through the network. If a packet structure was not available it would be necessary as the first stage of any protocol to devise a similar block structure.

A second factor in the adaptability of packet switching to network protocols is the predominance in protocols of short administrative messages. It is a fact that protocols employ a proportion of 'red tape' messages to set up the right initial conditions for a conversation, to acknowledge messages, diagnose errors and so forth. These short administrative messages probably amount to more than 50 per cent of the total of messages carried for any complex computer-organised task and this is true whatever kind of communication subsystem is used. Packet switching serves this kind of traffic very well.

The early packet networks vindicated the traffic assumptions on which their design was based. They showed the importance of speed changing and other measures to overcome terminal incompatibiity. Above all they verified that the majority of messages were short, in fact less than one packet long. So message assembly, packet re-sequencing and so forth, essential as they are, do not make up a large part of the network's operation.

By 1975 when the European Informatics Network was being designed[16] the communication subsystem was no longer a serious design problem but the treatment of terminals and the design of protocols remained controversial and difficult. Public packet-switched networks demanded higher standards of reliability and availability.

From 1975 onwards the development of public packet-switched networks was rapid. In fact, an early network in Spain[17] was the first network of this kind. The ARPA design was adapted to form the Telenet service in USA and the UK Post Office built an experimental packet communication system,[18] later to be replaced by a network to X25 standards. The first major packet network from an established carrier was Datapac in Canada[19] and France, after some experiments with RCP, introduced Transpac[20] with a distance-independent tariff. Figure 2.16 is a map of the first stage of development of the Transpac network. By this time, most advanced countries had announced plans for public data networks, some starting with circuit switching, some with packet switching and several having plans to install both services in due time.

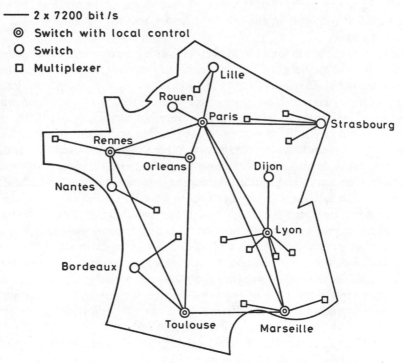

Figure 2.16   Map of the first phase of development of Transpac

References

Davies, D. W., and Barber, D. L. A.,
Communication Networks for Computers,
John Wiley and Sons, London (1973).

2. Jackson, P. E., and Stubbs, C. D.,
   'A study of multi-access computer communications',
   AFIPS Conf. Proc. Spring JCC., **34**, 491 (May 1969).
3. Fuchs, E., and Jackson, P. E.,
   'Estimates of distributions of random variables for certain computer traffic models',
   Comm. ACM, **13**, No. 12, 752 (December 1970).
4. Baran, P., Boehm, S. P., and Smith, J. W.,
   On distributed communications, Summary overview,
   Memorandum RM-3767-PR, Rand Corporation (August (1964)
   (Ore of a series of 11 reports)
5. Baran, P.,
   'On distributed communication networks',
   IEEE Trans. on Communication Systems, **CS-12**, 1 (March 1964).
6. Davies D. W., Bartlett, K. A., Scantlebury, R. A., and Wilkinson, P. T.,
   'A digital communication network for computers giving rapid response at remote terminals',
   Proc. ACM Symp. on Operating System Principles, Gatlinburg (1967).
7. Davies, D. W.,
   'Communication networks to serve rapid response computers', *Proc. IFIP Congress*, **72**, 650 (August 1968).
8. Scantlebury, R. A.,
   'A model for the local area of a data communication network—objectives and hardware organisation',
   Proc. ACM. Symp. Pine Mountain, Ga., 179 (October 1969).
9. Scantlebury, R. A., and Wilkinson, P. T.,
   'The National Physical Laboratory data communication network',
   Proceedings of ICCC, Stockholm, 223 (August 1974).
10. Roberts, L. G., and Wessler, B. D.,
    'Computer network development to achieve resource sharing',
    AFIPS Conf. Proc. Spring JCC., **36**, 543 (May 1970).
11. Brandt, G. J., and Chretien, G. J.,
    'Methods to control and operate a message-switching network'.
    Symposium on computer-communications networks and Teletraffic, New York, 263 (April 1972).
12. Heart, F. E., Kahn, R. E., Ornstein, S. M., Crowther, W. R., and Walden, D. C.,
    'The Interface Message Processor for the ARPA Network',
    AFIPS Conf. Proc. Spring JCC, **36**, 551 (May 1970).
13. Kahn, R. E., and Crowther, W. R.,
    'Flow control in a resource sharing computer network',
    Proc. ACM/IEEE Conf. on Problems in the Optimisation of Data Communication Systems, Palo Alto (October 1971).
14. Frank, H., Frisch, I. T., and Chou, W.,
    'Computer communications network design—Experience with theory and practice',
    AFIPS Conf. Proc. Spring JCC., **40**, 255 (May 1972).
15. Pouzin, L.,
    'Presentation and major design aspects of the Cyclades computer network',
    3rd IEE/ACM Data Comm. Symp., St. Petersburg, 80 (November 1973).
16. Porcet, F., and Repton, C. S.,
    'The EIN communication subnetwork principles and practice',
    Proceedings of ICCC, Toronto, 523 (1976).

17. Alarcia, G.,
    'C.T.N.E.'s packet switching network, its application',
    Proceedings of ICCC, Stockholm, 163 (1974).
18. Pearson, D. J., and Wilkin, D.,
    'Some design aspects of a public packet switched network',
    Proceedings of ICCC, Stockholm, 199 (1974).
19. Clipsham, W. W., Glave, F. E., and Narraway, M. L.,
    'Datapac network overview',
    Proceedings of ICCC, Toronto, 131 (1976).
    (Also three other papers on Datapac in this volume.)
20. Daret, A., Despres, R., Le Rest, A., Pichon, G., and Ritzenthaler, S.,
    'The French public packet switching service: the Transpac network',
    Proceedings of ICCC, Toronto, 251 (1976).

Chapter 3

Routing

3.1 INTRODUCTION

Successful operation of a data communication network is critically dependent on the provision of an adequate routing algorithm. In a circuit-switched network the routing algorithm operates during call set-up, whilst a route is being selected; in a packet-switched network the algorithm may either determine individually the routing of each data packet or else set up a route to be followed by a sequence of packets. Sophisticated routing methods have been used for many years in circuit-switched telephone networks. In the discussion that follows we shall see to what extent these methods can be carried over into the domain of packet switching. Indeed we shall find that in certain cases the technologies overlap to a limited degree.

The degree of difficulty of the routing problem in any network is strongly influenced by the network topology. In a star-connected network with full duplex links, Figure 3.1(a), each network node accepting and delivering user traffic is connected to a single central node through which all traffic must pass. Only the central node need be in possession of information defining the network topology; each destination node is served by a distinct link and the node routing table matches destination to output link. Thus the routing algorithm is one of great simplicity.

Another very simple arrangement is that of network nodes connected in a single ring, Figure 3.1(b). Here, if the links are duplex, traffic can reach any destination from any source either way round the ring. Again the routing algorithm can be quite trivial, needing no routing table as an essential feature. However, it is obvious that in many cases one way round the ring is a much shorter route than the other; here one may either provide a routing table at each node defining the shortest path to each destination or else by the node numbering system enable any node taking a routing decision to calculate which is the shorter path.

A network arrangement that can also make use of node numbering systems as an aid to the routing algorithm is that of the regular rectangular lattice,

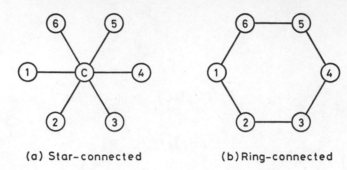

(a) Star-connected   (b) Ring-connected

Figure 3.1   Simple network topologies

Figure 3.2(a). In this case there are usually at least two shortest routes of equal length from a source to a destination (except in the case of immediately adjacent nodes). Node numbering is designed to indicate the row and column occupied by each node in the lattice. Each node needs to know how to direct traffic towards greater or lesser numbered rows and column numbers. This latter information may be presented in the form of a rudimentary routing table at each node.

In a tree-connected network, Figure 3.2(b), the addressing system can be designed to specify uniquely the path to be taken from one node to another; in such a network only one path exists between each node pair. The whole of the information necessary for the operation of the routing algorithm can be contained within the address; no routing tables are required in any node, only an indication of how to move up or down the network. In the illustration we show a simple construction in which one link leads from a node to the next level

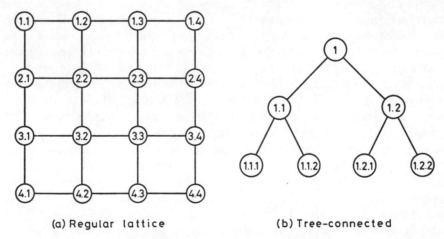

(a) Regular lattice   (b) Tree-connected

Figure 3.2   Simple network topologies

above, whilst two links lead to the level below; the latter number need not, of course, be limited to two.

As a final example of networks with very simple routing algorithms we mention the fully connected network, Figure 3.3(a). In this case every node has a direct link to every other node and possesses a routing table defining the unique link to be used to reach each destination. The routing algorithm could hardly be simpler.

These network topologies which lead to simple routing algorithms may be found in practice in certain special circumstances, but most real-life networks have much more complex topologies with irregular mesh configurations, Figure 3.3(b). Network node location is usually dictated by user need; the links joining the nodes depend on route and bandwidth availability and cost considerations frequently play a dominant part.

Route selection within an irregular mesh can be far more difficult than it is in the special cases considered above. By far the largest and best-known irregular mesh network is that of the public telephone system, extending via international links throughout the world.

Routing of calls within the circuit-switched telephone network is subject to certain particular constraints. Users or subscribers are each connected to a local office which may serve several thousand subscribers. For a whole range of reasons a user-to-user call must not pass through too many local offices. It is not economically sensible to provide direct trunk lines between all, or even most, local offices. Therefore the telephone system is provided with switching centres at several levels; the topology is hierarchical.

In the UK telephone network, local offices within a neighbourhood are connected by direct routes, known as 'junctions'. Provided capacity is available,

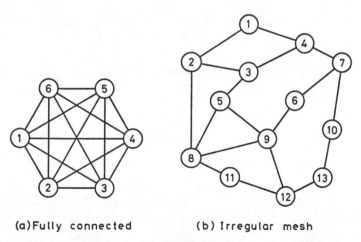

(a) Fully connected   (b) Irregular mesh

Figure 3.3   Other topologies

and provided the number of junctions included in a user-to-user call is limited, these routes are preferred. If capacity is not available or if too many junctions would be involved in a call, then the call is routed to the next level up the hierarchy, the group switching centre or GSC. GSCs are interconnected by trunks, but the GSC system is not fully connected. Any call is permitted to pass through three GSCs, but no more. If call completion can be made at the GSC level, subject to this constraint, then the higher levels of the hierarchy are not used in the call. However, should the call be over a longer distance or the lower

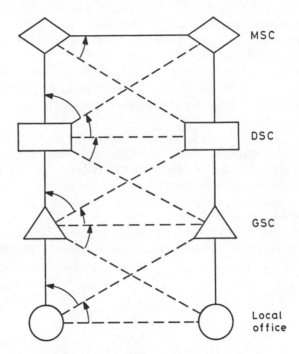

Figure 3.4   Hierarchical levels in a telephone network

levels of the hierarchy be fully loaded with other calls, then the call is routed to the higher levels of the hierarchy (the transit network), at district switching centre (DSC) or main switching centre (MSC) level. Main switching centres are fully connected in the UK via carrier systems. A schematic representation of the four levels of the hierarchy is given in Figure 3.4, in which the arrows represent the sequence of transfers of calls to higher levels if the lower levels are fully loaded. Subscriber and switching centre address numbering is designed to facilitate route-finding within the network. In this respect the system is similar to the lattice and tree-connected examples discussed above. Routing tables, as used comprehensively in packet-switched networks, are not required in such a configuration; they are, however, needed in tandem exchanges.

We see that the route chosen for a particular call depends both on the loading of the network and on the number of switching centres traversed. The dependence on loading introduces a degree of route adaptivity which we shall also find in the packet-switched context. The use of long-distance links at a higher hierarchical level is relevant when we come to consider very large packet-switched networks. Apart from these two points of similarity routing in packet-switched networks operates under different constraints. For example, the number of intermediate nodes traversed is not critical, as each packet is individually stored in each successive node. Perhaps the most important distinction is in the different addressing systems used; in circuit switching the destination address format of a call, used digit by digit, strongly influences the route taken by the call through the net (tables of alternative routes exist at some switching centres); in packet switching the addressing format need have little relation to the chosen route for each packet.

For an irregular mesh-connected packet switching network it is possible that the network designer may choose to dispense altogether with a formal systematic routing algorithm because the topology of the network may not be sufficiently known at each node or because the topology of the network is subject to change (for example in a military situation under enemy attack). In this case the packets may be forwarded either by *flooding* (multiple copies of a packet forwarded on all output links from a node) or by *random routing* (single copy of a packet forwarded by a node along a link chosen at random). The properties of these and other simple routing techniques are considered in detail in Section 3.4.

In modern packet-switched networks it is more usual to find a routing algorithm which tries to ensure a systematic progression of each packet from its source to its destination. In order to achieve this the routing process at each network node seeks to select for each packet the most appropriate output link on which to forward the packet. The packet header contains of necessity the destination address (or addresses for multiple destinations). Using the destination address obtained from the packet header, the routing process accesses a routing table to determine the choice of output link. The choice may be defined simply by seeking the shortest path or it may be complicated by an attempt to take into account local or global measurement of the loading of the network components, links and nodes. Routing of this kind was often called *directory routing* in the earlier days of networking. Its operation is strongly analogous to traffic behaviour in a road network, with signposts at intersections indicating the best routes for each destination.

The correct choice of routing algorithm may influence strongly the operation of the network. The network designer may seek to choose an algorithm that will allow maximum carrying capacity (by using multiple routes between source and destination) or, on the other hand, rapid transit may be more important, in which case a different routing algorithm might be used. Certainly the routing algorithm must be capable of rerouting traffic in the event of the failure of some part of the network.

3.2 TAXONOMY OF ROUTING ALGORITHMS

Routing in networks has been widely studied since the earliest days; many Ph.D. theses have been written on the subject and some very promising techniques proposed. Few of these techniques have been implemented in real-life networks. In this section we shall be concerned with algorithm classification. Most of the algorithms cited are considered in depth in later sections of this chapter.

Message switching networks have been known for a long time in the form of telecommunication networks with torn-tape switching centres. In these centres routing was carried out by human operators reading printed tape addresses and feeding tapes into selected tape readers for output.

Store-and-forward packet switching networks were first proposed in the context of military communications. An early discussion of routing in such networks may be found in Prosser,[1] the stress being on reliability and survivability. Since loss of network components is a real problem in this context, giving rise to changing topology, there is much to be said for routing techniques that do not require stored routing tables at each node. One such possible routing technique is that of random routing (see Section 3.4), whose performance is analysed in detail by Prosser, who categorises it as inefficient, but robust. The other type of routing technique considered by Prosser is that which uses a 'directory' or routing table in each node, giving greater efficiency, but also greater vulnerability in the face of component failure. Prosser indicated that the best routing algorithm would involve a blend of random and directory processes and promised a discussion of such a combination in a further paper. As far as can be ascertained this further paper was unfortunately never published.

During the middle-to-late 1960s much work on network routing techniques was carried out at the Rand Corporation by Baran and others. A convenient and comprehensive summary of this and other work may be found in the 1969 paper of Boehm and Mobley.[2] The emphasis is still on survivability of military communication networks. Boehm and Mobley were concerned to identify routing techniques which, whilst offering higher efficiency than flooding and random routing, are able to adapt well to changing circumstances. Adaptive techniques known in 1969 were classified by Boehm and Mobley into stochastic and deterministic processes; the former use estimates of the time required to reach a destination calculated from observations of messages passing through nodes, the latter compute the time required to reach a destination under ideal conditions from the structure of the network. Both processes may involve learning by the network nodes. A comparison of techniques was based on the way in which each was able to cope with the destruction, at random, of half the links in a 50-node network with 100 links; this is a rather extreme standard of comparison for general purposes, though appropriate in the military context.

Adaptive routing is clearly an important contender for routing in packet-switched networks, be they civil or military. Chiefly in the context of the ARPA network, Fultz[3] gives a valuable survey of adaptive routing methods, appraising them both by queueing theory and simulation techniques. Fultz adopts the same classification as Boehm and Mobley, stochastic and deterministic, but adds a third which he calls 'flow control' routing. Fultz's basic deterministic techniques are flooding, fixed routing, split traffic (bifurcation) and ideal observer routing. His stochastic techniques are random routing, isolated adaptive routing and distributed adaptive routing. Flow control routing relates to the ability of the network to refuse acceptance of new traffic when under pressure of heavy offered traffic and unable by diverting traffic to alternative routes to avoid congestion. We shall see later in the present discussion that routing and flow control interact to some extent. We would not, however, propose a method of routing integral with flow control as is almost implied by Fultz. Fultz's important contribution is his full treatment of distributed routing in the ARPA context.

Fultz's fellow-student, Gerla, discusses optimal routing in his Ph.D. thesis,[4] in the wider context of network design, introducing the important flow deviation approach to the solution of non-linear multi-commodity flow problems. A discussion of the flow deviation techniques appears in Chapter 10. Queueing theory and network flow theory methods are applied to a detailed analysis of deterministic routing policies. These methods are not readily applicable to stochastic routing policies.

Another very important thesis on routing in computer networks, by McQuillan,[5] followed in 1974, giving, in the first place, a very comprehensive review of network routing studies to that time. McQuillan then proceeded to classify the required network performance goals and categorised routing algorithms according to the ways in which they met these goals. As a basis for a classification of routing algorithms he postulated four routing doctrine functions:

control regime;
decision process;
updating process;
forwarding process.

These respectively govern the flow of routing information, produce the routing choices, update the routing information at all nodes and choose the paths for packets. Under the control regime function, McQuillan identifies four possibilities:

deterministic routing—fixed policy unaffected by changing conditions;

isolated adaptive routing—in which each node makes routing decisions based on purely local information;

distributed adaptive routing—in which nodes exchange information and the routing decisions are based on a blend of local and shared information;

centralised adaptive routing—in which nodes report local information to a routing centre, which in turn issues routing instructions to the individual nodes.

Having established a classification scheme for routing algorithms, McQuillan proceeds at length to discuss the construction of routing doctrines of various types, particularly the distributed algorithm used in the ARPA network. He identifies the problems associated with this algorithm, particularly that caused by the nodes acting too hastily on information shared between them, with consequent misrouting of traffic. We shall discuss this interesting problem in detail in Section 3.5. McQuillan's thesis concludes with a survey of the special problems of routing in heterogeneous networks and in very large networks.

Rudin[6] introduces yet another type of routing, which he calls 'delta' routing, in which a centralised network routing controller is used to determine routing decisions only when these cannot be made on the basis of local information. This doctrine, which we shall also discuss in detail later, may be expected to give optimum or near-optimum performance in many network applications.

Apart from the non-directory methods such as random routing or flooding, we shall discuss the main practically useful directory methods under two principal categories—*fixed* and *adaptive*. Fixed routing may be further subdivided into, firstly, the case in which only single routes are specified between any node and the required destination and, secondly, the case in which multiple alternative routes are allowed between any node and the required destination, a specified fraction of traffic being allocated to each. Adaptive routing we shall subdivide, following McQuillan, into *isolated*, *distributed*, *centralised* and, arising from the work of Rudin, *hybrid* (combination of isolated, distributed and centralised).

3.3   THE EVALUATION OF ROUTING DOCTRINES

In several quite distinct areas in computer science one meets design problems which, because of the strong parallels with activities already understood by people in their daily lives, are expected to be capable of quite simple, almost trivial solution. Route-finding in networks is one such activity, because people are well accustomed to finding their way around transportation systems.

Indeed the routing process involved in packet switching networks may be quite simple. To design a routing process based on flooding needs only a systematic duplication of packets to leave a node on all output links (excepting that on which each packet was received by the node). The process at the destination node must be able to recognise packets destined to that node and it may be necessary to recognise duplicates arriving later.

To design a routing process to use completely fixed routing requires that each node be able to recognise the destination of each packet, and to use this destination to access a *routing table* which will identify the unique link at the node on which each packet must be forwarded. The difficulty here lies in the calculation of the routing tables for all the network nodes. The simplest calculation will specify tables giving the shortest path between each source and

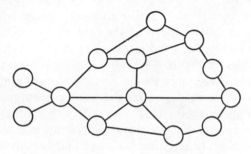

(a) Irregular mesh network

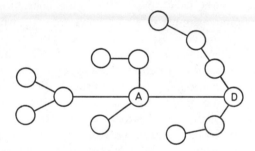

(b) Sink tree for node D

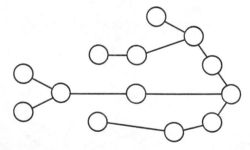

(c) Routing adjusted to distribute load

Figure 3.5　Adjustment of sink-tree routing to produce more even loading destination, effectively defining a *sink tree* for each destination in the network. A sink tree defines a set of paths, one from each network source, to one destination; the set of shortest paths to a destination is, by its very nature, tree-shaped. Consider the network of Figure 3.5(a); the set of shortest paths to the destination node marked D is as shown in Figure 3.5(b). The shortest path from any node to a destination is Markovian in character; this is to say that the previous history of a travelling packet (original source, nodes visited, links traversed) does not affect the designation of the shortest path to a destination from a particular node. If the traffic load matrix, in terms of flows between each source–destination pair, is known to the network designer and does not vary with time, then the fixed shortest-path routing tables can be modified to take advantage of spare capacity in parts of the network; the shortest-path routing tables may lead to unwelcome concentrations of traffic which can be dispersed by changing the tables. In Figure 3.5(b), if it is assumed that the flows from all nodes to node D are equal, note that a shortest-path routing doctrine places rather a large load on node A and on the link between nodes A and D. By adjusting the routing as shown in Figure 3.5(c) this situation is somewhat relieved, though, of course, other network components take an increased load.

The fixed route choice to a destination may be made to depend on the source from which the packet has come, a separate routing table entry being provided for traffic from each source which passes through a node to each destination. Figure 3.6 gives a simple example in which flows are split over more than one path, depending on the source of the individual packets.

The method just mentioned is one way of using more than one route for traffic between a node and a destination. Another method is to split the traffic between a node and destination, irrespective of source, deterministically in fixed proportions sent over two or more output links. The optimisation, given a static traffic matrix, of the specified proportions for each traffic flow is a network problem that has received much attention from network designers. It is more amenable to satisfactory solution using well-known analytic techniques (see, for example, Ford and Fulkerson[7]) than some of the less well-defined problems of adaptive routing which we shall meet later.

The aim of adaptive routing is to make each individual routing decision on

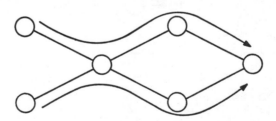

Figure 3.6   Non-Markovian routing

the basis of the current state of the network (state of network component operability and state of traffic). The practical problem is that each node routing decision process has to operate with incomplete information on the state of the rest of the network. At best the process will have access to the state of traffic in its own node and some indication of the position in its immediately neighbouring nodes; information on nodes and links further afield may well be incomplete and will certainly be out of date.

With these constraints in mind it should be obvious that the design of an optimised adaptive routing algorithm is a complex matter and that the prediction of its performance by analytic methods may present considerable difficulties.

The design of a basic, non-optimal, adaptive algorithm can be quite simple; it may be stated in terms of measurement of transit times, queue lengths, traffic flows, etc., with consequent diversion of traffic to this route or that. To optimise the performance of such an algorithm is the challenging task. Choice between rival possible adaptive algorithms is even less easy.

If the budget of a proposed network permits, then the simplest method of measuring the performance of a routing algorithm is to try it out on the real live network. In these circumstances alternative algorithms may be readily compared using real or specially generated traffic over the network itself. Performance with different traffic patterns can be assessed. This method has been used extensively in connection with the ARPA network,[8] where it has been possible to compare routing doctrines by analytic methods, by simulation methods and by measurement of real traffic performance on the network. The designer with all these tools at his disposal is fortunate indeed—and is rarely met in practice.

The more usual demand on a routing algorithm designer is that, given a network topology, a specification of link and node capacity and a definition of the predicted traffic matrix, he is expected to design an algorithm that will operate efficiently from the moment when the network is first switched on. The only two design evaluation methods at his disposal are mathematical modelling and simulation modelling.

In *mathematical modelling* use is made of the theories of queueing processes and of flows in networks, describing the performance of the network in a set of equations. Unfortunately the complexity of a packet switching network expressed in this way is formidable. The analytic method has been used with success by Kleinrock[9] and others,[10] but only if important simplifying assumptions are made in the mathematics. Perhaps the best-known is that of the 'independence assumption', under which packets arriving in a new node take on a new packet length; no less important is the assumption that no node ever runs out of packet buffers. The independence assumption is not a particularly drastic departure from reality, but, if the network designer is at all concerned with questions of congestion effects, then the infinite buffer pool assumption clearly rules this out of court. It is heartening in Kleinrock's work to see the good correspondence achieved between the results of analytic methods and those of simulation. It is doubtful whether the correspondence would be as good if extreme conditions, such as very heavy traffic overload or buffer famine, were postulated.

More recently techniques of diffusion analysis have been applied[11] successfully to queueing networks. This has allowed the elimination of some of the more unrealistic of the approximations and assumptions. Nevertheless simplifying assumptions are still essential to make analysis tractable.

Simulation

This brings us to the remaining evaluation tool at the designer's disposal, that of computer *simulation*. In simulation, the network and its operating system are modelled in terms of a purpose-written computer program. This should in no sense be an emulation, seeking to duplicate every small detail of network operation. Slyke, Chou and Frank[12] point out that a simulation model that seeks to cover every detail is an extremely expensive, wasteful and slow-running operation. For example, if a terminal polling operation is involved, then it would be wrong to simulate every distinct polling operation, because most of them would be negative. In simulation the time of a positive response to a poll can be predicted and the polling operation is activated in the simulation only at the appropriate time, thus avoiding wasting simulation time over the negative response polls. As a general rule one should only simulate the system features that are relevant; the skill of the simulation model designer lies in selecting the relevant features. However, it is dangerous to eliminate too much detail from the model; in assessing a routing algorithm one should describe the nodal queue-handling procedures and the routing process itself in full detail.

Having created a simulation model of a network, the experimenter applies simulated traffic to the model and observes the performance. The latter may be defined in many ways—means of transit times and flows, statistical distributions of transit times and flows, times and flows on specific routes, etc., etc. The exact choice of experimental parameters to be measured must depend on the nature of the network being simulated. It is a simple matter to replace one routing algorithm by another in the model and to obtain performance comparisons. Indeed tests on quite drastic changes of network operating system can be made simply and relatively inexpensively. Performance in the face of network component failure can be made the subject of specially designed experiments in which failure of specific components can be modelled.

The problem with both mathematical modelling and simulation modelling is the validation of the model. The ARPA case mentioned above provides the ideal situation in which modelling results can be compared with the performance of the network itself. In the absence of such a facility the model must be examined very critically and, in the case of simulation, consistency checks for correct operation of the model can and must be built into the model itself.

An essential feature of any routing algorithm, whatever its design basis, is that it must be utterly reliable. Correct operation of routing algorithms is difficult enough to determine without having the added complexity of detecting an error in the functioning of the algorithm arising from corruption of program code or data tables. Therefore it is essential that all program code and data table store transfers shall be rigorously checked for accuracy. Early networks did not include this precautionary measure and their performance suffered accordingly.

3.4 SIMPLE ROUTING TECHNIQUES

We have already touched upon two of the simplest routing techniques that require no routing tables or, indeed, any knowledge of network topology, however expressed. We shall now proceed to consider the characteristics of these techniques in a little more detail.

A node operating under a random routing doctrine, having ascertained that a packet needs forwarding (i.e. is not destined to a locally connected user destination), chooses by a random process the output link on which to consign the packet. It would generally make good sense if the packet were not directed back along the link by which it had arrived in the node, so this link should be excluded from the selection process. If the network designer considers that a pseudo-random number generator is wasteful of processor time and program storage space, then it might be worthwhile considering using the output links in rotation as each new packet is routed by the node, subject to the rule for not sending a packet directly back along its tracks. The mixture of successive packets handled by a node, destined to a whole range of destinations, might achieve a sufficiently random use of output links.

Packets thus transported by the network travel a random walk and do not progress systematically towards their required destination. For a given network it should be possible to calculate the probability distribution of the possible path lengths (in terms of links traversed or 'hops') required to reach the destination. There is bound to be a finite probability that some path lengths may be very long. It may therefore be wise to attach a hop count of links traversed to each packet, and to eliminate packets whose hop count exceeds a predetermined limit. (Provision of a hop count limit is also an essential precaution to avoid infinite paths when the destination is unreachable, for example when from a number of link failures the network becomes divided into two unconnected parts.) This has the disadvantage that no guarantee of packet delivery is given to the user. However, the doctrine of random routing has the twin merits of extreme simplicity and complete independence of any knowledge of network topology.

The other simple routing process that neither requires nor acquires a knowledge of network topology is that of flooding. A node needing to forward a packet (again subject to check that the packet is not to be delivered locally) makes as many copies of the packet as the node has output links, less one. A copy of the packet is sent out on all the links except that from which the packet was received by the node. The hop count is again used to limit the number of successive forwarding operations. The hop count limit must be set just to exceed the shortest path distance between the most distant source–destination pair. When a packet's hop count limit has been reached no further forwarding takes place and the packet copy is destroyed. A signal merit of this system is that at least one copy of the packet will reach its destination by the shortest path—and therefore in the shortest time. However, this is achieved at the cost of heavy overheads; a large number of packet duplications and abortive packet transactions are inevitably involved, which can impose a considerable load on the network. Destination nodes may need to check for duplicate packet arrivals and to destroy such packets. Unlike random routing, flooding will achieve delivery of each packet transported, provided the required destination is reachable. The process is simple and, like random routing, needs no knowledge of network topology.

Both these routing methods have much to commend them where a network is expected to be lightly loaded with traffic and to need the ability to continue to function in the face of loss of network components due to adverse conditions, such as attack by an enemy.

Techniques have been proposed by which network nodes, initially ignorant of network topology, acquire knowledge of this as successive packets are handled. For this purpose packets are required to carry, in addition to the destination address for which they are bound, the source address from which they have come. Hop counts, also known as 'handover numbers' are also carried. Routing is by random process in the first instance, but nodes are programmed to take note of the hop count and source address of each packet handled. A packet with a hop count of one has clearly come from a directly connected neighbouring node; thus neighbouring nodes are quickly identified, with their connecting link—the first entries in a rudimentary routing table. A packet with a hop count of two has evidently arrived from a source which is only two hops away over the link on which it has arrived; this provides more information as to network topology. The process proceeds by comparing the hop count for a given source address with the minimum hop count already registered; if the new one is less, then it is substituted for the previous one and the corresponding link is noted as providing the shortest known path to the particular network node.

This method has been called *backwards learning*, because the shortest paths to particular nodes are learnt by watching the traffic that has come from those nodes. As the process proceeds so the random element in the routing process wanes and the routing by the newly created routing tables takes over. Clearly the system is capable of adapting to loss of network components or other changes of topology, though this adaptation may take place extremely slowly and inefficiently. Such adaptation depends on each node continuing to take note of the source addresses of packets in transit, even after the network routing has apparently settled down to a steady state.

Backwards learning has been used in conjunction with *hot potato* routing,[13] so called because a node receiving a packet attempts to hand it on as quickly as possible to the next node, a reaction similar to that of a human being handed a hot potato! In hot potato routing a node ranks its outgoing links in order of descending suitability for reaching each network destination. The backwards learning provides routing tables for the hot potato process, though to achieve tables giving ranked order of output links for each destination demands a backwards learning process of some sophistication. One version of hot potato routing involves the node forwarding process in sending out a packet on the highest ranked output link that happens to be free for transmission at the moment of the routing decision. If no appropriate link is available then the packet has to wait and leaves the node on the first such link that becomes free. Another version of hot potato routing assumes the provision of short queues of packets awaiting output on each link, a limit being placed on the number of packets that may wait on each queue. The routing process in this case selects the highest-ranked output queue that happens to have space available. Either of these methods may well lead to unsuitable output links being chosen for traffic, with long and tortuous routes, just because the best route in particular routing decisions happens to be fully occupied momentarily. The very haste shown by the hot potato routing process is an undesirable characteristic. Greater deliberation can lead to greater efficiency.

Using a hot potato routing algorithm, but with pre-calculated routing tables as distinct from backwards learning, Healey[14] simulated a packet switching network with particular attention to its ability to withstand an applied traffic overload. The ability of the hot potato process to place a packet on any one of the output queues of a source node, however unsuitable the route so chosen, meant that queueing space would be found for an incoming packet from outside the network right up to the point where the node was full of packets awaiting output. This behaviour produced a solid lock-up with no traffic able to move towards destinations. It should be noted that packets were regarded in this experiment as individual entities with no notion of multi-packet messages or end-to-end protocol governing packet acceptance by source nodes for transmission through the network. Clearly the effect of the simple routing algorithm was to permit the acceptance of an excessive number of packets and to invite the network to fail by congestion. In work which followed this, Jolly and Adams[15] suggested a simple flow control to be used in conjunction with the hot potato routing. This was based on refusal of further traffic acceptance from source users whenever any of the output queue lengths in the node reached a pre-set level. When the output queue length fell below this threshold, acceptance of user traffic was resumed. This rather crude expedient had the effect of avoiding overfilling the net with traffic with consequent congestive failure. In the context of the experiments of Jolly and Adams it is also worth pointing out that it was found necessary to forbid hot potato routing of packets reaching their penultimate nodes. Traffic reaching a penultimate node was not allowed to be routed away from the link to the destination node; if the final link was congested, traffic was queued until this was available. These two changes to the basic hot potato routing doctrine allowed the network simulated to carry traffic moderately efficiently and to avoid congestive failure.

Fixed Routing

Of all the simple routing doctrines, perhaps the simplest and most obvious is that of *fixed routing*. Here routing tables are provided in each node by the network designer or by some network routing control centre. In the simplest form, fixed routing tables specify one particular link at each node to be used in reaching each particular destination; thus there is no choice mechanism involved in taking routing decisions. The routing tables may specify shortest paths between each source–destination pair. For a lightly loaded network this can be shown to give very satisfactory performance, with minimal transit times. If heavier loads are applied to such a network, then performance may degrade rapidly. This is because a set of shortest-path routing tables does not necessarily spread the traffic evenly over the network; certain nodes and links may become overloaded, whilst others have much spare capacity. If the traffic matrix is unchanging, then it is possible to recalculate the routing tables in such a way as to even out the network load. Such an action can be expected to improve the network performance, reducing delays and increasing the saturation load. If, on the other hand, the balance of the traffic matrix changes with time, then it is not possible to specify a set of fixed routing tables that will cope efficiently with all the patterns of traffic offered.

Despite these limitations fixed routing has been used in practice, for example in the airlines' SITA network.[16] Clearly some provision has to be made to take account of the possibility of failure of a link, which could disable a basic fixed routing system. In the SITA case this was done by storing in each node a complete set of substitute routing tables, one for each possible link failure throughout the network. Where possible, substitute tables were provided to allow for multiple component failure. If a link failed, then control packets were broadcast by the nodes at either end of the link, notifying all other nodes of the identity of the failed link; these nodes then changed their routing tables accordingly. In order to achieve a rapid passage of information, such control packets must be given a very high priority over other categories of traffic.

A similar system has been the subject of some simulation studies at the UK National Physical Laboratory (NPL),[17] in which it was confirmed that a small network could quickly recover from the effects of losing one link, rerouting all packets which were waiting to use the failed link. Clearly it is very difficult to design such a system to overcome the effects of the simultaneous failure of several network components.

Another network that uses what is basically a fixed routing doctrine, subject to provision for change in the face of failure, is the EPSS network. In this network a network control centre is intended to analyse reports from nodes, discover component failure and issue commands to individual nodes to change routing tables to take account of failures. When failures are repaired the control centre function will be to issue commands restoring the previously used routes.

Before leaving the subject of fixed routing, we will mention again the fixed routing doctrine whereby it is possible to use multiple routes between selected sources and destinations. The purpose of this technique is to cater for greater flows than can be carried by single routes. A further effect of use of multiple routes is to even out traffic over the network. To achieve this routing process each node where multiple routes are proposed must be given multiple routing tables, specifying for each destination the fraction of traffic that is to leave the node by a particular route. Figure 3.7 suggests how the proportions of traffic sent to each route may be made to depend on the relative route lengths. The system will be successful where the traffic pattern is fairly static. Where the traffic pattern is variable it may be still be possible to use multiple routes, but means must be provided whereby the splitting proportions adapt to the traffic demands. We shall see in the discussion of adaptive routing that such a system may well be practicable. However, it does not seem to have been adopted in practice for any of the major existing networks.

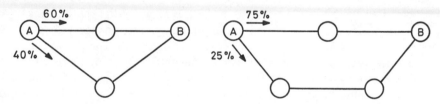

Figure 3.7   Flow splitting according to route length

3.5   ADAPTIVE ROUTING

Since packet networks first came on the scene, network designers have seen the advantages that might be conferred by a routing system that would adapt to current conditions, allowing when necessary the use of multiple routes, taking account of the failure or restoration of network links or nodes, accepting with ease the long-term addition of new nodes or deletion of existing ones. The prospect of such a routing system may be attractive, but its creation presents very considerable difficulty. The problem arises, of course, from the distributed nature of the network. Nodes need to take routing decisions to allow for events that are taking place in remote parts of the network and on which they have either no information or only out-of-date information. A great number of *adaptive routing* doctrines have been proposed; we shall discuss the more important of these.

In a road network, car drivers can hear routing information on their radios; in an ideal road network with a sophisticated information system they could take avoiding action and use alternative routes. This is possible because the routing information is handled by a separate system which is much faster in transmission than the vehicle. A central controller can receive radio reports from observers and send out advice to motorists accordingly. (One might comment in passing that, whereas this is easily possible for a road network, in practice it is not often achieved.) In packet networks the routing information travels by the same medium and at the same speed as the payload traffic. It is not sensible to provide a separate wide bandwidth system to handle routing and other control messages in a packet-switched network, with the payload traffic handled by low bandwidth circuits.

The idea of instantly available network-wide routing information in a packet network has its attractions. Using simulation modelling techniques we can analyse the theoretical performance of a network operating in this manner, though in practice it is impossible. Plessey Telecommunications Research Ltd.,[18] in a simulation study carried out for NPL, tested out a routing technique in which, as each network node took a routing decision, the node had a complete instant overview of the rest of the network. The routing algorithm, knowing queue lengths in all other nodes and the number of packets in transit on each link, computed the optimum next link to be traversed by the routed packet in order to reach its destination with minimum delay. The unexpected result of this simulation experiment was to show that mean delays obtained by the 'magic' (or ideal observer) technique were not significantly less than those observed when the routing doctrine was fixed, with the routing tables set for shortest paths for all traffic. It seems that though the 'magic' routing was done on the best currently available information, the changing pattern of traffic caused the routes which were optimal at the moment of choice to become suboptimal before the packets concerned reached their destinations. It is even possible that several nodes under this method might observe a lightly loaded section of network and all might attempt to channel traffic into this section, causing congestion therein. The defect of the magic algorithm was that it was not able to take account of future events.

The magic method is not, of course, possible in a real network, but the experiment illustrates what can be a disadvantage of several real-life routing algorithms—the fact that a section of the network may be reported to other sections as currently lightly loaded, with spare capacity. If the other sections, themselves embarrassed by congestion, all seek simultaneously to offload traffic to the lightly loaded region, then even worse congestion may be created. The fact that information reaching nodes is already out of date compounds the problem observed in the magic routing experiment.

Adaptive routing techniques used in real-life networks have to make what use they can of information available to them either locally (isolated adaptive routing) or transmitted around the network. If nodes are programmed to create routing information themselves and to share it with their neighbours, then this is a form of distributed adaptive routing. The alternative system, whereby nodes send status reports to a routing centre, which in turn issues routing instructions to all nodes is known as centralised adaptive routing. These different forms of adaptive routing all merit discussion in some detail, to which we shall presently proceed.

Before introducing the detailed discussion, we will mention a few other issues pertinent to adaptive routing.

Strict packet delivery sequence is of importance to many users, in that packets must be delivered to their destinations in the order in which they were originally accepted from the source user by the network. If the network routing is fixed and the flow control is arranged so that packets cannot overtake each other, then an assurance can be given that delivery of packets will be in correct sequence order without any further measures. If, on the other hand, the routing doctrine has an element of adaptivity built into it, then packets between the same source–destination pair may take different routes and may thus take different times to reach the destination node, therefore possibly arriving out of sequence order. In a network which employs adaptive routing and to which packet delivery order is important, then special means must be adopted to restore packet order before delivery is made to the destination user. This need arises in the ARPA network, where a sequence of packets forming a message is reassembled into order at the destination node before being delivered. In the ARPA network the reassembly protocol as originally specified was open to an interesting form of network lock-up. Reassembly space at the destination node was limited and, if two or more partly reassembled messages were held in reassembly space at a node with no more reassembly space available, then completion of reassembly was rendered impossible for all the messages—a state of lock-up. This problem was discussed extensively by Kahn and Crowther.[19]

In some cases network packet delivery order need not be vital, indeed reordering can be handled at the host and not by the network. Datagram network protocols do not necessarily demand absolute sequencing of delivered packets; in datagram networks adaptive routing can be used to full advantage. Some virtual call protocols, on the other hand, do, in the main, require correct delivery sequence; adaptive routing is then less relevant, unless packets are reordered by the destination node before delivery. However, a form of adaptive routing may still be relevant in the case of virtual calls whose route through the network is fixed at the time of call set-up; an attempt may be made to optimise the traffic carried by the call (and possibly the whole network) by choosing the best currently available route for the call. This kind of call with fixed route is used in the French PTT network, Transpac. Other types of virtual call involve virtual call interfaces only at source and destination nodes, with the network itself operating in datagram mode; this mode of operation is used in the Canadian Trans Canada Telephones network, Datapac. Here adaptive routing may be used freely.

Adaptive routing algorithms may be complicated by having totally different types of routes to be used by different types of packet. If a hybrid terrestrial/satellite network were built, then the satellite channels would offer wide bandwidth, but with appreciable transit delay, and the terrestrial channels might offer rather narrow bandwidth with short transit delay. The former would be ideal for large file transfers and the latter for short transmissions of packets used in interactive mode requiring rapid response.

Different routing may be applied to different types of packet even when the network has homogeneous transmission media. The routing doctrine may have regard to priority levels in the transmitted packets and may apply different techniques to the various levels. The file transfer/interactive packet dichotomy was made by Frank, Kahn and Kleinrock[20] when they proposed an 'excess capacity' routing doctrine for the ARPA network. McQuillan[5] also had comments to make on this mode of operation. This will be discussed later in this section.

Isolated Adaptive Routing

From a design point of view the simplest of the adaptive routing methods is that in which routing decisions are taken only on the basis of information available locally in each node; this is isolated adaptive routing. The nature of the local information required is a pre-loaded routing table, the current state (open or shut) of the outgoing links and the lengths of the packet queues awaiting the use of each link. The node need not possess information on the state of any other network components. The routing algorithm is programmed to make a choice between alternative routes, expressed in the routing tables, by a calculation based on queue lengths and knowledge of the network topology, expressed as a 'bias' towards the better links to be used in reaching each destination. In his survey of routing techniques[3] Fultz called this process the 'shortest queue plus bias' or $(SQ + B)$ method. Fultz recognised that the selection of the correct bias was critical to the success of this algorithm. If the bias B is set at zero, then effectively the routing choice is made to the currently shortest queue, as in 'hot potato' routing discussed earlier. With small B there is a strong tendency towards use of the shortest queue, which may, of course, be quite unsuitable as a route to the required destination. At the other extreme, if B is made very large, this factor will dominate the route choice process and the route to each destination will be effectively fixed, little account being taken of the current traffic conditions. Clearly an intermediate setting of bias must be chosen, if the routing algorithm is both to direct traffic efficiently and to adapt to changes in flows. Whether it is possible to select such a satisfactory inter-mediate bias setting is open to argument. Fultz presents results of simulations which tend to show that a satisfactory setting can be made.

A routing algorithm having somewhat similar properties was tested by simulation methods at NPL,[21] with the first object of increasing the maximum traffic handling capacity of the network. Routing tables pre-loaded in each node indicated the shortest path to be taken to each destination; these routes were designated as primary routes. If a second route existed (leaving the node on a different link, but not necessarily otherwise completely disjoint from the cor-responding primary route) which was of length equal to the primary route length in terms of number of links, but longer in actual distance, this was designated a secondary route of type A. If no type A secondary route existed, then a route using one additional link was designated a secondary route of type B. If no secondary route of type B existed, then no secondary route was designated. Numerical weights were allocated to each type of route, 3 to primary routes, 2 to secondary routes of type A and 1 to secondary routes of type B. Note that a simple calculation of this kind produces traffic routing proportions as shown in Figure 3.7. However, it is an elementary second step to combine the numerical weights with the queue length of packets awaiting transmission on each link; in fact, in the NPL experiment, each output queue was limited to five packets and the number of empty queue slots was added to the route weight in influencing route selection. An example will serve to illustrate the operation of this process. Consider a node, Figure 3.8, needing to route a packet to a destination; a primary route and secondary route of type B are available. The number of free spaces currently available on the output queue for the primary route is two and for the secondary route four. With this state of affairs the routing process, using a random number generator, will choose between the primary and secondary routes with a probability ratio of $3 + 2$ to $1 + 4$, giving

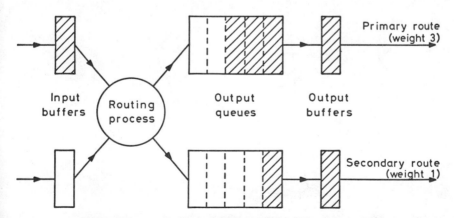

Figure 3.8   Flow splitting taking queue lengths into account

5 : 5; this gives an equal probability of using each route. If, on the other hand, the number of empty queue slots is respectively four and one, then the probability ratio will be $3 + 4$ to $1 + 1$, or $7 : 2$, so the bias is then towards the primary route. If one of the output queues is full, then the packet is sent to the other, whatever the number of empty slots. If both output queues are full, then the packet is deleted, to be received again later by retransmission from the previous node. There is a considerable parallelism between this routing method, which we term 'load-splitting', and Fultz's shortest queue + bias algorithm, and an even greater similarity between this method and Fultz's load-splitting routing algorithm which he terms 'bifurcated' routing.

The algorithm was tested in the first instance on a 10-node network, Figure 3.9, by measuring performance (throughput and delay) at various applied loads, using fixed shortest-path routing as a standard of comparison. It had been hoped that a network operated with this form of adaptive routing algorithm would carry a heavier general network traffic load than that carried under a fixed routing doctrine because of the expected ability to spread the load more efficiently. The results of the simulation experiment showed no improvement in maximum carrying capacity. However, when, with a moderately heavily loaded network, an additional stream of traffic was imposed between a selected source and destination pair, then a quite dramatic performance improvement was obtained.

The results of the latter experiment are illustrated in Figure 3.10, where a

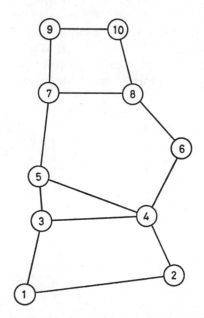

Figure 3.9   10-node network used in NPL routing experiments

Routing method	Overall throughput packet/s	Overall average transit delay ms	Overall average admission delay ms	Average throughput 1–8 packet/s	Average transit delay 1–8 ms
Fixed	3895	5.2	0.5	31	10.0
Overflow	3818	4.7	0.4	43	9.3
Bifurcated	3782	4.6	0.1	41	7.8

(a) Performance of network with no extra load

Routing method	Overall throughput packet/s	Overall average transit delay ms	Overall average admission delay ms	Average throughput 1–8 packet/s	Average transit delay 1–8 ms
Fixed	3866	8.3	7.9	246	34.0
Overflow	4049	6.2	2.1	300	11.7
Bifurcated	4144	5.8	0.3	342	10.2

(b) Performance of network with 10-fold increase
of applied load between nodes 1 and 8

Figure 3.10   Results of NPL routing experiments

comparison is made between fixed shortest-path routing, load-splitting and a further technique which we shall call 'overflow' routing. In overflow routing the primary route is used at all times unless in a node the output queue for a particular route is found to be full, when space is sought on the secondary queue (if a secondary route exists). Load-splitting was seen to be superior in terms of throughput and delay (for both general and stream traffic), overflow routing came second, with fixed shortest-path routing unable to cope with the additional traffic.

The Fultz and NPL simulations and the Fultz analysis have demonstrated that isolated adaptive routing may be used with success. However, it is important that certain shortcomings of the system should not be overlooked. Such routing adapts but slowly to distant events, be they component failure or accumulations of traffic causing congestion. Typically a chain of full queues has to form from the point of congestion back to a node where useful rerouting can take place, or back to the source before the traffic flow can be throttled. It goes without saying that this is a slow and cumbersome means of controlling the flow of traffic and of diverting traffic to take alternative routes. However, it is possible to provide other means of informing network nodes of distant events which may influence routing (we shall discuss the flow control aspects in Chapter 4); such a system has already been mentioned in the context of fixed routing, where recovery from component failure was discussed. The network designer may feel that the simplicity of some form of isolated routing, backed up by a failure (or congestion) notification system, has much to commend it.

Distributed Adaptive Routing

The technique which has hitherto been most popular in implemented networks is that of distributed adaptive routing. The best known example is that found in the network of the US Government's Advanced Research Projects Agency (ARPA).[8] The application of distributed adaptive routing in the ARPA network will be discussed in some detail.

The aim of the ARPA algorithm is to find paths of least delay for the traffic transported, and each node maintains a table of routes giving least delay to each destination, indicating for each the current best estimate of time required for the journey. At network set-up time the delay times are estimates based on network topology, but, as traffic is delivered to destinations, so the delay times are changed to transit times actually measured in the network. In the ARPA algorithm in its original form the delay tables are regularly exchanged between

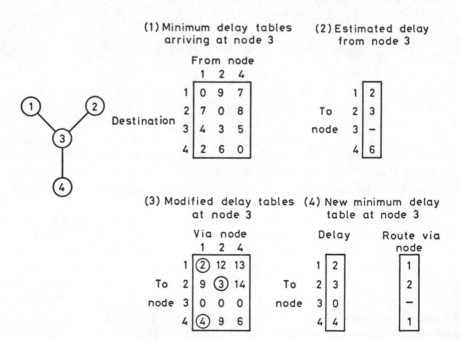

Figure 3.11   Exchange of routing information in the ARPA network

neighbouring nodes. When delay tables are exchanged each node enters a phase of recalculation of delays, based on the current queue lengths within itself and the delay times received from its neighbours. Figure 3.11 illustrates the receipt of minimum delay tables at an ARPA node and the subsequent recalculation of the local minimum delay and routing tables. (It is assumed that only part of the network is shown in Figure 3.11 and that other paths exist beyond the confines of this network fragment. In this example it will be seen that traffic from node 3 to node 4 is routed via node 1; this assumes that a route exists between node 1 and node 4 other than via node 3.) It is a simple process to discover by which neighbouring node traffic should be forwarded to reach its destination in the least time. The ARPA routing algorithm is also concerned with the accessibility of each network destination, since simultaneous outages of several components may isolate parts of the network. Accessibility is calculated using a separate method involving hop counts, but not concerning itself with delay estimates.

The exchange of delay tables between neighbouring nodes naturally requires a considerable amount of control packet traffic, possibly placing a substantial overhead on the operation of the network. Originally the update interval was ⅔ second; in measurements on the network it was shown that the delay table traffic accounted for nearly 50 per cent of the line bandwidth on one link of low bandwidth and an appreciable (though lesser) proportion of the bandwidth of the faster lines. Examination of the information exchanged showed that very often a transmitted delay table conveyed either exactly the same information or very nearly the same information as its predecessor. Clearly the synchronous exchange of delay tables was an expensive and unnecessary luxury. It was therefore proposed to change from synchronous to asynchronous updating. Delay tables would only be transmitted by nodes in which a significant change was detected, either in traffic intensity or in component operability. Re-computation of delay tables would only be undertaken either in the case of a detected local significant change or on receipt of a revised delay table from a neighbouring node. In the latter case it is quite conceivable that the new information might produce no change in computed least delays and therefore not require export of new delay tables. The key to this mode of operation lies in the definition of what constitutes a 'significant' change. Experiments by analysis and simulation by Kleinrock[9] and others have demonstrated that worthwhile improvements in network operating efficiency are attainable using the technique of asynchronous updating. An exhaustive analysis and comparison of the various delay table exchange techniques, synchronous and asynchronous, are to be found in Fultz's Ph.D. thesis.[3]

Promising though the asynchronous technique may be, it does not seem to have been adopted in the ARPA network. A change that has been adopted is to reduce the delay table exchange frequency on links of low bandwidth; this seems a simple and sensible expedient.

With synchronous updating the speed of adaptation to distant events is inevitably slow. Routing information percolating down one of the long transcontinental node chains of the ARPA network would take several seconds to cross the North American continent, taking ⅔ second per node. Thus notification of the failure of a network component, with consequent need for drastic rerouting, would take an appreciable time to take effect. During this time traffic would still be seeking to travel by the existing route, perhaps causing congestion near the location of the failed component. This state of affairs is a further argument for asynchronous updating, with recalculation of routes taking place in each node as soon as a significant change was detected; the built-in ⅔ second delay per node would no longer apply.

The process of controlling routing by exchange of minimum delay tables between nodes is indeed characterised by an ability to adapt quickly to reductions in delays, but, on the other hand, by a slow response to increasing delays; adaptation is rapid to 'good news', but slow to 'bad news'. This property of the ARPA routing algorithm is best illustrated by a simple example. Consider a set of four nodes connected in a chain, Figure 3.12; the chain may or may not form part of a larger network, with which we need not concern ourselves. For the sake of the discussion we assume that, in the lightly loaded state, the time taken to transfer a packet from one node to the next is one arbitrary unit of time. Thus to travel from node 4 to node 1 takes 3 time units; this time is entered in the minimum delay table at node 4 for traffic destined to node 1. The full set of minimum delay tables for the four nodes is shown in Figure 3.12, which also indicates the route to be taken in each case. Now imagine that a disturbance occurs in the traffic pattern, leading to extra traffic flowing from node 2 to node 1; this must increase the transfer time for packets going from node 2 to node 1. Let us assume that this time is increased from 1 arbitrary time unit to 5 arbitrary time units. The time for exchange of minimum delay tables arrives; node 2 notifies node 3 that its minimum time to node 1 is now 5 units; node 3 notifies node 2 that its minimum time to node 1 is 2 units. This happens because node 3 is not yet aware of the extra time taken from node 2 to node 1, though

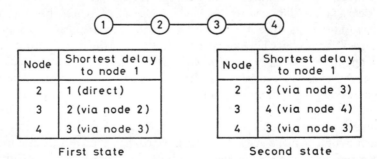

Node	Shortest delay to node 1
2	1 (direct)
3	2 (via node 2)
4	3 (via node 3)

First state

Node	Shortest delay to node 1
2	3 (via node 3)
3	4 (via node 4)
4	3 (via node 3)

Second state

Figure 3.12   Chain of four nodes illustrating routing update problem

traffic to node 1 from node 3 must, of course, have been passing through node 2. The result of this delay table exchange is somewhat chaotic. Node 2 calculates that the new minimum delay path to node 1 must go via node 3, taking 3 time units in transit. Node 3, having been given a delay of 5 units to node 1 by node 2, but only 3 units by node 4, computes the least delay path to node 1 to be via node 4, taking 4 units in transit. Thus traffic to node 1 is misdirected via nodes 3 and 4, and must eventually return down the chain, or, in the case of the chain being part of a larger network, node 1 traffic may reach its destination via a very circuitous route. The state of the minimum delay tables after such a recalculation is shown in Figure 3.12; note the 'ping-pong' effect on traffic for node 1 at nodes 3 and 4.

Clearly this mode of operation of the routing algorithm was unacceptable in the ARPA network and a modification of the original algorithm was devised and incorporated. This modification is termed the 'hold-down' technique, in which a node, which has detected an increased delay along what was formerly the minimum delay path to a destination, will continue to use the existing path until such time as its neighbours have been informed of the increased delay and have been able to re-compute their minimum delay tables. The effect of the modification is to distribute the routing decision amongst a group of neighbouring nodes; misrouting of traffic is avoided by allowing the nodes concerned to adapt collectively before the notification of increased delay is permitted to affect the routing. For comprehensive discussions of the hold-down technique as a solution to this defect in the original algorithm the reader should refer to McQuillan[5] and Naylor.[22]

One of the benefits expected from adaptive routing, as explained earlier, was the ability to spread the traffic flowing between particular source and destination pairs over more than one route, thus making effective use of any spare bandwidth. The ARPA routing doctrine which we have discussed in this section does not possess this property. In between delay table updates the route is fixed; at update time the preferred route may change and the traffic flow is then diverted, but this is not the same thing as the simultaneous sharing of more than one route for a particular traffic flow.

In Fultz's survey[3] of possible routing doctrines he proposes a combination of his 'SQ + B' technique, already mentioned in the previous section on isolated adaptive routing, with an update mechanism of the type in use in the ARPA context as discussed in the present section; he terms this technique shortest queue plus bias plus periodical update (SQ + B + PUA). Delay tables are exchanged between neighbouring nodes, but each local node has discretion to use a combination of queue length, bias and periodical delay table update information to compute the instantaneous best route to a destination at the time the decision is required. This routing doctrine potentially has the desired ability to share the traffic over more than one route, though it is not specifically designed for this purpose. The chief drawback to using this otherwise very attractive routing doctrine is the heavy computational load it may be expected to place on the node computer.

Another routing mechanism proposed for the ARPA network, but not implemented in practice, was the excess capacity method mentioned by Frank, Kahn and Kleinrock.[20] This aimed to use multiple paths efficiently, even during heavy traffic. The idea was to direct packets down the shortest path with excess (or spare) capacity available; thus several paths might be in use simultaneously from a node to a given destination. Simulation studies indicated that the method could be tailored to provide efficient routing with a variety of heavy traffic conditions. It seems that this method, like the others described here, relied upon the sharing of information between adjacent nodes, and must therefore be classed as a distributed system.

Centralised Adaptive Routing

The adaptive routing algorithms so far discussed use either locally available information or information exchanged between neighbouring nodes. We have commented how algorithms of this type adapt very slowly to distant events, because of the slow rate of flow of routing information through the network. Algorithm designers have therefore sought methods of basing routing decisions on a broader-based network-wide overview. One way in which an overview may be achieved is to establish a network routing centre, when centralised adaptive routing becomes the operative algorithm.

In centralised adaptive routing each network node will prepare status reports, giving current queue lengths, any component outages, etc., to be transmitted to the network routing centre. The centre, receiving status reports from all the network nodes, can, with a full overview of the network, determine the best routes to be used by all traffic flows. These best routes are specified in terms of routing tables which are despatched to the network nodes.

The times at which status reports are made to the centre and the times at which new routing tables are despatched to the nodes may be at regular intervals (synchronous) or only when a significant change has taken place (asynchronous). If synchronous operation is proposed, then the quantity of control information flowing in the network on behalf of the routing algorithm may be formidable, especially if the network is at all large, giving an excessive level of operating overheads. Asynchronous operation may result in a more tolerable flow of control information.

One might expect the network routing centre to produce optimal routes, with best use being made of the network capacity. This might indeed be the case, were it not for the unavoidable time lags in this form of routing. A delay occurs between the initial transmission of each status report from nodes and its receipt by the routing centre; for distant nodes this delay may be considerable. Conversely, after the centre has performed its routing computation, which may itself take some appreciable time, the time taken for the receipt of revised routing tables by all nodes can be equally significant. Thus the centre acts on information that is already partly out of date and despatches to nodes routing instructions that will be even more out of date when received. In a network in which the state of traffic flows is changing fairly rapidly it is difficult to see how this type of routing algorithm can hope to succeed.

A central routing controller may leave the network vulnerable to loss of routing control, should the central facility fail or part of the network become isolated. In this case the nodes would have to continue to use the most recently received routing tables. Some protection against failure could be given by establishing reserve routing centres at various points in the network, one or other of these to assume control in the event of loss of the central facility. Assumption of control by a subsidiary centre is a difficult operation to specify, as is the re-assumption of control by the main centre when this re-enters service or a break in communication is restored.

An analysis of the performance of a centralised adaptive routing algorithm may be found in Gerla,[23] who advocates this form of routing when compared with the other forms of routing which we have thus far discussed.

Hybrid Adaptive Routing

We have now seen that isolated and distributed adaptive routing both suffer to different degrees from myopia; they are either unaware of distant events or become aware of them very slowly. Centralised adaptive routing, on the other hand, has a network-wide awareness of events, but with a possible considerable time delay or phase lag. Such a control system could be unstable, producing a routing algorithm which swings wildly from one state to another as traffic changes.

Attempts have been made to find a routing system which combines the virtues of the various systems discussed so far, whilst avoiding their faults. We shall mention two such systems.

The first of these is 'delta routing', devised by Rudin.[6] In delta routing a central network routing controller is established. To this the individual nodes send status reports, either synchronously or asynchronously (both modes are considered by Rudin). The central controller takes a global view of the state of the network and sends routing commands back to the nodes in the light of its global view. This is similar to the centralised methods already discussed.

The essence of delta routing is to combine centralised with distributed routing. The central portion of the algorithm keeps track, acting fairly slowly, of the global situation; local discretion is allowed to the individual nodes so that they can react rapidly and independently to changes in traffic or local component status. The global information is somewhat out of date, but takes the widest view; the local information is up to date, but is myopic.

In delta routing the central controller sends routing tables to the individual nodes, but these are used in conjunction with local queue lengths in choosing routes to be taken by individual packets. Should there be several paths of almost equal merit from a node to a particular destination, then the routing algorithm is arranged so that local conditions shall determine which route is used by each packet. If the global overview shows that only one path is sensible, then the nodal routing decision is constrained to use this path. The 'delta' factor is a measure of the degree of discretion which is allowed to the node in each case.

The system operates by calculating expected journey times on the alternative routes. Figure 3.13 illustrates a routing decision to be taken at node A for traffic destined for node B. The alternative paths specified are via nodes 1 and 3. If the difference between the times via node 1 and node 3 is greater than the quantity 'delta', specified individually for this routing decision by the central controller, then all the traffic from A to B is sent by the quicker route. If the difference is less than 'delta', then the traffic is split between the two routes.

Rudin has carried out simulation experiments in which the performance of delta routing is compared with other routing doctrines involving distributed and centralised techniques. His conclusion is that, on the basis of maximised use of network capacity and of least delay times, delta routing is most successful. A further advantage of the scheme is that, should the central routing controller become isolated or fail, then the individual nodes may, at least for a time, continue to exercise sensible control over the routing of individual packets. The nodes then behave as they would in a form of isolated adaptive routing. Resumption of control by the central controller can take place very simply when communications are restored.

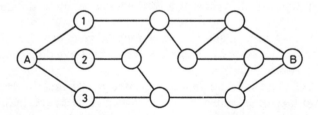

Time comparison at Network Routing Centre	Routing table sent to node A (Traffic A→B)	
	Primary	Secondary
Time (A→B) via 1 < Time (A→B) via 3 − δ	via 1	—
Time (A→B) via 3 < Time (A→B) via 1 − δ	via 3	—
|Time (A→B) via 1 − Time (A→B) via 3| ≤ δ	via 1	via 3

Figure 3.13   Delta routing

Delta routing does not seem to have been applied in practice in a real communication network, but has much to commend it. The computing load on the individual nodes should not be excessive.

The other hybrid technique we shall discuss is that of Chu and Shen.[24] These authors have proposed a hierarchical system of routing and flow control. In this system the network is divided up into areas of closely linked nodes. To each area is allocated a local routing controller, which receives status reports from its local nodes. Each controller computes routes in its own area and exchanges routing information, using high-priority control packets, with the other controllers. This technique aims to reduce the time lag between status report generation and the receipt of routing instructions, by providing local controllers. The network overview is achieved by using several controllers in communication with each other. Preliminary simulation studies of the technique have been carried out, but further studies will be necessary before it is clear whether the technique is worth developing further. It is interesting that routing is combined here with flow control aspects; we shall see in Chapter 4 how routing and flow control have an interaction.

3.6 ROUTING IN LARGE NETWORKS

Since their inception data communication networks have grown greatly in size, crossing international boundaries and even spanning more than one continent. The ARPA network, now of more than 60 nodes, originally of four, reaches from Hawaii across the USA into Europe, with nodes at London and Oslo; further expansion of ARPA is likely. The EIN and Euronet networks represent international cooperation within Europe. The airlines' SITA network spans the world. New national and international networks are on the way.

Increase in network size presents the designer of routing algorithms with new problems, which we shall discuss later in this section.

Building of larger networks is only one of the ways in which network scale is expanding. It is a natural development that designers of networks seek to interconnect networks. This has been happening for some years on an ad hoc network-to-network basis; international standards are now being sought to facilitate network interconnection.

The Influence of Network Interconnection on Routing

Various methods may be used for network interconnection; for example, a single node may be made common to two networks, with two halves, each appearing to the separate networks as ordinary network nodes, but having an internal interface across which packets are passed between the networks; alternatively a node in each network may be connected by means of a single link, with traffic on the link controlled by a specially devised protocol. The details need not concern us here. As far as routing is concerned, the problem is much the same whichever method of interconnection is used.

The network interconnecting nodes are commonly termed *gateways*. Conceptually a set of networks interconnected by gateways can be regarded as a single network of communication channels (the individual networks) linking together the gateway nodes. This concept holds the key to routing at inter-network level. By treating the problem as one of routing from gateway to gateway, economy and simplicity of the routing process are attainable.

A first essential is the establishment of a globally valid addressing system. In the first instance this may be established as a two-tier system, with each node designated by its address within its own network, and each separate network designated by its own unique identification. We shall see in the next section how it is possible in large networks to use a hierarchical addressing system to achieve economy of routing table size in individual nodes; hierarchies of considerable depth are proposed in the context of single homogeneous networks. We are here addressing the question of the interconnection of possible non-homogeneous separate networks, where a two-tier addressing hierarchy seems a natural first step. However, a multi-tier hierarchy may eventually be necessary if the number of interconnected separate networks becomes very large. In this case groups of networks might be established; inter-group communication could be via specially designated super-gateways. It remains to be seen whether network development on the world scale will demand such a solution.

The gateway principle avoids the need to provide every network node with complete routing tables specifying precisely the route to be taken to reach every node in every network. All that is needful is that each node shall have routing tables enabling the appropriate gateway to be reached for attaining the destination network. In the process several different networks may be traversed, with the packets passing from gateway to gateway. Within the individual networks packets may be contained temporarily within an envelope according to the format required by local protocol; the only address required of the envelope format is the local network address of the next gateway node to be visited. By making inter-network packets take the same format as domestic packets within any one particular network the routing process in ordinary network nodes need not be affected by the inter-network routing function. In the source or originating network, an inter-network packet seeks to reach the required exit gateway. In the destination or final network, the inter-network packet is routed from the final entrance gateway to the required destination node.

Path-finding within interconnected networks is only one of the problems with new features that have to be solved. Because of differing network standards other problems arise that can affect routing. The most important of these is the likelihood of different maximum packet sizes being applied in the various interconnected networks. A large packet arriving in one network may have to be split into two or more smaller packets in order to traverse another network with smaller limiting size *en route* to the destination. Packet splitting raises certain fundamental problems. It is possible to split packets at one gateway and reassemble the packets from the split parts at the next gateway. With fixed routing and fixed packet order, reassembly need present no problem. With adaptive routing, the component parts may arrive out of order and at widely distributed times, possibly presenting a reassembly problem. On the other hand the split parts may be sent on to the final destination as separate small packets to be reassembled on arrival. Packet reassembly, wherever it takes place, presents problems of lock-up avoidance and is best itself avoided if possible. It is conceivable that global routing policies may seek to avoid packet splitting by choosing routes through networks that do not demand packet splitting. Large packets may be constrained to avoid networks with low packet size limits, whilst small packets are free to use these.

We have seen that within single networks the finding of optimal routes is a severe one. On the global scale of several interconnected networks, with alternative global routes available as well as alternative routes within each individual network, the problem of finding optimal routes becomes extremely complicated. It will be even more difficult to obtain up-to-date synoptic information on which to base routing decisions. It could be wise to make the global routing doctrine as simple as possible, whilst allowing each individual network to preserve its local routing autonomy (and being as complex as is considered necessary to meet local needs). Such a simple global doctrine could be fixed routing, backed up by alternative reserve paths to take account of any component failure or other disastrous contingency.

The problems of routing in interconnected networks have received limited attention in the literature; notable papers are those by Cerf and Kahn[25] and, more recently, Sunshine.[26]

Hierarchical Routing

The problems of routing within very large single networks are somewhat different from those of interconnected networks. The designer is not concerned with problems of different standards and protocols; in single networks single standards can apply. Nevertheless routing in very large networks does present certain special problems, notably arising from the sheer scale of the operation.

Let us consider first the algorithm components in each node. The routing table, if it is to contain details of the route to every network destination, can become very large. We shall see that a system of area or hierarchical addressing can be applied to give economy of size of routing table. A greater difficulty is the identification of optimal routes within the large networks. A possible solution to this problem is a fundamental change in network organisation to a hierarchical structure, having much in common with long-established circuit-switched telephone network practice.

Hierarchical addressing systems for network routing have been proposed by Fultz[3] and, in greater detail, by McQuillan.[5] A recent very full analysis may be found in Kleinrock and Kamoun.[27] Groups of neighbouring nodes are designated as belonging to node clusters. In order to travel from a source to a destination in another cluster, the route specified in routing tables in the nodes will indicate the links to be traversed to reach the destination cluster. Only when the destination cluster is entered will the routing table specify the way to reach the required destination node itself. Thus routing tables in each network node list all the nodes in the cluster of which the node is a member, with the routes to be used in reaching them; all other network nodes, in other clusters, will be represented by cluster entries in the routing table. For example, in a network of 100 nodes, containing five clusters of 20 nodes each, each nodal routing table needs 23 entries (19 local nodes in the same cluster and four foreign clusters), as compared with 99 entries if the addressing and routing system is not hierarchic. The economy in routing table size is self-evident. The address field in packet headers can be divided into two zones, a cluster zone and a node zone.

Figure 3.14 indicates how a small portion of a hierarchically addressed network consisting of two addressing levels might be arranged.

We have given an illustration of a two-tier hierarchical addressing system. This gives considerable economy in routing table size and may be adequate for networks up to, say, four hundred nodes. There is no reason, however, why, in

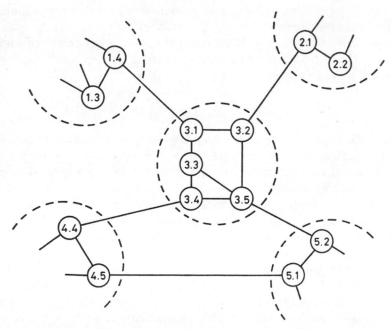

Figure 3.14   Two-tier hierarchical routing and addressing

even larger networks, a hierarchy of depth greater than two should not be used. This demands that super-clusters (or clusters of clusters) be established, with hyper-clusters (or clusters of super-clusters) in the next level above, etc., etc. Packets are routed up the hierarchy (from cluster to super-cluster, etc.) and across the hierarchy, until the address indicates that they have arrived in an addressing unit that contains the required destination node. They then progress down the hierarchy until they reach the destination cluster and finally attain the destination node itself. The economy of routing table size attainable by such a system is dramatic and has been analysed in detail by Kleinrock and Kamoun.

The penalty to be paid for the use of a hierarchical system is that until a cluster is entered, the path to a particular node is not specific. The cluster will be entered at the same point whatever the node sought. The result is that rather longer paths may be taken by packets than in a non-hierarchical system, where each path through the network is separately specified and may be separately optimised by one process or another. Kleinrock and Kamoun have recognised this trade-off and give an analysis of table length economy versus increase in path length. Their analysis extends to network sizes of 10 million nodes and hierarchical depths of up to 100. These numbers are well beyond present-day limits. However, Kleinrock and Kamoun recognise the clear benefits to be obtained in economy of routing table size for quite shallow hierarchical depths in nets of realistic size.

Hierarchical addressing can be used in conjunction with adaptive routing, but a routing scheme in which cluster membership is itself subject to adaptation is perhaps too complicated a concept. This places some restraint upon the freedom of an adaptive routing algorithm.

In larger networks it seems inefficient to establish the net on one homogeneous level with very long path lengths, in terms of links traversed, between source and destination. The hierarchical addressing system is capable of extension to a fully hierarchical organisation, in which the topology is connected as a hierarchy. This is the system adopted in circuit-switched telephone networks. The principle can very usefully be applied in the packet-switched context, though the detailed realisation will necessarily be very different. We have already, in the introductory section to this chapter, considered the broad nature of telephone network routing. In the packet-switched context we are thinking of a system in which users are connected only to the nodes at the lowest level of the hierarchy, in the same way as telephone subscribers are only connected to exchanges in the lowest level of the telephone hierarchy. Thus the higher-level nodes do not receive or deliver traffic directly.

A packet-switched network connected as a hierarchy is not likely to be as fully connected as a circuit-switched network. Nodes will be clustered into areas, as in hierarchical addressing, but, additionally, one node will be designated as a super-node or area node. Ten nodes per area may be a reasonable number. The area node may well be a more powerful device, in terms of processing power and storage, than the local nodes within an area. Each node in the cluster can reach the area node, either directly or through no more than two other local nodes. In a two-level hierarchy the area nodes of the various clusters will be linked together via links of greater bandwidth than the internal links within an area. Depending on the number of area nodes, it may be practicable to fully connect the area nodes. However, in a large network with, say, twenty areas, the cost of full connection could be prohibitive and a lesser degree of connection may be unavoidable. For very large networks with, say, fifty areas, then a third hierarchical level may, with benefit, be brought into existence. In this case clusters of areas will be served each by a hyper-node. It is most likely that the network designer will wish to fully connect the network of hyper-nodes (third level), using links of bandwidth several times greater than those at the second level.

A network thus connected is essentially a multiple-branched tree and, with the exception of alternative routes within areas on one level, there will be unique paths up and down the tree, i.e. packets on a given source–destination journey between areas are constrained to pass through unique super-nodes and (possibly) hyper-nodes. If this is the case then the routing definition is simple.

However, it can be argued that a tree-connected topology does not give the best possible performance for the equipment investment. We have postulated areas of nodes which connect to the other areas only by superior levels of the hierarchy. This is quite unlike the telephone hierarchy, where direct cross-connections between areas are common. In the packet switching context direct connections may be provided by a few direct links between neighbouring nodes in adjacent areas. The best routing policy may make use of these links for traffic needing to pass between nodes within the 'border regions' of adjacent areas, whilst other traffic uses the connection via the superior level.

The use of higher levels in packet switching will be predominantly for transporting long-distance traffic, with only short-distance traffic staying on the lowest level. In telephone switching, as we have already stated, the upper levels of the hierarchy serve as overflow routes where lower-level routes are fully loaded, subject to the constraint that the number of hops between switching centres shall not exceed a limited number. The philosophy of use in the two systems is thus slightly different.

Prediction of performance in a hierarchical network, particularly when cross-connections between adjacent areas are allowed, is very difficult. No attempt has so far been made to use analytic techniques for this purpose. The problem can be tackled by simulation, but even here the difficulties are formidable. We have seen how, to be meaningful, a simulation must not skimp on detail. In a very large network the number of nodes and links to be represented demands a very large simulation, which may run very slowly and demand much computing time for the production of adequate results.

An extensive study of a hierarchical network by simulation methods has

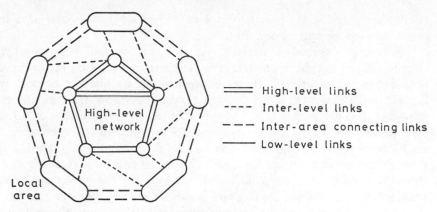

Figure 3.15   High-level network topology used in Logica simulation studies

been made by Logica,[28] under a study contract placed by NPL. In this study a two-level hierarchy containing five local areas, each of nine ordinary nodes and one super-node, ⸲⁰ nodes in all, was postulated. Figure 3.15 shows the topology of the whole network in outline, whilst Figure 3.16 shows the detailed topology of one local area. The operational regime was that of the datagram, with no concept of call or end-to-end control. The study was concerned with routing and flow control (or congestion avoidance). We shall report here the routing aspects of the work and the flow control aspects in the next chapter.

We see that the five local areas were connected in a ring with inter-area links. The five super-nodes were connected by one arrangement or another of wide bandwidth links. The routing policy laid down that traffic between non-adjacent local areas should always travel via the superior level. Traffic within one local area would normally not travel via the superior level. Traffic between adjacent local areas provides the case of interest; here there will be instances where it is beneficial to carry traffic via the high level and other instances

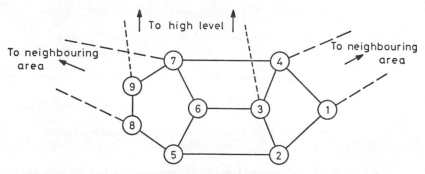

Figure 3.16   Low-level local area topology used in Logica simulation studies

(arising from traffic between border area nodes) where the inter-area links should be used for optimum performance.

An attempt was made to devise a system of overflow routing in imitation of circuit-switched telephone practice. For this purpose routes on the lower level were designated as primary routes between nodes in adjacent border areas. Secondary routes were to be via the higher level. A node finding a primary route fully loaded would send a packet towards the nearest high level node, in most cases passing through at least one other low level node. In order to ensure that the packet reached the high level, and was not diverted to some other low level route at an intermediate low level node, it was necessary for the node making the original decision to use a high level route to flag the packet accordingly. Intermediate nodes noted the flag and avoided rerouting the packet to the low level. The performance of the network operating with this policy was found to be somewhat inferior to that in which a simpler form of adaptive routing was specified.

The latter was simply a procedure in which primary, secondary and, occasionally, tertiary routes were specified between nodes, the switch from one to the other being made simply on the basis of the size of queues waiting to use the links concerned. Such routes might involve low level, high level or both, depending on the location of particular nodes. This method of routing closely resembles some of the localised adaptive policies discussed earlier in this chapter. As simulated, no transfer of routing information around the network was involved. It was clearly shown by this study that the provision of a super-node level was very helpful to network performance and that it was possible to devise a routing algorithm that took advantage of the second level. In the latter connection the attempt to imitate telephone practice was not particularly successful.

References

1. Prosser, R. T.,
   'Routing procedures in communication networks',
   IRE Trans. on Communication Systems, **CS-10**, 322 (December 1962).
2. Boehm, B. W., and Mobley, R. L.,
   'Adaptive routing techniques for distributed communications systems',
   IEEE Trans. on Communication Technology, **COM-17**, 340 (June 1969).
3. Fultz, G. L.,
   Adaptive routing techniques for message switching computer communication networks,
   University of California, Los Angeles, Report UCLA-ENG-7352 (July 1972).
4. Gerla, M.,
   The design of store-and-forward networks for computer communications,
   University of California, Los Angeles, Report UCLA-ENG-7319 (January 1973).
5. McQuillan, J. M.,
   Adaptive routing algorithms for distributed computer networks,
   Bolt, Beranek and Newman, Report 2831 (May 1974).

6. Rudin, H.,
'On routing and "delta routing": a taxonomy and performance comparison of techniques for packet-switched networks',
IEEE Trans. on Communications, **COM-24**, 43 (January 1976).

7. Ford, L. K., and Fulkerson, D. R.,
Flows in Networks,
Princeton University Press, Princeton, New Jersey (1962).

8. McQuillan, J. M., and Walden, D. C.,
'The ARPA network design decisions',
Computer Networks, **1**, 243 (August 1977).

9. Kleinrock, L.,
Queueing Systems: Vol. 2, Computer Applications,
Wiley–Interscience, New York (1976).

10. Pennotti, M. C., and Schwartz, M.,
'Congestion control in store and forward tandem links',
IEEE Trans. on Communications, **COM-23**, 1434 (December 1975).

11. Kobayashi, H.,
'Application of diffusion approximation to queueing networks', Part I,
Journal ACM, **21**, 311 (April 1974);
Part II,
Journal ACM, **21**, 459 (July 1974).

12. Slyke, R. van, Chou, W., and Frank, H.,
'Avoiding simulation in simulating computer communication networks',
Proc. National Computer Conference, 165 (1973).

13. Baran, P.,
'On distributed communications networks',
IEEE Trans. on Communications Systems, **CS-12**, 1 (March 1964).

14. Healey, R.,
Computer network simulation study,
National Physical Laboratory Report, COM64 (January 1973), (originally issued in earlier form, October 1970).

15. Jolly, J. H., and Adams, R. A.,
Simulation study of a data communication network, Part I,
Plessey Telecommunications Research Ltd., Report 97/72/78/TR.

16. Brandt, G. J., and Chretien, G. J.,
'Methods to control and operate a message-switching network',
Proc. Symposium on Computer-Communications Networks and Teletraffic, Polytechnic Institute of Brooklyn, 263 (April 1972).

17. Price, W. L., and Cowin, G. W.,
Simulation studies of the effect of link breakdown on data communication network performance,
National Physical Laboratory Report, COM77 (February 1977).

18. Adams, R. A., Jolly, J. H., and Smith, J. R. W.,
Simulation study of a data communication network, Part 3: Comparison of adaptive and fixed routing,
Plessey Telecommunications Research Ltd., Report 97/73/03/TR (February 1973).

19. Kahn, R. E., and Crowther, W. R.,
'Flow control in a resource-sharing computer network',
IEEE Trans. on Communications, **COM-20**, 539 (June 1972).

20. Frank, H., Kahn, R. E., and Kleinrock, L.,
'Computer communication network design—experience with theory and practice',
Proc. Spring Joint Computer Conference, 255 (1972).
21. Price, W. L.,
'Adaptive routing in store-and-forward networks and the importance of load-splitting',
Proc. IPIP Congress 77, Toronto, 309 (August 1977).
22. Naylor, W. E.,
'A loop-free adaptive routing algorithm for packet switched networks',
Proc. 4th ACM/IEEE Data Communications Symposium, Quebec, 7–9 (October 1975).
23. Gerla, M.,
'Deterministic and adaptive routing policies in packet-switched computer networks',
Proc. 3rd ACM/IEEE Data Communications Symposium, St. Petersburg, 23 (November 1973).
24 Chu, W. W., and Shen, M. Y.,
'A hierarchical routing and flow control policy for packet switched networks',
Proc. International Symposium on Computer Performance Modeling, Measurement and Evaluation, Yorktown Heights, 485 (August 1977).
— 25. Cerf, V. G., and Kahn, R.E.,
'A protocol for packet network intercommunication',
IEEE Trans. on Communications, **COM-22**, 637 (May 1974).
— 26. Sunshine, C. A.,
'Interconnection of computer networks',
Computer Networks, **1**, 175 (January 1977).
27. Kleinrock, L., and Kamoun, F.,
'Hierarchical routing for large networks: performance evaluation and optimization',
Computer Networks, **1**, 155 (January 1977).
28. Kerr, I. H., Gomberg, G. R. A., Price, W. L., and Solomonides, C. M.,
'A simulation study of routing and flow control problems in a hierarchically connected packet switching network',
Proc. International Computer Communication Conference, Toronto, 495 (August 1976).

Chapter 4

Flow Control and Congestion Avoidance

4.1 INTRODUCTION

In any communication system it is most important to have a free flow of traffic. If the capacity of the lines and nodes is always sufficient to carry the load, this free flow might seem to be guaranteed, but it is not so. The exit of packets at a destination might be impeded because a network cannot deliver packets faster than they are accepted. This restriction must quickly be passed back to the sender of packets to this destination or there will be a build-up of packets in the network. These are aspects of flow control, the means by which the network traffic is kept moving.

Although the network's carrying capacity will have been planned to cope with expected demands, many things can cause the capacity to be exceeded. It is simply not economic to provide capacity for any conceivable load variation so there will be occasional peaks in excess of the capacity. Even the statistical variation of traffic will eventually (if with low probability) give us an excess. Surges of traffic due to outside events or, unhappily, the results of planning not anticipating the extent of demand will strain certain networks at times. The design must be able to react sensibly to an overload. One result must be to restrict the acceptance of traffic for a while. If the network continues to carry all the traffic for which it was designed that will be the best it can do. So it must use its flow control mechanism to choke off demand. It must keep up these restrictive measures until more normal, unconstrained operation can take over.

If part of the subnet becomes over-filled with packets it can become impossible for packets to move. The queues into which they should be accepted are always full. This is called *congestion*. Some might refer to the flow restrictions mentioned above as congestion, but we reserve the term for the more unhealthy state in which traffic capacity is not fully used because the control measures have failed.

An extreme form of congestion is *lock-up*, a situation in which certain flows have stopped for ever, essentially because of a logical error in design. It can be illustrated by an analogy with a traffic circle, shown in Figure 4.1. This has

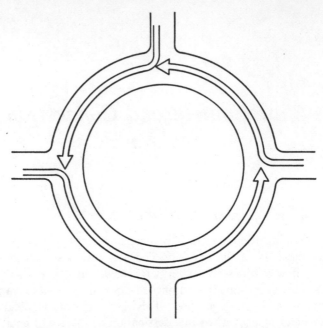

Figure 4.1   Lock-up condition in a traffic circle

three mutually interfering flows and the interference is caused by a faulty priority rule which favours traffic entering the circle. Unless the rules are changed the three flows will not start again. Buffer allocation and priority rules in packet networks can be chosen, wrongly, to cause such lock-ups. Figure 4.2 shows, also for the road network, how traffic restrictions can spread through a system. Packet networks do not have the large buffer capacity that roads possess, so the spread of congestion is more rapid. Adding more storage is not the answer because that adds delay. The spreading back of a traffic hold-up has only to loop back to the stream causing the delay and a complete lock-up of an indirect kind results.

Thus we have flow control, which regulates flows in normal operation and is principally a method of transmitting flow restrictions back to the place where the flows can be controlled and we have congestion avoidance which aims to prevent overloading of the network from spreading and causing more loss of performance than is really necessary. They are related, because the policies needed for congestion avoidance are enforced by the flow control mechanism.

Before we proceed to review the control of flow in packet-switched networks, we will consider briefly the type of problems encountered in the design and operation of circuit-switched telephone networks. In this case we have, instead of packets carried by the network, call attempts from subscribers to establish circuits to carry their conversations. The commodity that requires the application

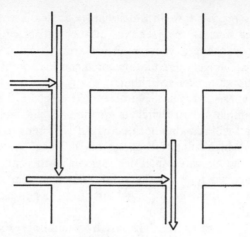

Figure 4.2   Spread of congestion in a street system

of flow control is the call attempt. Efficiency of operation of a telephone network may be expressed in terms of call completion rate—the percentage of all calls completed; this is loosely analogous to the packet throughput rate in a packet-switched network. A wide-ranging review of telephone network control principles may be found in Gimpelson.[1] He states that telephone networks have a maximum call-carrying capacity and that if the applied load exceeds this capacity, then the network will not even be able to support its full capacity. The problem arises because the public now has access (through the 'direct dialling' or 'trunk dialling' systems) to the long-distance circuits of the network, no longer needing to pass through human operator control. A call is established progressively as the call attempt is recorded in each successive exchange, with the temporary allocation of call registers and trunk bandwidth; these latter resources are held during the call attempt and also during the subsequent call if completion is achieved; both resources are available only in limited quantities. At peak load times many subscribers are trying to make calls and a great deal of the network equipment, exchanges and trunks, is being used in call attempts. Many subscribers, if their first attempt to obtain a circuit fails, will try again repeatedly, as often as is necessary to get through. The effect is cumulative, more resources are devoted to attempting to complete partially completed calls, and the proportion of calls completed (and hence the revenue earning of the system) goes down. If alternative routing is in operation, longer routes may be attempted at busy times, leading to the tying up of an even greater proportion of network resources.

If the peak load is focused in some region, because, for example, some natural disaster or some sudden event of regional importance occurs in a particular centre, then many call attempts may be made into this region, whilst the rest of the network is hardly under any strain. Call completion rate into the region suffers disastrously.

It is possible to reach a state in which hardly any calls are being completed. Indeed the call registers of one exchange may be full of calls awaiting access to a neighbouring exchange, whose registers are in turn full of calls seeking access to the first exchange; this situation could cause a complete lock-up, which has a direct parallel in packet switching.[2]

A subscriber whose call is not completed will be given the number engaged tone, but, in a simple circuit-switched system, all the facilities temporarily allocated to the call will remain allocated whilst he listens to this tone, and will only be cleared when he finally replaces his handset. A more sophisticated system will clear the allocated facilities as soon as the call is blocked, whilst generating the engaged tone for the subscriber. The reattempt rate may be reduced if a recorded message is played advising the subscriber to retry after some time interval.

Gimpelson is quite categoric that only by excluding excess calls from the network can a state of congestion be avoided in the telephone system at peak load. This requires a complex control system much more readily achieved in a stored program controlled exchange than in a Strowger or Crossbar exchange. Thus traffic flow control technology is advancing in parallel with the more sophisticated facilities offered by the system.

Access control needs to be sensitive enough to keep the network operating near the peak of the performance curve (provided that the demand load is great enough); the accepted load must not be allowed to pass beyond this point, because it takes much longer to extricate a system from congestion than it does for the congestion to form in the first place.

4.2 FLOW CONTROL IN PACKET NETWORKS

A well-designed flow control system is also a vitally important component of a packet-switched network. Packet flow may be controlled between neighbouring nodes, it may be controlled between source and destination network nodes, between source and destination host computers or between source and destination processes in the host computers. Figure 4.3 indicates the various points between which flow control may be applied in a packet switching network. Flow control at each level is concerned with ensuring that the rate of transmission of packets from the source shall not exceed the capacity of the destination to receive packets; it is further concerned to ensure that the load imposed on the transmission medium joining transmitter and receiver shall not exceed its capacity.

Point-to-point flow control systems are generally based on the acknowledgement of packets transmitted by the source and received at the destination. Acknowledgements may be either positive, indicating correct receipt, or negative, indicating either incorrect receipt or loss of packet. We shall examine later the details of various acknowledgement systems.

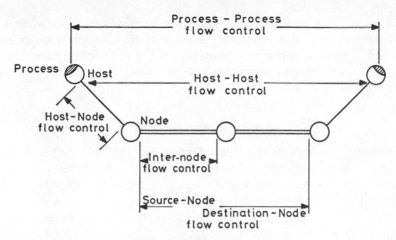

Figure 4.3   Levels of flow control

Between neighbouring nodes the protocol must be designed to ensure that the transmitter sends packets at a rate acceptable to the receiver. The protocol is concerned to protect the receiver node against over-filling of its packet buffers and against over-taxing its processing capacity. The transmission rate from the transmitter cannot, in a properly designed system, exceed the capacity of the transmission medium between the nodes; the latter is not protected directly by the inter-node protocol.

Between source and destination nodes the protocol must be designed to ensure that the source node does not accept packets from source users for transmission at a rate greater than that at which the destination user can accept them from the destination node. A second requirement is that the number of packets simultaneously in transit does not exceed the storage capacity of the network. The load applied to the network by one source–destination packet flow is unlikely to overtax its capacity, but the aggregate load between all source–destination pairs may quite easily do so. Protection against this kind of overload is not easy to achieve; if the number of packets in transit per source–destination pair is limited so that the maximum aggregate load is within safe limits, then at times when not all source–destination pairs are active the network will be under-run, even though the potential load between the active pairs could take up the spare capacity.

We therefore draw a distinction between the needs of flow control and those of congestion avoidance. The former is concerned with integrity of packet transmission and the protection of vulnerable entities (e.g. destination nodes) from overload; the latter is concerned with the protection of the network as a whole, or local parts of the network, from blockage due to an aggregation of excess traffic. The means adopted to achieve these objectives have features in common, but also differ in important particulars.

The present chapter will consider the principles of system design where these concern flow control and congestion avoidance. In Chapter 6 an extended description is given of two specific protocols, the HDLC link protocol and the X25 virtual call interface protocol; both these protocols contain important flow control features.

Link Level, Node to Node

The aim of flow control at the link level is, like that in all other dialogues within the system, to contribute to the efficient operation of the network. The particular contributions of link level flow controls are to the efficient use of the link bandwidth, including the integrity of the transmitted data, and to the efficient use of node buffers, including the avoidance of nodal congestion and of lock-up conditions.

The fundamentals of most inter-node protocols are that copies of transmitted packets are kept in transmitting nodes, to await either deletion when their correct reception is acknowledged by the receiving node or retransmission after a time interval if this acknowledgement is not received. Correct reception of a received packet depends upon buffer availability in the receiving node and upon the received packet itself passing some test of correctness. Such a test is usually based on a cyclic redundancy check which comprehends the data field and the header field of each packet; separate checks may be applied to these fields if desired.

The simplest inter-node protocol that can be devised handles packets one at a time; it need not even require an acknowledgement signal. In the early days of railways, trains were despatched on the time interval basis; a supposedly safe interval was maintained between the successive despatch of trains down a line. Some of the more spectacular disasters of the early railways were due to this mode of operation. In packet-switched networks packets could be sent from one node to the next on this basis, but no network designer in his senses would suggest this seriously. A safe-interval protocol must be designed to meet the worst case and therefore must take into account possible slow processing by the receiving node; such a safe time interval would be hopelessly long for most practical cases, leading to very inefficient use of the line bandwidth.

Keeping to the train control analogy, the early railways soon devised a block system in which signals passed between signal boxes, indicating 'train out of section' before a further train could be accepted; only one train was allowed in a block at one time. The analogue in packet switching is the acknowledgement signal. This can be used in the packet-at-a-time mode; a packet is sent by the transmitter, which then waits for an acknowledgement before the next packet is sent. Figure 4.4 illustrates the way in which this simple protocol works. Operating in this fashion there is no obvious need to distinguish packets one from another; a received acknowledgement should only refer to the most recently transmitted packet. With a perfect transmission system and infallible nodes there would be no need even to consider retransmission. A received acknowledgement would merely be the signal for the transmission of the next packet; neither data packet nor acknowledgement packet could possibly be lost; nodes need never run short of buffers, because, with one packet at a time operation on each link, adequate buffer provision can be simply calculated; received packets are therefore always accepted.

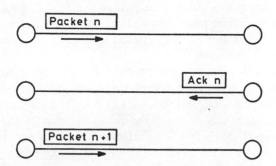

Figure 4.4   Exchange of packets between adjacent nodes under a simple protocol

In practice such perfect transmission and adequacy of packet buffering may not be found and provision has to be made for this in a practical inter-node protocol. If, because of noise on the line, a packet is not correctly received in the receiving node or, alternatively, buffer space is not available in that node, then the packet must not be acknowledged and the transmitting node must later send a second copy. This can be achieved in either of two ways; the transmitter may retransmit the packet if it has not been acknowledged before the expiry of a time interval (known as a 'time-out'); alternatively the receiving node may send a signal indicating the receipt of an incorrect packet or the receipt of a packet for which no buffer was available; this signal is often called a 'negative acknowledgement' (or NAK).

We will consider first the protocol in which acknowledgements are expected by the transmitter, in default of which within the time-out interval the most recently transmitted packet must be sent again. Not only may data packets be transmitted incorrectly, but also, since they travel via the same medium, acknowledgement signals may be faulty when they arrive at the transmitter. Thus a correctly received data packet may not be correctly acknowledged to the transmitting node. Alternatively the acknowledgement may arrive very late at the transmitter. Retransmission takes place in these circumstances, resulting very probably in the correct receipt of a second copy of the data packet at the receiving node. The protocol must be designed to allow the receiving node to distinguish between new data packets and repeat copies of previously received packets. This is simply done by providing an 'alternation bit' in the packet header, a device originally suggested by Bartlett, Scantlebury and Wilkinson.[3] This is a single binary digit, contained in the packet header, which alternates between its two possible states for successive data packets. Thus a node receiving a packet with alternation bit '0' expects the next data packet to have alternation bit '1'; arrival of a packet with '0' indicates that this is a second copy of the previously received packet. The alternation bit is also included in the acknowledgement signal, indicating unequivocally to the transmitter to which packet the acknowledgement signal refers. The packet header, including the alternation bit, is subject to the cyclic redundancy check. It is only in the highly unlikely event of the check operation failing to detect an error in the alternation bit that this protocol may break down.

We consider next the alternative protocol in which retransmission is based not on time-outs but on negative acknowledgements (NAKs). In a protocol of this type positive acknowledgements (ACKs) permit the transmission of a new data packet, whilst NAKs demand the retransmission of the previous data packet. One observes that a NAK signal may also be subject to errors on the line. It may be possible in the receiver to recognise even a faulty NAK, in which case retransmission can be initiated. If this is not possible, then this form of protocol may break down; in Chapter 6 the discussion of the HDLC protocol shows how this problem can be catered for. The time-out protocol with alternation bit gives a more convenient guarantee of correct packet exchange.

We have referred in this discussion to acknowledgement 'signals' and we have considered data flowing in one direction only. In this case the acknowledgement signals must travel as short control packets. More usually, data packets will travel in both directions between nodes and it is possible to include acknowledgement signals for one direction in the headers of data packets travelling in the other direction ('embedded acknowledgement'), thus using the line more efficiently. Indeed the extra bits required in packet headers to accommodate the protocol will be one for the data packet alternation bit and one for the acknowledgement alternation bit. Efficient operation of such a protocol would demand balanced data traffic in the two directions, which may not obtain in practice. To overcome this problem special short acknowledgement packets may be used if no data packet is currently ready for transmission.

Thus far we have considered data packet exchanges between adjacent nodes in which packets are handled one at a time. Correct acknowledgement is awaited before the next packet is sent. In the case of a very long line or a line of very high bandwidth, it is quite possible that this single packet mode of operation may be highly inefficient, with the line being idle for a great part of the time whilst acknowledgements are awaited. Therefore protocols have been devised in which several packets can be sent by a transmitter before the first of them is acknowledged.

In specifying a multi-packet inter-node protocol it is necessary to provide some means of distinguishing individual packets; this may be done by giving each packet a sequence number carried in the packet header. The simplest mode of using packet sequence numbers is for the receiving node to return acknowledgements (either as special packets or in data packet headers) indicating the sequence number or numbers of packet(s) to be acknowledged. The number of packets that may be transmitted before an acknowledgement is received is often called the 'window width'. Packet transmission is controlled by an algorithm which uses packet sequence numbers and the line window width.

We shall now outline the elements of a simple multi-packet inter-node transmission protocol. At the protocol initialisation time, it is of course necessary to set the values of sequence numbers in communicating nodes to the same value, typically 0. Thus the first packet to be transmitted by a node will bear sequence number 0 and the first packet expected to be received at its neighbour should also bear the sequence number 0. Let us denote the transmitted sequence number as N_t and the next expected received sequence number at N_r. Let us denote the window width as W.

At the start of communication the transmitter is allowed successively to transmit packets bearing the sequence numbers in the range $0 \leqslant N_t < W$. The receiver expects these packets to arrive in correct sequence order. As they arrive packets are checked for correctness; an incorrect packet is disregarded and may be considered 'lost'. Let the sequence number of a particular correctly received packet be S. If $S = N_r$, then the received packet is in correct sequence and it should be accepted for processing and onward transmission by the node, and an acknowledgement bearing the sequence number S sent to the transmitting node. If $S < N_r$, then the packet is a repetition of a packet previously correctly received by the receiving node; the second transmission may be due either to a lost or to a delayed acknowledgement packet; the receiving node should generate a further acknowledgement packet and send this to the transmitter, but otherwise ignore the packet. If $S > N_r$, then the packet is ahead of sequence, indicating that an earlier packet has been lost; such a packet should be ignored and not acknowledged.

Let us now consider the arrival of the acknowledgement packets at the transmitting node; as each arrives the node should delete the copy it has retained of the corresponding data packet. As packets are acknowledged so fresh packets may be transmitted; when packet 0 has been acknowledged packet W may be transmitted—and so on. We have already indicated in the above discussion that packets may get lost on links and that this applies equally to acknowledgement packets. If a received acknowledgement does not refer to the earliest transmitted packet awaiting acknowledgement, then, in this protocol, the node may safely delete all such packets up to and including that referenced by the acknowledgement packet. Against each copy of a transmitted packet will be noted a time (the time-out) by which the packet must be acknowledged; failing such an acknowledgement, then the node must retransmit the packet, using the original sequence number. Because, in the protocol being described, the receiving node will only accept packets in order, then it will be necessary to retransmit not only the earliest unacknowledged packet (possibly lost in transmission), but also all the later unacknowledged packets (which cannot be accepted out of order at the receiver).

An illustration may assist the understanding of this process. In Figure 4.5 we see the windows at transmitter (node A) and at receiver (node B). It is assumed that the window width is 3. Node A has sent out packets 3, 4 and 5, the last of which is still in transit to node B. Node B has received all packets up to and including 4. It has just acknowledged 3 and 4, and is now in a position to accept 5, 6 and 7, when they arrive in that order. When node A receives acknowledgements for 3 and 4 it will be able to transmit successively packets 6 and 7.

The process we have described is sufficient to ensure the correct exchange of packets between adjacent nodes. It has the merit that packets are invariably handled in correct order. If fixed routing is in use then packet sequence is preserved between source and destination nodes, which may be advantageous. It has the serious disadvantage of possibly requiring unnecessary retransmissions of correctly received out-of-sequence packets; this can result in inefficient use of link bandwidth.

A variation of the simple protocol allows the acceptance of packets out of sequence; this variation operates as follows. If the sequence number of an arriving data packet is in the range $N_r \leqslant S < N_r + W$, when it should be accepted and acknowledged, but checked against a list of previously correctly received packets (within the permitted range) in order to ensure that it is not a duplicate; if it is a duplicate, then it is destroyed, if not, the receiving node prepares to process it for onward transmission. If $S < N_r$, then the packet

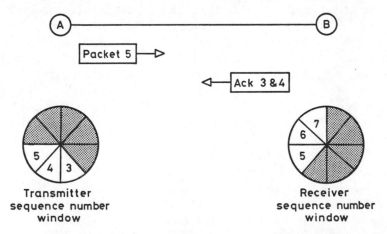

Figure 4.5   Packet numbering in an inter-node protocol

should be acknowledged, but otherwise ignored, being regarded as a duplicate. At the transmitting node each acknowledgement is taken to refer only to the specific previously transmitted packet bearing the corresponding sequence number; on correct acknowledgement this packet is deleted by the transmitting node. As in the sequential form of the protocol each packet awaiting acknowledgement bears a time stamp. At the expiry of the due time, in the absence of acknowledgement, retransmission of the packet takes place, but not, in this case, all later packets as well.

In this discussion we have assumed that sequence numbers start at some initial value and are then incremented indefinitely. In practice this would mean that an infinite number space would be required to accommodate the sequence number in each packet header; this is obviously impossible. What is more, an infinite range of sequence numbers is quite unnecessary. Cyclic sequence numbers can quite adequately permit recognition of individual packets. The optimum range of sequence numbers is a function of the number of packets that can be in flight between transmitter and receiver.

It is also possible to specify a simple inter-node protocol in which sequence numbers are not used. Communication between neighbouring nodes is then carried out on the basis of a set of logical channels, of which a limited number, say eight, are specified. Transmission of packets takes place one on each logical channel, used successively on the single physical channel; each packet bears an indication of the logical channel on which it has been transmitted. Once used, a logical channel cannot be re-used until the packet transmitted has been correctly acknowledged. If no logical channel is free, packet transmission is temporarily suspended. The receiving node returns an acknowledgement signal for each packet correctly received and stored. In order to distinguish newly received packets from duplicates, the 'alternation bit' device is employed. Acknowledgement signals take the form of the alternation bit of the packet to be acknowledged. These signals may be carried either in special control packets or else in the headers of data packets travelling in the other direction. If eight logical channels are in use, then the return of an 8-bit byte is sufficient to carry all the necessary acknowledgements, each bit corresponding to a different logical channel. This byte may be carried by all contrary direction data packets; a change of state of a bit indicates the correct receipt of a new data packet on the corresponding logical channel. Only on detection of a change of a bit may the corresponding channel be used for a further new packet. The number of logical channels provided corresponds in function to the window width of the two protocols discussed earlier; it sets the maximum number of packets that may be outstanding without an acknowledgement. The logical channels need not be used in any particular order; as each becomes free it can be used for a new packet.

In the foregoing we have concentrated on the function of the acknowledgement signal in informing a transmitter of the successful reception of its output. The timing of acknowledgement signals may play an important part in flow control. Immediate acknowledgement allows early transmission of fresh packets, whilst delayed acknowledgement retards transmission. Thus timing of acknowledgements is of paramount importance. A node which detects early warning of congestion may delay acknowledgements in order to cut down the packet flows impinging upon it.

We have suggested in the foregoing discussion that there is a range of different inter-node protocols, most of which will give satisfactory transmission of data from node to node. Inevitably some protocols are more efficient than others. Selection of the best protocol and its ruling parameters requires some analysis of performance, which can be carried out using simulation or analytical techniques. Danthine and Eschenauer[4] have carried out such a simulation study to compare the performance of the 1972 version of the ARPA inter-node protocol, a different protocol since used in ARPA (both these protocols use acknowledgements embedded in data packet headers) and a protocol using separate control packets for acknowledgements; the influence of the protocols on node buffer usage, transmission delay and useful throughput was considered.

The 1972 ARPA inter-node protocol used the principle, which we have already mentioned, of separate logical channels (eight in number). Time-outs were not involved in this protocol; instead, repeat copies of data packets were transmitted whenever the line would otherwise have been idle; repeats ceased only when an acknowledgement was received for the corresponding data packet. The second ARPA inter-node protocol, also based on logical channels, used retransmission on time-out, no automatic repeat transmissions being made; control packets were sent if the line would otherwise have been idle. Under heavy load these two protocols gave similar performance, but the second gave reduced delay under medium or light loads. The embedded acknowledgement method, however, meant that acknowledgement digits were not accessible to the node until the full-length data packet had been received. In order to allow earlier access to the acknowledgement digits, and therefore earlier freeing of the buffers holding copies of data packets ready for retransmission, the third inter-node protocol was devised. This used short control packets to convey acknowledgement signals. Danthine and Eschenauer give a full analysis of the relative performance of the three protocols, and conclude that though both the second and third are preferable the first, choice between them depends on which network resource is more valuable. The second protocol makes more efficient use of line capacity, whilst the third makes less demand on retransmission buffers in the nodes.

Other important parameters that must be well chosen are the number of logical channels to be used, or, alternatively, if logical channels are not used, the window width of packet sequence numbers. Correct choice will ensure good line utilisation; if the number of logical channels is too low or the window width too narrow, then the inter-node link will be under-used.

Adequate buffer provision in each node is essential; furthermore the pool of buffers must be managed in such a way that not all the buffers in a node may be allocated to a single link. If the latter is allowed to happen, then a direct store-and-forward lock-up, of the type described by Kahn and Crowther[2] can be created. Direct store-and-forward lock-up, should it occur, is extremely difficult to disentangle, but easy to avoid at the design stage by using a sensible buffer allocation discipline. A discussion of this problem follows in the section on congestion avoidance.

Subnet Level, Source Node to Destination Node

We have discussed at some length the reasons for inter-node flow control and have outlined some of the methods for achieving this. Many of the same concepts carry over into the network-wide field of source–destination flow control.

Source–destination protocols are concerned with the correct transfer of data packets at a rate which the destination host can accept from the destination node and which the network can support. To ensure the integrity of the data packets delivered to the host by the destination node, it is necessary that some form of test for correctness be applied in that node. It is not sufficient to rely upon the fact that each packet has been subjected to correctness tests on arrival in each node *en route*; this will have ensured that line errors will have been eliminated, but will not have taken account of errors that may have occurred in the nodes themselves. It is therefore necessary to provide a mechanism by which faulty packets may be retransmitted from the source node. This requires some form of end-to-end acknowledgement, with provision for retransmission in default after a time-out (or, alternatively, a negative acknowledgement system, though this may be prone to error due to loss or corruption of NAKs). The mechanism can be very similar to that used in the inter-node protocol. Note, however, that either the source node must (unlike intermediate nodes) retain copies of data packets until they are safely acknowledged by the destination node or else they must be obtainable from the source host whence they originally came. Note also that correct receipt of a packet in the destination node is not a sufficient condition for sending an acknowledgement to the source. It is essential that this should only be done when successful delivery of the packet to the destination host has been achieved.

Packet identification must be carried out by a packet numbering system which is common to source and destination. In networks of up to about 60 nodes, the present largest size, it may be reasonable for each source and destination node to maintain a permanent packet number register for each possible source–destination packet exchange. The sequence number will be cyclic, with a range sufficiently large to avoid confusion. Source and destination sequence numbers must be initialised to the same values and checks made to maintain synchronism. Indeed it may be sensible to resynchronise on a regular basis. In larger networks the number of source–destination pairs may make it impracticable to keep permanent sequence number registers for all node pairs; in this case the source and destination sequence numbering must be set up afresh for each new call. No sequence number registers would then be taken up by dormant source–destination pairs.

The requirement that a source shall not overtax a destination node with flow of data demands first of all that a check be made that the destination host is operative and that it is willing to accept transmission from the particular source. If transmission is made to a dead or unwilling host, then such packets would be undeliverable and would eventually clutter the network and, maybe, even cause congestion. If the network is to operate without a check on destination host availability, then the destination node must have discretion to take appropriate action; the latter may consist of returning the undeliverable packets to their source or destroying them (with or without returning an indication of this to the source). We shall have more to say about this point in our comments on host-to-host flow control.

The more normal status is that the destination host is available and that packet transmission may proceed. Packet flow must take place at a rate which the destination can accept. An element of flow control is afforded by the string of inter-node controls via which the packet is handed from node to node as it traverses the network. However, to signal down such a chain by means of full queues that a destination is accepting traffic at a rate slower than the source is emitting it, is a very loosely coupled and inefficient process; it requires the string of nodes to become congested before the source can be signalled to reduce the transmission rate. Therefore an end-to-end flow control is essential for efficient operation. It is a matter of some controversy whether such a flow control should be provided by the subnetwork, as in the case of the virtual call and similar systems, or by the host-to-host protocol, in which case the network can operate in a mode like that of the datagram.

Provision of an end-to-end flow control by the subnetwork may well be based on a windowing mechanism like that which has already been discussed in the preceding section. The choice of window width (number of packets allowed to be transmitted before an acknowledgement is received for the first) should be made to achieve the maximum transmission rate with the most efficient use of network bandwidth (minimum of retransmissions). Because a source may wish to transmit to a range of destinations at various distances, it is not necessarily correct to use the same window width for all source–destination pairs. Between widely separated nodes it may well be sensible to allow a large number of packets to be in flight—a wide window is used; nodes that are close together may require a narrower window. This can be achieved if each source node has a vector of window widths indexed according to destination.

Ideally the window width should be chosen so that the last packet allowed by the window is just finishing transmission from the source as the acknowledgement for the first packet is arriving back at the source; by this means transmission of packets would proceed uninterrupted at the optimum rate. It has been suggested[5] that each source–destination data exchange should discover its own optimal window width. This would be done by the source transmitting data packets until the first acknowledgement was received; receipt of the first acknowledgement would indicate the correct window width in terms of packets transmitted up to that point. This window width would then control the rest of the data flow. At first sight the self-discovery process may seem attractive. Consider, however, an acknowledgement delayed on its way back to the source, perhaps because of network congestion; the source would continue to transmit data packets until the delayed acknowledgement finally arrived. The window width would be excessive and therefore the flow rate would be excessive. Worse would be the case of a lost acknowledgement or set of acknowledgements, when the source might be even less well regulated. The more conventional course is to pre-set the window width according to the results obtained from either a mathematical model or a simulation model.

Packet delivery from destination node to destination host is usually (but not universally) required to be made in the same order as packet acceptance by the source node from the source host. Packet ordering places certain constraints on the end-to-end flow control, especially if adaptive routing is in operation within the subnet; in this case packets taking different routes between source and destination may be expected to arrive at the destination in an order other than that in which they were accepted at source. Some mechanism must be set up to re-establish order in the packet stream. The details of such a mechanism depend on whether packets are component parts of messages as in the ARPA network.[6]

A packet stream that does not need to be reassembled into messages can be handled in the following manner. Every packet carries a sequence number (S) which is specific to the particular source–destination packet flow; the sequence number will be cyclic with a modulus sufficiently large to avoid confusion. It is assumed that transmission from the source node is governed by a packet number window. The destination node maintains an expected packet sequence number $(EPSN)$ for every communicating source node. Packets arriving at the destination node are checked against the $EPSN$; if $S = EPSN$, then the packet may be output immediately to the host. If $S < EPSN$, then the packet is treated as a duplicate copy and is deleted (in the context of packet ordering we are not directly concerned with acknowledgement action). If $S > EPSN$, then the packet must be held by the node until packets with the earlier expected sequence numbers arrive. When the latter do arrive, then all packets with consecutive sequence numbers may be output in sequence. $EPSN$ is advanced to correspond to the next expected sequence number. Note that an acknowledgement need only be returned to the source to correspond to the last of the output packets, the others being acknowledged implicitly. If the subnet loses a packet, then the source node will, in the absence of an acknowledgement, retransmit a copy of the missing packet. Until the latter arrives at the destination node, the stream of output packets must be held up if absolute sequence order is to be maintained. Some applications may not demand absolute sequence integrity, in which case a missing packet may simply be omitted when a predetermined string length of packets is ready and waiting for output. The capacity of the destination node to store waiting packets must be taken into account in determining the length of such a string.

In the ARPA network messages of up to 8063 data bits are accepted from hosts for transmission. The maximum packet size is 1008 data bits plus overheads; therefore a message is broken up at the source node into up to eight separate packets, Figure 4.6, each of which must carry the identifier of the message together with a packet number within the message. ARPA allows multiple routes to be taken between source and destination (particularly in the event of component failure) and intermediate nodes do not attempt to maintain packet order; this network must therefore cater for message reassembly at destination nodes. The latter have a limited stock of reassembly buffers. In the original ARPA protocol reassembly buffers were allocated freely at the destination as each new packet arrived. The result of this was that the reassembly buffers might run out, filled by a number of partly reassembled messages, whose missing packets were held up in neighbouring nodes, unable to enter the destination node because of buffer starvation. Complete deadlock was produced in these circumstances; the condition called 'reassembly lock-up' has been discussed at length by Kahn and Crowther.[2]

The ARPA solution to the problem of reassembly lock-up was to establish a protocol whereby a reserved allocation of reassembly buffers was made for each message transmitted by a source node. A source node with a multi-packet message to send would first send a 'request for allocation' to which a destination

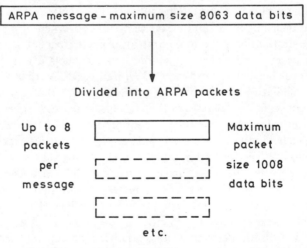

Figure 4.6   Split of ARPA message into packets

node with available buffer capacity would respond with an 'allocate' reply. On receipt of an 'allocate' notification, the source node was free to transmit the message, which would eventually occupy the allocated reassembly buffers at the destination before being finally output to the host.

Successful output to the destination host allowed the destination node to signal 'request for next message' (RFNM) to the source node. To avoid unnecessary overheads and time wasting, the reassembly buffers just vacated by the delivered message were held reserved for the next message from the particular source node. If, within 125 milliseconds, the source node sent in response to the RFNM a further message to the destination host, then the allocation of reassembly buffers was re-used. If, however, the source host did not provide a message quickly enough for the source node to transmit, then the latter sent a 'give back' signal to the destination, freeing the reserved reassembly buffers.

Up to eight separate messages may be in transit between any source–destination host pair. The source–destination protocol requires that messages are delivered in the same order as they were accepted for transmission by the source node. If several different hosts, maybe at different source nodes, all attempt simultaneously to send message streams to a single destination host, then the limited number of reassembly buffers at the destination will effectively limit the flow from each source host, provided any single host is prevented from monopolising the destination reassembly buffers.

Single-packet messages are not inconvenienced by the reassembly buffer allocation system. Such messages carry their own 'request for allocation', and are sent without a preliminary source–destination dialogue. If the destination node has no immediately available buffer, then the packet is deleted, but the request is noted. As soon as the destination node has a free buffer, an 'allocate' is sent to the source node which then sends again the single-packet message.

Flow control in the ARPA network has been the subject of many published papers, from which it is evident that the design has passed through many phases. A recent and comprehensive critique of the source–destination flow control in the ARPA network is contained in McQuillan and Walden.[6]

A network operating in datagram mode, without source–destination flow control, is vulnerable to malicious interference unless special steps are taken. For example, an attempt may be made to swamp communication with a particular destination (maybe for stock exchange manipulation purposes) by sending an excessively heavy stream of packets to the destination node. This stream may fill most of the packet buffers at the destination node and thus hinder delivery of other traffic. An effective counter to such a device is to maintain public and private destination addresses, the private address known only to privileged users. Non-privileged users always send to the public address, which is freely available under normal circumstances, only becoming unavailable if congestion sets in. Privileged users are assured of access to the destination via the private address.

Host–node Flow Control

In this section we shall be concerned with the flow control of traffic between the network customer devices and the nodes of the subnetwork to which they are connected. For convenience the term 'host' is often used as a general description of customer devices; however, these may range from large mainframe machines, through minicomputers (even microcomputers), to intelligent terminals and non-intelligent terminals. A wide range of protocols may be needed to handle the various types of connection to the network node. Some of these are discussed at length in Chapters 6, 7 and 8; here we are concerned only with the flow control aspects of the protocols. The conduct of the host–node protocol, where the connection is to a host computer, is shared between the node and the host. The latter provides a special program segment, called in ARPA a network control process, whose purpose is to conduct the protocols required to connect the host to the network. This facility may otherwise be provided by a special front end processor, but this solution is likely to be more costly and less effective. Where a non-intelligent host is concerned, the node must be responsible for the conduct of the host–node protocol, as in the ARPA Terminal Interface Processor (TIP).

The purpose of host–node and node–host protocols is quite simple—to avoid overtaxing the receiver by excessive transmission rate; since we are here considering a direct connection there is no risk of overloading the transmission medium. Data flow from a source host will be constrained by the amount of buffering available in the source node and by the rate at which the node is able to transmit packets into the network. The flow control must prevent excessive demands being made on buffers, especially if the latter are shared with other traffic passing through the node. Data flow from destination node to destination host will be limited by the rate at which the host computer can accept traffic. An overall constraint in both instances will be the bandwidth of the connection; this must be sufficient to avoid imposing a transmission delay which is significant compared with that of the subnetwork itself.

Another important consideration is that of fairness of treatment where several host connections are made to a single source node. The buffering and processing power of the network node must be fairly shared between the various connections. If different levels of traffic priority are involved, then this is an added complexity. Multiple connections from single hosts to several source nodes should cause no special flow control problems; if an end-to-end source node to destination node protocol is in operation, then traffic for particular destination hosts must flow over particular host to source node links during a single association; other associations with the same destination host may use other host–node links at either the same or other times.

Where several hosts are connected to a single node users may wish to establish communication between them on a local basis. Such traffic (called 'incestuous' by some) goes no further into the network than the local node. Here the flow control between hosts must rely entirely upon the host–node and node–host protocols.

Reliability of data transfer is as important at the host–node connection as anywhere else in the network. If the connection is over a short distance, then it may be possible to use a direct circuit with no provision for error detection and packet retransmission. The rare occurrence of an error on such a connection can be dealt with by the source host to destination host protocol, with retransmission allowed for at that level, provided the 'host' is an intelligent device. Where non-intelligent terminals are connected to the node, the node must provide terminal processor facilities such as are provided by the ARPA TIP. Errors over the line may be detected by character echoing at the terminal; the terminal protocol must allow for correction of errors by user action. A host remotely connected to a node over a data link with modems must communicate through a link protocol very like that of the inter-node link protocol, involving acknowledgements and retransmission.

The data transfer unit may not be the same as the packet carried by the subnetwork. In the case of ARPA the host–node data transfer unit is the message of up to 8063 bits, broken up into packets (maximum 1008 bits) within the node. If the data link is noisy, this could be a source of inconvenience, because full-length messages are approximately eight times more likely to be in error than are data packets travelling on a similar link within the subnetwork.

The host end of a link with a retransmission protocol must be driven either by a dedicated front end computer or by a network control process situated within the host itself.

Acceptance of traffic from the host by the network node depends on the source node to destination node protocol where any kind of 'call' is in operation. In ARPA the RFNM returned to the source node by the destination node is a signal for acceptance of a further message by the source node from the source host. The RFNM is not generated by the destination host until a successful message transfer has been made to the destination host. On the other hand, if the network accepts packets in a datagram mode, the constraint of an end-to-end protocol is not available to limit flow from a source host. We shall discuss possible methods of controlling flow in such circumstances in our consideration of congestion avoidance.

Host–host Flow Control

The two preceding sections have addressed the question of host–node and source–destination flow control protocols. Taken together these flow controls constitute a degree of host–host flow control, but it is normal to provide some form of separate control at the host–host level. This resides in the network control process referred to in the previous section, which is therefore responsible both for host–node and host–host relations.

The question whether flow control and other protocol matters should be the responsibility of the hosts or of the subnetwork has caused a degree of controversy. To some extent this argument follows the lines of that over virtual call and datagram. A substantial body of opinion holds that each level, host and subnetwork, must provide its own set of independent protocols. This argument rests on the proposition that the subnetwork should be allowed to control its own resources, whilst, independently, the hosts should control theirs.

At the host–host level it is a normal prerequisite of data transfer that an association shall be established before data is permitted to flow. The request for such a association to be set up comes from a user process within the host and is passed to the network control process for action. In the virtual call the willingness of the destination host to accept a call must be established, this 'willingness' involves identification and logging-on procedures. Even in the context of datagrams it may be expected that the willingness of the distant host to accept data packets from a particular source will be established before transmission of data commences.

Transmission of packets or multi-packet messages between source and destination host may either be conducted one data unit at a time along a virtual link, with several links active in order to allow several data units to be in simultaneous parallel transit, or else controlled by a windowing protocol with message sequence numbers which determine the number of messages which may be in transit at one time. Use of message sequence numbers clearly requires that the source and destination host network control processes shall first synchronise sequence numbers. In node-to-node and source node to destination node protocols we suggested that transmitter and receiver maintain permanent sequence number registers, which may need resynchronising from time to time. At the host level it is unlikely that each host will keep a permanent sequence number for communication with every other network host—hence the need to obtain agreement on sequence numbering each time a new conversation is set up. The number of messages allowed to be outstanding between source and destination is a matter for the network designer and may sensibly be made to depend on the distance between source and destination hosts. Depending on the choice of flow control method, the number of outstanding messages should be taken to determine either the allowable number of logical channels or the allowable message number window width.

The host–host flow control process should seek to provide fair shares of the communication facility for contending host processes. It is a matter of network management policy whether the maximum number of processes should be able to communicate at the lowest acceptable rate or whether fewer processes should communicate at a somewhat higher rate.

If multiple host to source node connections are provided, then it may be sensible to allow a network control process seeking to establish an end-to-end connection, but encountering a refusal from the first source node tried, to attempt to establish the liaison via another node with which it has a connection.

Process-to-process Flow Control

User processes exist within host computers and access the network via the medium of the host network control process. In the preceding section we have considered communication between hosts controlled by the network control process. The flow of data between user process and network control process must be governed in part by the relationship between source and destination network control processes. The flow is also governed by a user process level relationship. Access to a destination host process is usually via log-in and password procedures. The progress of the inter-process conversation, once this is set up, is subject to the rate at which source and destination processes operate (CPU speeds, store access times, etc., etc.) and therefore each process pair must reach agreement on the conversational protocols to be observed. These are not necessarily related to the communication medium through which the conversation is carried out; however, the fact of network transit delay compared with effectively instantaneous communication via a direct connection may have an effect on the nature of the inter-process protocol.

4.3   CONGESTION AVOIDANCE SYSTEMS

We define congestion in packet networks as a state in which network performance is degraded in some way because of an excessive number of packets in transit within the network. The performance degradation might be a reduction in throughput despite no corresponding reduction in applied load or a greater delay encountered by packets in traversing the network; these features of performance degradation are likely to be encountered together. Congestion may be local, confined to a limited region of a network, or, more seriously, it may be general throughout a network. In the extreme case congestion may be so severe that all or almost all traffic comes to a standstill, with little or no traffic being delivered to destinations or being accepted from sources. It goes without saying that this is a deadly state for a data communication network to enter and is to be avoided at all costs. We shall concern ourselves therefore in the network context with the causes of congestion, methods of congestion avoidance and methods of recovery from congested states.

Congestion is a state which may affect most transportation systems. Wooden logs in a river are carried efficiently until individual movements begin to interfere one with another. Up to a point an increase in packing density of logs should give an increase in throughput, but there comes a point where a further increase in packing density produces interference between logs and the total throughput may fall. Even greater packing density may lead to a state in which the logs lock together in a mass and the flow rate in the channel falls to zero.

Road traffic behaviour is more closely akin to the behaviour of a packet-switched network. In the road system we have a network of transportation channels, roads, intersections, etc. Traffic flows through the road network in streams between a vast number of different source–destination pairs. These streams constantly merge and diverge at the various intersections and branch points. Maximum delivery rate (vehicles reaching their destination per unit time) is achievable when the number of vehicles on the roads does not exceed a certain level. On occasions, such as public holidays, when the number of vehicles on the roads is excessive, traffic jams form and progress of individual vehicles becomes very much slower. Indeed it is all too easy to attain a condition in which hardly any vehicles are reaching their destinations. This is due to interference between the flows of streams of vehicles and between the flows of individual vehicles.

Causes of Congestion

In a packet-switched network the basic resources are link bandwidth and node buffer storage, both fundamental to the operation of a store-and-forward system. Data links can carry offered traffic up to their maximum capacity, allowing for overheads; unlike roads, their performance is hardly likely to degrade because of excessive traffic; they are not themselves liable to congest. They may, of course, because of their limited capacity, contribute to congestion development. Congestion in packet networks is more a matter of exhaustion of the stock of free node buffers. Free flow of traffic is dependent on the existence of a pool of free buffers in each node to receive the forwarded traffic. In a congested network packets arrive in new nodes only to find no buffer available to store them; they are therefore, depending on the network protocol, either

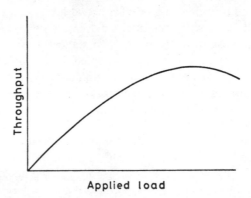

Figure 4.7   Throughput versus offered load in a network subject to congestion

subject to retransmission from the previous node or from the source node or host. The more severe the degree of congestion, the greater the proportion of network resources devoted to retransmission; therefore the delivered traffic may fall. This phenomenon is also well known in telephone networks.[1]

The relationship between offered load and network throughput for a network subject to congestion is shown in Figure 4.7. As the offered load increases up to the point of onset of congestion, the throughput increases uniformly with the offered load. As congestion becomes noticeable the rate of increase of the throughput falls and eventually a maximum is reached. In a poorly controlled network, further increase in applied load produces a reduction in throughput. That network performance should be degradable on account of excessive offered traffic is clearly an undesirable state. A more acceptable performance characteristic is shown in Figure 4.8, where throughput initially increases linearly with

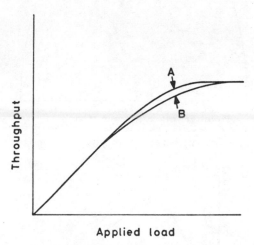

Figure 4.8   Desired throughput versus offered load characteristic

offered load, then tails off slightly to reach a maximum at which it remains irrespective of any further increase in 'offered load. The way in which the maximum is reached may be important; for designers interested in extracting the maximum performance from their network, curve A is obviously to be preferred to curve B. The shape of the curve between the linearly increasing portion and the maximum will be a function of the network congestion avoidance system.

In Figure 4.9 we illustrate the generally quoted[7] relationship between the number of entities currently within a transportation system and the system throughput. A relationship like this relates cars per kilometre to cars per hour and expresses the performance of a typical road which, unlike a data transmission path, contains storage. It shows that, for a given flow rate there can be two states, free flowing and congested. This relationship illustrates more clearly the nature of congestion, with its close dependence on the number of entities simultaneously in transit. Ideally any transportation system should be operated as near the maximum of this curve as possible. We shall shortly consider means

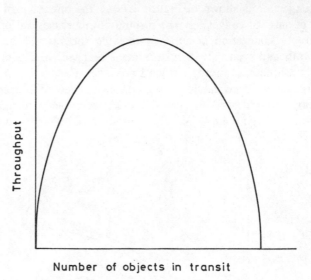

Figure 4.9   General relationship between throughput and number of objects in transit

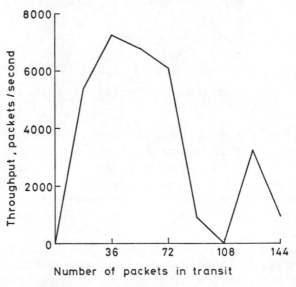

Figure 4.10   Network throughput versus number of packets in transit

of achieving this in the packet network context. The theoretical function illustrated in Figure 4.9 suggests that a certain amount of interference between packets occurs even at light loads and that the relation between applied load and throughput may cease to be linear well before congestion effects become otherwise measurable. A significant experimental result was observed in some network simulation by Plessey[8] for NPL. Figure 4.10 shows the observed relationship between network throughput and the number of packets simultaneously in transit within the network. The number of nodes in the network simulated was 18; the plotted points therefore each represent integral numbers of packets per node. The maximum throughput was observed in the region of three packets per node, 54 in total. Zero output, complete lock-up, was observed for six packets per node. The result is remarkable in the light of the total number of packet buffers (and dynamic packet storage on data links) available within the network; this amounted to some 400 storage buffer locations.

General congestion arises, therefore, when the amount of traffic in transit is such that too many packet stores are occupied in the nodes, leading to an excess of retransmission activity and consequent loss of performance. The cause is clearly due to lax control on packet acceptance at source nodes.

Congestion may occur on a localised basis if part of a network contains an excess of traffic, even though the network as a whole may be lightly loaded. This may happen if a network bottleneck impedes the free flow of traffic.

Deficiencies in node procedures may also permit the development of local congestion. Consider two nodes connected by a simple link, Figure 4.11. Each has a pool of buffers. If the entire pool of buffers in each node is occupied by packets seeking to reach the neighbouring node, then no buffers will be available for acceptance of traffic from the neighbour. Under these conditions no traffic can successfully be exchanged over the data link. This state is that which Kahn and Crowther[2] discussed and entitled 'direct store-and-forward lock-up'.

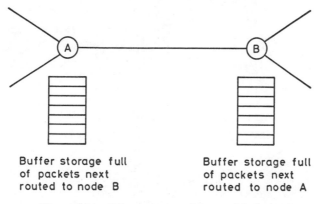

Buffer storage full   Buffer storage full
of packets next   of packets next
routed to node B   routed to node A

Figure 4.11   Direct store-and-forward lock-up

The same authors also discussed another form of lock-up, which can also arise in the ring topology of Figure 4.12. If the buffers of node A are all full of packets seeking to reach node C, node B is full of packets seeking to reach node D, C full of packets for E and D full of packets for F, then once again we have a condition in which packets arrive in nodes to find no free buffers available and traffic locks up completely. This condition was termed 'indirect store-and-forward lock-up'. Direct and indirect lock-up are similar to the lock-up mechanism of roads shown in Figures 4.1 and 4.2.

Both direct and indirect store-and-forward lock-up are due to faulty design of node operating system. In particular they arise because all packet buffers in one node are permitted to be allocated to one output queue. The prevention of direct store-and-forward lock-up is quite simple; only a limited number of packet buffers may be allocated to a particular queue. Indirect lock-up is much more difficult to cure.

Methods of Congestion Avoidance

Congestion can arise from several causes—a general excess of traffic within the network, network bottlenecks and faulty design of node operating systems. Congestion avoidance requires different measures to meet each of these conditions.

A general excess of traffic is due to insufficiently firm control on acceptance of traffic at source nodes. We must now consider what means are available for strengthening the control on traffic acceptance.

We have observed in the discussion on flow control that a limit may be placed on the number of packets in current transit between a source node and

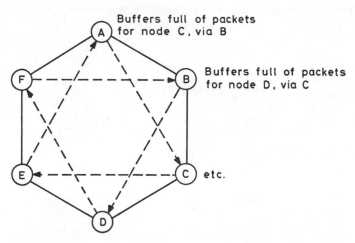

Figure 4.12   Indirect store-and-forward lock-up

a destination node. Packets awaiting their turn to traverse the network may be made to wait in host storage, outside the network. It is possible, by placing a low limit on the number of packets allowed to be in transit between each network source–destination pair, to ensure that the total number of packets in simultaneous transit will always be below the level at which general congestion becomes noticeable. This solution is unattractive, however, because in practice not all source–destination pairs will be active at once and active pairs will be unnecessarily restricted in their throughput.

It is necessary to place some limit on the number of packets outstanding per source–destination pair or per individual call, if virtual calls are being operated, but this limit should not be made unnecessarily low in order to try and avoid congestion. Some other mechanism must be sought.

We observed earlier that transportation systems in general perform best if the number of packets in transit is limited to a certain known level (Figure 4.9). If it were possible to prevent the transit packets exceeding this level, then perhaps good performance could be ensured. A network scheme to achieve this purpose was first mooted by Davies.[8] This was the isarithmic scheme which depended on a system of permits to control packet acceptance for transmission. In this scheme each network node was initially allocated a stock of permits. Each incoming packet, irrespective of its destination address, was required to acquire a permit at the source node before it was accepted from the host. If no permit was available, then the packet had to wait in the host until a permit became available. Once a permit was acquired, the packet was accepted and began its journey to its destination, notionally accompanied by the permit; acceptance of a packet implied unit decrement of the local node permit pool. At intermediate nodes the travelling packet was not subject to isarithmic control. At the destination node, as soon as the packet was successfully handed over to the destination host, the permit was freed and added to the permit pool held at the destination node. This pool controlled acceptance of incoming traffic from hosts connected to the destination node.

If all source nodes output as many packets as they received from other source nodes, then this scheme would adequately control traffic below the congestion level. Each active source–destination pair would be allowed to exchange traffic at a rate determined by its share of the available permits; the more pairs that were active, the less traffic that would be allowed per pair. (Note that if some nodes holding permits had no source traffic, then these permits would remain unused and the total throughput would be correspondingly reduced.) However, the balanced traffic limitation was unrealistic; network traffic between communicating nodes is not usually balanced. Therefore additional provision is required within the isarithmic scheme to take account of unbalanced traffic. This can be done by placing a limit on the number of permits that any node is allowed to hold in its free permit pool. If the free permit arising from successful delivery of a packet is not acceptable in the permit pool of the destination node, because the latter is already up to quota, then the free permit must be sent elsewhere. The way in which this is done might be expected to have a strong influence on the performance of the network. Practical implementation of an isarithmic system would require some kind of regular check on the number of permits. This would take account of permits accidentally lost by the network and of those wrongly created on account of some system malfunction.

An extensive series of simulation experiments[10] was carried out at NPL to study the performance of an isarithmically controlled network. Initially the isarithmic control was applied to an 18-node network which had been discovered, in early simulation experiments,[11] to be prone to complete failure due to congestion. Figure 4.10 illustrates the relationship between throughput and numbers of packets in transit for this network without isarithmic control. We observed that best performance was obtained for three packets per network node. In applying the isarithmic scheme to this network it was found that five permits per node gave optimum throughput, illustrating the point made in the preceding paragraph on the method of handling free permits. Some of these would be waiting in permit pools for new incoming traffic, whilst others would be in transfer between nodes. Hence more permits per node were required than the number given by dividing the desired maximum number of packets in transit by the number of nodes. Introduction of isarithmic control gave complete protection against congestive failure even when very excessive offered loads were applied.

With the 18-node network measurements were made of the effect of changing the permit pool size on the admission delay (average time spent by each packet awaiting acceptance by the network). The relationship between admission delay and size of permit pool is shown in Figure 4.13 for a network containing five

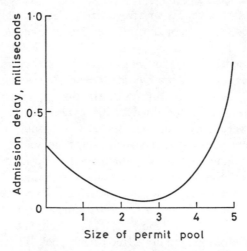

Figure 4.13   Admission delay versus size of permit pool

permits per node. Clearly, a minimum admission delay was attainable for a permit pool size of two or three. If more permits had been allowed to wait in the permit pool, then some nodes would have had a stock of permits in excess of their needs, whilst others were unnecessarily denied permits. If the permit pool were made too small, then many permits would have been in process of redistribution and would not be available for their proper function.

The redistribution of free permits between nodes was carried out in the original simulation experiments by carrying them in special short control packets. This was potentially wasteful of line bandwidth and a change was made to transporting them in the headers of data packets whenever one of these was available. If none was available at the time of permit transfer, then a special control packet was generated. A range of permit redistribution doctrines was simulated; some of these attempted to take account of the different offered load at various source nodes, whilst others simply offered surplus permits to immediate neighbour nodes. The changes in pattern of admission delay arising from the various redistribution doctrines were minimal, therefore transfer to immediate neighbours, the simplest mode, was taken as standard.

Further simulation experiments were carried out at NPL on a 10-node network operating under a somewhat different node operating system and link protocol. Full details of this work may be found in Reference 10. For the present purpose it is sufficient to contrast the behaviour of this network with and without isarithmic control. Relationships between admission delay, transit delay (travelling within the network), throughput and applied load are shown in Figures 4.14 and 4.15. There is fundamentally little difference between the performance with and without isarithmic control. Admission delay at light applied loads was slightly greater for the isarithmically controlled system, whilst transit delay was considerably less at very high applied loads under isarithmic control. Maximum throughput was marginally less with isarithmic control.

It is notable in these experiments that neither the non-isarithmic nor the isarithmic system failed due to congestion in the face of heavy applied load. It is therefore worth examining in a little more detail the features of the non-isarithmic system simulated. If this can be shown to be safe against congestion, then there is no reason for the introduction of the additional complexity of an isarithmic control system.

Flow control on the acceptance of new traffic at source nodes was based on buffer availability. Buffers were drawn from the node buffer pool up to a maximum number per node output queue; in the NPL experiments a range of output queue limits from five packets to ten packets was tried. Best performance in terms of least delay in transit was obtained with a queue length limit of five or six packets; a queue length limit of ten packets gave considerably longer delays in transit, which is a result to be expected. Throughput was little affected by changes of output queue length.

As new packets were offered by the source host to the network node they each successively entered a single packet input buffer. Whilst in this buffer their destination was read and the node routing algorithm selected the output queue they should join. If this output queue length was already up to the limit, then the packet was not moved from the input buffer, but remained there, effectively blocking the acceptance of further traffic from the host. Periodic attempts were made by the node to transfer the blocked packet to the output queue. When this

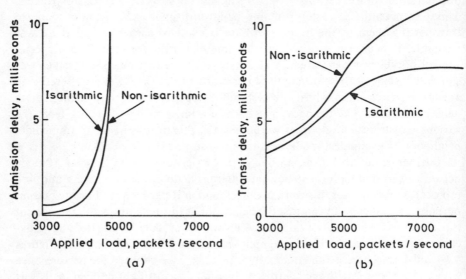

Figure 4.14   Delay versus applied load

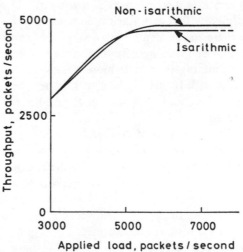

Figure 4.15   Throughput versus applied load

transfer was finally effected, the input buffer was freed to allow further packets to seek acceptance.

This method of flow control depended on local conditions, namely packet queue lengths, and was therefore easy to implement. Its operation was essentially crude; input flow was stopped whenever a packet could not be placed on an output queue, irrespective of the possibility that later packets following in the input flow might wish to join nodal queues with plenty of room. Nevertheless the simulation experiments showed that performance was acceptable and that congestive failure was successfully avoided.

It was further observed in the simulation experiments that different packet buffer limits had to be set for input source traffic and for transit traffic, already travelling within the network. Failure to provide different limits produced a congested state, with acceptance of excess source traffic. By allowing one or two buffers per output queue to be reserved for transit traffic, a degree of priority was accorded to the latter; a fundamental principle for successful network control is that delivery of packets already within the network should take priority over the acceptance of new traffic. Reservation of one or two buffers out of the five or six packet buffers per output queue was found to be sufficient. This result is confirmed by the analytic and simulation results of Lam and Reiser;[12] it is notable that their results showed optimum throughput for a ratio of reserved buffers to total buffers very similar to that observed in the NPL simulation experiments.

Note that this method of flow control, used in isolation, responds poorly to a reluctant destination host. If packets seek to reach a particular destination which is either dormant or dead, these packets will be undeliverable; it requires a set of full queues extending back from destination to source before the flow can be stopped. Clearly a combination of congestion avoidance based on packet buffer availability, as discussed in this section, and source–destination flow control, as discussed earlier, constitutes a powerful means of network control.

Adaptive routing may have a profound effect on the success of congestion avoidance based on source node buffer availability. If the choice of output queue to be joined by an incoming packet extends to several queues, depending on the existence of space on these queues, then the control on the incoming flow will be weakened. Adaptive routing may allow the acceptance of considerably more traffic and several queues per node may become full. It is to be expected, and this was confirmed in the simulation experiments, that a network so controlled will congest and fail. If congestion avoidance is to be based on source node buffer availability, then adaptive routing should be permitted to operate in the network only in regard to transit traffic, i.e. traffic that has left the source node; fixed routing should apply in source nodes to all newly accepted packets.

Flow control based on node buffer availability has also been the subject of simulation studies at the Gesellschaft für Mathematik und Datenverarbeitung.[13] This has been concerned also with avoidance of direct store-and-forward lock-up and uses a system of buffer categories in each node. As each packet progresses along its path, the packet category is incremented by one at each successive node. As the packet category increases, so the packet is allowed access to additional buffer categories. New traffic seeking to enter a source node is limited to the lowest buffer category and is made to wait for admission if this buffer category is temporarily exhausted. This principle has been applied at GMD to both virtual call and datagram networks.

Control of packet admission according to source node buffer availability depends on the detection of signs of congestion in the source nodes themselves and does not readily react to congestion occurring elsewhere. If the network can tolerate additional control traffic, then it is possible to inform source nodes of congestion occurring elsewhere. Schemes of this type have been suggested for the Cyclades network by Pouzin[14] and for the Aramis network by Pineda.[15] The basic idea is that a node running short of buffers or having an almost full queue or queues signals to earlier nodes that traffic flow must be cut down. Pineda suggests that a node informs its neighbours of any output queues that are in difficulty; the neighbours are equipped with expanded routing tables that indicate which neighbouring output queues each traffic stream needs to join. Thus individual traffic streams causing congestion can be eased off, whilst those not involved in congestion can still flow freely. Pouzin's idea is somewhat similar; instead of measuring queue lengths, the system monitors link loadings. Link loads up to 70 per cent of full capacity are regarded as safe, no action being taken; link loads between 70 per cent and 80 per cent cause the source nodes contributing to the loads to be signalled to reduce the contributing flows; link loads over 80 per cent cause the offending streams of packets to be discarded. Both these schemes are more complex than the source node buffer availability scheme, but this may be acceptable if the simpler scheme should prove inadequate in some context.

We have suggested in the foregoing that the presence of bottlenecks in networks may lead to congestion. No sensible network topology will include bottlenecks. However, such bottlenecks may occur because of temporary component failure. Simulation experiments[16] at NPL on the 10-node network (Figure 3.9) investigated network performance with failure of a major network link. It was shown that the source node buffer availability congestion avoidance mechanism allowed the network to continue operating safely, though at a reduced throughput.

We shall concern ourselves in the next section with some problems of network interconnection. We observe here that an inter-network gateway may constitute a topological bottleneck, carrying an excess of traffic. It may be wise to provide at least two gateways between each pair of interconnected networks. Failing this the gateway node must be of greater power and buffer capacity to cope with the possible extra load. Correct dimensioning in relation to expected load is essential.

Congestion due to faulty design of node procedures has also been mentioned. In particular it is clearly essential that packet buffer allocation shall be correctly handled. We have seen how allocation of all packet buffers to one output queue can produce direct store-and-forward lock-up. We have also seen how source node packet buffer handling has a dominant effect on the acceptance of new traffic; adaptive routing must be used with care in this context. There are many aspects of node operating systems which must be designed with care if congestion is to be avoided.

Recovery from Congestion

Clearly it is desirable to detect the onset of congestion and to successfully avoid it; nevertheless, if the network enters a congested state, it is wise to provide means of recovery. Unlike vehicles in a road system, or other solid objects, we are dealing with data packets which are ephemeral in nature. The network can free itself by deleting the blocked traffic, freeing the full buffers and starting all over again. This may well be a feasible solution if copies of all data packets in transit are held by source hosts and can be retransmitted after time-outs according to a host-to-host protocol. Nevertheless a serious hiatus in network performance will have taken place and users may become dissatisfied, especially if this condition occurs frequently. Complete loss of data packets is unlikely to be acceptable to any class of user.

Packet deletion is a feature of the Cyclades network.[17] If any packet entering an intermediate node cannot be found a packet buffer, then this packet is deleted automatically and retransmission from the source host is expected. One can see that in the presence of a heavy load this policy will lead to inefficient running of the network, with an excessive proportion of resources devoted to packet retransmission. The effect is potentially almost as bad as a congested network without provision for packet deletion. As an occasional expedient for coping with purely local congestion, packet deletion is quite acceptable, provided, of course, that the host protocol guarantees retransmission. The host protocol is bound to be somewhat complicated on account of this system; not only may data packets be deleted, but control packets may suffer the same fate. This means that correctly delivered data packets may be retransmitted and delivered a second time, if the corresponding acknowledgement suffers deletion.

When congestion was feared in the ARPA network a rather novel suggestion was made for overcoming it.[2] This involved the provision of what amounted to a duplicate network, normally not carrying traffic, which was brought into action if a lock-up occurred. The duplicate net was created by reserving a proportion of link bandwidth and node buffer storage. Once a lock-up had been diagnosed, the blocked packets were released by transfer onto the duplicate net. Special allocation of link bandwidth and node buffers was bound to be an expensive expedient. In practice most of the potential ARPA lock-ups were all avoided by redesign of the node procedures; indirect store-and-forward lock-up was left as an improbable event.

Where network lock-ups have occurred in practice, it has usually depended on the network operators to use ad hoc means of freeing the log jam, because built-in unjamming procedures may be too complex or expensive to provide. It is also difficult to foresee all the possible ways in which a network may be become locked up. It is certainly effort well spent to analyse potential lock-up situations very carefully at the design stage and to build in preventive measures to avoid them. In this case prevention is much easier than cure.

4.4 SPECIAL PROBLEMS

Our discussion of flow control and congestion avoidance has so far been concerned with networks in general, such as have been built in the last ten or twelve years. Current trends, to larger networks and to interconnected networks, may lead to new design problems in matters concerning flow and congestion.

Interconnected Networks

In the last four years considerable attention has been paid to the problems of inter-networking—so much so that the International Network Working Group was set up, now more formally constituted as IFIP Working Group TC 6.1. Topics addressed have included global addressing and routing techniques, levels of network interconnection and the functions required of the inter-network interface, often called a 'gateway'. Less attention has been paid to problems of flow control and congestion avoidance in the context of interconnected networks.

In addition to the categories of flow control we considered in section 4.2, it is likely that certain additional provisions must be made for inter-networking. These are flow control with a transmission window mechanism between source node and first gateway, gateway to gateway for all intermediate networks, and final gateway to destination node. Retransmission protocols may exist at each of these stages, making a source node to destination node retransmission protocol unnecessary. However, delivery confirmation can only be given on a source–destination basis.

The gateway nodes must be provided with an adequate packet buffer pool to cater for the likely level of inter-network traffic. Cerf and Kahn[18] suggest that message reassembly should not take place at gateways; this implies that packet ordering need not be maintained if adaptive routing disrupts packet order. If fragmentation of packets is necessary because of different network packet size limits, Cerf and Kahn maintain that the only logical place to locate the reconstruction process is in the destination host (this is because the last network entered may have the least packet size limit, so that the last gateway has to fragment packets). This philosophy goes against the widely held view that packet networks should deliver a data stream exactly equivalent to the received data stream.

Because of reliability requirements it is probable that at least two routes should be provided between any pair of interconnected networks. This may mean that two separate gateways join two nets or that the alternative access route is via some other network. Whatever means are adopted the gateway nodes are likely to form a bottleneck; if much inter-network traffic is to flow, then there will be contention for the gateway resources. Traffic held up for lack of access to the gateway may begin to pile up in nodes adjacent to the gateway. This is a potential source of congestion.

The various congestion avoidance schemes we have discussed may perform in different ways in this context. Isarithmic control may enter a locked-up state unless care is taken. The danger is that traffic seeking to leave one net, but with each packet still engaging a permit of that net, may be held up for lack of a permit in the second net, the latter being occupied by packets seeking to leave the second net and enter the first, and vice versa. Clearly a packet exchange system must and can be devised that avoids this type of lock-up.

Congestion avoidance by source node buffer availability is unlikely to operate well in an inter-network context. Evidence of congestion at a bottleneck is fed back slowly to remote source nodes, which therefore react slowly.

Perhaps the most suitable form of congestion avoidance mechanism in this context might be of the type mentioned in section 4.3 as suggested by Pouzin for the Cyclades network.

Very Large Networks

As with network interconnection attention has been given to routing and addressing in very large networks, but the subject of flow control seems to be neglected.

Because of the long distances possible between sources and destinations any window-based flow control must clearly allow different window sizes, depending on the distance involved; if this is not done, then very slow data flow rates may be encountered on the longer paths.

In any call connection type of protocol the call set-up time is bound to be large; there really is no way round this in a single homogeneous large network. Perhaps the arguments for the datagram mode of operation are stronger in large networks. Certainly it is important that provision should be made for efficient transfer of single packets not forming part of a longer stream.

The larger the network, the more difficult it will be to specify an efficient congestion avoidance algorithm. Congestion in part of a large network may be due to excessive flows emanating from some other, possibly quite remote, area. Again the Cyclades idea of signalling the source node to reduce a particular flow has its attractions.

The wisest course is not to build very large homogeneous nets because of the various difficulties of controlling them. We have already suggested in the chapter on routing that large networks should be constructed with a hierarchical structure.

Hierarchical Networks

By hierarchical networks we understand those in which source and destination nodes are all on the lowest level of the hierarchy. Higher-level nodes and links are provided solely to establish efficient communication between nodes on the lowest level; the higher-level nodes do not accept traffic from users nor deliver traffic to users.

Flow control in a hierarchy will exist on a node-to-node basis and on a source–destination basis; flow control between hierarchy levels is afforded by the inter-node protocols applying to inter-level links. The latter may be no different from any other inter-node protocols or, on the other hand, extra inter-level flow control provisions may be included.

Because of the limitation of traffic acceptance to the lowest level, congestion avoidance by source node buffer availability is unlikely to prevent the higher-level components from becoming congested. This effect was observed in the Logica simulation experiments[19] mentioned in Chapter 3. The latter were concerned with a two-level hierarchy, Figures 3.15 and 3.16, in which the upper level became congested to the point of breakdown. An attempt to avoid this by reducing the window width in the inter-level flow control protocol was not successful. Use of the isarithmic flow control technique in the upper level was successful in avoiding congestion; admission to the upper level was made conditional on acquisition of a permit.

It seemed intuitively correct to impose a flow control system which gave greater priority in node buffer allocation to traffic seeking to leave a level for a lower level; at the lowest level, to traffic about to leave the network. Second priority might be given to traffic moving about on the same level. Least priority should be given to traffic seeking to enter a higher level; at the lowest hierarchical level this represents traffic seeking to enter the network from users. This scheme has much in common with call flow control practices in telephone systems. It was simulated in the two-level hierarchy, but performed no better than the expedients already mentioned.

As yet no evidence is available on practical problems arising from greater hierarchical depths, though there is no reason to expect that these should be insurmountable. The operational advantages of reconfiguring a large homogeneous network as a hierarchy are unquestionable, particularly when better response times and simpler routing doctrines are required.

References

1. Gimpelson, L. A.,
   'Network management: design and control of communication networks',
   Electrical Communication, **49**, 4 (1974).
2. Kahn, R. E., and Crowther, W. R.,
   'Flow control in a resource-sharing network',
   IEEE Trans. on Communications, **COM-20**, 539 (June 1972).
3. Bartlett, K. A., Scantlebury, R. A., and Wilkinson, P. T.,
   'A note on reliable full-duplex transmission over half-duplex links',
   Comm. ACM, **12**, 260 (May 1969).
4. Danthine, A. A. S., and Eschenauer, E. C.,
   'Influence on packet node behavior of the internode protocol',
   IEEE Trans. on Communications, **COM-24**, 606 (June 1976).
5. Belsnes, D.,
   'Flow control in the packet switching networks',
   Proc. Eurocomp, 349 (1975).
6. McQuillan, J. M., and Walden, D. C.,
   'The ARPA network design decisions',
   Computer Networks, **1**, 243 (August 1977).
7. Agnew, C.,
   'Dynamic modeling and control of congestion-prone systems',
   Operations Research, **24**, 400 (May 1976).
8. Davies, D. W.,
   'The control of congestion in packet-switching networks',
   IEEE Trans. on Communications, **COM-20**, 546 (June 1972).
9. Jolly, J. H., and Adams, R. A.,
   Simulation study of a data communication network, Pt. I.,
   Plessey Telecommunications Research Ltd., Report No. 97/72/78/TR (September 1972).
10. Price, W. L.,
    'Data network simulation: experiments at the National Physical Laboratory, 1968–76',
    Computer Networks, **1**, 199 (May 1977).
11. Healey, R.,
    Computer network simulation study,
    NPL Report COM64 (January 1973) (originally issued in earlier form, October 1970).
12. Lam, S. S., and Reiser, M.,
    Congestion control of store-and-forward networks by input buffer limits,
    IBM Research Report RC6593 (June 1977).
13. Raubold, E., and Haenle, J.,
    'A method of deadlock-free resource allocation and flow control in packet networks',
    Proc. International Computer Communication Conference, Toronto, 483 (August 1976).
14. Pouzin, L.,
    Congestion control based on channel load,
    Reseau Cyclades Report MIT-600 (August 1975).
15. Pineda, L.,
    'Le controle de flux dans le reseau Aramis',
    Journées de travail, modelisation et simulation de reseaux d'ordinateurs, IRIA, 95 (February 1976).

16. Price, W. L., and Cowin, G. C.,
   Simulation studies of the effect of link breakdown on data communication network performance,
   NPL Report COM77 (February 1975).
17. Pouzin, L.,
   'Presentation of major design aspects of the Cyclades computer network',
   Proc. 3rd ACM/IEEE Data Communications Symposium, St. Petersburg, Fla., 80 (November 1973).
18. Cerf, V. G., and Kahn, R. E.,
   'A protocol for packet network intercommunication',
   IEEE Trans. on Communications, COM-22, 637 (May 1974).
19. Kerr, I. H., Gomberg, G. R. A., Price, W. L., and Solomonides, C. M.,
   'A simulation study of routing and flow control problems in a hierarchically connected packet switching network',
   Proc. International Computer Communication Conference, Toronto, 495 (August 1976).

Chapter 5

Packet Broadcast Systems

5.1 INTRODUCTION

The term *network* seems to imply a mesh or web of links joining nodes, but this is only one of many structures that can be applied to computer communication. In the typical mesh network each link has a specific function, it transports data between a certain pair of nodes. In this chapter we consider packet communication systems in which the transmission medium is not point-to-point but allows several stations to communicate—like a radio channel, for example. If the transmitting station can be heard by all the others it is truly a *broadcast* system. We shall also meet radio systems where there are many listeners but not all stations are mutually within range.

Broadcast systems exist without radio transmission. They have been in use for many years in the familiar 'bus' or 'highway' of a computer system, used sometimes for processor–store access and, more often, to reach a set of peripheral controllers. The well-known 'multi-drop' or 'multi-point' line is a data communication system with broadcast properties because all the stations are in contact with the controller over a single transmission medium.

Common to all these systems is the problem of *contention*. Broadcasting of messages is no problem—everyone hears and only the addressee need act. The problem is caused by the access of many transmitting stations to one channel. Who or what decides the allocation of the channel's time? A fixed cycle of access corresponds to time division multiplexing and is called time division multiple access or TDMA, but this is inefficient for sparsely used channels in computer communication and we are looking for a dynamic or adaptive method of sharing the channel. The scheme of *polling* used in multi-point lines carries a big overhead if traffic is low or uneven. New methods of handling the contention problem are needed.

The transmission may be achieved in several ways—by use of ground radio, by means of geostatic satellite transponders or by means of wide bandwidth cables. Figure 5.1 illustrates these systems with one station sending. The other stations can transmit at other times and, with a radio system of limited range,

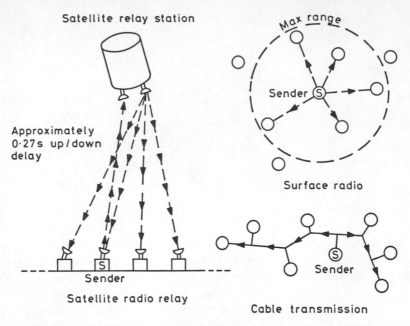

Figure 5.1 Broadcast packet systems: satellite, radio and cable

channels could be re-used in a distant area. For the sake of clarity we adopt in this chapter the following terminology. Packet radio systems are said to consist of several types of device—packet terminals, packet repeaters and packet stations. A packet terminal may be a simple unintelligent terminal or a large mainframe computer or a device lying between these extremes of complexity; it is equipped with the means of transmitting and/or receiving radio signals. A packet repeater is concerned with creating radio paths between terminals and stations or between pairs of terminals; repeaters receive, store, inspect and transmit packets. The function of a packet radio station is to perform routing, flow control, accounting and other functions for the whole system. In satellite systems we have packet terminals, in the form of ground stations with associated computers or simple devices; we also have packet repeaters in the form of the geostatic satellite transponders, though packets are not normally stored or inspected in this case, merely retransmitted. In broadcast cable systems the basic requirement is for a number of packet terminals, represented by transceivers attached to the cable and to the computing devices.

The common feature of satellite, packet radio and wide band cable systems is the transmission of packets from packet sources via a common communication channel. Each packet is received at a number of other packet terminals (acting as destinations) and the packet header is inspected at each terminal to determine whether or not the packet is destined for the particular terminal. Packets found to be addressed to other terminals are ignored, those addressed to the terminal are passed on to it. In the satellite case, packets are transmitted to the satellite using one transmission frequency (the *up* channel) and, there being no storage provision within the satellite, immediately retransmitted by the satellite on a second frequency (the *down* channel). All terminals are listening to the down channel and therefore correct reception at the original transmitting terminal can be taken to indicate correct reception at the desired destination terminal. A satellite system thus needs no formal acknowledgement as in the node-to-node protocols discussed in the previous chapter, though formal acknowledgements may be necessary in the case of radio and cable systems. All three systems, satellite, packet radio and cable, suffer from the possibility of a clash in transmission, when two or more transmitting terminals overlap. In packet radio and cable systems the transmitter can listen in to the medium before transmitting and only transmit when this is clear; this does not altogether avoid clashes, as simultaneous or almost simultaneous transmission can still take place. In satellite systems the problem is severe, due to the time interval required to transmit up to the satellite and down again, about 270 milliseconds; transmitters cannot listen effectively to each other; clashes only become known when the retransmission arrives from the satellite. In all these systems the resolution of this *contention* for use of the transmission medium is pre-eminently important. A great deal of thought has gone into designing systems to perform this function efficiently; this will be the subject of the greater part of this chapter.

Important advantages of satellite systems over conventional terrestrial data networks are the wide bandwidth available, the high accuracy of transmission and the high availability of the transmission medium. Cacciamani[1] states that the American Satellite Corporation has several networks in use with multiple numbers of 1.344 Mbit/s data links, both point-to-point and broadcast. On an earth station basis the data rate may be as high as 60 Mbit/s. Error rates of 1 bit in 10^8 and better are currently being achieved and the system availability is better than 99.99 per cent. This compares very well with the record of terrestrial systems such as the ARPA network.

To take full advantage of such performance when using satellite links in a hybrid satellite/terrestrial system, it would be necessary to provide terrestrial connections to the satellite earth terminal with performance equal to the satellite link. With the present state of terrestrial transmission technology the latter is likely to be the limiting factor; wide bandwidth terrestrial links are very expensive; therefore it may not be possible to use the satellite potential to the best advantage.

For this reason a new type of earth station has been designed with a lesser specification, but with the great advantage of cheapness; lesser bandwidth requires a smaller antenna dish, thereby considerably reducing the cost. Cacciamani notes, for example, a simple packet terminal capable of operating at data rates up to 112 kbit/s and costing less than $100 000. These packet terminals are intended to be located very close to broadcast systems user devices, thus obviating the need for long and expensive land-based connections of comparatively limited capacity. Such packet terminals can even be mobile, mounted on vehicles, an important consideration in military and other contexts. The greatest portability is possible in packet radio systems, where hand-held or pocket terminals are quite feasible.

The technology of all broadcast systems, whatever their nature, has a great deal in common, though the problems of contention resolution are somewhat different and require different techniques for their resolution. Much of today's technology has sprung from developments of the ALOHA system, which is a ground radio system. We shall therefore consider this system first, then proceed to a discussion of the more complicated ground radio systems; this will be followed by an account of satellite broadcast systems and cable broadcast systems.

5.2 PACKET RADIO SYSTEMS

The ALOHA system is essentially a UHF packet broadcast system created for very pragmatic reasons (including the poor quality of local telephone lines) by a team at the University of Hawaii; it first became operational in 1970. The system covers the Hawaiian Islands, Figure 5.2, and is centred on the island of Oahu. Inexpensive access is afforded to central time-sharing computer systems for several hundred terminal users. In the first instance communication was limited to a large group of terminals in the Honolulu district within direct radio range of the central station. User-to-user communication is also catered for.

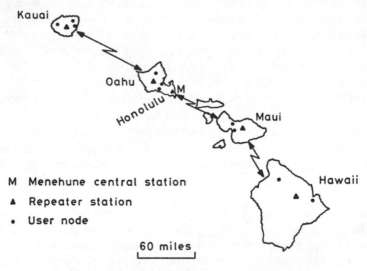

M Menehune central station
▲ Repeater station
• User node

60 miles

Figure 5.2   The ALOHA network coverage

The Basic ALOHA System

The aim of the ALOHANET is to provide cheap and easy access for a large number of terminal users to central computing facilities. A summary of the ALOHA project may be found in Binder *et al.*[2] User-to-computer communication is via a 100 kHz random-access channel at 407.350 MHz; the broadcast return channel, computer-to-user, is also of 100 kHz bandwidth at 413.475 MHz. Direct user-to-user communication is not catered for (user-to-user communication is possible by transferring data to the central switch and then forwarding it to the destination user) and, until the addition of packet repeaters, the system was logically equivalent to a star-connected network. The central communications processor, the *Menehune* (or packet station), located at Honolulu on Oahu, which receives packets from users and is responsible for sending packets to them, is an HP 2100 minicomputer. Menehune is a Hawaiian name for an imp—a reference to the ARPA node. The packet transmission data rate is 9600 baud, packets consisting of a header (32 bits), a header parity check field (16 bits), and up to 80 bytes of data, followed by a data parity check field (16 bits). Maximum size packets are therefore 704 bits in length and take about 73 milliseconds to transmit; propagation time is negligible in comparison.

Control of the broadcast channel from the central computer to the users presents no problem, because only one transmitter is using the channel. Packet headers contain user addresses which enable individual receivers to identify the traffic intended for them. The user-to-computer channel, referred to above as random-access, could have been apportioned to individual users by a fixed allocation scheme, such as frequency division multiplexing or time division multiplexing. However, the nature of terminal traffic is almost always bursty and a fixed allocation would hardly make the best use of the communication medium, hence the choice of a random-access scheme.

This scheme, known as pure ALOHA, allows a packet terminal to transmit packets at times which are completely independent of packet transmissions from other terminals. A natural consequence of this independence of action is that packets from different sources may be transmitted at the same time and therefore collide or overlap as they arrive at the Menehune central station; an overlap that affects only the smallest fraction of transmission time has the same effect as an overlap of complete packets; both packets are irretrievably corrupted. Figure 5.3 indicates the way in which overlaps may occur. Packets subject to such overlap are rejected by the Menehune and the fact of overlap is made known to the respective transmitting terminals by absence of the acknowledgement signal which would otherwise be sent by the Menehune to the packet terminals. Packets refused by the Menehune on account of an overlap are retransmitted by the packet terminals after a time-out period. It is plainly obvious that an immediate retransmission of packets by these terminals, or, indeed, retransmission after a fixed, uniform time interval, would just result in a second overlap; therefore retransmission takes place at each terminal after a random delay. Clearly the number of overlaps is a function of traffic intensity; the greater the traffic, the greater the probability of overlaps. It is also essential that acknowledgement packets should be sent with highest non-preemptive priority from the Menehune to the packet terminals; otherwise unwanted retransmission may occur.

Error control on the broadcast channel (Menehune to packet terminals) presents difficulties. Ideally this should be on the same positive acknowledgement basis as the error control in the other direction on the random-access channel. However, acknowledgement packets destined to the Menehune would have to contend for the random-access channel in just the same way as data packets. Binder *et al.*[2] state that, because of this contention, at full channel loading each random-access packet must be retransmitted an average of 1.7 times; thus each data packet or acknowledgement packet must be sent 2.7 times on average before it is successfully received. In an error-free situation, to ensure that the acknowledgement is successfully transmitted by the packet terminal, the Menehune must send the data packet 2.7 times on average, even though the packet may have arrived correctly the first time. Where errors occur, the multiple transmissions from the Menehune will be essential if an acknowledgement system is to operate correctly. This is evidently very wasteful of bandwidth and can be avoided by not using acknowledgements in this channel, relying on low error rates and a system of reporting errors to the user, who may decide to repeat a transaction. Where, for particular users, this is not acceptable, a system of positive acknowledgement may be introduced on a selective basis.

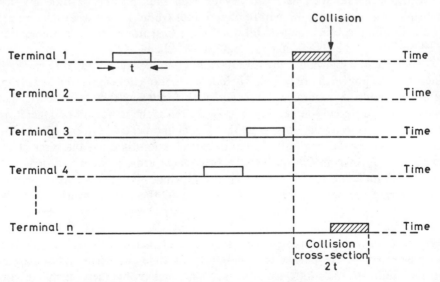

Figure 5.3   Packet timing in pure ALOHA

To analyse the performance of the basic ALOHA system we need to know the distribution on the channel of two kinds of packets, original packets and retransmissions. In order to simplify the problem let us assume that, taken together, they have a Poisson distribution. This characterises the total use of the channel, but only a certain proportion of the packets carried are successful, non-colliding packets, and these alone constitute the throughput of the channel. The Poisson assumption says something about the way retransmissions are timed, but it is probably accurate enough if the period over which retransmission is likely to occur is rather longer than the average inter-packet interval. A further simplifying assumption is that all packets have the same length, hence the same transmission time, t. It is convenient to measure traffic in terms of the number of packets per interval t.

Let G be the total traffic (average number of packets on the channel in time t) and S the successful traffic or *throughput*. Clearly if p_0 is the probability that a packet will avoid collision then

$$S = G\, p_0$$

A packet will collide with another if its start is within time t of the start of any other packet. The 'collision cross-section' is $2t$. (In Figure 5.3 the tail of a packet from terminal 1 is just caught by the leading edge of a packet from terminal n.) The probability of zero events within time $2t$ in this Poisson distribution gives the value of p_0 and hence, from the above equation,

$$S = G\, e^{-2G}$$

If we review the assumptions for realism, the important ones are the Poisson assumption and the constant packet length. The Poisson assumption implies a large population of contending stations. With few stations it seems that the channel can be better used than this equation says. A finite number of terminals, with some offering much more traffic than others, should obtain somewhat better channel utilisation (because a terminal never interferes with itself). The practical case in which packet lengths are not constant gives a lower effective channel utilisation.

Figure 5.4 shows the relationship between S and G. S is plotted on the horizontal axis because this is the offered traffic, whenever the system is still working, that is, when all packets eventually get through. Increasing S to a certain point increases G, but beyond that point our assumptions fail. The effect of the congestion so brought about is that retransmissions fail at a rate which creates even more retransmissions and the system blocks completely.

A more detailed study of the statistics reveals a worse phenomenon. With Poisson distribution at *any* value of S there is a finite probability of blocking within a given time T and this increases towards unity if the time T is increased without limit. So, with an infinite population of transmitters, at any traffic level there will eventually be a runaway situation. The practical situation is not so

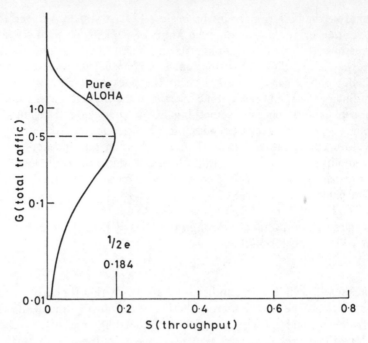

Figure 5.4   Performance of pure ALOHA

bad, however, because, with a finite population of users, the system exhibits much greater stability. A suitable lengthening of retransmission time adds stability. Since each station can observe the total channel traffic, a control mechanism should be feasible.

Pure ALOHA makes use, at best, of about 18.4 per cent of the available channel bandwidth, which is a disappointingly poor performance. Nevertheless, if wide bandwidth is cheaply and readily available this performance may be adequate for particular applications.

The Slotted ALOHA System

The low maximum throughput rate of pure ALOHA arises from the high practical probability of packet collision, which in turn is due to the total lack of discipline in packet transmission from packet terminals. Various proposals have been made for improving the channel utilisation. The first of these we shall consider is the so-called 'slotted ALOHA' system, which is a direct development from pure ALOHA. In slotted ALOHA packet terminals are not allowed total freedom in choosing packet transmission times; instead, the channel time is divided up into segments, each of duration t seconds (the transmission time of a full packet). All packet terminals are provided with a system synchronised clock which indicates, at each terminal, the start of each transmission segment. The individual transmitter timing is such that, allowing for propagation delay, the start of any packet arrives at the central receiver at the beginning of a packet time segment. Collisions may still occur, but now the amount of channel time wasted per collision will be always one transmission segment, compared with the possible maximum of two segments in pure ALOHA; the collision cross-section is reduced from $2t$ to t. Figure 5.5 illustrates the timing of packets in slotted ALOHA.

On the basis of the same traffic assumptions that were made for pure ALOHA, the relationship between successful throughput and offered channel traffic is given by

$$S = G\,e^{-G}$$

This relationship is plotted in Figure 5.6, where we see that the theoretical maximum useful throughput is 36.8 per cent of the channel capacity, twice that of pure ALOHA.

Both pure and slotted ALOHA systems are inherently unstable if large numbers of terminals are active; excessive traffic leads to more collisions, which in turn lead to additional retransmissions; eventually useful throughput can reduce to almost zero, whilst the channel becomes fully loaded. Lam and Kleinrock[3] have analysed the stability of the ALOHA systems.

The discussion of pure and slotted ALOHA has assumed an infinite population of users. For a less than infinite user population, Abramson[4] gives the following expression for slotted ALOHA with N separate user stations

$$S = G\,(1 - G/N)^{N-1}$$

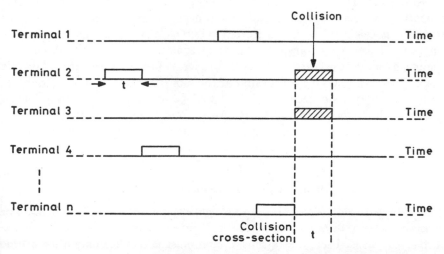

Figure 5.5   Packet timing in slotted ALOHA

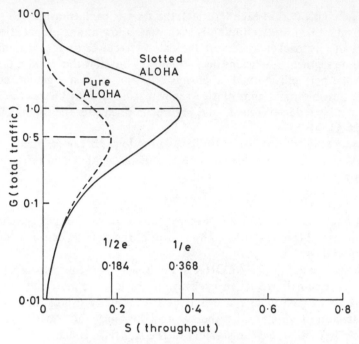

Figure 5.6   Performance of slotted ALOHA

As one would expect, in the limiting case, $N \rightarrow \infty$, this equation reduces to

$$S = G\,e^{-G}$$

Abramson carries the analysis further, giving results for slotted systems supporting two classes of users at different packet transmission rates. From his results it is evident that, if the slotted ALOHA channel is lightly loaded, a single large user may transmit data at a significant percentage of the total channel data rate; the latter may be well in excess of the 36.8 per cent obtainable when all users are seeking to transmit at the same data rate. This condition has been termed 'excess capacity' and may well be important in a lightly loaded system, if the traffic consists of transmission from a large number of terminals operating in interactive mode, together with a small number requiring occasional bulk file transfer.

Timing of Retransmissions in ALOHA

We have already observed that in a packet broadcast system immediate or constant delay retransmission of collided packets would result in inevitable further collisions. Therefore retransmission must take place only after a time interval to be chosen at random by the packet terminals. In slotted ALOHA the retransmission delay must evidently be an integral number of packet transmission periods. A practical system may specify a maximum retransmission delay of, say, K transmission periods, with retransmission spread uniformly over this time (probability of retransmission in a particular transmission period being $1/K$). The choice of the value K will affect performance; if K is made too small, then second collision probability is increased; if K is made too large, then the time taken by the system to successfully transmit a packet will be excessive. An useful analysis of this problem is given by Kleinrock,[5] who gives relationships between channel throughput (S), channel traffic (G), retransmission delay (K) and system delay (T). The theoretical channel efficiency (36.8 per cent) is only approached as $K \rightarrow \infty$; unfortunately this is accompanied by $T \rightarrow \infty$, an unacceptable condition. The range of realistic values of K extends from 2, channel efficiency attainable about 30 per cent, to 15, channel efficiency attainable about 36 per cent. For G (channel traffic) of 1, the system delay is in the range 40 to 50 packet transmission periods, which is surprisingly large. Lower delays are attainable for lower G, but this is at the cost of lower throughput (S).

In the original ALOHA system an attempt was made to minimise retransmission time when the channel was lightly loaded, whilst avoiding frequent retransmissions (leading to channel saturation) when the channel was heavily loaded. For this purpose the packet terminal was programmed to make three attempts at retransmission at relatively short intervals, after which either the user was informed and required to re-initiate the process or else a longer retransmission interval was interposed.

Collision Avoidance Systems

The low bandwidth utilisations of pure and slotted ALOHA systems have led to many proposals for increasing utilisation by means of slot reservation schemes or channel sensing schemes. The object of slot reservation schemes is to reserve a particular future time slot of the transmission medium for a particular transmitter, thus ensuring that collisions do not take place. We shall see that such slot reservation schemes are able to achieve the required greater efficiency, but, naturally, at some cost in overheads, either in terms of allocation of part of the bandwidth for reservation purposes and/or increased complexity of the transmission timing process in the transmitting terminals. Slot reservation schemes are often found in the context of satellite systems, where they represent the only practical method of improving performance for a simple transponder satellite; we shall defer detailed discussion of them to a later section of this chapter.

Because the maximum propagation delay in a ground radio packet broadcast system is small compared with the packet transmission time (say, one/tenth or less), better channel utilisation is obtainable if the packet terminal wishing to transmit a packet first listens to the channel before transmitting; if the terminal wishing to transmit detects that the channel carrier is active, then it waits until the channel becomes quiet, testing for this at intervals. This is the principle commonly used for aircraft voice communications. However strictly the 'listen before talk' rule is applied in packet radio, there may be collisions because of the time it takes for the packet from one terminal to reach another. If the unguarded interval is very small compared with the time taken to transmit a packet, the probability of collision need not be high, but if many stations are waiting to jump in at the end of another's transmission, collision could be more frequent than necessary.

In the packet radio context the mode of operation in which packet terminals listen to the broadcast channel has come to be known as Carrier Sense Multiple Access (CSMA). The principle was first suggested by Wax of the University of Hawaii in an internal memorandum of 1971.

We have seen how packet radio was first developed in the ALOHA sense with packet radio terminals all within direct radio communication with one central packet radio station. Pure and slotted ALOHA channel multiplexing techniques are primarily applicable to this sort of network; two channel frequencies are used, one to the central station and one from it. The techniques we now discuss can be applied to a more general form of packet radio in which individual packet terminals need not be within radio range of each other; packet radio repeaters may be used to collect traffic from packet radio terminals and to hand these on, either to other repeaters or to a central packet radio station. This network can also be used as a general communication network rather than as a star network with central computing facility. Traffic can pass from terminal

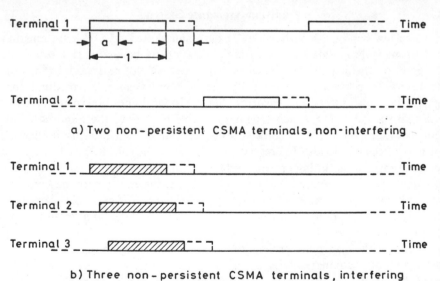

a) Two non-persistent CSMA terminals, non-interfering

b) Three non-persistent CSMA terminals, interfering

Figure 5.7   Packet timing in non-persistent CSMA

to terminal, and may or may not need to travel via a central packet radio station. One common channel frequency may be used for all traffic, whatever its direction.

An extremely full account has been given by Kleinrock and Tobagi[6] of the various ways in which CSMA can be applied; the reader is directed to this source for the mathematical analysis of the performance of these modes of operation. We shall here give an outline of the basic principles and of the performance to be expected from each operational mode.

In the most basic form of CSMA the packet terminal with a packet to transmit, commonly called a 'ready' terminal, senses the channel and, if it finds it idle, immediately transmits its packet. If the channel is not idle, the packet terminal schedules a further attempt at transmission at a random time with a probability distribution obtained by sampling of a specified retransmission delay distribution. When the time for another attempt arrives, the packet terminal repeats the process. In this simple form of CSMA the broadcast channel is not time slotted and transmissions may start at any time. In Figure 5.7 we show the way in which the channel is used; it is assumed that packet transmission time is 1 unit time and the fraction—packet propagation time divided by packet transmission time—is a. In a successful transmission the channel is busy for a period of $1 + a$ time units. If, after the beginning of a transmission, no other packet terminal transmits during the period a time units, then no collision occurs and the packet having the channel will be successfully transmitted. Figure 5.7(a) shows transmission from two terminals, non-interfering, whilst Figure 5.7(b) shows transmission from three terminals, interfering; in the latter case both terminals 2 and 3 begin transmission during the vulnerable signal propagation time at the beginning of terminal 1's transmission—causing transmission from all three terminals to collide. This mode of CSMA operation is termed 'non-persistent' by Kleinrock and Tobagi; because of the ability to begin transmission without reference to a synchronous time frame, it is further categorised 'unslotted'.

It is plain that if all packet terminals are prevented from transmitting during the period a, then successful transmission can be guaranteed. This is not practically possible, but, as in slotted ALOHA, a worthwhile performance improvement can be obtained by dividing the channel time into slots of width a units and constraining all packet terminals to begin new transmissions only at the beginning of one of these small time slots. Note that, unlike slotted ALOHA, where the time slot is of length equal to the packet transmission time, we have here a time slot which is equal to the packet propagation time (the latter may be expected normally to be a small fraction of the former). This mode is known as slotted non-persistent CSMA.

The problem of scheduling a time for a further sensing of the channel when the channel is currently sensed to be busy can be tackled in rather a different way. This is the so-called persistent CSMA mode, more generally known as

p-persistent, where the parameter p determines the probability that the packet terminal delays its transmission. If the parameter p is set at 1, then the ready packet terminal, on sensing that the channel is idle, immediately transmits its packet with probability 1. If the channel is not idle, the packet terminal listens to the channel until it becomes idle and then transmits with probability 1. The object of this procedure is to avoid the channel being unnecessarily idle (as may be the case with delayed retransmission in non-persistent CSMA or in the ALOHA systems). However, this mode of operation can be seen to be inefficient in practice, because two packet terminals may be listening in to the busy channel; when it goes idle, both will transmit, with certainty causing a collision. Thus 1-persistent CSMA is not a satisfactory mode of operation. Slotting the channel into mini time slots does not resolve this problem for $p = 1$.

If p is less than 1, then, depending on the chosen value, a significant

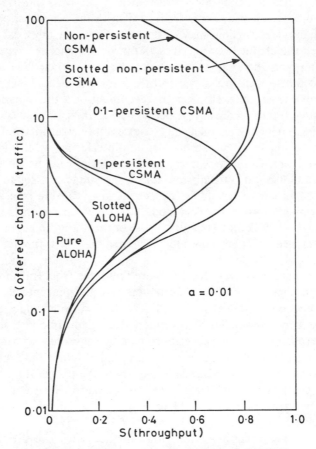

Figure 5.8   Performance of ALOHA and CSMA
(reproduced by permission of L. Kleinrock)

performance improvement may be obtained. The aim is to avoid the conflict certainty when $p = 1$, whilst still reducing the channel idle time as much as possible. The operation of the p-persistent CSMA may best be understood in the slotted case. A ready packet terminal senses the channel and, if it finds it idle, then with probability p it transmits its packet; with probability $1 - p$ it delays transmission by one time slot (a time units, the normalised propagation delay). At the beginning of the next time slot, if the packet was not transmitted, the process is repeated. Should the channel be busy when sensed, the packet terminal waits until it becomes idle and then proceeds as above.

We have therefore to consider the relative performance of several practical operational modes of CSMA (slotted 1-persistent mode is not a practical proposition):

unslotted non-persistent

slotted non-persistent

unslotted 1-persistent

slotted p-persistent.

The performance of each of these systems depends *inter alia* on the value of a. In Figure 5.8 we show the relationship between throughput and applied load for $a = 0.01$. Figure 5.9 shows the maximum throughput attainable for each system, also for $a = 0.01$. The value of a has a very strong influence on performance; Figure 5.10 shows how channel capacity varies with a. This figure demonstrates clearly the superiority of the CSMA protocols over ALOHA protocols for all values of a less than 0.2; this range of propagation delay is appropriate to a packet ground radio network with 1000-bit packets on 100 kbit/s channels for distances up to about 400 miles, a much greater distance than would be found in practice in a UHF system.

Protocol (a=0.01)	Channel capacity
Pure ALOHA	0.184
Slotted ALOHA	0.368
1-persistent CSMA	0.529
Slotted 1-persistent CSMA	0.531
0.1-persistent CSMA	0.791
Non-persistent CSMA	0.815
0.03-persistent CSMA	0.827
Slotted non-persistent CSMA	0.857
Perfect scheduling	1.000

Figure 5.9   Maximum channel throughput in ALOHA and CSMA
(reproduced by permission of L. Kleinrock)

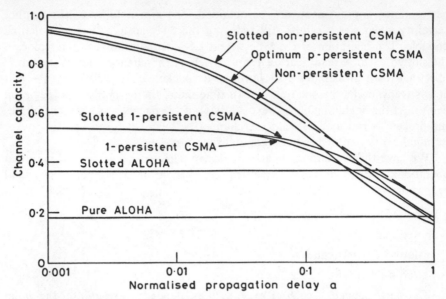

Figure 5.10   CSMA and ALOHA channel capacities as functions of normalised propagation delay (reproduced by permission of L. Kleinrock)

Looking at the performance comparison in terms of capacity, it is natural
to ask why the additional complexity of p-persistent CSMA is worthwhile,
compared with slotted non-persistent CSMA. The answer lies in the performance
in terms of transit delay. Figure 5.11 gives delay as a function of throughput
for the various protocols. This shows that optimised p-persistent CSMA gives
less delay at higher throughputs than does slotted non-persistent CSMA. This
is to be expected, as p-persistent CSMA is aimed at transmitting as soon as
possible and minimising channel idle time.

The Problem of Hidden Stations

In the discussion of ground radio packet systems it has been assumed that
all packet terminals are able to hear each other's transmissions directly. Because
of obstacles and the intervening distance, this may not always be the case.
Packet terminals that are all able to communicate with a single central station
may not necessarily be able to hear each other. Kleinrock gives an analysis[5]
according to the number (N) of separate groups of packet terminals that are
mutually unable to hear each other (to simplify the analysis each group is
assumed to have an infinite population). Figure 5.12 shows how the performance
of two forms of CSMA degrades with increasing N. For $N = 2$, performance
is already worse than it would be if slotted ALOHA were the operating mode.
For greater N the performance declines asymptotically to that of a pure ALOHA

system. This result is very much to be expected, because CSMA depends on packet terminals listening to each other. In a satellite network direct listening to other terminals is impossible; ground radio with large N resembles a satellite system in some respects.

A proposal to overcome this problem in ground radio packet systems is Busy Tone Multiple Access (BTMA).[7] In this mode a narrow band is allocated to a busy tone transmission which is activated by the central station at all times when the latter is receiving a transmission from a packet terminal. This busy signal is received at all packet terminals, which may listen and detect whether the central station is busy receiving a packet from another packet terminal. Because the busy tone band is narrow it may take longer to detect a transmission in this band than it does for detection of a transmission under CSMA with the full channel bandwidth. In transmission scheduling BTMA behaves rather like

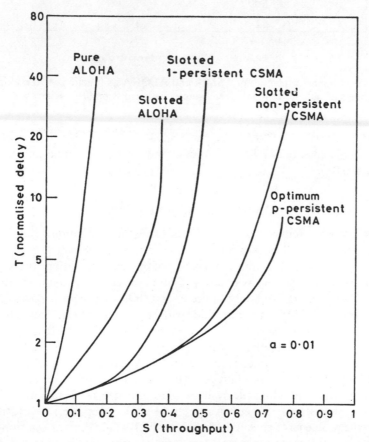

Figure 5.11 CSMA and ALOHA transmission delays as functions of throughput (reproduced by permission of L. Kleinrock)

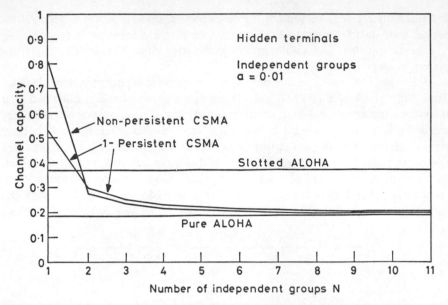

Figure 5.12   Channel capacities of CSMA and ALOHA as functions of the number of groups of hidden terminals (reproduced by permission of L. Kleinrock)

unslotted non-persistent CSMA. For a bandwidth of 100 kHz, Kleinrock gives the maximum capacity of BTMA as 0.680, and for 1 MHz, maximum capacity 0.720 ($a = 0.01$).

Packet Radio with Repeaters

Thus far our discussion of the various forms of contention resolution has assumed either that all packet radio terminals are within radio range of each other or that they are all within radio range of one central station. If the packet terminals are of low power, as one would often expect to be the case, then the size of such a network is plainly limited. To establish adequate coverage over a greater area it is necessary to introduce packet radio repeaters. Packet terminal transmissions are first picked up by repeaters and retransmitted, possibly at greater power, either to other repeaters or to a central packet radio station. When repeaters were introduced into the ALOHA network itself, these repeaters were very simple devices. The first repeater was located on Maui (Figure 5.2); further repeaters, extending the system, were intended for Kauai and Hawaii. Figure 5.13 shows an arrangement of central station, repeaters and terminals. To avoid the problems of packet duplication which would have arisen from radio range overlap, the repeaters were hard-wired to read packet addresses and to retransmit (on the same frequency) only those assigned to the particular repeater.

Thus single paths were implemented through the ALOHA net. Repeaters were designed to retransmit packets both in the random access and broadcast channels.

The ALOHA central packet station communicated with groups of terminals through repeaters, each serving several terminals. The repeaters received a packet, stored it in its entirety, checked that it should be retransmitted and then retransmitted it on the same frequency. A repeater could not receive and transmit simultaneously on the same frequency. Therefore the Menehune was constrained to order its transmissions so that successive packets, with no inter-packet interval, were not required to be handled by the same repeater.

In order to provide system redundancy in more complex networks, the coverage of various repeaters may be made deliberately to overlap and packet transmission may be picked up at more than one repeater. This mode of operation has much in common with the flooding technique which we first encountered in our discussion of packet routing. If flooding is to be the operative mode in a packet radio system, with each repeater automatically sending on each packet that it receives, then means must be provided within the system to prevent perpetual retransmission of packets. This can be done by including handover numbers in packet headers, the numbers being incremented each time a packet passes through a repeater. A limiting value should be placed on the handover number; when this value is reached, no further retransmission takes place. Because this mode of operation involves multiple copies of packets it is important that the packet header contain a unique packet identification so that the destination can detect duplicate packets and discard them.

Flooding is not necessarily the best way in which to operate a packet radio

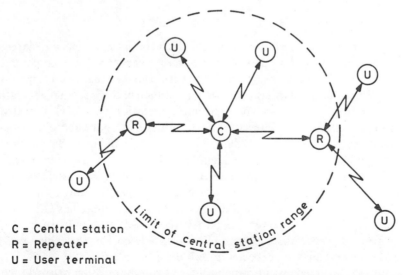

C = Central station
R = Repeater
U = User terminal

Figure 5.13 Central radio station communicating with users via repeaters

network with repeaters. The latter can be made to discriminate between packets and decide, on the basis of the packet destination address, whether or not they should be retransmitted. This could imply that there should be a single route from source to destination, such a route being specified in the packet header. It would be the role of the central packet station to calculate routes for all desired traffic exchanges and to notify packet terminals of the full route specification in each case; the route specification must travel with each packet transported. In such a system adaptation of the routing to take account of device outages would be the function of a central packet station, which must notify route changes to the packet terminals.

Despite the low error rate expected in packet radio, it is still necessary to provide packet sum checks. Where packets travel over single routes (without multiple repeater transmission) it is a simple matter to provide an acknowledgement protocol between communicating devices. Packets correctly received are acknowledged, whilst those received incorrectly are not acknowledged, but are subject to retransmission after a time-out. End-to-end flow control may be established between source and destination for exactly the same reasons as were advanced in the context of terrestrial networks in Chapter 4.

Acknowledgement protocols in a system operating packet flooding do not make very good sense. The requirement would be that a packet will be retransmitted unless all repeaters in range have correctly acknowledged it. Such a retransmitted packet may have arrived correctly at some repeaters and not at others; discrimination between first arrivals and repeats is plainly necessary. Flooding, though a simple enough basic concept, has too many disadvantages.

5.3 SATELLITE SYSTEMS

The application of geostationary satellites to communications antedated the use of packet-switched data networks by several years. Commercial communication satellites began working in 1965 with the internationally sponsored Intelsat I. Since that time Intelsat has seen the launch of three further generations of satellites; Intelsat IV was brought into operation in 1971. World-wide coverage is afforded within Intelsat, three satellites stationary above the equator over the Pacific, Atlantic and Indian Oceans being sufficient. By the present time many other communications satellites have been brought into operation; this proliferation has been accompanied by dramatically falling costs (the annual cost of each voice circuit fell by a factor of 38 between Intelsat I and Intelsat IV). The cost of earth stations, initially as much as $5 million, has fallen, partly due to increased satellite power and partly due to less ambitious specification. Earth stations for specialised data applications now cost in the region of $100 thousand; this cost may be expected to fall even further.

Satellites can provide point-to-point links in communication networks, channel capacity being split by frequency or time division multiplexing. A 50 kbit/s link between the US continental ARPA network and the Hawaiian ALOHA packet radio network was provided as early as 1973 via Intelsat IV. At about the same time a transatlantic satellite link (7.2 kbit/s) was provided, allowing nodes in Norway and England to join the ARPA network. Both these satellite connections were on a point-to-point basis with a fixed channel capacity.

The elegance of satellite applications in packet switching only really becomes apparent when the whole (or a large part) of a transponder bandwidth is devoted to multi-access operation, the up channel at one frequency operating in multi-access mode and the down channel at another frequency operating in broadcast mode. Earth stations transmit packets at the full available bandwidth. The satellite retransmits packets, also at the full available bandwidth, and downward packets are received at all earth stations visible to the satellite antenna. By reading packet header addresses earth stations recognise those packets destined to them and ignore all others. This method of operation has a very great deal in common with the packet radio systems which we have already discussed. The greatest difference between satellite and ground radio systems lies in the time of flight of the transmitted signals. Because of the need to maintain exactly the 24-hour orbit time required of a geostationary satellite, it must be maintained at a height of about 36 000 km above the equator. The total time of flight (up plus down) of a signal is therefore between 240 and 270 milliseconds, depending on whether the satellite is directly overhead or towards the horizon. Because of the high bit rates at which packets are transmitted, a number of packets may be transmitted before the first of these returns to earth. Therefore in a satellite system there is no possibility of using a contention resolution system of the carrier sensing variety, which we discussed in the context of packet radio. The pure and slotted ALOHA systems may be applied in just the same way as in packet radio, but the proportion of bandwidth which can be used in these systems is low, as we have already seen. The simple theory of broadcast channels shows maximum channel utilisations of 18.4 per cent and 36.8 per cent for pure and slotted ALOHA respectively. For satellite systems the only practicable methods of improving on the inadequate performance of slotted ALOHA are those which are based on channel reservation techniques.

In packet radio a collision between two packets is detected at the transmitting station by the absence of an acknowledgement from the receiving station; thus positive acknowledgements (either hop-by-hop or end-to-end) are mandatory in a packet radio system. In a satellite system they are not really necessary because packets transmitted from the satellite are received at all earth stations (including the original transmitter). Thus a station correctly receiving a packet which it transmitted 270 milliseconds earlier has a very good degree of assurance that the packet is at almost the same time being correctly received at the intended destination. Certainty of correct reception is not possible, because local conditions at the destination earth station may be unfavourable, but correct reception at the original transmitter indicates with certainty that no packet collision occurred in the multi-access channel. The destination station can request retransmission of a packet which did not collide, but was otherwise in error, error detection being carried out by an integrity check.

Multi-access Reservation Systems

Reservation systems aim to make better use of the available satellite bandwidth. They can be applied in the context of all broadcast systems, but are particularly useful in the case of satellite packet systems. They operate by reserving future time slices for transmission from a particular terminal. Reservation systems depend for their correct operation on the good behaviour of all the transmitting terminals. The latter are physically free to transmit at any time, but only by conforming to the reservation discipline can they ensure that packet collisions will either be eliminated or drastically reduced (depending on the details of the reservation system).

In all reservation systems a proportion of the satellite bandwidth has to be sacrificed in order that transmitting terminals may record their bids for future time slots. This proportion can be very small, so that, at least in theory, most of the satellite bandwidth is available for, and can be used for, data packet transmissions. An additional cost to the user is the somewhat greater complexity required in the ground stations.

Several algorithms have been proposed for the operation of multi-access reservation systems. We shall first discuss two systems, operating under rather different principles, respectively due to Roberts[8] and to Hwa.[9] Roberts's method has become known as 'Reservation ALOHA'. The bandwidth is divided into fixed length time slots as in slotted ALOHA; each slot is large enough for one data packet, and may be reserved by one of the ground terminals. After every M data packet slots one slot is divided into V small slots, which are provided for the packet terminals to enter their requirements for future reservations and also

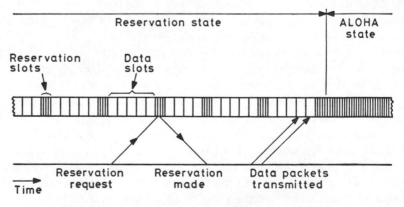

Figure 5.14   Sequence of events in reservation ALOHA

for packet acknowledgements. A terminal holding a packet or packets for transmission transmits a request for the requisite number of packet slots (maximum reservation is eight) using one of the V mini-slots selected at random. Thus the V mini-slots, occurring once every $M + 1$ full-size slots, are accessed in a slotted ALOHA mode. If the reservation request does not collide with a request from another terminal, then it will be received at all ground terminals which, by simple addition, are able to add the number of requested reserved slots to the tally of future reserved data packet slots that each holds. Figure 5.14 shows the sequence of events in which a terminal requests a future reservation for two packets, the reservation does not conflict with a request from any other terminal and the requesting terminal calculates in which future slots to transmit its two packets.

Effectively all the waiting packets for which a reservation has been made join one 'queue in the sky', the length of which is known at all times to all ground terminals. Each terminal is responsible for recording which future slots are reserved for its use; no terminal need concern itself with the details of reservations made by other terminals. The process can be seen to be one of 'dead reckoning', which can only succeed if no errors are made by any terminal. It is of vital importance that the reservation information retransmitted by the satellite to all terminals shall be correctly received (if there is no collision). For this reason Roberts suggests that three independently sum-checked copies of the reservation data be sent; by this means the probability of all three copies being in error can be in the region of 1 in 10^{-7} for a channel error rate of 1 in 10^5. If a reservation packet collides with another, then this will be obvious to the originating terminals and a retransmission of each reservation request will be made in the next available reservation slot, again using a random selection to choose the particular mini-slot.

It is evident that the choice of the value of M, the number of packet slots available between each reservation slot, is an important factor in determining the performance of the system. We have seen that each terminal can reserve up to eight slots; if there are N active terminals, then up to $8N$ data slots may be reserved. If $8N$ is greater than M, then some reservations may carry over beyond the next reservation slot; if then each terminal is allowed to request reservation of eight further slots, the system becomes overloaded, with ever-increasing queues of packets with future reservations at the ground terminals; in such a case packet delays would rapidly become excessive. The solution is quite simple; each ground terminal is constrained to a limit of eight future reserved slots at any time. The satellite will continue to carry and deliver data packets quite happily and will not overload. Only if contention for the reservation slots becomes excessive will the satellite performance degrade; the number of mini-slots provided per reservation slot must be related to the number of ground terminals and to the likely traffic activity to be expected from them.

In a lightly loaded state it may happen that no reservations are outstanding at a particular time. In such a case the use of the M reserved data packet slots reverts to a slotted ALOHA mode divided up into mini-slots. A reservation request may be transmitted in any mini-slot, with no requirement to wait for up to M data slots to pass by. Once a successful reservation has been made the system enters the reservation mode and reservations must be made in the special reservation slots. Should the number of reserved slots again fall to zero, the slotted ALOHA mode is again entered—and so on. In the mini-slots (224 bits in Roberts's original proposal) it may be possible to send small data packets, without setting up a special reservation.

We now consider a different system of slot reservation, which is due to Hwa,[9] who calls it *conflict-free multi-access* (CFMA). Reservation ALOHA, which we have just discussed, has the problem of conflict in accessing the reservation mini-slots, though conflict is eliminated from the data packet slots. CFMA completely avoids all conflict on the satellite multi-access channel. As in reservation ALOHA the multi-access channel is divided into time frames, each of which in CFMA contains three sections, an R-vector, an A-vector and an I-vector. The R-vector contains mini-slots for placing requests for future reservations. The A-vector contains acknowledgement mini-slots for previously received packets. The I-vector is divided into data packet slots. Each ground terminal has its own allocated mini-slot in the R-vector, the number of mini-slots being equal to the number of terminals, N. Thus access to the R-vector is effectively in time division multiplexing mode. If the number of data packet slots in the I-vector is m, then this is the maximum number of reserved slots that a terminal may request; the terminal may thus make a bid for the whole of the I-vector. A distributed arbitration algorithm present in each ground terminal determines the actual allocation to each terminal of slots in the I-vector. This is achieved by allocating a priority order for each of the m data

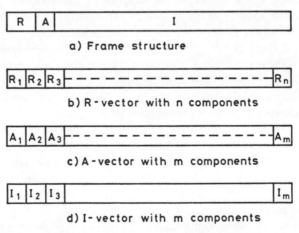

a) Frame structure

b) R - vector with n components

c) A - vector with m components

d) I - vector with m components

Figure 5.15   Vector fields used in CFMA

packet slots. In the simplest case with $N = m$, the priority order for each slot is different; in this case every terminal has one slot for which it has first priority, another for which it has second priority for that slot and so on down the pecking order to the least priority. If a particular terminal has made no reservation bid, then a chance to use its slot goes to the terminal with second priority. Figure 5.15 gives an indication of the division of channel time into the various kinds of vector. If all terminals have made a bid for at least one slot, then each will be allocated its first priority slot and no terminal will be allocated more than one slot. As regards overheads on the satellite channel, Hwa gives figures which suggest that the overheads for a system of 64 users, 64 data slots of 1000 bits each, are somewhat less than 2 per cent; this is surely a small price to pay in terms of channel bandwidth overheads.

Used in a satellite application the A-vector may be superfluous, as all broadcast transmissions from the satellite are received at all ground terminals. Used in a ground radio system the A-vector is evidently essential because, as we have already noted, acknowledgements must be made in these systems.

A new proposal, applicable only to a packet radio system, is worthy of note; this is the MLMA, *multi-level multi-access*, method of Rothauser and Wild.[10] This method also addresses the problem of contention resolution between terminals using a common communication channel. It differs from the systems so far described in relying upon the ability of all terminals to access in overlapping mode the channel reservation slots; this is possible because it is assumed that all terminals use the channel in bit-synchronous mode, which in turn places a limit on the diameter of the system which operates under MLMA. Effectively, for a 1000 bit/s radio channel the system diameter is limited to 30 km.

The mechanism of MLMA avoids wasteful contention for the reservation slot. Logically, there is little difference between this and Hwa's scheme already cited. The latter has the advantage that it is not limited to a restricted system diameter. A performance comparison is given for MLMA against ALOHA and CSMA; this shows that, for the conditions chosen (1000 active terminals, 1000-bit packets, three-level MLMA), MLMA approximates closely to the theoretical performance limit—as indeed do all the reservation schemes. Figure 5.16 shows how delay varies with throughput for ALOHA, CSMA and MLMA.

Yet another variation on the reservation theme is found in Borgonovo and Fratta,[11] who propose a slotted ALOHA system which automatically switches to a reservation mode whenever a collision occurs; this is known as RUC, *reservation upon collision*.

It is not easy to evaluate the performance of these and other systems for reserving satellite or radio bandwidth because assumptions have to be made, not only of the arrival processes of traffic at the packet terminals, but also of the mix of traffic in terms of packet and message lengths. Also in the case of Roberts's reservation ALOHA system, assumptions must be made for the

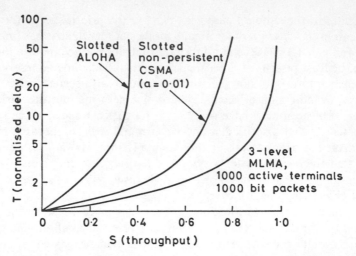

Figure 5.16 Comparison of delay as a function of throughput for ALOHA, CSMA and MLMA

number of mini-slots per reservation slot, the number of data packet slots between reservation slots, the nature of the randomising process for retries after reservation collisions, etc. In the case of Hwa's conflict-free system, choices must be made of the number of data packet slots per frame and, if the number of packet terminals is not equal to the number of packet slots, the way in which slot priorities are allocated to terminals.

Based on stated assumptions (50 kbit/s channel, 10 active stations, half traffic is single packets, half is blocks of eight packets), Roberts gives a set of comparisons between systems (FDMA, TDMA, ALOHA and reservation ALOHA), which show that reservation ALOHA is superior in terms of delay except at very low channel loadings (less than 10 per cent), where the overheads of reservation ALOHA are not worthwhile; in terms of cost for a given delay, reservation ALOHA is much cheaper except where very low delay is demanded, when its cost is similar to that of slotted ALOHA.

Despite the obvious additional complexity of the reservation systems, because of the regime to be observed by all the ground terminals, the better performance and better channel utilisation seem to weigh overwhelmingly in favour of such systems if satellites are to be used to the best advantage in packet switching operations.

In the packet radio context Kleinrock[12] gives an extremely thorough and detailed comparison of nine different access modes, including a dynamic reservation system similar to that we have just described. In this comparison the reservation scheme performs better than almost all the others for all the conditions considered, particularly, of course, at the heavier loads. At light loads, with a small number of terminals, there is a real risk that a system operating in reservation mode may unnecessarily delay packets in waiting to place a reservation. This is where Roberts's reservation ALOHA scheme scores in switching back to slotted ALOHA for reservation purposes when no reservations are outstanding.

A variation on the reservation schemes applicable to satellites may be found in a scheme suggested by Ng and Mark.[13] This depends, not on a contention resolution algorithm built into each ground terminal, but on intelligent processing capacity in the satellite itself. Time at the satellite is divided into up-link and down-link frames, each of which is of duration at least as long as the round trip time (up and down, about 270 milliseconds). Each frame contains a 'header' and data packet slot; in the up-link header the ground terminals report the lengths of their waiting packet queues to the satellite. The satellite computes the slot allocations to each terminal in the next up-link frame and signals these immediately to the terminals in a down-link frame. The allocation algorithm may operate under any one of many queue disciplines. Ng and Mark comment that the mathematical analysis of their proposed system is formidable, but the performance of a simplified mathematical model is in good agreement with that of a more exact simulation model. Allowing for the differences in operational assumptions, the performance of the system is little different from that of the other reservation systems already considered. The trade-off is between added complexity in the satellite and in the ground terminals; if there are many ground terminals, then it may be worthwhile considering locating the more complex logic in the satellite itself.

Practical Satellite Packet Systems

Despite the large amount of effort which has been put into the theoretical study of satellite packet system performance, the number of practical experiments (outside the military context, of which we cannot speak) is remarkably low. As we have already observed, satellites have been in use for some years to provide point-to-point links in data networks. Only two experimental systems have been known to make use of the unique properties of satellites, namely multi-access to the satellite and broadcast return signals over very wide distances. These experiments involved, in the first place in 1973, the University of Alaska, the NASA Ames Research Centre and the University of Hawaii. A more ambitious experiment began in 1975 and involved Bolt, Beranek and Newman, the University of California at Los Angeles, University College London, the Comsat Corporation, the Linkabit Corporation and the Norwegian Defence Research Establishment. This experimental system is known as Satnet and makes use of an Intelsat IV-A satellite and four earth stations in the region of the North Atlantic Ocean. An account of the multi-access protocol in use may be found in Jacobs, Lee and Viterbi.[14] This is known as the *contention-based demand assignment protocol* (CPODA) and is based on a distributed reservation algorithm in which each transmitting station requests future reservations according to the number and size of the packets it holds for transmission; reservations are thus tailored to packet size and are not necessarily all of maximum packet size. The processing load placed upon stations is somewhat greater than in a simple reservation system and may be unacceptable for small inexpensive stations. To overcome this objection a hybrid system has been proposed in which large stations partake in the distributed algorithm, but small stations refer to one or more designated large stations to make reservations on their behalf. In 1977 the protocol underwent extensive evaluation on the Intelsat system.

A description of an evaluation tool designed for use in this context is to be found in Treadwell *et al.*;[15] it provides a flexible means of relating network performance to details of the internal network behaviour. Time-stamped packets are closely observed as they traverse the network. Several of the access modes mentioned in this chapter are to be tried out. The results of the evaluation are not yet available, but are expected shortly.

5.4   PACKET CABLE SYSTEMS

With the aim of providing convenient and flexible communication between locally distributed users and hosts, various packet cable systems have been designed and implemented. Distributed multi-processing is well accommodated by the medium.

Systems have been developed by Mitre (Mitrix[16]), Bell Telephones (Spider[17]), University of California at Irvine (Distributed Computing System, DCS[18]) and Xerox (Ethernet[19]). Mitrix and Spider employ a central minicomputer acting as a network control centre. DCS and Ethernet employ distributed control. A ring configuration is used in DCS and Spider, whilst Mitrix implements two one-way busses using CATV technology; Ethernet uses a branching two-way passive bus. We shall briefly consider each of these systems except Spider (which does not operate in channel contention mode and is therefore irrelevant to this discussion), but concentrate on Ethernet, which is most closely related to conventional broadcast systems.

Mitrix, established in 1970, uses TDMA, with slots assigned to users by a network control computer. Requests for slot assignments are made by users communicating with the control computer via special time slots dedicated to this purpose. Logically this is very like the various kinds of reservation systems which we have just considered. The system performs efficiently for synchronous or very heavy duty cycle traffic. However, the transactions to be serviced are usually neither synchronous nor high duty cycle. Therefore other schemes have been considered at Mitre. Mitrix II, developed for applications at the Central Intelligence Agency, uses a dual-mode slotted TDMA bus. This dedicates certain slots to the synchronous, very high duty cycle traffic and other slots to be shared by bursty users in a slotted ALOHA mode. Utilisation of the ALOHA slots is improved by use of an adaptive retransmission technique described by Meissner, Segal and Tanigawa;[20] rapid retransmission is permitted if the ALOHA mode traffic is light, whilst the mean retransmission time is extended if the ALOHA mode traffic is more intense.

DCS provides communication between a collection of minicomputers connected by a ring configuration. The system is of modest proportions, with the emphasis on low cost. The whole system is process, not processor, oriented. Process migration between hardware is catered for. The ring operates in a conventional mode, packets circulating once, being removed at the interface which introduced them. In both Spider and DCS, provision is made for removing a faulty interface unit from the ring, thus avoiding breaking the ring. The system does not, of course, operate in multi-access broadcast mode.

Ethernet, which operates in a truly multi-access broadcast mode, is of more interest to us in the present context. Xerox have built an operational Ethernet which supports 100 nodes along a kilometre of cable. The interface from a terminal connects via a bit-serial interface and a transceiver to the Ether cable; we shall refer to the interface plus transceiver as a station. As in Mitrix, a packet is broadcast and heard by all destinations; it is accepted only at the destination station corresponding to the packet destination address. The access mode is a development of CSMA, already encountered in packet radio systems. The physical configuration of the transceiver allows the transmitting station to listen-in to the common medium whilst transmitting a packet. This allows any collisions to be detected immediately they occur and not, as in packet radio, by the absence of an acknowledgement after an interval of time. Colliding packets interfere with each other so as to be unrecognisable by a receiver. The mode of operation is often called *listen while talk* (LWT), as distinct from the *listen before talk* of CSMA.

A station with a packet to transmit operates thus; it first listens to the Ether (packets are phase encoded) and transmits immediately if the Ether is idle, but defers to any transmission already in progress (i.e. it waits). Once it hears the transmission cease, the station immediately transmits its packet. If no other station has also been waiting, the station will acquire the Ether and packet transmission should be successful. If, however, another station has also deferred, then it too will immediately transmit when the previous transmission ceases. The result is a packet collision, which causes all conflicting transmissions to fail. The significant feature of Ethernet is that the failure will be immediately apparent at all transmitting stations and the conflicting transmissions can be aborted without further delay. This feature allows better use to be made of the communication resource by avoiding the full-length transmission of collided packets which is not avoidable in either packet radio or packet satellite modes.

Clearly, a packet collision may occur even if a station transmits on to an apparently idle Ether. This is because of the signal propagation time on the

Ether cable. Once a transmission has been in progress for a period of twice the maximum propagation delay, then no further risk of collision exists; all other stations will remain in deferring mode.

Because of the small, but finite, risk that a pair of packets may appear to collide at one station, but, because of propagation delays, they are clear of each other at other stations, a station detecting a collision injects a short burst of noise onto the Ether cable in order to ensure that the collision is detected at all stations.

After a packet collision each station waits for a randomised interval before again listening to the Ether and repeating the process. It is evident that a change in performance would be derived if stations deferring were to wait for a randomised interval after deferring before transmitting a packet. This should be the subject of analysis, but, speaking qualitatively, the result should be fewer packet collisions at heavy loads, at the expense of an increased transit delay at light loads.

The Ethernet system adapts the length of the randomised post-collision wait to depend on the level of traffic; the mean retransmission interval is made to depend on the frequency of collisions.

As in all broadcast systems, successful operation depends on the good behaviour of each station. If a station neglects to adjust its retransmission interval with increasing traffic or sends very large packets, it can usurp or monopolise the Ether. The system contains low level software in each station to prevent this from happening.

The Ethernet system contains no end-to-end acknowledgement protocol and packet delivery is not guaranteed; high probability of successful delivery is usual. Users are expected to provide higher level protocols which check on the correct delivery of packets.

A more recent proposal by Agrawala et al.[21] for a slightly more elaborate Ethernet-like protocol includes provision for acknowledgement signals between receiving and transmitting stations. These authors also take into account the effect on Ethernet performance of the interaction between communications processor and host processor, in particular the delay in clearing the communications processor packet buffer due to the limited processing rate of the host processor. Greater efficiency is attained by creating a deliberate artificial collision (by transmitting a burst of noise) if a packet begins to arrive which the station cannot cope with because of lack of buffers. The creation of a deliberate collision avoids the transmission of a full packet in these circumstances, thus saving time on the Ether as in the case of colliding packets, mentioned above.

It is interesting to note that the Mitre Corporation now takes the view[22] that the LWT mode of operation is to be preferred for low duty cycle, bursty users. It is seen to provide a very simple low-cost solution to the subscriber interface problem, since it does away both with the need for slot reservation requests and with the need for a central adjudicating network controller.

5.5 HYBRID SYSTEMS

In the preceding chapters and the present chapter we have considered in turn distributed terrestrial networks consisting of nodes and data links, and the broadcast systems of the present chapter. We shall now discuss the ways in which these different data communication media can be used in conjunction.

The characteristics of the different systems are quite different. Bandwidth of a terrestrial network is an expensive commodity, so that throughput of such a network may not be very great; on the other hand the delays in transit can be relatively small. Such a network caters well for interactive traffic, but not so well for bulk file transfers. At the other extreme, satellite systems provide massive bandwidth at low cost, but suffer from the inevitable satellite delay of 270 milliseconds; if retransmissions are necessary then the delay may be several times greater. Such a system is ideal for bulk file transfer, but could be quite inadequate for interactive traffic.

Packet radio systems are limited in geographical range, but have considerable advantages of cheapness; they cater well for the mobile terminal. Packet cable systems make use of CATV techniques, but, for timing considerations, are even more limited in physical size than are packet radio systems. The response time of packet radio can be quite rapid and that of packet cable very rapid. Packet radio has modest bandwidth capability, but packet cable has considerable bandwidth.

Clearly it is possible to serve local communities by packet radio or even by packet cable; the longer inter-community links may be made by satellite or by long-distance land lines. The nodes serving as gateways between cooperating systems must be designed so as to take full account of the different system characteristics; considerable storage capacity may be necessary to allow for different system speeds.

Where it is desired to provide in the one system for different types of traffic, two packet media may be designed to operate in parallel, traffic being directed to the one or the other depending on the nature of the traffic itself. One such system has been analysed in considerable detail;[23] this consists of a terrestrial network operated in parallel with a satellite system. As we shall see, it is notable for yet another system of access to the satellite multi-access channel.

The terrestrial network is organised into local areas of several nodes, joined by short-distance land lines. The local areas are interconnected by longer-distance land lines. Each local area contains one node with access to the satellite. Huynh et al. discuss two fundamentally different modes of operation. In the first of these the satellite multi-access channel is used according to the slotted ALOHA algorithm. In the second the system operates under the MASTER algorithm (Multi Access Satellite with Terrestrial Retransmission). In the MASTER system no retransmissions are attempted on the satellite multi-access channel; if a collision occurs, then the packets which have collided are redirected mandatorily to the terrestrial network. The aim is to avoid the unstable property of the satellite link under slotted ALOHA, where the throughput, as we have seen, can fall to zero in the presence of excessive offered traffic.

In a later paper,[24] Huynh et al. categorise a contention system as one in which throughput increases to a maximum and then decreases as system load increases; they categorise a queueing system, by which they mean the store-and-forward terrestrial network, as having the characteristic of throughput increasing to one (i.e. normalised load) as the system load increases. The whole of the MASTER philosophy hinges on this distinction. We would comment that a terrestrial network may not be so well-behaved. As we have seen in our discussion of flow control in store-and-forward networks, it is quite possible for the throughput of such networks to rise to a maximum with increasing applied load and then to decrease, eventually to zero, if the applied load is further increased. To avoid this condition of a store-and-forward network it is necessary to apply congestion avoidance controls.

Extensive analysis has been performed on the hybrid network operating in slotted ALOHA and MASTER modes. Much of the interest centred around the routing philosophy. The aim of the routing doctrine was to minimise overall delay, whilst achieving the maximum throughput. The doctrine adopted in both cases was deterministic, the fraction of inter-area traffic initially directed to the satellite channel being a parameter of the experiment. No local area traffic was sent via the satellite.

The results obtained showed disappointingly little difference between the slotted ALOHA and the MASTER systems. MASTER was shown to work better than ALOHA under certain circumstances only. The link capacity assignment, determined by the cost ratio of ground and satellite channels, determines which system is better. As predicted in the design philosophy, the satellite channel under MASTER was somewhat less sensitive to small changes in traffic.

The further suggestion was made that the satellite channel should be used on a reservation basis, but that the reservations should be set up by using the ground network. This suggestion makes sense provided that the delays in transmission via the ground network are substantially less than those via the satellite. The advantages over reservation ALOHA, where a distributed reservation algorithm operates via the satellite channel itself, are not great, if, indeed, they exist at all.

As we have already suggested, the main benefits of a hybrid system should be obtainable where the division of traffic between satellite and ground network is made according to the characteristics of the traffic, interactive or bulk data transfer. This distinction was not made by Huynh et al., but is well brought out by Maruyama,[25] who discusses a heuristic method for capacity, flow and priority assignments in a hybrid network; network cost minimization is also addressed. In this work the satellite links are dedicated and are not used in contention mode. However, Maruyama believes that extension of the method to shared satellite channels should present no difficulty, given that delay models with more practicable assumptions become available.

The tendency in current terrestrial network design seems to be towards virtual call systems of the more rigid kind in which resources are reserved per call. Efficient use of broadcast system bandwidth is dependent on the more flexible multiplexing schemes which we have discussed in this chapter. Use of broadcast facilities for virtual calls has not, as far as we know, been studied; it may present new problems of protocol design. Networking in the freer context of datagrams is well catered for in broadcast systems.

References

1. Cacciamani, E. R.,
   'Developments in data communication',
   Infotech State of the Art Report on Future Networks (July 1978).
2. Binder, R., Abramson, N., Kuo, F. F., Okinaka, A. and Wax, D.,
   'Aloha packet broadcasting—a retrospect',
   Proc. National Computer Conference, 203 (1975).
3. Lam, S. S., and Kleinrock, L.,
   'Packet switching in a multi-access broadcast channel',
   IEEE Trans. on Communications, **COM-23**, 891 (September 1975).
4. Abramson, N.,
   'The throughput of packet broadcasting channels',
   IEEE Trans. on Communications, **COM-25**, 117 (January 1977).
5. Kleinrock, L.,
   Queueing Systems. Vol II: Computer Applications,
   Wiley–Interscience, New York (1976).
6. Kleinrock, L., and Tobagi, F.,
   'Random access techniques for data transmission over packet-switched radio channels',
   Proc. National Computer Conference, 187 (1975).
7. Tobagi, F., and Kleinrock, L.,
   'Packet switching in radio channels: Part II—the hidden terminal problem in CSMA and the busy-tone solution',
   IEEE Trans. on Communications, **COM-23**, 1417 (December 1975).
8. Roberts, L. G.,
   'Dynamic allocation of satellite capacity through packet reservation',
   Proc. National Computer Conference, 711 (1973).
9. Hwa, H. R.,
   'A framed ALOHA system',
   Proc. PACNET Symposium, Sendai, Japan, 109 (August 1975).
10. Rothauser, E. H., and Wild, D.,
    'MLMA—a collision-free multi-access method',
    Proc. IFIP Congress 77, Toronto, 431 (August 1977).
11. Borgonovo, F. and Fratta, L.,
    'A new technique for satellite broadcast channel communication',
    Proc. 5th ACM/IEEE Data Communications Symposium, Snowbird, Utah, 2–1 (September 1977).

188 COMPUTER NETWORKS AND THEIR PROTOCOLS

12. Kleinrock, L.,
    'Performance of distributed multi-access computer-communication systems',
    Proc. IFIP Congress 77, Toronto, 547 (August 1977).
13. Ng., S. F. W., and Mark, J. W.,
    'A new multi-access model for packet switching with an intelligent satellite',
    Proc. International Computer Communication Conference, Toronto, 117 (August 1976).
14. Jacobs, I., Lee, L.-N., and Viterbi, A.,
    'CPODA—a demand assignment protocol for SATNET',
    Proc. 5th ACM/IEEE Data Communications Symposium, Snowbird, Utah, 2–5 (September 1977).
15. Treadwell, S. W., Hinchley, A. J., and Bennett, C. J.,
    'A high level network measurement tool',
    Proc. Eurocomp 78, 35 (May 1978).
16. Willard, D.,
    'A time division multiple access system for digital communication',
    Computer Design, **13**, 79 (June 1974).
17. Fraser, A. G.,
    'A virtual channel network',
    Datamation, **21**, 51 (February 1975).
18. Farber, D. J.,
    'A ring network',
    Datamation, **21**, 44 (February 1975).
19. Metcalfe, R. M., and Boggs, D. R.,
    'Ethernet: distributed packet switching for local computer networks',
    Comm. ACM, **19**, 395 (July 1976).
20. Meisner, N. B., Segal, J. L., and Tanigawa, M. Y.,
    'Dual mode slotted ALOHA digital bus',
    Proc. 5th ACM/IEEE Data Communications Symposium, Snowbird, Utah, 5–14 (September 1977).
21. Agrawala, A. K., Bryant, R. M., and Agre, J.,
    'Analysis of an Ethernet-like protocol',
    Proc. Computer Networking Symposium, NBS, Gaithersburg, Maryland, 112 (December 1977).
22. Meisner, N. B., Willard, D. G., and Hopkins, G. T.,
    'Time division digital bus techniques implemented on coaxial cable',
    Proc. Computer Networking Symposium, NBS, Gaithersburg, Maryland, 104 (December 1977).
23. Huynh, D., Kobayashi, H., and Kuo, F. F.,
    'Design issues for mixed media packet switching networks',
    Proc. National Computer Conference, 541 (1976).
24. Huynh, D., Kobayashi, H., and Kuo, F. F.,
    'Optimal design of mixed-media packct switching networks: routing and capacity assignment',
    IEEE Trans. on Communications, **COM-25**, 158 (January 1977).
25. Maruyama, K.,
    'Designing mixed-media communication networks',
    Proc. Eurocomp 78, 241 (May 1978).

Chapter 6

Communication Protocols and Interfaces

6.1 INTRODUCTION

At all levels of a computer network, from the communications subsystem to the computers and terminals that connect to it, we are confronted by a large variety of geographically distributed pieces of hardware. They are designed to cooperate in the execution of tasks for the network user. The events that occur in this complex environment are unpredictable in terms of their nature, their sequence and their timing.

This point can be illustrated by a simple example. Consider a task that involves the output of a file onto a lineprinter and in which the transfer takes place through a packet-switched network. The computer now has no simple direct way of establishing whether the device is ready to start receiving the data. Even assuming that such knowledge is obtained and the transfer begins, what will happen if the lineprinter runs out of paper? During the data transfer a sensible procedure to be adopted by the computer would be to input data into the network at the rate at which the lineprinter could accept them; but internal network behaviour could result in bunching of the transmitted packets and an instantaneous arrival rate higher than the printer could cope with. The network might also deliver the information to the device in the wrong order, lose pieces of information or corrupt it. The problems of controlling remote devices are not new and have been solved for connections via leased or dial-up lines. As for the extra problems created by packet switching technology some are solved by the communications subnet as part of the service it offers; others have to be resolved by the computer and devices that connect through it. For example, it was naive to worry earlier about the speed matching between the computer and lineprinter. The lineprinter connects to the network through a link level procedure which allows the device to accept data at a rate it can handle. As a matter of fact the computer does not have to worry at all about the device speed, for it can attempt to send at some maximum attainable rate. Depending on the nature of the network, the maximum attainable rate is controlled by the communication subnet or by procedures between the communicating devices. Whichever method is used the end result is the same, namely the avoidance of congestion in the communication subnet from accepting packets at a rate greater than that at which they can be delivered.

Two very important points follow from the previous discussion. Firstly, a device connected onto a packet-switched network must have some intelligence. The minimum required is that it should operate the procedures of the interface between the communication subnet and itself. Unintelligent devices must connect to the network through intelligent ones. Secondly, a number of procedures must be defined, both in the communication subnet and in the computers around it, to ensure the reliable execution of user tasks. These procedures entail the exchange of information between geographically separated hardware, and are implemented through software processes. Two such processes, which are usually separated physically, cooperate to implement the procedure.

Two processes running in different geographical locations must use the exchange of messages to coordinate their action and achieve 'synchronisation'. This message exchange must follow carefully designed procedures. Such procedures are called *protocols*. Their main characteristic is the ability to work where the timing and sequence of events can be unknown and where transmission errors are expected.

The concept of a protocol has been introduced earlier in the book. What we shall do in this chapter is to provide an abstract definition of a protocol and the framework for its operation. In looking at the requirements that a protocol has to satisfy for the performance of a variety of network tasks, we shall discover that they have some requirements in common. This will lead to the concept of levels of protocol and of interfaces between adjacent levels. We shall discuss in detail link level procedures and in particular, the High-level Data Link Control Procedure (HDLC) which is defined by the International Standards Organisation (ISO). Such procedures, according to our definition, are protocols since they operate via processes located in different hardware. They give a very useful insight into many of the problems that have to be solved for providing reliable data transfer in a network environment. We shall continue with packet level protocols and describe the specification of the X25 interface between public packet-switched data networks and subscribers to these networks. X25 is a recommendation of the International Telephone and Telegraph Consultative Committee (CCITT). This interface is implemented using three protocols. We shall describe the functions of these protocols and discuss some implementation problems. The chapter will conclude with a general discussion on the design of communication protocols and the unified access of network facilities.

Protocols

The term 'protocol' can be used to describe the procedures for the exchange of information between processes not only in a network environment but also in multiprocessor systems for controlling the interaction of parallel processes, in real-time applications for controlling a number of different devices, and in other systems where there is no fixed time relationship between an event occurring and the action implied by that event.

Protocol functions are accomplished by the exchange of messages between processes. The format and meaning of these messages form the logical definition of the protocol. Rules of procedure determine the actions of the processes cooperating in the protocol. The set of these rules constitutes the procedural definition of the protocol. Using these concepts we can now give a formal definition of a protocol as: the logical and procedural specification of the communication mechanism between processes. The logical definition constitutes the syntax, while the procedural one forms the semantics of the protocol.

The functions of the communication subnet protocols have been discussed in earlier chapters. Most important among these are error, flow and congestion control, and routing strategies. Error control protects the integrity both of user data and of control messages exchanged between the subnet protocols. Flow and congestion control enables the communication subnet to share its resources among a large number of users, providing each one with a satisfactory service without endangering its own operation. Routing strategies, as well as optimising the utilisation of the subnet resources, also increase the availability of the subnet services by providing alternative routes between two points in the network. In spite of the fact that these functions are provided in the communication subnet some must be repeated in protocols implemented between computers in the network. This is because the communication subnet has no control over the operation of a task or the sharing of resources between tasks in these machines. The exact functions performed by the protocol stem from the task it has to perform and the character of the environment in which it must perform it. The functions in their turn define the procedural or semantic part of the protocols, the implementation of which must use an appropriate logical or syntactic structure.

Processes

Protocols are implemented via processes and the operation of a protocol is achieved by the exchange of messages between processes. To understand protocols it is therefore important to have a clear notion of what is meant by a process, and how processes cooperate to achieve the protocol functions. We shall define a process as being a logical or a virtual processor. A process is self-contained and unaware of the fact that the real processor that serves it shares its resources amongst a number of active processes. Once this is stated we can list the characteristics of a process. It must have processing capability, that is, a claim on a real processor (CPU) plus a program. It must have something to process and this can arrive from outside the process in the form of a message.

Process input occurs at logical software ports. Through these ports a process receives messages from processes residing either in the same, or in other computers. A set of private data defines the current state of a process and determines the action to be taken on receipt of a message. The result of the computation performed by a process is sent out through an output port; again the process can have a number of these ports. Figure 6.1 demonstrates our concept of a process.

Let us now consider, by means of an example, how a protocol operates. The most simple process is one which receives a single message, processes it and returns a message as reply. There is no relation between this event and any other that takes place before or after it. The process that originates the message must know the address of the destination process and this is included in each message. This address must also uniquely identify the destination processor which in its turn must have knowledge of the destination process. The process of origin, when despatching the message, enters a state in which it is waiting for a reply on one of its ports. It does this by making the appropriate change to its data. The destination process performs the function specified in the message, constructs an output message containing the results of the operation and the originating process address, and sends it out through an output port. Now it is free to accept messages from any other process in the system. When the reply message is received at the originating process it is checked to make sure that it is from the expected source before it is accepted. When the message is accepted the process state will change to 'no message expected' on that input port. For this very simple protocol all that is needed is a syntax to define the format of the messages and very simple semantics.

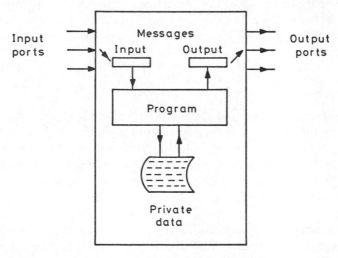

Figure 6.1   Model of a process

The enquiry–response protocol described above in its very simple form is implemented a great deal in the communication environment. One example is the echo process, where a message is received and returned unaltered to the originating process. The enquiry–response protocol can be made more elaborate

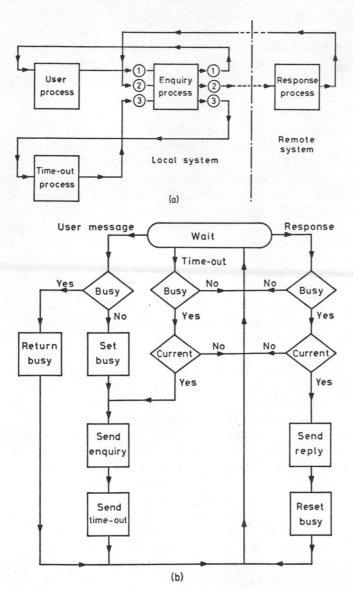

Figure 6.2   Enquiry response protocol: (a) block diagram of process communication; (b) enquiry process flow chart

to bring in features normally associated with more complex protocols. For example, it can attempt to ensure that the reply is received at the enquiry process by employing a scheme of acknowledgements and retransmissions to cope with lost messages. This is not normally implemented because in this particular protocol the repetition of the whole procedure would be simpler than an acknowledgement and retransmission scheme and result in no more traffic. The enquiry process would set a timer whose expiry time was long compared to the time within which the response was expected. If no response had been received when the timer expired, the process would repeat its message. This time-out procedure can be implemented as another process on the same processor as the enquiry process.

Let us now trace the sequence of events in the enquiry–response protocol as seen from the enquiry process end. First something or someone, which we call the user, must request for such an interaction to occur, see Figure 6.2(a). This arrives on input port 1 as a message to the process. The process constructs a message and despatches it to the response process through output port 2, the reply from which is expected on input port 2. At the same time it constructs a message for the time-out process. The message contains a time t and data. It is sent out on output port 3. The time-out process will return the data part of the message after time t through input port 3. Finally the enquiry process manipulates its private data so that it defines a state for the process during which it is expecting a message at input port 2 and is not prepared to accept further requests from port 1. If the next event to occur is the receipt of the response on port 2, a message is formulated and returned to the user via output port 1 and the process returns to a non-busy state having completed its task. In that state it will be prepared to accept further user requests. Let us now consider what will happen when the time-out associated with the completed task occurs. If in the meantime the process has become busy and has despatched another message, it may mistake this time-out as associated with its current activity. This can be avoided by labelling each new activity differently from the previous ones and by including that label in the data sent to the time-out process. The enquiry process will then be able to distinguish and act upon the current time-out and discard all others. An alternative is to enhance the time-out protocol so that time-outs can be cancelled as well as set. If the current time-out occurs before receipt of the response, the enquiry message is sent again. This mechanism creates another problem. If the original response was not lost, but unduly delayed in the network, its arrival completes the operation. The response to the second enquiry can then arrive during the next activity and again must be recognised from the activity label as an old response and discarded. Figure 6.2(b) shows a flow chart for the process operation.

Most protocols need to perform functions that require the exchange of several messages over a period of time and with a complexity much greater than that of the simple enquiry response protocol. To accomplish such a task, the processes cooperating in the protocol implementation must be aware of the state that their task has reached at any point in time. It is important that synchronisation is achieved and maintained between processes for the duration of the task. Before they start execution of a task, two processes form an association by establishing a call. The call is established between process ports. A number of messages are then exchanged between processes to initialise parameters associated with the call and to achieve synchronisation. From then on, if synchronisation is maintained, each process has the correct view of the state of the protocol. Error recovery procedures are provided to ensure that if synchronisation is lost it is re-established during the protocol operation. Finally when the task that the protocol is performing has been completed or if it is not required further, the call between the processes is closed down.

Protocol Implementation

A protocol is defined in terms of its syntax and semantics and has to be implemented between two processes. An implementation definition describing the actions of each process is required. Process actions can be described in terms of process states and events which cause transitions between those states. An event is the arrival of a message at a process. When a process is in a particular state it defines the subset of messages that can be received and the action that should be taken on receipt of any of these. If another known message is received, then synchronisation has been lost and the process must enter the appropriate error recovery part of the protocol. After receipt of a message from one of the input ports, the process can enter an intermediate state during which it formats and despatches an output message. Figure 6.3 demonstrates this state transition principle. Actions must be defined for all allowed messages. In Figure 6.3, an

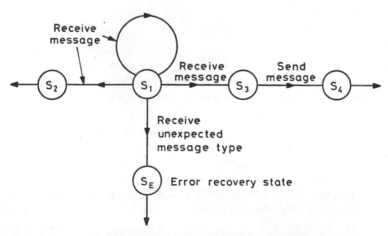

Figure 6.3   Example of state transitions

event causing no change to the state has been shown by a loop that starts and ends on state S_1. The error recovery actions could depend on the actual type of the unexpected message. The actions must be unambiguous, so the receipt of a specific message type must lead to a unique state.

The description of protocol implementation using state diagrams becomes difficult in the case of complicated protocols with a very large number of states. An alternative method for protocol description is the use of a high level language. This is less prone to errors than the state diagram method. It also has the advantage of describing the protocol functions in the medium in which they are to be implemented thus avoiding discrepancies between description and implementation. Both these methods which provide an implementation tool give a more precise definition of protocol semantics than a natural language description. It has therefore been suggested that they should form part of the protocol definition itself.

When a precise definition of a protocol has been achieved, it must be tested for correctness. This has sometimes been done by testing the implemented protocol and all the functions required of it and correcting errors that are discovered, but such an exercise can prove cumbersome and expensive and can lead to the acceptance of inadequate protocols if changes prove difficult. Methods have been developed for applying formal proving techniques to protocol definitions. Such techniques can be a useful design tool. Nevertheless until recently they have hardly been used because they are difficult and complex to apply and proofs can only be obtained for the simplest of cases. They are a very promising area of research and should prove valuable in the future. A more detailed discussion of these techniques will be given in Section 6.5 of this chapter.

Protocol Structure

Some of the functions required by tasks in a computer network are common to all tasks. The most important of these is the transporting of data between processes without error. This function is partially provided by the packet-switched communication subnet. The processes running in the host computers of the network view the communication subnet as a 'lower level' which provides the communication function and they need not be aware of the internal structure of the communication 'system'. It can even be replaced by another, as long as the interface it presents to the process above it offers the same functions and characteristics. Figure 6.4(a) shows the view of processes P_1 and P_2 of the lower level system that provides the communication facility. The system itself might have a complicated internal structure, but this does not concern P_1 and P_2. They are cooperating to implement a protocol whose nature is dependent on the lower level characteristics. The protocol between P_1 and P_2 may in its turn provide an enhanced service for another set of processes P_3 and P_4. For these, the communication system includes P_1 and P_2. Their view of the system is through a well-defined interface between P_3 and P_1 on the one side and P_4 and P_2 on the other. P_1 and P_2 might also be capable of supporting a number of processes at the same time, thus providing a multiplexing function. If P_1 and P_3 are not located on the same computer then their interface will have to be implemented using protocols. For example, if we introduce an error-prone physical link, a *link level protocol* will have to be employed to ensure the correctness of the messages exchanged between the processes. The introduction of this protocol, which closes locally, does not affect the overall structure of the system. It is merely a substitute for a direct connection. This is illustrated in Figure 6.4(b).

The network structure or architecture is therefore a hierarchical one consisting of a number of layers. There is no unique layered structure arrived at by some formal procedure but only good and bad solutions. A good solution should be flexible, efficient, easy to implement and should enhance the understanding of the system. The modularity of this approach minimises the interdependency

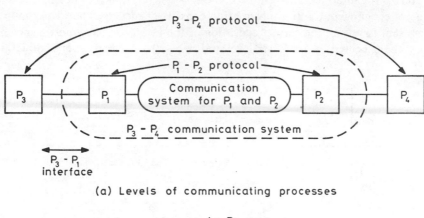

(a) Levels of communicating processes

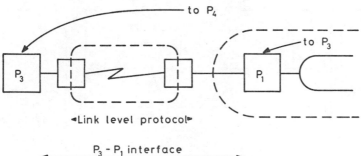

(b) The insertion of a physical link introduces another protocol which closes locally and does not affect the overall structure

Figure 6.4   Layers of communication protocols

between the various components of the network. The definition of the structure should make no assumptions as to how the functions are implemented or distributed on network components.

This layered structure is commonly referred to as onion skin architecture. Figure 6.5 is a schematic diagram of this approach. In this diagram layer n provides a service to layer n + 1, its 'user'. To do this it utilises the functions of the n − 1 layer to communicate with other entities at layer n in the network. Protocols usually are the communication rules between entities *at the same level*. The structure of the levels below or above n is not known to layer n itself. Each layer implements a set of functions to offer an enhanced service to the layer above it. There is an exception to this rule when a protocol or protocols is employed between two adjacent levels to provide a secure path between the two as in the example in Figure 6.4(b). Therefore the overall structure can have internal substructures.

Across the interface between the n and n + 1 layers control information and data are exchanged. Control information consists of messages between the two layers sent to ensure the correct operation of the interface, to request a specific task to be executed by the lower level and to report on progress or completion

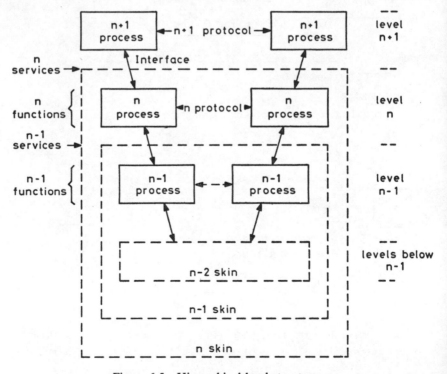

Figure 6.5   Hierarchical level structure

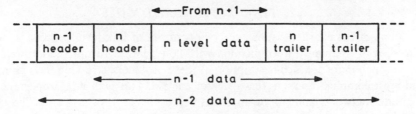

Figure 6.6   Message structure

of a task to the higher level. The data passing across the interface are either control messages associated with the protocol and destined for the remote n level process or data to be delivered to the remote $n + 1$ level. A process therefore has three interfaces: two physical ones between the higher and lower levels, and a logical one with its partner in the protocol. Whatever the functions or contents of messages sent from the higher to the lower level for delivery to the remote process, these are transparent to the lower levels.

The onion skin architecture leads to a layered structure of messages within the network as shown in Figure 6.6. The header added at each level is associated with the operation of that level of protocol and can, for example, include numbering for sequence and error control and source identification. As the message progresses through the lower levels, more information is added. When it starts rising through the levels at the remote end the header and trailer information is stripped, processed and the data passed to the next level. Figure 6.7 shows the onion skin structure of the messages; notice that the onion skin order is reversed from that of the protocols in Figure 6.5. This hierarchical framework is dynamic above the communication subnet level. A network task should have the freedom to create its own structure and configure a system to meet its own functional requirements. In doing this it might utilise a number of standard processes. This kind of freedom is important to allow an efficient implementation of a variety of distributed tasks with differing requirements.

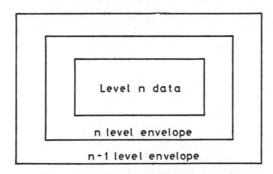

Figure 6.7   Message onion skin layers

6.2 LINK LEVEL PROTOCOLS

Some of the characteristics and the operation of link level procedures were discussed in Chapter 4, in connection with flow control. In this section we shall give a much more detailed description of these protocols, stressing their primary and most complex function, that of error control. This is of vital importance in computer networks and can be applied to all other levels of protocol. The exact operation of error control protocols depends on the characteristics of the system beneath the protocol. It is advantageous from our point of view to take as our example a system which is a physical link, because its characteristics are well-defined and predictable. Figure 6.8 shows a block diagram of the error control protocol and its function. Two processes wish to cooperate and execute a task. To accomplish this task they need to exchange messages according to a protocol. They must therefore have available a transport system that will carry messages between the two but such a transport system can be unreliable and corrupt or lose messages. This will cause the protocol of the two processes to fail, unless the processes themselves implement mechanisms to correct the shortcomings of the transport system. The transport system can of course be used by a number of processes all requiring the same degree of reliability. It therefore makes sense not to replicate the error control protocol in each and every process, but to define it as an independent level, servicing several processes, and converting the unreliable transport medium to a reliable communication facility. In this section we shall assume that the transport system is a physical link and shall consider its characteristics in defining the error control protocol. In other cases the transport system might be a packet-switched communication network or similar medium. We shall discover that the mechanisms we invent for error control will be suitable, after minor additions, to perform flow control as well.

Frame Structure

Link level protocols must be capable of detecting errors in arbitrary bit sequences because the higher level processes are entirely free to choose any binary sequence to implement their protocols. No method can be devised which detects errors in a continuous arbitrary data stream. The way to make errors detectable is to transmit data in blocks with a Cyclic Redundancy Check (CRC).

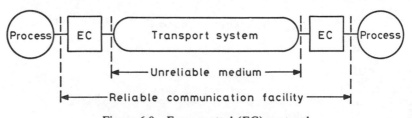

Figure 6.8   Error control (EC) protocol

This method of error control involves the 'division' of a block of data by a predefined bit sequence and the transmission of the 'remainder' of that division as part of the data block. The receiver performs the same division sum and checks whether the remainder it has obtained is the same as the transmitted one. If this is the case, it can with a high degree of confidence assume that the data received in that block is correct. If the calculated and received remainders do not match, the block of data is assumed wrong and discarded. A description of the operation of cyclic redundancy is given in the Appendix to this chapter (Section 6.6).

A number of schemes have been devised to separate data into frames for transmission. The aim of all these is to preserve transparency of user data. That is to say, if special characters or bit sequences are used to define the beginning and end of a block, some other mechanism must be devised to allow the same bit sequence to be transmitted as part of the user data without signalling the end of frame to the receiver. Three variations on the frame format are shown in Figure 6.9. The first of these, Figure 6.9(a), carries in its header a byte (DFL) whose binary value indicates the length of the data field in octets. To determine the length of the data field the header information must be used while the frame is arriving, for this reason the header itself is protected by a Cyclic Redundancy Check. A second CRC checksums the whole of the frame from the first bit of the frame level control to the last bit of the data. The two bytes of frame level

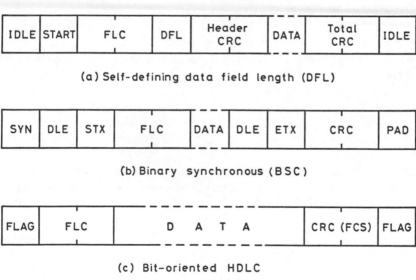

(a) Self-defining data field length (DFL)

(b) Binary synchronous (BSC)

(c) Bit-oriented HDLC

FLC ≡ Frame level control

FLAG ≡ '01111110'

Figure 6.9   Frame format types

control, included in all the framing mechanisms, are used for the implementation of the link level protocol. The framing used in Figure 6.9(a) is known as 'self-defining data field length'. When frames are not being transmitted the line is filled with idle characters. On detecting the start character, the receiver checks the correctness of the first three bytes received using the CRC of the header. If correct, it accepts the next n bytes and checks the correctness of the whole frame. If the header information has been corrupted and the CRC check fails the receiver starts looking again for start characters which of course can be repeated in the data field. This does not matter, for the CRC check will only be satisfied when the beginning of a correct frame is encountered.

The binary synchronous (BSC) framing mechanism, see Figure 6.9(b), uses a set of ISO 7-bit codes to delimit the frame. Like the previous one, it is byte-oriented and the data is expected to be an integral number of octets. The characters that signal the beginning of the frame are DLE followed by STX; those that signal the end are DLE followed by ETX. To avoid abnormal termination of the frame due to the user data repeating a delimiting sequence, the transmitter inserts another DLE character after every occurrence of DLE in the user data. The mechanism searching for delimiting characters at the receiver accepts DLE only if it is followed by ETX and ignores it if it is followed by another DLE. Before delivering the data field to the user, a pair of consecutive DLE characters is replaced by a single one. The characters are inserted for transparency after the CRC has been calculated by the transmitter, and are removed before it is checked by the receiver.

The final framing structure shown in Figure 6.9(c) is the bit-oriented HDLC. The frame is delimited by 8-bit flags consisting of one zero, six ones, followed by one zero (01111110). The last two bytes of a frame contain the CRC, while the first two are used for frame level control. Data transparency is preserved by the insertion of a 0 bit by the transmitter whenever there is a sequence of five contiguous 1 bits occurring anywhere in the frame from the beginning of the frame level control to the end, including the last five bits of the CRC. The receiver examines the frame contents and discards any 0 bit which follows five contiguous 1 bits.

Nowadays there are several large-scale integrated chips on the market which perform all the framing functions of link level protocols, including insertion and removal of characters or bits for transparency and calculation of the CRC. In packet-switched networks where the information is transported in discrete units, the use of these link level protocols does not require any additional processing to divide the data into blocks for transmission.

Error Correction

The frame structure allows errors to be detected and blocks of data or packets contained in these frames to be discarded. A protocol must therefore

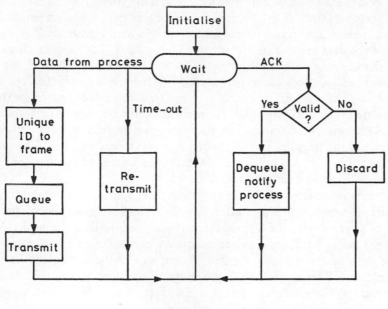

(a) Sending

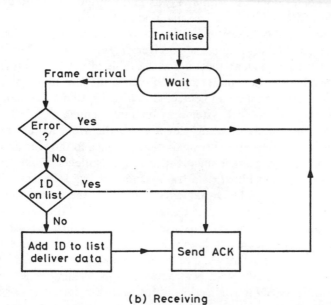

(b) Receiving

Figure 6.10 Non-sequential protocol flow diagrams

be found to enable recovery from this loss of data. This can be done in theory by associating a unique identifier with each frame which is transmitted on the link. Such an identifier is allocated to a block of data to be transmitted and placed in the frame level control field of the frame. The transmitter keeps a copy of the data and the identifier associated with it. The receiver checks this identifier in a received data frame. If it has not received a frame with the same identifier before, it considers this as a new frame and delivers the data to the higher level as well as returning a special acknowledgement frame to the transmitter. The acknowledgement frame contains no data. The frame level control field marks the frame as an acknowledgement type, and also returns the identifier of the frame received. The receiver also stores the identifier so that it can check if it receives a duplicate. If a duplicate is received the receiver returns an acknowledgement for it and discards it.

Upon transmission of a frame, the transmitter starts a timer associated with that frame which will expire after time t. If an acknowledgement from the receiver arrives before the timer expires, the copy of the data will be erased and the timer stopped. If no acknowledgement arrives within time t (which can occur if the data or the acknowledgement frame was corrupted on the link), the transmitter will retransmit the frame. Regardless of which kind of loss caused the retransmission it will result in the reception of an acknowledgement, provided that no further error occurs. This type of protocol can cause frames to be accepted at the receiver in a different sequence from that in which they were transmitted. For example, if frame A was transmitted before B but A was corrupted, then B is correctly received first and passed to the higher level. Figure 6.10 shows the logic of operations of this non-sequential procedure for the transmitter, Figure 6.10(a), and the receiver, Figure 6.10(b). The only synchronisation needed in this protocol is for the table of known identifiers at the receiver to be empty at the initial stage. Of course the idea of an infinite set of available identifiers cannot be implemented in a real system. We shall see later in this section how a practical system can be implemented.

In many systems it is necessary to preserve the sequence of transmitted packets. This can be achieved with small modifications to the scheme described above. We simply choose as the unique identifier the integers from 1 to infinity and assign these to transmitted data frames in ascending sequence. The transmitter sets a sequence number variable (SN) to 1 and the receiver an expected sequence number (ESN) to 1 on initialisation. SN=1 is allocated to the first frame to be transmitted and then incremented by 1. When the first frame is received at the receiver it checks that the SN of the frame is the same as its own ESN; accepts the frame, acknowledges it, and increases ESN by 1. The receiver will discard frames with SN < ESN as duplicates and acknowledge them again. Frames with SN > ESN indicate a loss of frame due to corruption and are also discarded by the receiver. The transmitter uses a time-out mechanism to retransmit unacknowledged frames. Figure 6.11 shows the operation of the

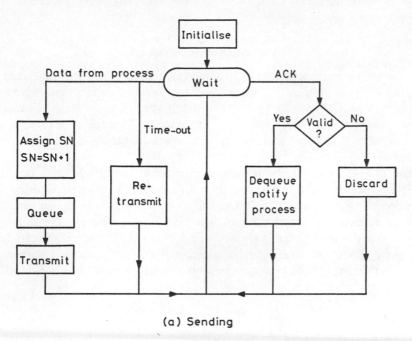

(a) Sending

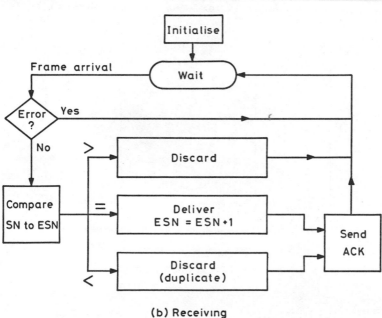

(b) Receiving

Figure 6.11   Sequential protocol flow diagrams

transmitter Figure 6.11(a) and receiver Figure 6.11(b) in the sequential link level protocol

The Alternating Bit Protocol

A practical implementation of a non-sequential protocol was described in Chapter 4.[1] This protocol has been used by, amongst others, the Advanced Research Project Agency's (ARPA) network in the USA and by the European Informatics Network (EIN) in Europe. Here we shall recapitulate some of the features of the protocol and explain its operation using a state diagram description.

The protocol operates by defining a number of logical channels (such as eight) and transmitting one frame at a time on each of these. During the operation of the protocol, data frames are transmitted on a logical channel, each frame carrying a parity bit, which alternates between successive data frames. When a data frame is transmitted with parity 0, the next data frame with parity 1 on the same logical channel will only be transmitted when an acknowledgement for the previous frame has been received. The parity of the

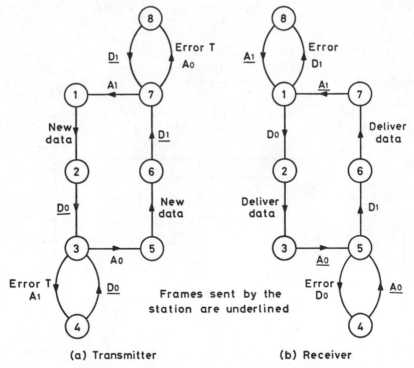

(a) Transmitter   (b) Receiver

Figure 6.12   Alternating bit protocol state diagrams

frame and the logical channel number on which it is transmitted are coded in the frame level control field. The use of more than one logical channel in this scheme ensures that no loss of link bandwidth occurs because of waiting for acknowledgement of a data frame transmitted in a logical channel. The syntax of this protocol is simple and comprises the definition of the data and acknowledgement frames. The semantics of the protocol are the actions associated with the transmission and receipt of these frames.

We shall describe the semantics of the protocol in terms of the state diagrams of the receiver and transmitter shown in Figure 6.12 for one of the logical channels. We assume that an initialisation procedure will synchronise transmitter and receiver so that each is in its respective 1 state. In this state the transmitter is waiting for data to transmit while the receiver is expecting a data packet with parity 0. In the figure this is shown by the notation D_0 on the arrow leaving state 1 of the receiver. Transmitted frames are shown by underlined symbols. On receipt of new data the transmitter enters state 2 and transmits the data frame. The transmission of data frame with parity 0 labelled D_0 causes the transmitter to enter state 3. A time-out counter is also started. When the receiver in state 1 receives frame D_0 it enters state 2, delivers the data to its destination, returns the acknowledgement A_0 and enters state 5. In this state it is waiting for the receipt of the next data frame with parity 1. The receipt of the acknowledgement at the transmitter causes the transition from state 3 to 5 after the previous data frame is deleted from the store. In state 5 the transmitter is waiting for data to transmit. This new data will now be transmitted with parity 1. The same operation is repeated for the parity 1 transmission. Thus during operation the data is sent in successive data frames which carry alternating parity.

If data or acknowledgement frames are corrupted on the link the time-out mechanism at the transmitter will cause it to retransmit the last transmitted data frame with the same parity. If the acknowledgement was lost then the receiver will get a duplicate copy of the frame last received and will enter error state 4 or 8 and retransmit the last acknowledgement, having discarded the duplicate frame. In the state diagram we have included a feature which, though not essential, can improve efficiency. This is that both transmitter and receiver retransmit their last transmitted frame when a frame is received in error at either. This can speed up error recovery when frames are corrupted. These actions are indicated by the transition marked 'Error' on the diagram.

One very remarkable feature of this protocol is that it will reach synchronisation even if it is not initialised but this can result in the loss of one frame of data. Figure 6.13 shows a program language description of the protocol using an Algol-like structure. The receiver coding is very simple requiring only a single procedure.

For full duplex data transfer a number of logical channels are implemented in each direction of the link. To improve the efficiency of the protocol a data frame carries the parity status of all the receivers at the end of the link from

RP = Receiver parity
TP = Transmitter parity
FP = Frame parity
AP = Acknowledgement parity
TS = Transmitter state
Initial conditions: RP $\neq$ TP, TS = READY

TRANSMITTER	RECEIVER
Transmit new frame	**Frame received**
IF TS=READY THEN	IF NO ERROR AND FP$\neq$RP THEN
BEGIN	BEGIN
FP:=TP;	DELIVER DATA;
	RP:=FP;
TRANSMIT FRAME;	END
QUEUE FRAME;	AP:=RP;
START TIMER;	SEND ACKNOWLEDGEMENT
TS:=NOT READY;	
END	

Receiving Acknowledgement
IF NO ERROR AND AP=TP THEN
  BEGIN
  DEQUEUE FRAME;
  STOP TIMER;
  TP:=MODULO 2 (TP+1);
  TS:=READY;
  END
ELSE RETRANSMIT;

Time-out
RETRANSMIT;

Retransmit
FP:=TP;
TRANSMIT QUEUED FRAME;
RESTART TIMER;

Figure 6.13   Alternating bit protocol program description

which it is transmitted. Therefore, when data flows in both directions, no special acknowledgement frames have to be sent if there is a data frame to transmit.

6.3 HIGH-LEVEL DATA LINK CONTROL PROCEDURES

A sequential link level protocol which has been the subject of standardisation by the International Standards Organisation (ISO) is the High-level Data Link Control (HDLC). It uses the bit-oriented framing structure which was described in the previous section. The syntax of the protocol is defined in 'Elements of procedure'[2] and the semantics are defined in 'Classes of procedure'.[3] The syntax is general enough to allow the definition of a number of link level protocols with different operational characteristics. As well as their importance as internationally agreed standards these protocols give a good insight into the mechanisms which can be employed at any level for error and flow control.

The frame structure, which appears as an independent ISO standard,[4] also defines the way in which the cyclic redundancy check is coded (see the Appendix, Section 6.6) and the coding of the two octets of frame level control. The word used to describe the cyclic redundancy check is *frame check sequence* (FCS). The first transmitted byte of the frame level control is used as an address field while the second is reserved for control and identifies the frame type. If required the address field can be extended to any number of octets. The control field associated with extended numbering is two octets long.

The Window Mechanism

We return now briefly to the more general problem of transporting a sequence of packets through a transmission medium that can cause corruption, duplication, loss, and out of order arrival of packets at their destination. The aim is to devise a protocol which can recover from all of these. Corruption of data can be detected by employing a cyclic redundancy check and discarding packets that have been received in error. In the previous section the general principle of operation of a procedure that preserves packet sequence was described. It required the sequential numbering of packets by the sender and the acceptance of packets by the receiver in sequence. Retransmission or timeout by the sender of packets not acknowledged would recover from packet loss.

In a practical implementation of a sequential procedure several modifications to this simple picture must be introduced. Some of these are to improve the efficiency of operation in particular situations. For example, if the procedure is implemented across a network the receiver might store packets received out of sequence until any missing ones arrive. This takes into consideration that the network can cause packets to arrive out of order. If the receiver always discards these the transmitter will be forced to retransmit unnecessarily and occupy more network resources. Other modifications have to be introduced in the packet numbering scheme because it is not feasible to employ a scheme which numbers packets from one to infinity.

Nevertheless it is worth considering the operation of infinite numbering schemes in more detail. One of the attractive features of such a hypothetical scheme is that no confusion can arise between any of the transmitted packets as they are all uniquely numbered. We assume that the two cooperating processes go through an initial connection phase after which the transmitter starts numbering its packets from one. At any instant of time, the transmitter has transmitted n packets for l of which it has received acknowledgements, where $l \leqslant n$. At the same instant the receiver has received and acknowledged m

packets, where $l \leqslant m \leqslant n$. Figure 6.14(a) shows the state of transmitter and receiver at time t. If the next frame received is not $m + 1$, it can be discarded or stored. If stored the receiver does not return an acknowledgement, other than for packets up to m, until the next expected frame $m + 1$ is received. The return of an acknowledgement with the number k implies that frames up to and including k have been correctly received. In many protocols (including HDLC) what is actually returned is the number of the next expected frame, in our example $k + 1$. When this is received by the sender it acknowledges all outstanding frames up to and including k.

In the distributed environment of computer networks, where no knowledge of the state of the transmission medium or the process at the other end is directly available, it is desirable to limit the number of packets that can be unacknowledged between any source and destination. This avoids flooding the transmission medium with packets that cannot be delivered to their destination at the speed

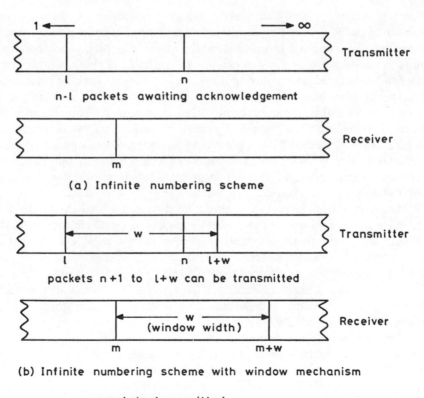

(a) Infinite numbering scheme

(b) Infinite numbering scheme with window mechanism

$l \leqslant m \leqslant n$ n-packets transmitted
l-packets transmitted and acknowledged
m-packets received and acknowledged

Figure 6.14   Infinite numbering scheme

with which the source can enter them. This maximum outstanding number of packets is referred to as the window w. If such a window is implemented in the example shown in Figure 6.14(a) the number of packets awaiting acknowledgement $(n - 1)$ is not allowed to exceed w, that is $(n - 1) \leqslant w$. This limit on the number of outstanding packets ensures that the lower levels in a network are not flooded by packets between a single source–destination pair. It also allows the receiver to do two things: to control the flow of information by delaying acknowledgements to the sender and to be able to allocate resources like storage sensibly as it cannot expect to receive more than the window width of w packets. The window mechanism is illustrated in Figure 6.14(b). The returning of an acknowledgement by the receiver will advance the receiver's window of expected packets. The receipt of an acknowledgement by the transmitter advances its window and allows it to send more packets. If at any time the transmitter has the maximum number of outstanding frames w, it must cease transmission until it receives acknowledgements from the receiver to advance its window.

The restriction on the number of outstanding frames imposed by the window mechanism provides an excellent way of controlling flows at any level. The window must be large enough so that under uncongested conditions of the transmission medium, and when the receiver can absorb the packets as fast as the source transmits, then the flow of packets is not inhibited. Under these conditions the window size is such that, before the sender has to stop transmitting, acknowledgements will have time to return to it and advance the window. Any slowing down of the acknowledgements by the receiver or increase of delays in the transmission medium due to congestion will have the desired effect of slowing down the flow. In the practical implementation of communication protocols where the numbering of packets is restricted to a finite range, the window also serves to avoid confusion between packets that by necessity carry the same number.

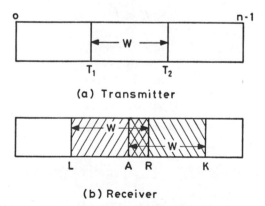

Figure 6.15   Modulo N numbering

When a finite number range is used packets are numbered modulo n from 0 to $n - 1$ and the packet following the $(n - 1)$th is numbered zero. Because of the time-out retransmission mechanism, the possibility exists of duplicate packets being generated by the sender. The window mechanism must be such as to separate the number range of new packets expected at the receiver and those that are retransmissions. Figure 6.15 illustrates the operation of modulo n numbering with window w.

At a certain instant the transmitter, in part (a), has received acknowledgements for all transmitted packets up to and including that with number T_1. It can therefore transmit packets $[T_1 + 1]_n$ to $T_2 = [T_1 + w]_n$ where the square bracket and subscript n denote modulo n arithmetic. At the same time the receiver, in part (b), has received all packets up to and including A and has returned an acknowledgement to the transmitter. If this acknowledgement has correctly reached its destination the transmitter can expect to receive new packets in the range $[A + 1]_n$ to $K = [A + w]_n$. If at that time the highest number received in that range is R, it implies that the left-hand bound of the transmitter $T_1 \geq L$ where $L = [R - w]_n$ therefore have the double inequality $L \leq T_1 \leq A$. This represents the receiver's view of the transmitter's window position. Another obvious inequality is $A \leq R$. The highest number of a new packet that can be received is K and the relative size of modulo numbering n and window w must be such as not to confuse this packet with a retransmission of the lowest number packet L. No confusion can arise if no zero is encountered in the process of obtaining the integer K from L by the repeated addition, modulo n, of one. In other words when L and K are in the same numbering sequence, all the frames that can be received have distinct numbers. We therefore have only to consider the case of an embedded zero between L and K. If there are n_1 frames on the left of zero up to L and n_2 frames on the right of zero up to K, we obtain $L = n - n_1$ and $K = n_2$. To ensure that no new or retransmitted packets bear the same number we must have

$$K < L$$

Therefore

$$n_2 < n - n_1$$

or

$$n_2 + n_1 < n$$

The total number of frames that can be received is:

$$N = n_1 + n_2 + 1$$

including the embedded zero.
We obtain

$$N < n + 1$$

or, as both N and n are integers:

$$N \leq n$$

From Figure 6.15(b) we see that N can take any value up to and including $2w$. The maximum value $2w$ is obtained when $A = R$. Therefore, if we are always to meet the criterion $N \leqslant n$ for distinguishing retransmitted and new packets, we must have $2w \leqslant n$. This gives us the maximum size of window, for it implies that

$$w \leqslant n/2$$

This relationship ensures that no confusion arises between new transmissions and retransmissions so that protocols can be built which store out of sequence arrivals to make the most efficient utilisation of resources. It must be pointed out that it offers no safeguard for the situation where the transport medium can delay the delivery of duplicate packets excessively.

In link level protocols the characteristics of the transmission medium are more predictable than those of a packet-switched network. The medium cannot cause out of order arrival of packets or frames, nor can it duplicate them. The maximum limit of response time can be calculated accurately and time-outs can be set for optimum error recovery. In HDLC, time-out recovery is in most cases a second order recovery mechanism and other methods are used in conjunction with it. We shall return to the error recovery mechanisms of HDLC later in this section. HDLC uses two alternative numbering schemes: one is modulo 8 and the other modulo 128. Figure 6.16 shows the coding of the control field for the data carrying or *information* frame for the modulo 8 numbering. The information frame type is identified by the zero in the first bit of the control field. The sequence number of the frame is coded in the 3-bit N(S) field where

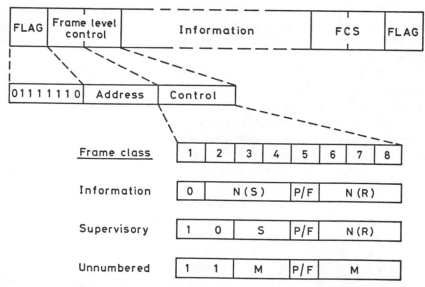

Figure 6.16   HDLC frame: coding of the control field

bit 2 is the low order bit. The next bit, bit 5, is a polling bit and we shall describe its function later. The last three bits (6–8) carry the next expected frame number for data flow in the opposite direction. This enables acknowledgements to be carried in information frames when these are passing in the opposite direction. Seven frames can be outstanding in HDLC with modulo 8 numbering and, although the receiver cannot distinguish in the event of error whether a frame is a new one or a retransmission, this is resolved by the transmitter when the response to the error is received. This can be achieved because sequence is preserved in the link and the receiver only accepts frames in sequence. We shall discuss this further when we return to error recovery in more detail.

For modulo 128 transmission the same format of the control field applies except that the fields for $N(S)$ and $N(R)$ are extended to 7 bits each and the control field now is 2 octets long. From now on in discussing HDLC we shall assume a modulo 8 numbering but all the arguments can be extended to modulo 128 operation. When no data is being transmitted in the other direction of a link a special supervisory frame is employed to carry the acknowledgement number $N(R)$.

Stations, Commands and Responses

The numbering and window mechanism of HDLC are described in the 'Elements of procedure', and are employed by all HDLC protocols. The elements of procedure also define a number of building blocks only a subset of which is used to define individual protocols. These building blocks are the HDLC stations and the frame types that can be exchanged between stations to accomplish the protocol functions. The ISO terminology for a protocol defined using these elements is *Class of procedure*.

Historically HDLC was developed for unbalanced link level operation with one master station on the link controlling one slave or a number of slaves. The master station is responsible for initiating all data transfers and for initialising and controlling the link. The master station in HDLC is called a *primary* and the slave a *secondary*. Two unbalanced HDLC configurations are shown in Figure 6.17: the first of these, Figure 6.17(a), shows a point-to-point link with a primary station at one end and a secondary at the other; the second, Figure 6.17(b) is a multidrop configuration with a number of secondary stations controlled by a single primary. This unbalanced link configuration is most suited to connecting unintelligent and semi-intelligent devices to a mainframe computer. In this situation the mainframe comprises the only intelligence in the system and it is reasonable that it has overall control of the terminals connecting to it either directly or through a front end.

In a distributed network the switching nodes of the communication subnet and the computers connecting through it are of equal status and every one needs

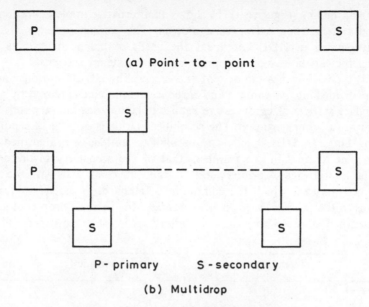

(a) Point - to - point

P - primary   S - secondary

(b) Multidrop

Figure 6.17   Unbalanced configurations

to have the ability to initiate link connection and disconnection. In this environment a balanced point-to-point link configuration is essential. This balanced mode of operation can be achieved by having a primary station at each end of the link which communicates with a secondary at the opposite end. The concept of the station now becomes very similar to that of a process. Figure 6.18(a) shows a balanced configuration implemented with a primary–secondary pair at

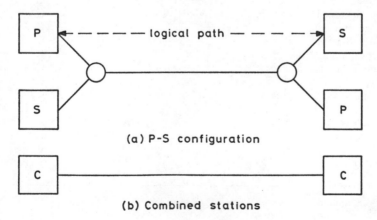

(a) P-S configuration

(b) Combined stations

Figure 6.18   Balanced configurations

each end of the link. Figure 6.18(b) shows an alternative implementation of the balanced system using a *combined station*. The combined station has been specially defined in HDLC to meet the needs of balanced systems and it combines the capabilities of both primary and secondary stations.

Many types of frames can be sent and received by HDLC stations and these types are divided into *commands* and *responses*. Commands are sent by primary to secondary stations. Responses are replies to commands and are sent from a secondary to a primary station. The combined station is capable of sending and receiving both. In HDLC only the secondary stations are identified by an address. The address in the frame is that of the secondary involved in the particular interchange. A primary station transmits commands with the address of the secondary for which the command is intended. A secondary transmits responses to the primary with its own address. In the multidrop configuration illustrated in Figure 6.17(b) each secondary station has a distinct address. A

Name	Mnemonic	Function
Information	I	C/R
Supervisory		
Receive ready	RR	C/R
Receive not ready	RNR	C/R
Reject	REJ	C/R
Selective reject	SREJ	C/R
Unnumbered		
Set normal response mode (extended)	SNRM	C
Set asynchronons response mode (extended)	SARM(E)	C
Set asynchronous balance mode (extended)	SABM(E)	C
Disconnect	DISC	C
Set initialisation mode	SIM	C
Request initialisation mode	RIM	R
Unnumbered poll	UP	C
Reset	RSET	C
Unnumbered information	UI	C/R
Exchange identification	XID	C/R
Unnumbered acknowledgement	UA	R
Disconnected mode	DM	R
Request disconnect	RD	R
Frame reject	FRMR	C/R

C—command;   R—response;   C/R—can be used as either

Figure 6.19   HDLC frames

secondary acts on command from the primary which contains its own address and replies with a response containing the same address. In the balanced configurations, Figure 6.18, each end of the link has a unique address (again associated with the secondary function) and commands are sent by each with the other's address while responses contain the sending end's address. This distinction of commands from responses via the address field in the case of point-to-point balanced configuration is necessary because in an HDLC class of procedure the same frame type can be used as command or response with different effect on the protocol operation.

The complete set of frame types is shown in Figure 6.19 which also indicates whether they can be used as commands, responses or both. The frame types are also classified as *information, supervisory* or *unnumbered* and are distinguished according to the formats shown in Figure 6.16. The setting to 0 of the first bit of the control field identifies information frames. Supervisory and unnumbered frames are identified by the presence of 1 in the first bit of the control field and are distinguished from each other by the value of the second bit which is set to 0 for supervisory and 1 for unnumbered frames. There is only one frame of the information type and this is the frame which carries the data or packets across the link. The 2-bit supervisory function (S) field in the supervisory frames allows four types of these frames to be defined. They are all associated with the control of data flow and recovery from loss of data due to corruption of information frames. All four carry the N(R) number which indicates the expected information frame number. The 5-bit modifier (M) field in the unnumbered frames allows the definition of up to 32 frames. Twenty of these frames have been defined and are primarily for setting up, closing down, and reporting the state of the link level procedure. Figure 6.20 shows the coding of the S and M fields for all the types of HDLC frame.

The fifth bit of the control field is used to implement polling and check pointing mechanisms. This bit is known as a *poll* bit when used in commands and a *final* bit when used in responses. A secondary or combined station receiving a command with the poll bit set to 1 must at the earliest opportunity reply with a response with the final bit set to 1.

We shall now look in more detail into the use of the various frame types in HDLC.

Modes of Operation

The origins of HDLC lie in link level protocols for unbalanced multidrop configurations. For this reason, what is referred to as the *normal response mode* (NRM) of operation is that the secondary transmits responses to a poll from the primary. In a configuration operating in this mode a secondary obtains permission to transmit frames when it receives a command from its primary with the poll bit set. It will then transmit a series of frames and indicate

Frame	S-bits	
	3	4
RR	0	0
RNR	0	1
REJ	1	0
SREJ	1	1

Supervisory

Frame		M-bits				
		3	4	6	7	8
SNRM		0	0	0	0	1
SARM	DM	1	1	0	0	0
SABM		1	1	1	0	0
SNRME		1	1	0	1	1
SARME		1	1	0	1	0
SABME		1	1	1	1	0
DISC	RD	0	0	0	1	0
SIM	RIM	1	0	0	0	0
UP		0	0	1	0	0
UI		0	0	0	0	0
XID		1	1	1	0	1
RSET		1	1	0	0	1
FRMR		1	0	0	0	1
UA		0	0	1	1	0

Unnumbered

Figure 6.20 HDLC frames: table of control field codings

completion of this transmission cycle by setting the final bit to 1 in the last frame of the transmitted sequence. This hands control back to the primary and the secondary must wait for another poll before it can transmit again. If a secondary has no data to transmit it will hand control back to the primary immediately by returning a receive ready (RR) frame with the final bit set to 1.

As well as the normal response mode there also exists an *asynchronous response mode* (ARM). In this mode a secondary can transmit at will and does not have to wait for a poll from the primary. Point-to-point balanced or unbalanced configurations can be operated using this mode. Multidrop configurations are sometimes operated in what is known as contention mode where the stations connected together can transmit freely. Two stations transmitting simultaneously will cause corruption of data. Contention mode can only operate successfully when this probability of simultaneous transmission is small. One can therefore see a small proportion of applications that might require to operate in ARM on multidrop configurations and this is not forbidden by HDLC. In a protocol operating in either response mode stations can request the transmission of frames simultaneously. Nevertheless the protocol can be implemented on half as well as full duplex lines. It is a lower level function, implemented possibly in hardware to arrange alternate transmission on half duplex lines.

Before a link protocol can start operating the two ends must synchronise by initialising their respective transmit and receive sequence numbers for information frames. They can use the same mechanism to resynchronise in the event of an error which cannot be recovered by the protocol itself. The setting mode commands shown in Figure 6.19 are used for this purpose. Three pairs of commands are used to indicate to the other end not only the basic mode of operation (normal or asynchronous), but also the type of station and the numbering scheme (normal or extended). This is a useful feature when communicating in a circuit-switched environment where you do not know the communication protocol employed by the remote station. A primary sends a set normal response mode (SNRM) to set up the link operating in the normal response mode with a numbering scheme modulo 8. Alternatively it will transmit set asynchronous response mode (SARM) to operate in the asynchronous response mode. Combined stations only operate in asynchronous response mode and are distinguished from primary–secondary operation by sending *set asynchronous balanced mode* (SABM). All three modes of operation can work with modulo 128 numbering and the commands used for this are, *set normal response mode extended* (SNRME), *set asynchronous response mode extended* (SARME) and *set balance response mode extended* (SBRME). When a set mode command is sent to a secondary or combined station it responds with an unnumbered acknowledgement (UA) to complete the operation.

For stations operating in extended mode the control field is extended to 2 octets to accommodate the seven bit number fields in the information and supervisory frames. The extra octet remains unused in the unnumbered frames. The control field formats for extended mode of operations are shown in Figure 6.21 where the bits marked X are unused.

Frame Rejection

An HDLC procedure works in one of the six modes of operation and must include in its vocabulary the appropriate set mode command, the UA response and the disconnect (DISC) command. The DISC command is sent by a primary or combined station to close down the link operation. Further unnumbered

Frame class	Control field bits															
	1	2	3	4	5	6	7	8	9	10	11	12	13	14	15	16
Information	0		N (S)						P/F			N (R)				
Supervisory	1	0	S	S	X	X	X	X	P/F			N (R)				
Unnumbered	1	1	M	M	U	M	M	M		X	X	X	X	X	X	X

U- unspecified , X - reserved and set to zero

Figure 6.21   HDLC extended mode of operation: control field

frames can be included in the procedure to provide extra functions. In the majority of the unnumbered frames the information field is not present. In the few that do contain an information field, it forms an extension of the control field to carry data for the link level operation, unlike that of the information (I) frame itself which is transparent to the link level procedure.

One of the unnumbered frames which is contained in most procedures is *frame reject* (FRMR). This can be used as either a command, a response or both. This frame type was originally defined as a response only. When used as such it is still referred to as *command reject* (CMDR). Its function is to allow the receiver to inform the transmitter of the receipt of a frame that either cannot be understood or contravenes a rule of the protocol. If the offending frame is a command then a FRMR (CMDR) response is returned; if it is a response a FRMR command is returned. The frame reject is one of the unnumbered commands which contains an information field, the size of which is 20 bits or 36 bits for modulo 8 or modulo 128 (extended) mode of operation respectively. For a particular implementation these fields can be padded with zeros to match the character width being used. Figure 6.22 shows the format of the FRMR information field. The first 8 bits (16 bits for extended mode) contain the control field of the received frame which caused the FRMR transmission. Each of the last four bits when set to 1 specifies the reason for the rejection of the frame as follows:

W indicates either an invalid frame or an HDLC frame that is not part of the subset implemented by the station.

X indicates that the frame contained an information field which is not permitted for its type.

Y indicates an information frame with a data field which exceeded the maximum data field that can be accommodated by the station.

Z indicates that the control field contained an N(R), the number of the next expected frame, which acknowledges frames that have not been transmitted.

If all these bits are set to 0 the frame is rejected for an unspecified reason.

The N(S) and N(R) returned with the FRMR are the numbers of the frame next to be transmitted and next expected respectively at the station sending the FRMR.

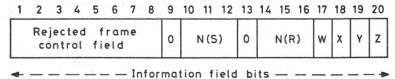

Figure 6.22   HDLC frame reject: information field format

When a station sends a FRMR it enters a 'frame rejection' condition and expects to receive a set mode command to reinitialise the link. In the primary–secondary configuration only the FRMR response (CMDR) is employed. It acts as a request by the secondary for reinitialisation as well as providing the primary with information about why this is necessary. The inclusion of the secondary's next expected frame N(R) in the CMDR indicates to the primary which information (I) frames have been correctly received by the secondary prior to issuing the CMDR. Once the CMDR is issued no other I frames are accepted by the secondary except to make use of the acknowledgement number contained in the N(R) assuming that the CMDR was not issued because of a bad N(R) count in the first instance. The inclusion of the secondary's next frame to be transmitted allows the primary to compute whether all information frames that have been transmitted were correctly received, before the CMDR was issued. The returning of the control field of the offending command enables a monitor process at the primary to diagnose any incompatibilities of operation between the two stations.

The Rest of the Unnumbered Frames

The *unnumbered information* frame (UI), which can be a command or a response, allows data to be transmitted outside the HDLC window mechanism. Such data is protected by CRC and when corrupted on the line will be lost and not recovered at the link level. One of the uses envisaged for this facility is in facsimile transmission where each information frame might carry a single line for a picture and the loss of it does not greatly affect the final result.

The *unnumbered poll* command (UP) can be used by a primary or combined station to send a poll instead of using the P bit in one of the other commands. The poll bit in the UP command must be set to 1. A primary can send this command with a group address polling a number of secondaries at the same time. Therefore it provides a group poll capability. This command does not contain an information field.

The *set initialisation mode* command (SIM) is used to reinitialise the link and in that respect it performs the same function as a set mode command. The difference between the two is that SIM also initiates station-specified procedures to initialise other link level control functions which are implementation dependent. The operation is completed by the receipt of a UA response. *Request initialisation mode* response (RIM) is sent by a secondary to prompt its primary to send a SIM command.

The *reset* command (RSET) is used by a combined station during the data transfer phase to reinitialise the data flow only in one direction of the link. The data flow from the station that has issued the RSET is initialised. Its effect for that direction of flow is identical to issuing a set mode command.

The *exchange identification* command and response (XID) is used by the stations to exchange information on the capability of each. These frames can contain an information field, the format and contents of which are defined by the class of procedure using this facility. The XID response is sent as a reply to the XID command.

A combined or secondary station can send a *request disconnect* response (RD) to ask to be placed in disconnected mode. This should result in a DISC command closing down the communication link. A station in a disconnected mode does not wish to set the link up and send or receive information. It replies to set mode commands with a *disconnected mode* response (DM). The DM response has one further use. When sent unsolicited to a primary station when the link is not set up, it is interpreted as a request to that primary to set up the link by sending a set mode command.

Classes of Procedure

The types of stations, the operational modes and the large number of frame types described above might not only confuse the reader but also the implementer of HDLC procedures. They can also be combined in a variety of ways to produce a variety of protocols. The classes of procedure define a well-ordered structure for choosing these protocols. They do not attempt to provide an implementation guide for any single HDLC protocol.

We have seen that control is vested in the primary station and response in the secondary station while the combined station has both. Any station included in a link procedure can also act as a source or sink of data or both. Let us consider two examples. First the unbalanced configuration shown in Figure 6.17(a) comprising a primary and secondary station, one at each end of the link. If we wish to use this for transporting data in one direction, say from secondary to primary, then the primary acts as a sink of data only, while the secondary acts as a source. To achieve this function we need to define an HDLC procedure in which the information (I) frame is used as a response only. For transporting data in both directions then primary and secondary act as both source and sink and the I frame must be both a command and a response. For our second example we consider the balanced configuration of Figure 6.18(a) comprising a primary and secondary pair at each end of the link. In a balanced configuration the capability of each end is the same, therefore in any non-trivial configuration we must have both source and sink capability at each end of the link. We can achieve this by giving the primaries source and the secondaries sink capability and using the I frame as a command only. Figure 6.23 shows the HDLC station building blocks.

Having chosen the station configurations, their role as sources or sinks of data and the mode of operation, one has chosen the basic frame types of an HDLC procedure. For example, if the I frame is only a command then the frame which acknowledges correct receipt of data, that is the *receive ready*

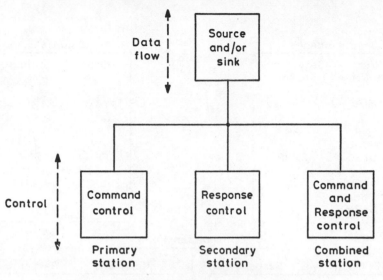

Figure 6.23   HDLC stations

(RR), needs to be only a response. The classes of procedure define a basic repertoire of frames to be used for constructing both unbalanced and balanced classes of procedure. Twelve optional functions are also provided which modify this basic repertoire either by adding frames or deleting frames. Figure 6.24 shows the proposed structure of the basic repertoire and optional functions to be used in the classes of procedure.

Information Transfer and Error Recovery

We shall describe the data transfer phase of the protocol by means of an example with information flow in one direction. The configuration we shall describe is unbalanced point-to-point as shown in Figure 6.17(a). We shall also consider error recovery and discover that once again HDLC has a variety of offerings to suit all tastes. In the example the primary acts as a sink and the secondary as a source of data, so the information frame is a response. The link operates in the asynchronous response mode, therefore the secondary can transmit to the primary at will. The physical link is capable of two-way simultaneous transmission. Each end of the link transmits contiguous flags, which indicate the 'active channel state', whenever it is capable of operating.

When the line from the secondary is in the 'active channel state' the primary can initiate the setting-up procedure by transmitting a SARM command. This, as all other commands, will contain the address of the secondary. When transmitting the set mode command the primary starts a time-out mechanism, which will trigger a retransmission of the command if no response is received

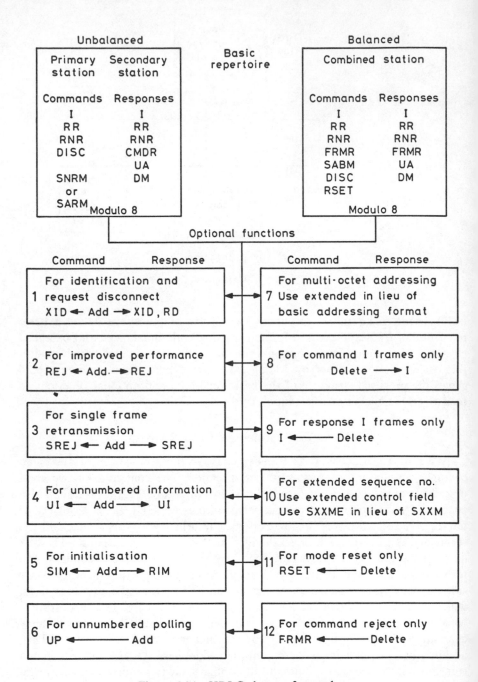

Figure 6.24 HDLC classes of procedure

from the secondary within time t. The value of t is a function of the link speed and must be large enough to allow sufficient time for the response to return to the primary. When the secondary receives the SARM it has one of two choices. If the protocol includes the *disconncted mode* (DM) response, it can reply with DM indicating to the primary that it is not prepared to set up the link at the present time. If it is prepared to set up the link then the secondary responds with an *unnumbered acknowledgement* (UA). As the secondary acts as a source of data it has associated with it a send state variable $V(S)$ which it sets to zero when responding with UA. When the primary, acting as a sink, receives the UA response it sets a receive state variable $V(R)$ to zero. The receipt of the UA response complctcs the setting-up and initialisation procedure. If the SARM command is corrupted on the link it will be discarded by the secondary and will be retransmitted after time-out by the primary. If the UA returning to the primary is corrupted, the situation is slightly more complex, because the secondary, as soon as it returns a UA and sets its send state variable to zero, can start transmitting data in I frames. This can result in an information frame being received by the primary before the setting up is completed. To avoid confusion the primary ignores any frames received correctly other than a UA after sending SARM. It will eventually time-out and retransmit the set mode command. It is worth noting that the possibility of receiving data frames before completing the set-up procedure in this example could be avoided if the primary was the source of data.

When the link set up procedure is completed satisfactorily the secondary can start transmitting I frames. Before transmission the I frame is given a sequence number $N(S)$ equal to the current value of the send state variable $V(S)$ and $V(S)$ is then incremented by 1, using modulo 8 addition. The information part of the frame and the number, $N(S)$, associated with it are stored until an acknowledgement is received from the primary indicating that the frame has been correctly received. With modulo 8 numbering a maximum of seven frames can be outstanding awaiting acknowledgement. When the primary receives an I frame it will check whether the sequence number of the frame is equal to that of the expected frame. That is to say if the $N(S)$ of the frame is equal to $V(R)$, the primary's receive state variable, the primary will then accept the I frame and pass the data contained in it to the level above it. The receive state variable will be incremented by 1 modulo 8. After $V(R)$ is incremented, a receive ready (RR) command, with $N(R)$ set equal to $V(R)$, the number of the next expected frame, is returned to the secondary to acknowledge the receipt of the information frame. A station receiving an information frame with the correct sequence number is not obliged to accept it. It can if necessary stop the data flow by returning a receive not ready (RNR) frame. What it must do, when receiving an I frame with the expected sequence number, if it wishes to stop the data flow, is either to accept that frame and acknowledge it as above using an RNR or not accept it and simply return an RNR with $N(R)$ equal to the V(R) which has not been updated by the receipt of the I frame. As soon as the data sink is again prepared to receive data it sends an RR to the source. When the source receives an RNR it will stop transmitting I frames until it receives an RR. This can cause a deadlock situation if this RR is corrupted on the link and never received. To avoid this, a procedure that can be followed is for the source to keep retransmitting the frame next expected by the sink at fixed intervals of time. When this is received, if the sink is still in a receive not ready state, it will retransmit RNR, otherwise it will accept and acknowledge the frame with an RR. The deadlock danger now disappears because the changing from receive not ready state does not rely on a single event involving the transmission of a frame that can be corrupted.

HDLC provides four methods for recovering from loss of I frames. These methods are not all entirely independent. The most basic of them is the time-out recovery which has been discussed earlier in the context of other link level protocols. In HDLC a station transmitting I frames starts a time-out counter on transmission of the first data frame. Subsequently if the timer is running on transmission of an I frame, it implies that previously transmitted I frames are awaiting acknowledgement, and no further action is taken. When an N(R) is received, in any supervisory frames, acknowledging *some* of the oustanding I frames, the time-out counter is restarted; if it acknowledges all the outstanding I frames the timer is stopped. It will be restarted when a new I frame is transmitted. In our example with flow in one direction the N(R) field of the I frame is unused, but for full duplex information transfer the N(R) of the I frame always contains the current value of the receive state variable V(R) of the transmitting station. Therefore, if an I frame is available for transmission when an acknowledgement has to be returned to the other station, the I frame is transmitted instead of an RR frame. The N(R) count received at a source acknowledges the correct receipt of all previously transmitted and unacknowledged frames up to but not including frame number equal to N(R). If the timeout counter expires at a data source the station will initiate retransmission of unacknowledged I frames.

To improve the efficiency of the error recovery mechanism the capability of sending negative acknowledgements is provided in the protocol. Two supervisory frames are included for this purpose, these are *reject* (REJ) and *selective reject* (SREJ). If an I frame is discarded by a station because of a frame check sequence (FCS) error then the next I frame received will not be the expected frame and the sequence number N(S) will be different from the receive state variable V(R) of the station. This and subsequent frames can be discarded awaiting the retransmission on time-out of the missing frame followed by the discarded frames. With the negative acknowledgement capability provided by the REJ frame, the sink, as soon as it receives an out-of-sequence frame, replies with REJ containing in the reject frame's N(R) field the current value of the receive state variable. The receiving station will then discard all other I frames with no further action until it receives the frame with the expected sequence number. When a REJ frame has been sent no other reject can be issued until the frame number referred to in the N(R) of the REJ frame is received. The time-out mechanism must still be employed to recover in situations where the REJ frame is corrupted on the link. A station receiving REJ will first process the N(R) carried by it which acknowledges all previously transmitted I frames up to and including frame numbered $[N(R) - 1]_8$. It will then start retransmitting all I frames from N(R) upwards. If when the station receives REJ it is transmitting an I frame it can, if it wishes, abort that transmission which is now wasting link bandwidth. Aborting a frame is accomplished by transmitting at least seven contiguous one bits without inserting zeros. Receipt of seven contiguous one bits is interpreted as an abort and the receiving station ignores the frame. The abort mechanism is provided in the large-scale integrated chips which perform the framing and polynomial check sequence function.

Link efficiency can be improved even further by using the selective reject (SREJ) capability. In this case a station expecting frame number L and receiving frame $[L + 1]_8$ accepts this and subsequent frames but issues a selective reject with N(R) equal to L. When the source station receives the SREJ it only retransmits the frame with the same number as the N(R) of the SREJ frame. Only one selective reject at a time can be outstanding. The SREJ capability is most useful for very long terrestrial links or satellite links where the transmission medium can store a large number of frames. In such cases the extended numbering scheme is used and the source station can transmit a large number of frames before an indication of whether a frame has been correctly received reaches it from the sink.

The final scheme that can be employed by HDLC procedures for error recovery is poll/final bit checkpointing. This works on the following principle for a source which is a primary or combined station, i.e. has command capability. The station sets the poll bit to 1 in a command it transmits. A station is not allowed to send a second command with the poll bit set until it receives a reply to the first poll in a response with the final bit set. Only in the event of a time-out occurring can it repeat a poll command even if it had no response to the previous poll. This is done to cope with the situation where either the command carrying the poll or the response containing the reply was corrupted on the link. The station receiving the polling command must reply at the earliest opportunity with a response with the final bit set. The response that will contain the final bit during the normal data transfer phase will be either an information frame or a supervisory frame containing an N(R) with the current value of the receiver state variable V(R). If I frames in the direction of transmission of the poll command have not been hit by errors then the N(R) contained in the response with the final bit set must acknowledge all I frames transmitted before or concurrently with the frame carrying the poll. If it does not acknowledge these frames then an error must have occurred and the station which issued the poll will start retransmitting frames from the one numbered N(R), the number contained in the response with the final bit set.

The above error recovery procedures can be combined to produce a protocol that is robust and efficient. They must nevertheless be combined carefully to avoid interference between them, which on certain occasions can cause erroneous behaviour of the protocol. As an example we consider one such case. To illustrate our example we shall use the format adopted in an Annex to the HDLC 'elements of procedure' which contains a large number of typical situations encountered under the various operational modes. Figure 6.25 shows the notation used to describe the frames. In the actual examples the activity of a station is marked on a horizontal axis which indicates time. Each example shows the cooperating station at each end of the link with two horizontal axes showing each one's activity. The beginning of the frame indicated by a short vertical line shows the time at which the transmission of a frame begins; the end of the frame indicated by a similar vertical line marks the time at which the frame has arrived completely at the receiver. A more correct, but less useful, interpretation of the times is that they represent the starting and closing flag of frames at some point on the link. Let us now consider a special situation in our example of one way data transfer and see how we can recover from an error situation using firstly REJ as primary error recovery mechanism and time-out as secondary and secondly SREJ and time-out. The particular situation is shown in Figure 6.26. The secondary station has transmitted a series of very short I frames. The primary has been busy in receiving these and has only had the opportunity to acknowledge them when the secondary stops transmission having sent the maximum number of frames allowed. The acknowledgement gets corrupted on the link and the secondary soon times out and starts retransmitting from frame

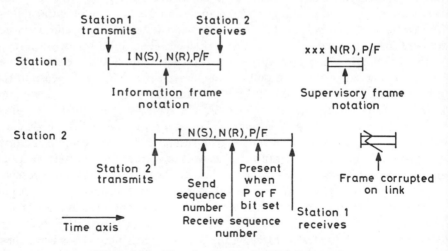

Figure 6.25   Notation for use in HDLC examples

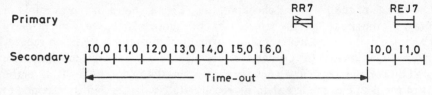

Figure 6.26   Error recovery using reject and time-out

number 0. When the primary receives the frame zero again it treats it as a new frame and assumes that frame number 7 was corrupted. This is a misinterpretation of the real situation. If the primary uses the REJ command this should not matter. The primary will respond with REJ with N(R) equal to 7 and ignore subsequent I frames until 7 arrives. Receipt of the REJ at the secondary will acknowledge all outstanding frames and retransmission will cease, recovering link synchronisation. The REJ itself does not cause retransmissions because no outstanding frames remain. If SREJ was used instead of REJ then confusion could arise because the I frames retransmitted after time-out will be again interpreted by the primary as new frames and this time they will be stored as such and a SREJ issued to recover the supposedly lost frame number 7. This occurs because no unique separation exists in the transmission window between the numbers of retransmitted and new I frames. This, coupled with the fact that the time-out error recovery mechanism can cause the retransmission of I frames already correctly received, can confuse the situation. Nevertheless it is essential to employ a time-out mechanism. This is to enable recovery when control frames are lost or when the last I frame in a sequence of frames is discarded owing to errors on the link. In the latter case the receiver has no way of detecting the loss as no out-of-sequence frame is received.

To avoid confusions arising from retransmission on time-out the HDLC specification recommends that instead of a secondary station retransmitting the total number of outstanding frames: either the last transmitted frame is retransmitted or if available a new frame is transmitted assuming the number of outstanding frames awaiting acknowledgement is less than eight. A receiving station which employs SREJ should not respond with it when receiving an I frame with an N(S) one less than the receive state variable. Returning to our example of Figure 6.26 the use of SREJ will now cause no confusion. The secondary will retransmit I frame 6 and the primary will not respond with SREJ as 6 is one less than its V(S). This still does not resolve the deadlock. What will actually happen is that the secondary will retransmit on time-out N times and then declare the link as non-operational. Or it could be that a station using SREJ also employs REJ and responds with this in the above situation, resolving the deadlock. It is more satisfactory in error recovery if the source of data has command capability, i.e. it is either a primary or combined station. The station may then enquire on time-out the status of its partner with a supervisory frame and make use of the poll/final checkpointing. This is shown in the example of Figure 6.27; the situation is the same as that of Figure 6.26, but now the primary is the source and the secondary would normally respond with SREJ to recover from error. On time-out the primary retransmits the last transmitted frame with the poll bit set; the secondary when it receives this does not send a SREJ as the N(S) of the frame is one less than its receive state variable, but it responds to the poll bit by sending an RR with the final bit set. When this is received at the primary it acknowledges all outstanding frames and no retransmission is initiated by the poll/final bit checkpointing.

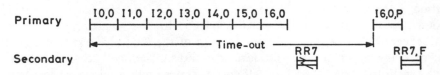

Figure 6.27 Improved time-out recovery using poll/final checkpointing

Data Flow in both Directions

In the unbalanced configuration that we have been discussing, with a primary communicating to a secondary, full duplex data transfer is achieved by employing the I, RR, RNR and REJ or SREJ frames as both commands and responses. Each direction of flow has its own pair of send and receive state variables. At each station, primary or secondary, the V(R) of one direction and the V(S) of the other direction of flow are stored. In the case of an I frame the N(R) and N(S) of the frame carry the current values of these variables. V(S) is increased by 1 modulo 8 after transmission of an I frame.

In the balanced configuration shown in Figure 6.18(a) each primary–secondary pair at opposite ends of the link handles one direction of

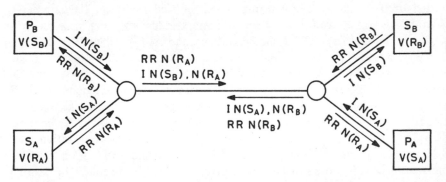

Figure 6.28 Data transfer in full duplex balanced configuration using primary secondary pairs

transmission. The difference between the balanced configuration and the combined station is in the setting up and disconnecting of the link. The data transfer phase of the link is similar in both. Figure 6.28 shows the logical and physical flow of I and RR frames for the primary–secondary configuration. Primary P_A communicates with secondary S_A. The primary acts as a source of data and the I frame is a command, while the secondary is the sink and RR frames are responses. Although logically the data flows and their control are independent, advantage is taken of the flow in the opposite direction. If a secondary, say S_A dispatches an RR, this is not transmitted if the primary of that end of the link, P_B, has I frames to transmit. The $N(R_A)$ of the RR is carried in the I frame from P_B. This figure can be seen as logically describing the operation of the combined station, showing the receive and transmit functions separately.

The setting-up procedure of the primary–secondary combination for balanced operation is shown in Figure 6.29(a). The primary P_A at one end of the link sends a SARM command and starts its time-out counter. Receipt of a UA from the distant secondary causes it to set its send state variable $V(S_A)$ to zero and completes the set-up cycle. If no UA is received before the time-out expires the primary will retransmit SARM. SARM is retransmitted if necessary N times after which the primary stops and the link is declared as unusable. When a SARM is received and the link is not set up, it will act as a trigger for a SARM to be sent by the primary of that end of the link, to set up the other direction of flow. It will also be passed to the secondary which will set its receive state variable $V(R_A)$ to zero and respond with a UA. If a SARM is sent by any primary during the data transfer phase then it acts as a reset for one direction of flow. It is normal practice in HDLC that the receipt of a set mode command during data transfer phase reinitialises the link and is used as a means of resynchronising.

There is a danger in using this to reset one direction of flow. If there is an instantaneous loss of power at one end of the link, when power is restored the initialisation procedure will come into effect. In our example it will send SARM.

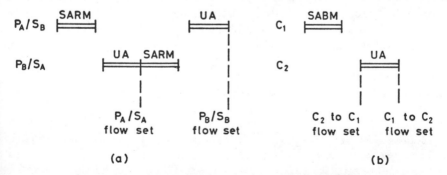

Figure 6.29   Balanced configuration setting-up procedures

The other end of the link will not have noticed anything wrong and will interpret this as a reset in one direction and simply respond with a UA. The end experiencing problems has now no way to initiate reinitialisation of both directions of flow. It is for this reason that the set mode command is better used as a global reset and the RSET command employed for reinitialising one direction of flow.

Figure 6.29(b) shows the setting-up procedure for the combined station configuration. Here a single SABM sets up the link. Receipt of SABM causes a combined station to set to zero both its send and receive state variables and respond with UA. The receipt of UA sets these variables to zero at the station which initiated the set mode command.

To close down the link in similar fashion to the set mode command procedure the primary–secondary pair has to exchange a pair of DISC commands acknowledged by UA responses. The combined station needs only to send one DISC acknowledged by one UA response. In the balanced configuration either end of the link can initiate the setting-up procedure by sending set mode commands. Similarly either end can reset or close down the link.

6.4   THE X25 INTERFACE

Packet-switched communication subnets offer computers and terminals connection at a variety of levels and interfaces. The internal structure of the subnet is independent of these interfaces. The experimental packet-switched networks that came into operation in the late nineteen-sixties and early nineteen-seventies employed a datagram transport mechanism in which the packets made their way through the communication subnet independently of each other. Each packet carried a destination address which was used at intermediate nodes to choose an output link according to a routing algorithm. Although the transport mechanism was the same in all these networks there were substantial differences in the interface they offered to the host computers. The ARPA communication subnet, for example, has knowledge of associations or links between processes established across the network. It controls the flow of packets at the host-to-network interface on individual association basis by accepting messages. The association between processes is established between the hosts by the host-to-host protocol without the participation of the subnet but the subnet needs to have knowledge of the association once established. The ARPA procedures bear a similarity to the virtual call concept although the transport mechanism is purely datagram. The Cyclades network in France and the European Informatics

Figure 6.30   Datagram format

Network (EIN) offer their host computers a simple datagram interface through which packets with full addresses flow independently of each other. Figure 6.30 shows a possible format for packets across such a datagram host-to-network interface. A source and destination address is included in each packet. The facilities field contains requests for special network services. Some examples of these are the delivery confirmation, which invokes the return of a control packet by the network to the source host to indicate successful delivery of the packet, and the non-delivery diagnostic which results in a network response to the source when a packet cannot be delivered to the destination. The non-delivery diagnostic packet will indicate to the source the reason for non-delivery and return the identifier field of the original datagram. This field allows the source host to identify the packet referred to in the non-delivery diagnostic.

The worldwide adoption of packet switching technology saw the standardisation by CCITT of a single packet level protocol for interfacing to public data networks. It has also led to a new type of packet-switched communication subnet pioneered by the French postal administration in the Transpac network. This network controls the flow of data within the subnet by establishing a chain of virtual calls along the path of the data. Other networks offering public services, for example Datapac in Canada, operate internally in the datagram mode. The French Transpac solution has also been adopted for a communication subnet to connect a number of data bases in the European Economic Community (EEC), the Euronet project.

The CCITT recommendation which defines the user-to-network interface or, in CCITT terminology, the interface between *data terminal equipment* (DTE) and *data circuit terminating equipment* (DCE), is known as the X25 recommendation.[5] The CCITT practice is to define a number of services, the facilities offered by the services and how these facilities are accessed by the subscribers. The X series recommendations relate to data transmission. The first of these recommendations X1[5] defines the international classes of service in terms of link speeds and their usage, e.g. asynchronous, synchronous. These services are to be offered on digital data networks and packet-switched networks.

User class of service	Data signalling rate (synchronous) bits/sec
8	2 400
9	4 800
10	9 600
11	48 000

Figure 6.31 CCITT recommendation X1: user classes of service for public data networks. Packet mode of operation

The recommendation specifies four speeds of operation for connecting to packet-switched networks. These are user classes 8 to 11 and are shown in Figure 6.31

Recommendation X2 defines the facilities to be offered by the various services and Figure 6.32 is a table of these facilities for the packet mode of

User facilities	Classes of service			
	1-7	8-11		
		DG	VC	PVC
Assigned for an agreed contractual period				
Permanent virtual circuit PVC	E	-	-	E
Closed user group	E	A	E	-
Closed user group with outgoing access	A	A	A	-
Packet assembly and/or disassembly	E	-	-	-
On per call basis				
Abbreviated address calling	A	FS	FS	-
Datagram (DG)	FS	A	-	-
Virtual call (VC)	E	-	E	-

−not applicable   E - international facility   FS-for further study
A-optional national or international facility

Figure 6.32   CCITT Recommendation X2: packet-switched services user facilities

operation. Three basic facilities are defined. The first is the datagram (DG) which will allow the subscriber to receive and send self-contained packets from and to anywhere else in the network. The second is the permanent virtual circuit (PVC) which allows two DTEs to have a permanent association on respective logical channels. They exchange a number of packets on these channels; the network undertakes to deliver these to their destination in the same order as they entered the network. It also incorporates the notion of a sequence of packets and the user can mark a number of consecutive packets as such. This indication is passed on to the destination. The third facility is the virtual call (VC) which is the switched equivalent of the PVC. While in a PVC the association between two DTEs is always present; in the VC the association is established for a period of time and then terminated. Figure 6.32 shows that some of the packet-switched facilities can be accessed via classes of service 1–7, the asynchronous and synchronous classes for the circuit-switched services. Of particular interest is the *packet assembly–disassembly* facility, only relevant to non-packet-switched services. This converts character or binary streams to packets for a network subscriber. This facility is used to provide connection for character mode terminals and enables them to communicate with DTEs operating in the packet mode.

X25 Architecture

The X25 recommendation comprises three levels of protocol. In the form agreed by the CCITT sixth plenary assembly in 1976 it gives access to the virtual call and permanent virtual circuit facilities. It allows the multiplexing, on the same physical circuit, of connections between a DTE and a number of other DTEs on the network. Each of these logical connections makes use of a virtual circuit defined at the third level of X25. All three levels of the interface are independent of each other and the first two of these could be replaced by any other protocol that performs the same function. The third level is the one that actually gives the interface its identity and a replacement of it will result in a different interface. The three levels of X25 close locally across the DTE/DCE interface. This means that all exchanges across the three levels of the interface have only local significance. Some of these exchanges enable the DTE to pass requests to the network which imply non-local actions within the network transport system before they can be completed. In our picture of the onion skin architecture of communication systems, the communication between two remote processes using an X25 interface to connect to the network can be represented as in Figure 6.33.

The user or DTE access to the packet switch is via a data circuit. This can be a leased or dial-up connection and in many of the countries which are implementing public networks it will be an analogue circuit in the telephone network. Digital circuits with fast switching technology are being brought into operation and, because of their superior error characteristics, these are going to be used for data transmission early on. A hybrid situation will exist for some time where most of the trunk circuits will be digital but the local circuits up to the user premises will be analogue. The operation of digital circuits will be according to CCITT recommendation X21 which provides for fast digital addressing for the establishment of circuits as well as the operation of leased circuits. The need to accommodate the hybrid solution for the transitional period has resulted in recommendation X21 bis which defines the addressing procedure for establishing switched circuits by users accessing the digital network via

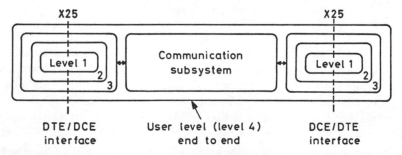

Figure 6.33   Communication using X25 interface onion skin architecture

analogue lines. The X21 bis interface is compatible with the existing V24 recommendation for connection to the telephony network using modulator–demodulator devices (modems). The first level of the X25 interface incorporates the X21 and X21 bis recommendations and as such it specifies the electrical and procedural characteristics for the operation of the data transmission circuit.

The second level of the interface is an HDLC link level procedure to ensure the correct exchange of data between DTE and DCE. An HDLC data frame carries a single packet, across the X25 interface.

The third level is the packet level of protocol and as indicated earlier this is the level which gives X25 its character of a virtual circuit interface to a packet-switched service. It provides the ability to establish calls using virtual circuits and to send and receive data. A window mechanism associated with each virtual circuit performs flow control. Reset and restart facilities allow recovery from errors at the interface. Calls can be closed down and virtual circuits freed so that they can be used for other calls.

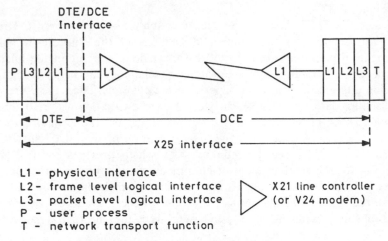

Figure 6.34   DTE/DCE interface block diagram

Figure 6.34 shows the physical configuration of the DTE/DCE interface for X25. The reader who is familiar with CCITT terminology for telephony circuits used in data transmission will notice the difference between DCE in that context and in the X25 interface. The DCE for data transmission over telephony circuits is the modem on the customer premises and the DTE/DCE interface is operated according to the V24 recommendation. In the case of X25 the DCE extends into two levels of software L2 and L3 inside the network switching computer. The logical structure of the interface is shown in Figure 6.35. The ability to have a multi-channel logical interface at the packet level is shown as a local protocol. The user process, on the other hand, will communicate with a remote process and implement a protocol across the network.

The Packet Level

The packet level of the interface comprises a number of logical channels each with a unique identifier. The number of possible channels is 15 groups of 255 channels each. The group is identified by 4 bits and the channel by 8 bits in the packet header. The binary value of these fields denotes the group and channel number. There is a one-to-one correspondence between DTE and DCE channel numbers. The range of logical channels which can be used by the DTE is specified by the network administration. The logical channels are used to offer two facilities on the packet-switched network, namely the permanent virtual circuit and the virtual call.

A permanent virtual circuit is a permanent association between two DTEs. When the two lower levels of X25 are operational a DTE can send packets containing data to the network, addressed to the logical channel allocated to a particular permanent virtual circuit. The network will deliver these to the destination DTE. In the same way a DTE can receive data on such a circuit from the other member of the association at any time. No call set-up or clearing action is needed; thus the permanent virtual circuit is similar to a point-to-point private line.

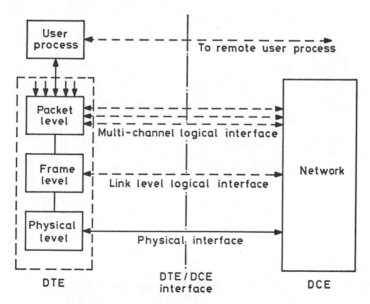

Figure 6.35   X25 interface logical structure

A virtual call is a temporary association between two DTEs and is initiated by a DTE sending a call request packet to the network, on a free logical channel. The X25 specification recommends that the DTE chooses the free channel with the highest channel number. The call request packet must explicitly contain the destination address. As a result of the receipt of the call request packet, the network will send the called DTE an incoming call packet on the free logical channel with the lowest channel number. A called DTE has the choice of accepting or rejecting the call. The calling DTE will receive a response indicating whether or not the called DTE has accepted the call. If accepted, the virtual call enters the data phase. When for any reason a virtual call cannot be established, the network will return a clearing packet to the calling DTE indicating the reason. Either DTE may clear an established call. Figure 6.36 shows the logical structure of an association using X25.

A DTE can have many permanent virtual circuits and/or virtual calls active at the same time. These calls will be to a number of other DTEs in the network and the packets associated with these calls all share the same physical link and error control procedures of level 2. Figure 6.37 illustrates this multiplexing of data streams. Whatever the internal structure of the network it will in its turn multiplex packets from several DTEs onto its fast internode links. The bandwidth of these links must therefore be shared between the active network users so that a minimum throughput per call can be guaranteed. It is also important for the network not to accept packets from a source at a rate higher than the destination

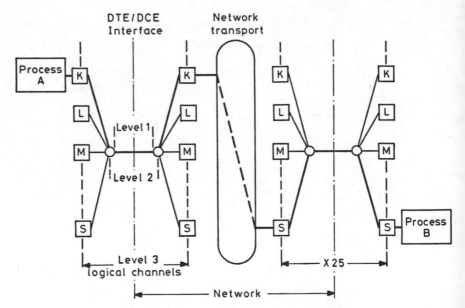

Figure 6.36   VC or PVC between two DTEs

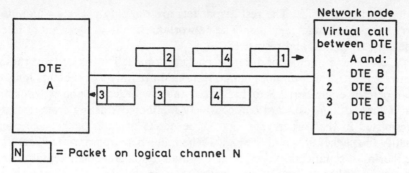

Figure 6.37   Interleaved packet flow

can receive them. To achieve this each logical channel implements a flow control scheme by employing a window mechanism. The flow control scheme is available to the DTE as well as to the DCE, so that a subscriber can control the rate at which it receives data. An interrupt facility allows two DTEs communicating via a virtual circuit to exchange short pieces of information in interrupt packets. They can therefore be employed to resolve conditions where neither end process can accept data and the logical channel flows have ceased.

In the event that the two ends of an association can only resolve their problems by clearing the flow in a logical channel, X25 provides the facility of resetting virtual calls and permanent virtual circuits. The *reset operation* clears the logical channel of all data packets and reinitialises the flow control. A *restart* facility clears *all* virtual calls and resets permanent virtual circuits associated

General format identifier		Octet 1				
		Bits	8	7	6	5
Data packets	Sequence numbering scheme modulo 8		x	0	0	1
	Sequence numbering scheme modulo 128		x	0	1	0
Call set-up and clearing, flow control, interrupt, reset and restart packets	Sequence numbering scheme modulo 8		0	0	0	1
	Sequence numbering scheme modulo 128		0	0	1	0

Note: A bit shown as 'x' may be set to either '0' or '1'

Figure 6.38   General format identifier

with a particular DTE. The restart packets are the only packets which do not carry a logical channel identifier. The network itself will, in the event of internal problems, reset calls and restart DTEs.

X25 defines a number of different packet formats. The majority of these are control packets which do not contain data and are only a few octets long. Bits of an octet are numbered 8 to 1. Bit 1 is the low order bit and is transmitted first. Octets of a packet are consecutively numbered starting from 1 and are transmitted in that order. The first three octets of each packet are used to identify the packet type and the logical channel where appropriate. Octet 2 and the four most significant bits of octet 1 contain the logical channel number and the group number. When these are not used, as in the case of the restart packet, they are set to all zeros. The four most significant bits of octet 1 distinguish between two possible window mechanisms for flow control. They are called the *general format identifier*. Octet 3 contains the code for the *packet type*. Figures 6.38 and 6.39 list the general format and packet type identifiers. Bits marked

Packet type		Octet 3 Bits							
From DEC to DTE	From DTE to DCE	8	7	6	5	4	3	2	1
Call Set-up and clearing									
Incoming call	Call request	0	0	0	0	1	0	1	1
Call connected	Call accepted	0	0	0	0	1	1	1	1
Clear indication	Clear request	0	0	0	1	0	0	1	1
DCE clear confirm	DTE clear confirm	0	0	0	1	0	1	1	1
Data and Interrupt									
DCE data	DTE data	x	x	x	x	x	x	x	0
DCE Interrupt	DTE interrupt	0	0	1	0	0	0	1	1
DCE interrupt confirm	DTE interrupt confirm	0	0	1	0	0	1	1	1
Flow control and reset									
DCE RR	DTE RR	x	x	x	0	0	0	0	1
DCE RNR	DTE RNR	x	x	x	0	0	1	0	1
	DTE REJ	x	x	x	0	1	0	0	1
Reset indication	Reset request	0	0	0	1	1	0	1	1
DCE reset confirm	DTE reset confirm	0	0	0	1	1	1	1	1
Restart									
Restart indication	Restart request	1	1	1	1	1	0	1	1
DCE restart confirm	DTE restart confirm	1	1	1	1	1	1	1	1

Figure 6.39   Packet type identifier

CALL REQUEST and INCOMING CALL Packet format

8	7	6	5	4	3	2	1
0	0	0	1	logical channel group number			
logical channel number							
0	0	0	0	1	0	1	1
calling DTE address length				called DTE address length			
DTE address								
				0	0	0	0
0	0	facility length					
facilities							
call user data							

CLEAR REQUEST and CLEAR INDICATION Packet format

8	7	6	5	4	3	2	1
0	0	0	1	logical channel group number			
logical channel number							
0	0	0	1	0	0	1	1
clearing cause							
diagnostic code							

DTE and DCE CLEAR CONFIRMATION Packet format

8	7	6	5	4	3	2	1
0	0	0	1	logical channel group number			
logical channel number							
0	0	0	1	0	1	1	1

CALL ACCEPTED and CALL CONNECTED Packet format

8	7	6	5	4	3	2	1
0	0	0	1	logical channel group number			
logical channel							
0	0	0	0	1	1	1	1

Coding of clearing cause field in clear indication packet

	8	7	6	5	4	3	2	1
DTE clearing	0	0	0	0	0	0	0	0
Number busy	0	0	0	0	0	0	0	1
Out of order	0	0	0	0	1	0	0	1
Remote procedure error	0	0	0	1	0	0	0	1
Number refuses reverse charging	0	0	0	1	1	0	0	1
Invalid call	0	0	0	0	0	0	1	1
Access barred	0	0	0	0	1	0	1	1
Local procedure error	0	0	0	1	0	0	1	1
Network congestion	0	0	0	0	0	1	0	1
Not obtainable	0	0	0	0	1	1	0	1

Figure 6.40 Call establishment and clear packet formats

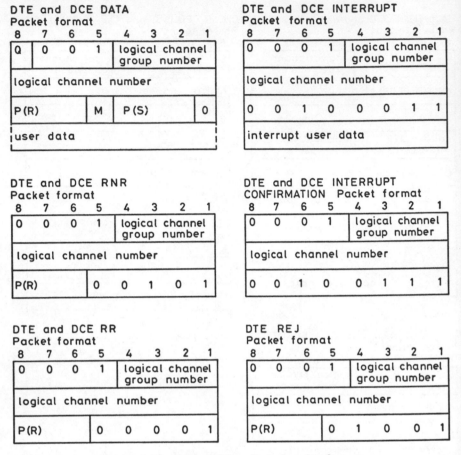

Figure 6.41   Data and flow control packet formats

with an X in these tables can be either 0 or 1. Their use is discussed later in this section. Figures 6.40 to 6.42 show the packet formats of X25 and the coding of control bytes.

Call Set-up and Clear

The formats of the call request and incoming call packets are identical and are shown in Figure 6.40 together with the call confirmation and clear packets.

The sequence of events for establishing a virtual call between two DTEs is as follows. The calling DTE will send to the network a CALL REQUEST packet on a free logical channel. It is recommended to use the highest number channel free. This packet must contain the called DTE address. Depending on the local implementation of the interface it either will or will not contain the

RESTART REQUEST and
RESTART INDICATION
Packet format

8	7	6	5	4	3	2	1
0	0	0	1	0	0	0	0
0	0	0	0	0	0	0	0
1	1	1	1	1	0	1	1
Restarting cause							
Diagnostic code							

RESET REQUEST and
RESET INDICATION
Packet format

8	7	6	5	4	3	2	1
0	0	0	1	logical channel group number			
Logical channel number							
0	0	0	1	1	0	1	1
Resetting cause							
Diagnostic code							

DTE and DCE
RESTART CONFIRMATION
Packet format

0	0	0	1	0	0	0	0
0	0	0	0	0	0	0	0
1	1	1	1	1	1	1	1

DTE and DCE
RESET CONFIRMATION
Packet format

0	0	0	1	logical channel group number			
Logical channel number							
0	0	0	1	1	1	1	1

Coding of restarting cause field in
restart indication packets

	8	7	6	5	4	3	2	1
Local procedure error	0	0	0	0	0	0	0	1
Network congestion	0	0	0	0	0	0	1	1

Coding of resetting cause field in
reset indication packet

	8	7	6	5	4	3	2	1
DTE reset	0	0	0	0	0	0	0	0
Out of order	0	0	0	0	0	0	0	1
Remote procedure error	0	0	0	0	0	0	1	1
Local procedure error	0	0	0	0	0	1	0	1
Network congestion	0	0	0	0	0	1	1	1

Figure 6.42 Restart and reset packet formats

calling DTE address. There are some circumstances where the inclusion of the calling DTE address is essential. This is when the DTE is known by more than one address. Multiple address DTEs are a possibility and are going to be offered by some networks, for example Transpac, to provide sub-addressing for local complex configurations. The address field length is dynamic and the lengths of the two addresses are coded in the fourth octet using 4 bits for each. The binary value of these 4 bits is the length of the appropriate address in semi-octets.

The addresses follow with the called DTE address first. Each digit of the address is represented in binary coded decimal in a semi-octet. Starting from the high order digit of the address this is coded in bits 8–5 of the fifth octet, the next digit in bits 4–1, the next in bits 8–5 of the sixth octet and so on, until the whole of the address is coded. For addresses with an odd number of digits, bits 4–1 of the last octet are all set to zero to round up the address space to an integral number of octets.

As well as the address field the CALL REQUEST packet can contain a facilities field specifying special facilities required by this call. Only the calling DTE can request these facilities and the called DTE has to accept them or refuse the call. Some of these facilities are described in more detail later on. Finally the CALL REQUEST packet may contain up to 16 octets of user data.

The facilities and user data fields are delivered to the called DTE in an INCOMING CALL packet completely unchanged. If the CALL REQUEST packet contained only the called DTE address, the INCOMING CALL packet would contain the calling DTE address and possibly the called DTE address. The logical channel number chosen by the DCE for sending the INCOMING CALL packet will be the lowest free number available at that interface. In the event of a call collision on a logical channel, the DCE will proceed with the call from the DTE and will presumably transfer the incoming call to another free channel. The call collision situation will not occur if the DTE always uses the highest free channel number unless only one logical channel remains free. In the event of a call collision under these conditions the incoming call will be dropped and a clear indication will be returned to the remote DTE with the clearing cause field indicating 'number busy', see Figure 6.40. If the called DTE wishes to accept the call, it returns, on the same logical channel, a CALL ACCEPTED packet to the DCE. The network then sends a CALL CONNECTED packet to the calling DTE.

The called DTE can reject an incoming call by returning a CLEAR REQUEST packet to the DCE instead of the CALL ACCEPT. In that case the called DTE cannot use that logical channel number for an outgoing call until it receives a CLEAR CONFIRMATION from the DCE. The called DTE does not have to give a reason for rejecting a call, but if it chooses it can set the diagnostic code field and return it in the clear request packet. This will be delivered to the calling DTE in a clear indication packet with the clearing cause field set to all zeros. The calling DTE must then return a CLEAR CONFIR-

MATION packet. If for any other reason the network is unable to set up a call for a DTE it returns a CLEAR INDICATION with the clearing cause field coded appropriately. The table in Figure 6.40 gives all possible clearing causes and their coding.

When the CALL ACCEPTED packet is returned to the DCE by the called DTE, it enters the data phase of the call and can start sending data packets on the logical channel. The data phase for the calling DTE is entered when it receives the CALL CONNECTED packet. The data phase of the virtual call can be terminated by either end sending a CLEAR REQUEST. Figure 6.43 illustrates the call establishment, data and clearing phases of a successful virtual call.

The recommendation gives a state diagram description of the call set-up and

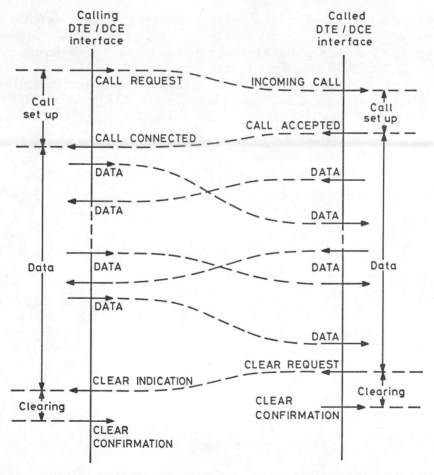

Figure 6.43   Call establishment, data and call clear phases of a VC

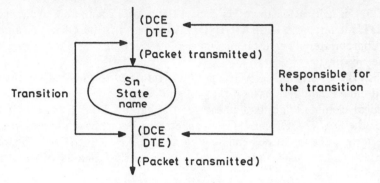

Figure 6.44   State diagram notation

clear phases of the interface. Each logical channel can be described in terms of one of seven states. These states describe the combined DTE/DCE operation and are not logical states of the process implementing one side of the protocol at the DTE or DCE. They would be more correctly described as sub-phases of the call set-up and clear phase itself. The notation used to describe these states or sub-phases of the interface is shown in Figure 6.44. The transition between the sub-phases is shown in Figure 6.45 for the call set-up and in Figure 6.46 for

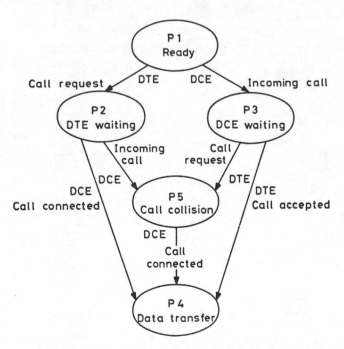

Figure 6.45   Call set-up state transition diagram

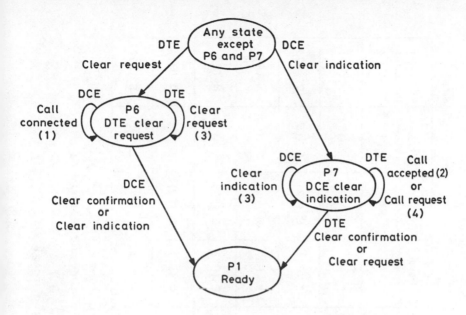

(1) Possible only if the previous state was DTE waiting (P2)

(2) Possible only if the previous state was DCE waiting (P3)

(3) Takes place after time-out

(4) Possible only if the previous state was Ready (P1) or DCE waiting (P3)

Figure 6.46   Call clear state transition diagram

the call clearing phase. If we look at Figure 6.45 we see that the transmission of a CALL REQUEST packet by the DTE on a logical channel in the ready state (P1) causes the interface to enter the DTE waiting state (P2). The DTE process enters a DTE waiting logical state as soon as such a transmission is initiated. At that instant in the DCE's view the state of that channel is still 'ready' (P1); it will only enter the sub-phase of call set-up described by P2 when it receives the CALL REQUEST packet. When the DCE responds with CALL CONNECTED it enters the data transfer phase (state P4). This state is not reached by the DTE until it receives the CALL CONNECTED packet.

The table of Figure 6.47 shows the action taken by the DCE on receipt of a packet from the DTE on a particular logical channel. The action is dependent on the DCE's view of the state of the interface. There are three actions indicated. *Normal action* is taken on receipt of a packet which in the current state of the interface forms part of the X25 procedures and actions as described in this section. For example with the DCE in the ready state (P1) the receipt of a CALL REQUEST from the DTE is an expected event and from the table we

State as perceived by the DCE / Packet from the DTE	Ready P1	DTE waiting P2	DCE waiting P3	Data transfer P4	Call collision P5	DTE clear request P6	DCE clear indication P7
CALL REQUEST	N (P2)	E (P7)	N (P5)	E (P7)	E (P7)	E (P7)	D (P7)
CALL ACCEPTED	E (P7)	E (P7)	N (P4)	E (P7)	E (P7)	E (P7)	D (P7)
CLEAR REQUEST	N (P6)	N (P6)	N (P6)	N (P6)	N (P6)	N (P6)	N (P1)
DTE CLEAR CONFIRMATION	E (P7)	E (P7)	E (P7)	E (P7)	E (P7)	E (P7)	N (P1)
DATA, INTERRUPT, RESET FLOW CONTROL	E (P7)	E (P7)	E (P7)	N (P4)	E (P7)	E (P7)	D (P7)
INCORRECT FORMAT	E (P7)	E (P7)	E (P7)	E (P7)	E (P7)	E (P7)	E (P7)

N-normal, E-error, D-discard

The new state to be entered is shown inside the brackets

Figure 6.47   Action by DCE on receipt of frame by DTE

see that the new state to be entered, indicated by the figure in brackets, is state P2 DTE waiting. In the state P2 the DTE is waiting for either a CALL CONNECTED for a successful call or a CLEAR INDICATION if the call is unsuccessful. The DTE is allowed to abandon a call and it does this by following the CALL REQUEST by CLEAR REQUEST before it receives a response to the former. Scanning down the second column of the table of Figure 6.47 we see that in the DTE waiting state the DCE considers as normal the receipt of CLEAR REQUEST from the DTE. Any other frame from the DTE is an *error* which will cause the DCE, as in all cases of error, to transmit a CLEAR INDICATION and enter state P7. In particular the receipt of a CALL REQUEST in this state is an error. Therefore if the DTE sends a CALL REQUEST on a logical channel and a time-out is started after which if no response has been received from the network the call is retried, the procedure to follow is to send a CLEAR REQUEST first and then retry the call. It can do this on the same channel after receipt of CLEAR CONFIRMATION from the DCE or, if it does not want to wait, it can try the same call on another channel. Returning to the table the third action is *discard* which appears in the last column. This indicates that the DCE will simply ignore the frame and take no further action. This is to avoid a deadlock situation when synchronisation is lost at the interface. If the table was describing the DTE's actions on receipt of frames from the DCE the discards would shift from state P7 to state P6. Finally the interface does allow either end to send CLEAR packets even when in the ready state (P1); this is to enable each end to ensure synchronisation.

Data Transfer and Flow Control

Data packets can be sent at any time using permanent virtual circuits or, after a virtual call has been established, using logical channels. Data packets are identified by setting to 0 the low order bit (bit 1) of the third octet. The remaining 7 bits of that octet are used for flow control, see Figure 6.41 for packet formats. The data field of the packets starts from the fourth octet and can be any number of bits, not necessarily an integral number of octets, up to the network imposed maximum. The preferred maximum data field length in X25 is 128 octets, although any number which is a power of 2 between 16 and 1024 can be chosen to define the maximum data field length in octets.

Each data packet transmitted or received by a DTE on a given virtual circuit is sequentially numbered modulo 8. The first data packet to be transmitted in a given direction after the virtual circuit has been established (or after resetting) is numbered 0; that is, it has a send sequence P(S) equal to 0. The P(S) number is binary coded in bits 2–4 of the third octet.

The send sequence number associated with each data packet is required to maintain the integrity of the transfer of data packets on the virtual circuit. It allows both the DCE and the DTE to detect the loss of data packets as well as to control the flow of data packets across the DTE/DCE interface.

Each packet also carries a packet receive sequence number P(R) which is used to authorise the transmission of additional data packets. The P(R) number is binary coded in bits 6–8 of the third octet. If a DTE or DCE wishes to authorise the transmission of one or more data packets on the DTE/DCE interface and there is no data flow in the reverse direction in which to carry this information, it can transmit a RECEIVE READY (RR) packet. If temporarily a DTE or DCE cannot accept data packets on a logical channel, it can transmit a RECEIVE NOT READY (RNR) packet. This condition is cleared by the transmission of an RR packet.

The maximum data field length of a data packet to be transmitted on a virtual call may be established independently at each end of the virtual circuit. When different maximum packet sizes are used at each end of a virtual call, the number of data packets arriving at the destination DTE may be greater or smaller than the number originally sent by the source DTE.

A packet of user data will not in general be combined with other packets which have already been received by the network, or which are sent after it. If the destination maximum packet size is less than that of the source, the network will have to divide a packet into two or more packets. To indicate to the destination the boundaries of the original packet, the network makes use of bit 5 of the third octet, known as the 'more data bit', to define a logical sequence of packets. A packet sequence consists of consecutive packets with the more data bit ON plus a packet following these with the more data bit OFF. Only maximum length packets can have the more data bit set. The source DTE can make use of the more data bit to define a logical sequence of data that cannot fit into one packet. The network then has the freedom to recombine these packets if necessary. For example, if the destination DTE packet length is greater than that of the source, a packet sequence from the source, which is defined by the use of the more data bit, can be delivered to the destination as a sequence consisting of a smaller number of packets. This can be an advantage to the receiver in that it does not need to allocate unnecessary packet buffers which are never filled up because the sender implements a smaller packet size.

The eighth bit of the first octet is used to indicate two different levels of data and is known as the data qualifier. The concept of data level has been introduced in X25 to cater for the situation, as in the case of terminal handling, where there are two destination processes: intermediate process and end process. One level of data is transparent to the intermediate process and is passed to the end process unchanged, e.g. text to be displayed at a terminal. When only one level of data is being transmitted on a logical channel, this bit must be set to zero. If the more data bit is used to define a multi-packet sequence, this must be transmitted without change of the data qualifier bit.

The maximum number of sequentially numbered data packets that a DTE or DCE is authorised to transmit and have outstanding at any given time may never exceed the window size. The value (between 1 and 7) of the window size is a constant, agreed with the network authority at subscription time. The transmission of more data packets is authorised by updating the window boundaries. The lower window edge is updated upon receipt of a P(R) greater (modulo 8) than the last P(R) received.

An example of window operation is shown in Figure 6.48 where the window size $w = 3$ permits a maximum of three packets to be outstanding at a given time. In this example the lower window edge, or last P(R) received, is 3. Since $w = 3$, the first data packet not authorised for transmission has send sequence number 6. As packets are transmitted and P(R)s returned, the lower and upper window edges rotate.

If a DCE receives a packet outside the window size it will consider this as a procedural error, and will initiate a reset procedure on that logical channel. The use of the RNR packet can inhibit the transmission of data packets within the window. This mechanism cannot guarantee to stop the flow of packets. This is because by the time the RNR arrives at its destination further frames may have been transmitted by level 3 on that logical channel. To drop these frames at the receiving end will cause the call to be cleared as no retransmission at this level is provided. This is an area where some clarification is needed in the operation of the level 3 procedures.

The normal data packet transmission sequence can be bypassed by the use of non-sequenced interrupt packets. Interrupt packets carry only one octet of user data, and are delivered to the destination DTE even when it is not accepting data packets. They contain no send or receive sequence numbers. An interrupt confirmation packet must be received by a DTE before it can send another interrupt packet. The return of confirmation in the case of interrupt implies that the interrupt has been received and acknowledged at the destination DTE/DCE interface. That is to say that, unlike the confirmation of other actions like clear, reset, etc., the interrupt confirmation is end-to-end.

As we saw earlier, the general format identifier caters for the definition of packets numbering schemes modulo 128. For such schemes, packets are num-

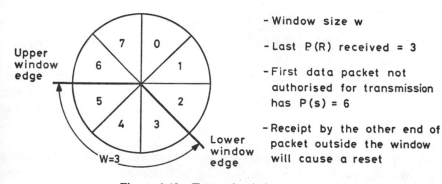

Figure 6.48   Transmit window operation

bered from 0 to 127 and the window size can be up to 127. The purpose of this extended window is for very long links with large transmission delays. The packet formats for data and flow control have to be appropriately modified to allow 7-bit fields for P(R) and P(S). It must also be stressed that although there is a great similarity between the data transfer control frames of level 3 and those of HDLC level 2, their purpose and function is entirely different. The primary function at level 3 is flow control while at level 2 error control.

Reset and Restart Procedures

The reset procedure is used to reinitialise a virtual call in the data phase or a permanent virtual circuit. It removes in each direction all data and interrupt packets which may be in the network. The reset procedure can be initiated by either end of an association or by the network. The resetting is completed when a reset confirmation packet has been received by the end (DTE or DCE) which initiated the reset.

The formats of the reset packets, and the coding of the reset cause field by the DCE, are shown in Figure 6.42. After the reset the lower window edge related to each direction of flow at the DTE/DCE interface, and the number to be allocated to the first packet to cross the interface, are set to zero.

A restart procedure is used at the DTE/DCE interface to clear all virtual calls and reset all permanent virtual circuits. If a restart is initiated this will cause clears and resets at the far end of all associations of the restarting DTE. The restart packet formats are shown in Figure 6.42. Restart packets do not carry a logical channel identifier.

An important point to be made is that both these actions can cause the loss of packets that have been acknowledged at the local DTE/DCE interface. Therefore something above X25 is needed to recover from a reset or restart initiated by the user or network and to resynchronise the data flows in a communication.

Optional User Facilities

The section in X25 which defines optional user facilities is not complete and is designated for further study. The facilities described there are proposals which will be discussed in the present study period by the appropriate study group at CCITT. These facilities fall into two classes: those requested by the DTE on a per virtual call basis and included in the facilities field of the CALL REQUEST packet; and others which apply to a particular DTE/DCE connection.

Two that come into the first category are 'reverse charging' and 'flow control parameter selection'. In the reverse charging facility, the calling DTE indicates that it wishes the called DTE to be charged. In Flow Control Parameter

Selection a flow control class is chosen by the calling DTE. This specifies either the window size w, the maximum data field length, or both.

Three facilities which fall into the second category are: 'reverse charging acceptance', 'one-way logical channel' and 'packet retransmission'. The implementation of one or more of these facilities is agreed with the network administration for a particular DTE/DCE connection. In reverse charging acceptance the DTE agrees to accept incoming calls which request reverse charging. One-way logical channel reserves a number of logical channels exclusively for incoming, or exclusively for outgoing calls. Packet retransmission allows the DTE to request the retransmission by the DCE of packets (at level 3). This is accomplished by the use of REJECT packet (see Figure 6.41 for the packet format). The value of $P(R)$ in this packet must be greater than or equal to the last $P(R)$ transmitted by the DTE. The DCE on receipt of the REJECT packet starts retransmitting packets with $P(S) = P(R)$.

Another important facility in the context of public data networks which has been discussed, but is not included in the present X25 definition, is the 'closed user group facility'. A closed user group is protected from unauthorised access. A call from a non-group member is refused by the network, thus giving an extra level of protection against attempts to access information by network subscribers who are not authorised to do so.

The Link Level

The second level of X25 is an HDLC link level procedure. Its primary purpose is that of error control. The recommendation refers to this protocol as a 'link access procedure' (LAP) and allows two variants to be used, both compatible with ISO definitions. These two variants are called LAP and LAP B. LAP B was introduced into the recommendation during the 1976–1980 study period after the approval of X25 during the 1976 CCITT plenary. It brings X25 into line with the ISO preferred procedure for balanced operation using the combined station concept.

LAP is a balanced procedure made up from two unbalanced configurations back to back with a primary and secondary at each end of the link. The configuration is as shown in Figure 6.28. Turning back to the chart of Figure 6.24, LAP is made up of the unbalanced basic repertoire and incorporates optional functions 2, 8 and 12. LAP B is similarly made up from the basic repertoire of the balanced box and incorporates the optional functions 2, 8, 11 and 12.

The receive not ready (RNR) at level 2 can be used to stop accepting information frames and provide an extra level of flow control. There is nevertheless a danger in doing this because, as well as stopping the flow of data meant for the processes above level 3, it also stops the flow of control packets to level 3. This is an interesting problem and one that occurs in any hierarchical structure. It is worth considering in some more detail its effect on the operation of the communications interface, taking as an example levels 2 and 3 of X25. Let us first assume that in a particular implementation buffers at a DTE are released when acknowledgements are received at the link level. This is a reasonable assumption if the packet-switched network offers great reliability and virtual calls are rarely cleared or reset because of communication subnet failures. Under such conditions no other mechanism over and above X25 needs to be employed to effect error recovery and once confirmation is received from the subnet at level 2 that the data has been correctly received the buffer can be cleared. Under these conditions a level 2 RNR can be sent if the DTE runs out of buffers; this will stop all flows to level 3 virtual calls and permanent virtual circuits. Buffers at the DTE will still be released when level 2 acknowledgements are received. If the busy condition implied by the RNR lasts for a long time what will happen is that not only flows of data to the DTE will have stopped, but also flows from the DTE to the network will eventually stop as the windows at level 3 cannot be updated. When a large proportion of the buffers is occupied by outgoing data the level 2 RNR will then create an unnecessary slowing down of the outward flow. It will actually result in a number of start–stop cycles which will make the local congestion worse.

When an end-to-end acknowledgement scheme is employed over and above the X25 interface the use of RNR at level 2 becomes even more dangerous. In such schemes the DTE employs a protocol with the remote DTE to establish that data has been received correctly at its destination. A copy of the data is kept locally until such confirmation is received in case it is necessary to retransmit it. In this environment level 2 acknowledgements do not release buffers.

As we have discussed earlier the RNR at level 3 is not very effective as a method of flow control either. We must therefore conclude that the primary flow control mechanism in X25 is the window at level 3. Receive not ready at level 2 must be used with care and to some extent its use will be dictated by the local configuration. For example if levels 2 and 3 are physically separated then level 2 resources like buffers can be independent of level 3 and in this case RNR at level 2 is important.

The difficulties we discussed above occur because there is interference between the various levels. This occurs when functions at these levels attempt to control a common resource. Great care must be taken that these mechanisms do not interfere destructively.

The Physical Level Interface

The physical level, level 1, of X25 can operate by employing existing CCITT procedures as described in the V24[6] recommendation. These procedures enable the DTE to operate over a leased analogue circuit connecting it to a packet switching node or concentrator. The V24 procedures are extended in recommendation X21 bis[5] to allow access to the digital circuit-switched network using an analogue circuit. The analogue circuit operates between the customer's premises and the circuit switch node. Procedures for sending and receiving addressing information enable a DTE to establish switched circuits with other DTEs which have access to the digital network. When the circuits reaching the customer's premises are digital then the X21 procedures are employed. Similar to the other physical level procedures, X21 defines the physical, electrical and procedural characteristics of the interface.

The X21 interface operates over eight interchange circuits. Their function is defined in recommendation X24 and their electrical characteristics in recommendation X27 (alternative electrical characteristics for the DTE are specified in X26). The table in Figure 6.49 lists these circuits. Four of these circuits are: ground, common return and two timing circuits. Signal element timing provides bit timing, the byte timing is a national option and is not always present. The timing circuits are driven by the DCE. The other four circuits provide the transmission and control facilities of the interface. Data is transmitted from the DTE on the 'transmit' circuit and received on the 'receive' circuit. Figure 6.50(a) shows the four data and control circuits.

We are not proposing to cover the X21 procedures in detail, but give the general principle of its operation through an example. Let us consider the establishment of a successful call initiated by the DTE and also the data and clearing phases of the interface. The X21 recommendation defines a number of combined states of the interface in a similar fashion to the packet level of X25. Figure 6.50(b) takes the reader through the example and indicates at the bottom these combined states. In accordance with CCITT definitions we call the binary states of the control and indication circuits OFF for binary 1 and ON for binary 0. In the ready state of the interface all four circuits are in a binary 1 steady state, and either DTE or DCE can initiate the procedure for establishing a call.

Circuit	Name	From DTE	From DCE
G	Signal ground		
Ga	DTE common return	x	
T	Transmit	x	
R	Receive		x
C	Control	x	
I	Indication		x
S	Signal element timing		x
B	Byte timing		x

Figure 6.49   X21 interchange circuits

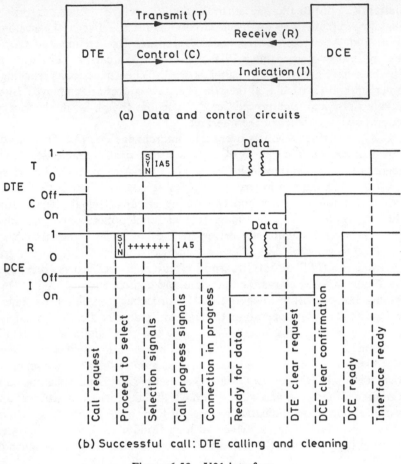

(a) Data and control circuits

(b) Successful call: DTE calling and cleaning

Figure 6.50   X21 interface

The DCE does this by sending SYN characters on the receive circuit, thus bringing the interface to the incoming call state.

In our example the DTE is indicating its wish to make a call by changing the control circuit from the OFF to the ON state and the transmit circuit from 1 to 0. This causes the interface to enter the call request state. When the DCE is ready to accept addressing information from the DTE it transmits a SYN synchronising character and then a series of characters in IA5 format the interface enters the proceed to select state. During this state the DTE transmits the address of the remote X21 DTE to which it wants to connect; the address is coded in a series of IA5 characters. The eighth bit of each character, the parity bit, offers a single bit error protection. The DCE replies with call progress signals transmitted on the receive circuit. In our example, as we assume the call is successful, the call progress signals will simply indicate that fact and identify the remote DTE as an extra security measure. The data phase, during which information transparent to the interface flows between the two DTEs, is entered by the DCE, changing the state of the indication circuit from OFF to ON. Data can then be exchanged between the two DTEs until either decides to terminate the call. In Figure 6.50(b) the local DTE makes a clear request by changing the control circuit state to OFF. After that the DTE cannot send any further data. It must nevertheless be prepared to receive data from the DCE until the DCE completes the call clearing phase by changing the state of the indication circuit to OFF. Finally the return of the transmit and receive circuits to the steady 1 state brings the interface back to the ready state.

During the call establishment phase a call collision between incoming call and call request can occur. This is resolved by the DCE abandoning the incoming call and allowing the DTE to proceed with the outgoing call.

The X21 procedures for operating leased circuits are much simpler. Here a change of the control or indication circuits declares the appropriate end's intention to transmit data. When both circuits have changed to the ON state the interface enters the data phase. The interface specification is not complete in this area and the procedures for terminating the data transfer phase for leased services are, in the CCITT terminology, for further study.

6.5 A UNIFIED VIEW OF PROTOCOL DESIGN

The X25 interface described in the previous section is a step towards a unified but modular design of an interface for the data networks of the future. The use of X21 at the physical link level of the interface will enable the network subscriber to access a packet-switched service via the fast digital network if the two networks coexist. He can also, by making use of the same connection, call another subscriber directly through the circuit-switched network. DTEs can then make the best choice of transmission medium to suit the pattern of the data to be transmitted. We can divide the traffic characteristics into three broad classes. The first of these is bulk data which could be transmitted most efficiently using a direct link between two DTEs, obtained via X21. The second is interactive traffic and transfer of small to medium size files associated with the real-time use of computers; this kind of traffic is best carried at present via packet-switched networks offering a virtual call interface.

A third class of traffic which will be increasing very rapidly in the near future is associated with transactions which need to exchange a small number of short messages to complete their task. Examples of this type of interaction are credit validation, point of sale terminal and cash dispensers. In all these cases what is required is the exchange of a small number of short messages between a terminal and a computer. At first a message from the terminal identifies the customer, by the use of a code, and indicates the credit or cash required. A second message from the computer confirms that the transaction can proceed. Finally the terminal must confirm the completion of the transaction, so that the computer can update its files. This type of traffic is best served by a datagram facility. Such a facility is being discussed at present in CCITT.

Another interface which is being discussed at CCITT is for simple DTEs which only require one virtual call at a time and do not need the multiplexing function of X25 level 3. For this type of DTE a simplified interface is possible. This has become known as the 'frame mode' DTE as the packet level of X25 becomes redundant. Some of the proposals for this interface envisage a simple level 3 to enable the DTE to establish a call. During the data transfer phase only the link level procedures are used to carry the data across the interface.

An important consideration in the design of interfaces is that subscribers connected to the network via one of these can communicate to all other users irrespective of the interface they employ to connect to the network. This requirement implies that facilities are independent as far as possible from interfaces and are accessible from a number of these. The complexity of some of these protocols and the overall requirement that they should work effectively in a varied environment requires that they should be reliable. Protocol proving techniques have already been applied to some of the basic communication protocols and problems with protocol operation have been identified. This is an area which will expand in the future and will play a useful role in system design.

The Datagram Facility

The datagram facility can be seen as a number of distributed processes. Each process supports several users on full duplex ports and connects to all other datagram processes on the network. Figure 6.51 illustrates this concept. A user of the datagram facility can send data to any other subscriber of this facility by sending packets containing the destination address to the datagram process to which he is connected. The datagram process will examine the address

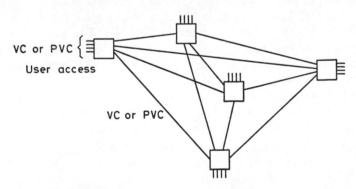

Figure 6.51   Fully-connected network of datagram processes

and, if the packet is directed to another user connected to the same process, it will output it through the appropriate port. If it is for a remote user it will establish the destination datagram process and send it along the appropriate interprocess port. The datagram processes will control the input of packets from its various users in such a way as to share equally among them the available resources.

Let us now consider how this abstract concept of a fully-connected datagram network can be incorporated in a virtual call network and accessed via an X25 virtual call interface. The user access ports and the interprocess ports can be implemented through virtual circuits, using either the virtual call or the permanent virtual call facilities. In this fashion the internal network mechanisms of flow control can be used to control the flow of datagrams. A datagram process can then be located at each of the switching nodes or concentrators of the X25-based network. The datagram process carries an address so a virtual call can be established to it via the X25 interface. The datagram service is thus viewed as independent of the particular interface and can be accessed not only via X25 but also via the frame mode DTE.

Protocol Verification

The aims of protocol verification are the same as those for program verification and proving. Techniques developed for the latter have been used in protocol verification.[7] An alternative approach has been the use of state diagram description of protocols.[8] Any protocol verification must be preceded by a clear definition of protocol functions and goals. The verification should establish that these functions are performed by the protocol as defined and that the goals are reached. As in program proving another important result of verification is to show that no infinite loops or deadlocks are possible in the protocol.

The ultimate aim of these techniques is to design automatic or semi-automatic protocol verifiers. These are programs which help the protocol designer to prove the correctness of his protocol. They usually require the protocol to be defined in some symbolic language either specially devised for the purpose[9] or an existing high level language, for example Algol.[10]

All protocol verification methods require the protocol to be described in a formal unambiguous way. This formal definition of a protocol does in its own right improve the likelihood that a correct protocol or a protocol with fewer errors is defined. With this aim in mind it is clearly an advantage if the formal definition required for proving is the same or very similar to the one to be used for coding the protocol. We shall also see later on, when we give a brief description of program proving techniques, that this method involves making assertions at key points of the program, which provides an ideal way of documenting and explaining the protocol.

Even if the goal of protocol verification and proof cannot be achieved satisfactorily, the steps we are forced to take towards it can be justified on their own merit. Most of the techniques used to date have their limitations but progress has been remarkably fast since the beginning of 1978.[11] These encouraging results, plus the fact that ultimately there is no other way to make sure that a protocol works, makes study in this area very important. Without formal proofs we can never be sure that obscure faults do not remain in protocols even after fairly thorough exercising and testing.

The various components of X25 have attracted the attention of the protocol provers and have become a vehicle for trying new techniques. This is for two reasons: first that the techniques have just become capable of handling protocols of this complexity; second because of the importance of these protocols as international interfaces to the public data networks. The techniques have been applied to X21 which forms level 1 of X25[12] and to call set-up and clearing phases of the packet level, level 3.[8]

Program Proving Techniques

In the application of program proving techniques to protocol verification the first step is the algorithmic, or program, description of the protocol. The basic technique of proving the protocol is to attach at each point in the program a statement of what we believe to be true about the value of the various variables, flags and booleans at that point. These statements are called assertions. The truth of an assertion at each point follows from the truth of the assertions at all points previous to it in the program. For this reason this is known as the 'inductive–assertion' method. The technique has been developed for proofs of programs [13,14,15] and has been adopted for use in protocols.

The difference between program and protocol proving using inductive–assertion techniques is in the complexity of the model. Both programs and protocols can be modelled in terms of processes. A program can consist of one or more collocated processes. In its simplest form of a single process it must have at least one input and one output port. In more complex situations, as well as the input and output ports, other ports are used to communicate between a number of processes. A protocol is modelled similarly using two processes located remotely and communicating via a number of ports through a communication medium. The basic difference and extra complexity comes from the characteristics of the communication medium and the distributed nature of the communicating processes. We cannot rely any more on the input to our processes not being lost, nor can we guarantee that it will be an expected input. To cater for this kind of situation we provide mechanisms in each process to cope with unexpected events and take appropriate action. Time-outs are introduced to avoid lock-ups due to the loss of information. These time-outs in their turn introduce the possibility of duplicated information arriving at a destination, which will occur when the communication medium unduly delays the delivery of packets. These considerations make protocol operation more complex and the choice of the assertions more difficult.

Anyone who has written a program must, without recognising it, have included assertions at key points of the program. These take the form of consistency checks which do not contribute to the execution of the task but might cause an abnormal termination or a warning message to be printed. For example before calculating the square root of N one might check that $N \geqslant 0$. In program proving, as each assertion follows from all previous ones, it is important for the proof that a complete set of these is established. This is the most difficult part of the procedure and in the case of complex programs failure to prove that one assertion follows another can be due to an intermediate step having been overlooked. Consider two consecutive points in a program, say A followed by B. The assertion at A is the relationship $R_A(X,Y,Z)$ between variables X, Y and Z. At B the assertion is expressed in terms of the relationship $R_B(X,Y,Z)$. The relationship can take the form of a single function of the variables or a number of equalities or inequalities which define acceptable boundaries of the variables. Assume that in going from point A to point B we have the assignment statement $Y = E$, where E is an expression. The way to prove that R_A and $Y = E$ imply R_B is to substitute E for Y in R_A. If the result is a relationship that is R_A or is implied by R_A then we know that R_B follows from R_A and the assignment $Y = E$. For example if R_A is $Y > 0$ and R_B is $Y > 1$ with $E = Y + 1$, if we substitute $Y + 1$ for Y in R_B we get $Y + 1 > 1$ which is the same as R_A: $Y > 0$.

For a complete proof of a protocol we must define the total set of assertions and prove that, for any pair of assertions A and B such that B can be reached from A in a single step, then A together with the action between A and B implies B. Part of our assertion must also be that for any possible input at a process port the output bears the correct relation to that input. Having achieved this we have proved that if a process associated with the protocol makes an output it will be the correct output and the protocol will progress. What we have not proved is that the protocol will progress, i.e. it does not loop indefinitely. To prove that a protocol will progress all loops in the system must be identified and for each loop an integer function F identified. Each time round the loop, F must decrease by at least one and the loop terminates when F becomes less or equal to zero. For an example let us return to the enquiry–response protocol described in Section 6.1, page 193. One of the input ports of the enquiry process receives the time-out message which causes the message to be retransmitted, see Figure 6.2. This gives the possibility of an infinite loop if the response process is not operating. Clearly a counter must be set in the enquiry process which decrements by one after each transmission. Retransmissions must cease when this counter reaches the value zero and an appropriate message is returned to the user process.

The completeness of our proof relies on having modelled the behaviour of the processes and the communication medium correctly and on having taken into account all possible inputs, as well as on having followed every possible path in the protocol and verified the assertion. This is not an easy task and these techniques have to date only been used to verify simple protocols like the non-sequential alternating bit protocol.[7]

Finite State Description

In Section 6.2, page 206 we described the alternating bit protocol in terms of a number of states of the transmitter and receiver; see also Figure 6.12. Any protocol can be expressed in terms of the states of the processes that cooperate to implement it. The main limitation of this approach is that for more complex protocols the number of states becomes extremely large. From the finite state description of each element of the protocol we can construct the transition diagram for the overall system. A protocol which can be described by two processes, one with n and the other with m states, has a total of $n \times m$ possible states of the overall system. Not all of these states are reachable if the protocol is properly initialised. To construct the state diagram of the overall system, reachability analysis can be used. This involves the formal definition of adjoint states. For a protocol implemented between processes A and B the adjoint states of a state S_A of process A are those states of process B in which that process can exist when process A is in state S_A. The combined states of the system can be constructed by the set of all adjoint states.

We shall illustrate the combined state description through an example of the alternating bit protocol. The separate states of transmitter and receiver of

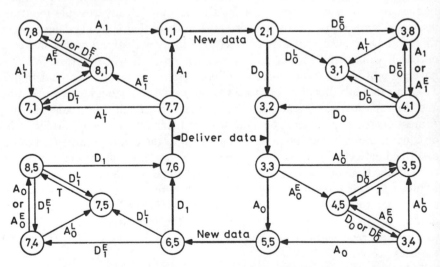

Figure 6.52   Alternating bit protocol combined transition diagram

this protocol are shown in Figure 6.12. In constructing the combined state diagram we shall make three assumptions which restrict the total number of these states to 20 from the possible total of 8 × 8. The first assumption is the 'empty medium' abstraction.[8] This considers only the states that are reached when the communication medium does not contain any messages associated with the protocol. The second assumption is that the protocol is initialised, i.e. both transmitter and receiver are in their respective 1 states. The third assumption is that the medium only contains one message at a time. The resulting transition diagram for the overall system is shown in Figure 6.52. The notation used is that the appearance of a message type, acknowledgement or data of either parity, along a transition line indicates a message sent by the appropriate process which is no longer in the communication medium. This implies that it has been received either correctly or in error, erroneous receipt is indicated by E superscript on the message type. The message can also be lost and this is indicated by L superscript. The combined states are indicated by (A, B) where A is the state of the transmitter and B of the receiver. In all cases when a message is sent the possibilities of correct or erroneous arrival and loss must be considered. Some interesting features of this protocol can be illustrated by considering the total combined state space without any synchronisation restrictions. What can be shown is that this protocol will, if not synchronised, achieve self-synchronisation with possible loss of one data message. Another interesting discovery is that if the one message at a time assumption is removed, the protocol, while completely out of phase at the two ends, can continue to function around a loop of transitions through the error states 4 and 8. This is an unstable condition that only persists if the two ends continue transmitting simultaneously. A starting state for this condition is the combined state (2,7).

In the above example the unstable loop condition is interesting but causes no real problems. The discovery of such unwanted loops is a very important part of the state diagram verification. Of particular interest are stable loops that actually modify or damage the function of the protocol.

6.6 APPENDIX: CYCLIC CODES FOR ERROR DETECTION

'Cyclic redundancy checks' are widely used for error detection in networks. The most common use is for detecting errors on links and in this application the complete operation is performed using hardware. At the present time a variety of chips using large-scale integration is available for this purpose. This same method of error detection can also be used for error recovery at the higher levels in the network if extra protection is required. In this case the 'cyclic redundancy check' can be performed in software fairly economically using table look-up techniques.[16] Cyclic codes are also capable of providing a degree of error correction but this is extremely cumbersome to operate and is not commonly implemented.

In discussing the way in which cyclic codes operate and in developing their theory it is useful to work in a framework in which binary information is represented as a polynomial.[17] That is to say then in a k-bit sequence each bit represents the coefficients 0 or 1 of a $k - 1$ polynomial. For example a message 101101 is represented by the polynomial $1 + x^2 + x^3 + x^5$. The polynomial is written low order to high order because it will be transmitted serially, high order first, and we indicate signal flow as occurring from left to right.

These polynomials obey the laws of algebra with the exception that addition is modulo 2. Adding the coefficients of two terms of the same order we get:

$$1 + 1 = 0 \qquad 1 + 0 = 1$$
$$0 + 1 = 1 \qquad 0 + 0 = 0$$

and the sign is immaterial i.e. $-1 = +1$ which makes subtraction and addition equivalent. In this, as in ordinary algebra, every polynomial can be factored into prime irreducible factors in only one way.

A cyclic code is defined in terms of a generator polynomial $P(x)$ of degree n. $P(x)$, by operating on the polynomial defined by the k bits of a message to be transmitted, generates a code polynomial which is divisible by $P(x)$. The code polynomial is transmitted instead of the original message. For example a code polynomial can be formed by multiplying the message polynomial (of degree less than k) by the generating polynomial $P(x)$.

The method used in practice has the advantage of resulting in a code polynomial defining a bit stream in which the high order bits are identical to the original k-bit message and the low order bits are added check symbols. To encode a message polynomial $G(x)$ using a generator polynomial of order n, we divide $x^n G(x)$ by $P(x)$ and add the remainder $R(x)$ of the division to $x^n G(x)$ to form the code polynomial

$$x^n G(x) = Q(x)P(x) + R(x)$$

where $Q(x)$ is the quotient. Since in modulo 2 arithmetic, addition and subtraction are the same, we have the code polynomial $F(x)$ defined as

$$F(x) = Q(x)P(x) = x^n G(x) + R(x)$$

The multiplication of $G(x)$ by x^n makes the first polynomial on the right-hand side have zero coefficients in the n low order terms while $R(x)$ is of degree less than n. Therefore the k highest order coefficients of $F(x)$ are the same as those of the polynomial $G(x)$, which are the message symbols, the low order n coefficients are the coefficients of $R(x)$, and these are the check symbols.

It is worth mentioning that if $P(x)$ has x as a factor then every code polynomial generated will have x as a factor and therefore the zero order coefficient will be equal to zero. Therefore in this case $P(x)/x$ provides the same amount of information. For this reason $P(x)$ is always chosen to be non-divisible by x.

Let us now consider an example of the above. We choose $k = 10$ and $n = 5$ with the generator polynomial $p(x) = 1 + x^2 + x^4 + x^5$, to encode the message

$$1\ 0\ 1\ 0\ 0\ 1\ 0\ 0\ 0\ 1$$

corresponding to the polynomial

$$G(x) = 1 + x^2 + x^5 + x^9.$$

By long division we divide $x^5 G(x)$ by $P(x)$ and find the remainder $R(x) = 1 + x$, thus:

$$x^5 G(x) = (1 + x + x^2 + x^3 + x^7 + x^8 + x^9)P(x) + (1 + x).$$

The code polynomial is found by adding the remainder $(1 + x)$ to $x^5 G(x)$, giving:

$$F(x) = (1 + x) + (x^5 + x^7 + x^{10} + x^{14})$$

which defines the bit stream:

$$1\ 1\ 0\ 0\ 0\qquad 1\ 0\ 1\ 0\ 0\ 1\ 0\ 0\ 0\ 1$$

where the first five bits are check digits and the following nine are the original message.

Error Detection

An encoded message containing errors can be represented by

$$H(x) = F(x) + E(x)$$

where $E(x)$ is a polynomial with non-zero terms in each erroneous position. With modulo two addition $F(x) + E(x)$ is the coded message with the erroneous bit positions complemented.

If the received message $H(x)$ is not divisible by $P(x)$ then an error has occurred. On the other hand if $H(x)$ is divisible by $P(x)$ it can mean one of two things, either that $E(x) = 0$ or that $E(x)$ itself is divisible by $P(x)$. In either case we have no alternative but to accept $H(x)$ as containing the correct message. An error pattern $E(x)$ is detectable if and only if it is not divisible by $P(x)$.

In choosing $P(x)$ it is important to know the error pattern of the transmission medium on which the error code is to be used. For example $P(x)$ must be such that an $E(x)$ due to a burst error on telecommunication circuits is not divisible by $P(x)$ for a large proportion of these errors. Recommendation V41 of CCITT[6] defines a generating polynomial of order 16 suitable for use on communication lines. This results in a 16-bit check pattern to be generated and transmitted with the message. The recommended polynomial is of the form

$$P(x) = 1 + x^5 + x^{12} + x^{16}$$

At the beginning of the appendix we mentioned that cyclic codes have the ability to provide error correction as well as error detection. The error correction capability of the code is related directly to the error detection. For example any code capable of detecting all double errors is capable of correcting all single errors. If a single error occurs we can try to correct it by changing each binary digit. Any change other than the digit in error will generate a double error which will be detected. Therefore only correcting the erroneous digit will produce a code polynomial. More generally any code capable of detecting all $2r$ errors can correct any combination of r errors. Such an error correction scheme implemented on large messages is extremely expensive in processing time.

Implementation

Let us consider the series of operations for coding a message represented by a polynomial $G(x)$ using the generating polynomial $P(x)$ of order n. $G(x)$ is multiplied by x^n and the resulting polynomial is divided by $P(x)$ to obtain the remainder. The division is performed in modulo 2 arithmetic. Figure 6.53(a) gives an example of such a division while 6.53(b) shows the same division employing only the coefficients of the polynomials. The modulo 2 arithmetic has simplified the division considerably. Also the quotient of the division is not required.

The sequence of operations to obtain the remainder of the division can be described as follows:

(1) The highest order bit of the divisor (which defines the order of $P(x)$) is aligned with the highest order non-zero bit of the dividend and subtracted from it (the same as addition).

(a) Repeat the above, replacing the dividend by the result of the subtraction.

(b) Repeat step (a) until the difference is of lower degree than the divisor.

The final difference is the remainder.

$$
\begin{array}{c}
& 1X^3 + 1X^2 + 0X + 1 \\
\hline
1X^2 + 0X + 1 & \overline{\smash{)}\,1X^5 + 1X^4 + 1X^3 + 0X^2 + 1X + 0} \\
& 1X^5 + 0X^4 + 1X^3 \\
\hline
& 1X^4 + 0X^3 + 0X^2 + 1X + 0 \\
& 1X^4 + 0X^3 + 1X^2 \\
\hline
& 0X^3 + 1X^2 + 1X + 0 \\
& 1X^2 + 0X + 1 \\
\hline
& 1X + 1
\end{array}
$$

$$
\begin{array}{c}
& 1101 \\
\hline
101 & \overline{\smash{)}\,111010} \\
& 101 \\
\hline
& 10010 \\
& 101 \\
\hline
& 0110 \\
& 101 \\
\hline
& 11
\end{array}
$$

(a)   (b)

Figure 6.53   Modulo 2 division

The hardware to implement this algorithm is a feedback shift register and a number of modulo 2 adders (which are the same as 'exclusive or' gates). The number of shift register stages required is the same as the order of the generating polynomial. The shift register is initialised to all zeros and the dividend is shifted through from left to right, high order bit first. As the first 1 is shifted off the end, the divisor is subtracted by the following procedure:

(1) In the subtraction, the highest order term of the divisor always cancels the highest order 1 of the dividend. As this is shifted off the end of the register, this part of the subtraction is done automatically.

(2) Modulo 2 adders are placed so that when a 1 shifts off the end of the register the divisor, excluding the high order bit which has been taken care of, is subtracted from the contents of the shift register. The register then contains the difference, which is shifted until another 1 comes off the end, and the process is repeated. This procedure continues until the entire dividend has been shifted into the register.

The register than contains the remainder resulting from the division.

Figure 6.54 illustrates a register that performs the division by the polynomial

$$1 + x^2 + x^4 + x^5.$$

In encoding a message polynomial $G(x)$ we first multiply it by x^n where n is the order of the generator polynomial. This in practice means attaching n zeros beyond the low order bit of $G(x)$. The remainder is obtained when the k message bits plus the n trailing zeros have been shifted through the shift register. The n trailing zeros are then replaced by the contents of the shift register to form the code polynomial.

Check Sequence in HDLC Frame Structure.

In practical implementations feedback shift registers are directly coupled to the input and output of link level procedures. Logic circuitry detects the

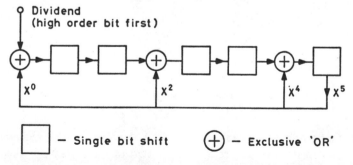

Figure 6.54 Shift register for dividing by $1 + x^2 + x^4 + x^5$

beginning and end of frames. It operates a number of gates to form and despatch the polynomial check sequence in the case of a transmitter or to form and compare the remainder in the case of a receiver. The polynomial check sequence for HDLC is referred to as the 'frame check sequence' (FCS).

In HDLC the flag sequence indicates the boundaries of a frame. If such a flag fails to be inserted between frames the receiver will then interpret two frames as one. Furthermore the shift register on receipt of the first frame plus FCS will be all zeros if no error has occurred. This is the correct bit pattern for starting the next division and the receiver will not detect the obliteration of the flag separating the two frames. The frame will be accepted and passed to the higher level as a correct frame. The frame format can also be satisfied as the address and control field of the first frame are correctly received. This problem occurs because for correct reception the initial and final bit pattern in the shift register is the same. To avoid this the coding of the polynomial check sequence is modified in HDLC[4] to make these different.

The CCITT generating polynomial

$$P(x) = 1 + x^5 + x^{12} + x^{16}$$

is used to divide

$$x^{16}G(x) + x^k L(x)$$

where k is the order of $G(x)$ and

$$L(x) = \sum_{n=0}^{n=15} x^n$$

this extra term, in modulo 2 arithmetic, inverts the 16 high-order bits of $x^{16}G(x)$. It is also equivalent to initialising the shift register to all 'ones'.

The transmitted bit pattern is the original message with the inverted remainder of the division appended to it. Expressed as a polynomial this is:

$$FR = x^{16}G(x) + R(x) + L(x)$$

where the remainder $R(x)$ is given by

$$Q(x)P(x) = x^{16}G(x) + x^k L(x) + R(x)$$

On receipt, the following division is performed

$$[x^{16}FR + x^{k+16}L(x)]/P(x)$$

which can be rewritten

$$x^{16}[x^{16}G(x) + x^k L(x) + R(x)]/P(x) + x^{16}L(x)/P(x)$$
$$= x^{16}[Q(x)P(x)]/P(x) + x^{16}L(x)/P(x)$$

The first numerator is divisible by $P(x)$. Therefore, at the receiver, if the transmission is error free, the remainder is that of the division of the constant second term and is equal to

$$1 + x + x^2 + x^3 + x^8 + x^{10} + x^{11} + x^{12}$$

With this method both the receiver and transmitter invert the 16 high order bits and this is implemented by initialising the shift registers to all 'ones'. The remainder itself is also non-zero and has the bit pattern (for low to high order)

$$1\ 1\ 1\ 1\ 0\ 0\ 0\ 0\ 1\ 0\ 1\ 1\ 1\ 0\ 0\ 0$$

In this way the HDLC frame sum check ensures that two frames concatenated with their correct FCS values will not check as a whole. So the missing of a flag between frames is detected.

References

1. Bartlett, K. A., Scantlebury, R. A., and Wilkinson P. T.,
   'A Note on Reliable Full-Duplex Transmission Over Half-Duplex Links',
   CACM, **12**, No. 5, 260 (1969).
2. *Data Link Control Procedures—Elements of Procedure (Independent Numbering)*,
   ISO/DIS4335, International Standards Organisation (1976).
3. *HDLC—Classes of Procedure*,
   ISO/TC97/SC6/N 1501,
   International Standards Organisation (1977).
4. *Data Communication—High-Level Data Link Control Procedures—Frame Structure*,
   ISO 3309, International Standards Organisation (1976).
5. 'Series X Recommendations',
   The Orange Book, VIII.2,
   International Telecommunications Union, Geneva (1977).
6. 'Data Transmission Over the Telephone Network: Series V Recommendations',
   The Orange Book, VIII.1,
   International Telecommunications Union, Geneva (1977).
7. Stenning, N. V.,
   'A Data Transfer Protocol',
   Computer Networks, **1**, No. 2, 99 (1976).
8. Bochman, G. V.,
   'Finite State Description of Communication Protocols',
   Proc. Computer Networks Protocol Symposium, Liège, F3-1 (1978).
9. Brand, D., and Joyner, W. H.,
   'Verification of Protocols Using Symbolic Execution',
   Proc. Computer Networks Protocol Symposium, Liège, F2-1 (1978).
10. Hajek, J.,
    Automatically Verified Data Transfer Protocols
    Proceedings of the ICCC, Kyoto, 749 (1978).
11. Sunshine C. A.,
    'Survey of Protocol Definition and Verification Techniques',
    Proc. Computer Network Protocols Symposium, Liège, F1-1 (1978).
12. West, C. H., and Zafiropoulo, P.,
    'Automated Validation of a Communications Protocol: the CCITT X21 Recommendation',
    IBM, Journal of Research and Development, **22**, No. 1, 60 (1978).

13. Floyd, R. W.,
    'Assigning Meanings to Programs',
    Proc. Symposia in Applied Mathematics, Vol. **19**, AMS, Providence, R.I., 19
    (1967).
14. Hoare, C. A. R.,
    'An Axiomatic Basis for Computer Programming',
    CACM, **12**, No. 10, 576 (1969).
15. *Proceedings of an ACM Conference on Proving Assertions About Programs*,
    ACM, New York (1972).
16. Boudrear, P. E., and Steen, R. F.,
    'Cyclic Redundancy Checking by Program',
    AFIPS, Proc. Fall Joint Computer Conference, 9 (1971).
17. Peterson, W. W., and Brown, D. T.,
    'Cyclic Codes for Error Detection',
    Proc. Institute of Radio Engineers, **49**, No. 1, 228 (1961).

Chapter 7

High Level Protocols

7.1 THE HOST'S VIEW OF THE NETWORK

The traditional view of a single computer controlling a number of peripheral devices in a master–slave relationship is not appropriate in the distributed network environment. To make full use of the new facilities offered by distributed networks the nature of operating systems will have to change. These will become less autonomous and will cooperate on an equal basis with other intelligent devices to execute tasks. Ultimately the idea of any centralised control and of operating systems will be replaced by that of a network of cooperating processes. Experimental packet-switched networks like the ARPA net in USA, the Cyclades network in France and the international European Informatics Network (EIN) had these goals in mind. The communication subnet would offer a facility for all its hosts to access each other's resources. We shall use the term *host* to describe any intelligent device capable of connecting to a packet-switched network. No distinction will be made between a host which offers computing resources and a host which acts as a terminal concentrator. The latter handles terminals and controls their interaction with a remote computer, via a protocol. It constructs packets from character streams from the terminals and despatches them through the packet-switched network to the computer, as well as converting packets from the computer to character streams to be sent to the terminals. Such a host in the ARPA network is called a 'terminal interface processor' or TIP.

We can divide the use of network facilities by hosts into three broad classes of varying degrees of sophistication. The simplest of these is when the communication subnet simply replaces physical lines of communication like leased or dial-up circuits. The communication is between computers and terminals which are compatible and the computer knows the exact type of terminal or terminal concentrator with which it is communicating. In the second class, advantage is taken of the ability to access a variety of hosts from a terminal and to exchange information between dissimilar hosts. To achieve this we must define a number of standard communication protocols to be used for communication between dissimilar hosts. This approach enhances the facilities available to the user and moves towards the idea of a network of computers. Both the first and second class are using the network for accessing a number of remote services. Although the second approach enables wider access and communication between hosts, the hosts are still seen by the user as separate entities. The move towards standard procedures for exchange of information above the basic communication levels brings us towards the third level of sophistication. Here the aim is to achieve a truly distributed network of computers which cooperate to execute user tasks. In such an environment the multiplicity of systems is hidden from the user. In this chapter we shall concentrate on the problems of the second class of goals, namely of achieving compatibility in communication between dissimilar hosts in a bilateral connection.

In describing the design of protocols for distributed access we shall not concentrate on a particular communication subnet or network interface. The X25 interface described in Chapter 6 is clearly going to play a major role but it will coexist with other extant and future communication interfaces. The current trend is to design a standard communication service called the *transport service* offering a number of facilities accessible via primitives at the transport interface. This interface is standard throughout the network of hosts. Upon it and its facilities we can build protocols for the communication between hosts. Such protocols will make possible the file transfer, remote job entry, and terminal access between systems.

These protocols, including the uniform transport service, have been called high level protocols. They will encompass procedures up to the application level

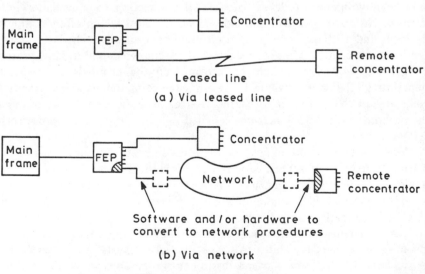

(a) Via leased line

(b) Via network

Figure 7.1   Remote access

of software. It is worth stressing that what is being modelled is an abstract system. When accessing a host which implements these protocols we expect it to behave according to our view of this abstract system. We do not care how this is achieved internally in each host. Each implementation will be different and will be dictated by the requirements of the local operating system. This is not just a compromise solution making the best of existing systems. It is very important that systems should have the freedom to develop and take advantage of new methods, both in hardware and software.

Remote Access

We shall now consider the simplest case of replacing a physical link with a network and discuss the advantages and disadvantages of this. Figure 7.1(a) shows a hypothetical configuration of a mainframe computer which, through a front end processor, supports a number of terminal concentrators with a variety of terminals. These can be interactive devices such as teletypes and VDUs, or input/output devices such as card readers and lineprinters, or storage devices like discs and tapes. We assume that one of the device concentrators is located remotely and accessed through a leased line. The remote concentrator is permanently connected to the system and the mainframe has a fixed view of the devices it owns and controls. The network of devices is connected in a hierarchical tree structure, with the front end processors and concentrators forming nodes.

The major advantage resulting from the replacement of the permanent connection by a switched one is that a number of devices of the type supported by the mainframe and connected to a number of concentrators of the same type can access the mainframe. It is also possible for such clusters of terminals to connect at different times to a number of similar mainframes which are available in the network. This will allow terminals to obtain a better service and to switch between mainframe computers depending on availability and load. Other advantages are a lower error rate offered by the network compared with that of a leased telephone line and the financial saving. The latter comes from the fact that only local connections to the switched network are required permanently. The network charges are per duration of call in a circuit-switched network and per packet in the case of a packet-switched network. The comparative costs between leased lines and switched networks depends of course on the total utilisation of the original leased line. If the utilisation were very high then the permanent leased circuit solution might be the most economic. Nevertheless the cost to the user of a particular service is subject to other constraints. Charging practices, particularly in Europe where the Postal Administrations are monopolies, do not always reflect the cost of the service provided. Tariffs might be set at a particular level to encourage users to follow the Administration's policy.

When communicating via a network it will be necessary to provide some extra hardware and software at both ends to implement the network procedures, see Figure 7.1(b). For example, to connect to a public packet-switched network an X25 interface will be required. The data across the original link must also be converted into packets for transmission and reconverted to the form expected by the original system on receipt. This is not difficult, and the greatest problem that might occur is the change in the timings for the exchange of information with the remote terminal or device. However, unless the packet-switched network is used to connect the mainframe to a single terminal concentrator on a permanent virtual circit via X25, another problem arises. If the circuit is switched and is used to connect a variety of concentrators and their terminals, the mainframe's static view of its own tree-structured network and the devices it controls is lost. Some mechanism must be introduced to update dynamically the map of devices available to the mainframe. Devices that connect dynamically to the mainframe for a specific task are not under the control of the mainframe in the sense that once that task is completed the mainframe is not free to use them at will for other tasks.

Manufacturers are already responding to the appearance of public data networks and are converting proprietary network configurations to extend through the medium of public data networks. The main contribution they are making is to provide X25 interfaces at their front ends and terminal concentrators. The advantages to be gained by the user from such modifications are the flexibility of a more dynamic environment, and improved reliability. They still leave unanswered the demand for compatibility between a variety of systems.

Distributed Access

We make the distinction between remote and distributed access. Distributed access is the ability to communicate with any host in the network and not only with hosts that support your own procedures. This compatibility can be achieved in two ways. The first of these is for a network of m hosts using n different procedures, where $n \leqslant m$, to implement each other's protocols. This will require one of the hosts to map from its own procedures to that of the remote host with which it is communicating. Returning to our example of Figure 7.1 the front end processor implements the procedures of a variety of terminal concentrators and terminals. This can become impracticable if a large number of protocols is involved.

The second solution is to define standard network protocols above the communication level. Already with X25 all hosts connected to the network at the packet level can send and receive packets to and from anywhere else in the network. The higher levels of protocol will require the definition of standard messages to be exchanged between processes. These, in the case of an X25 network, will be carried in the data field of the information frame. The definition of standard procedures within the network to perform a number of functions, will require each host to map its own local procedures into the network standard. Therefore each host needs only to implement a single mapping per function. An important consideration is the design of protocols that are efficient. This requirement can be met by designing protocols which perform these functions at the most appropriate level. As an example let us consider the communication between a computer and a terminal. The terminal generates characters, a sequence of such characters comprises a command, upon which the application in the computer takes some action. The required actions are similar in a variety of systems. The difference lies in the coding of the command. A network standard command is needed which can be mapped into the local system procedures. It will also be wasteful in network utilisation and offers no extra advantage if we connect across the network at the character level, that is to say send each character generated in a single packet. The computer has to wait until a complete command is received before it can process it. Therefore we should connect at the message or command level, saving in both communication subnet and computer resources.

This requirement of performing the mapping at the correct level can be met by incorporating the network protocols within the main computer connecting to the communication subnet. Alternatively if the local system does consist of a front end and a mainframe computer, communication between the two must be at the process level and achieved by the exchange of messages between processes. None of these goals can be achieved effectively in present-day operating systems which at best are too centralised; at worst they are not very efficient in providing the real-time environment required. The present trends are to provide such facilities in computers and we should expect to see, during the nineteen-eighties, systems that are more flexible in accommodating distributed access in an efficient manner.

The high level protocols can be defined without reference to any existing systems. The early development of these concepts and the framework or architecture with which they function will formulate the requirements for systems which are to support them. The goals are therefore twofold: firstly to define procedures which can enable the communication between inhomogeneous computers and terminals in a network environment, and secondly to provide the basis for the development of distributed systems.

Distributed Processing

The high level communication protocols will enable us to define a number of network-wide functions that can be performed according to a network standard. If these are designed correctly, they will take us towards a framework which can be used for distributed processing. In the distributed processing environment we have to define a universal inter-process communication scheme. The high level protocols will then be seen as a number of distributed utilities that can be employed by the user or application level processes to perform specific functions.

Distributed processing will enable resource sharing in networks. As indicated at the beginning of this section resource sharing has been the ultimate goal of the research networks. By resource sharing[1] we mean that the computers interconnected via a communication subnet can call on each other's resources to execute a total task for the user. The system under which they cooperate to achieve this makes possible the access of a remote resource with the same ease as it would for a local one. In fact the aim is to build a facility in which access to a resource is uniform and independent of whether it is local or remote.

In Section 6.1 of Chapter 6 we gave the definition of a process and modelled the operation of a protocol on the communication between two processes. We shall extend this concept to describe all distributed resources and functions in terms of processes. For example, in such a network an interactive terminal and a file can both be modelled in terms of processes. Therefore the operation of displaying a file on a terminal can be modelled in terms of process communication. The physical terminal and file are driven and accessed respectively via their associated processes. The organisation of such a system of asynchronous processes is achieved through a distributed kernel or nucleus, the task of which is to schedule the processes and provide the necessary protection between them. The distributed kernel, the computers and the communication subnet make up the distributed processing environment. We shall return to this problem at the end of this chapter.

7.2   THE TRANSPORT SERVICE

Public data networks have focused attention on interfaces for accessing communication subnet services. In a fast developing technology for computer communications there will be a variety of transmission methods. These will include public and private, distributed as well as local, networks. Techniques like packet and circuit switching will be used side by side with local wire broadcast networks, satellite channels, multi-drop and point-to-point circuits. Each transmission service has its own characteristics. This implies that processes which connect via a variety of transmission media or networks will have to implement different procedures for each of these media. This is because the sophistication and services of the transport systems vary. Even in a packet-switched environment we can have differences in service characteristics between a datagram and a virtual call interface. The latter offers flow control on a per call basis and arrival of packets in sequence; these services have to be provided by the host for datagrams. The virtual call, as defined in X25, does not provide end-to-end security and if a call is reset by the network, the user must provide recovery mechanisms of his own.

The notion of a transport service is that of a universal communications interface which offers to processes uniform facilities independent of the underlying communications medium. The transport interface can be viewed as the upper interface of a transport protocol. The interface is constant, irrespective of the communication subnet services. The protocol itself is very much a function of these services. We therefore have the definition that a transport protocol bridges the gap between services available and facilities desired.[2] The transport protocol functions can be very trivial or very complex depending on the underlying medium. Figure 7.2 illustrates how this fits into the hierarchical picture of communication protocols.

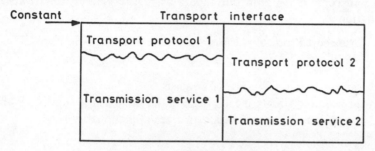

Figure 7.2 Transport protocol—bridging the gap between transmission services and a set of standard facilities

For connecting a host to a packet-switched network four levels of protocol are required.[3] The physical link, the link access control and packet transfer procedures are provided by the communications subnet. The three levels of X25, see Section 6.4, Chapter 6, are examples of these three levels of protocol. The fourth level is the transport protocol with a universal upper interface, see Figure 7.3. Before designing a transport protocol we must have a clear idea of the facilities it has to provide to the processes above it or, looked at from above, the functional requirements imposed on the transport services from the processes that are its users. We must also consider which of these services are already provided by the transmission medium underneath. The transport protocol is

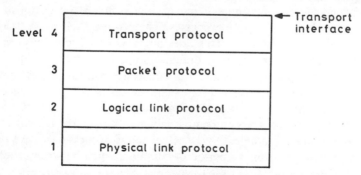

Figure 7.3 Communication protocols hierarchy

therefore a function of the required facilities (F) and the services (S) offered by the communication subnet:[4]

$$\text{Transport Protocol} = TP\,(F,S)$$

By defining a universal set of facilities we reduce F to a constant and the transport protocol becomes a function of the communication subnet services only. Returning to our definition of level structure in Chapter 6, page 198, and Figure 6.5 in conjunction with our model of Figure 7.3, we can rewrite the above equation as:

$$\text{Transport Protocol} = \text{Level 4 Services} - \text{Level 3 Services}$$
$$= F - S$$

where subtraction is the difference of two sets.

When the required standard facilities are the same as the services S offered by level 3 the transport protocol becomes a zero functionality level.

Transport Interface

To define the transport interface we need to consider the functional requirements for the communication between processes. In Section 6.1 of Chapter 6 we saw that a process is a virtual processor with a number of input and output ports. In a distributed environment, processes cooperate to implement protocols and execute tasks for their users, which can be higher level processes. Processes are event driven; an event is associated with the receipt or despatch of a message. Before two processes can exchange messages they must be aware of each other's existence, and when a series of messages has to be exchanged for the completion of a task there must be a notion of connection or association between processes. At any instant of time there can be a number of processes at a single host in association with remote ones and all system resources like store, CPU and communication bandwidth must be shared fairly between these.

Processes within a single host are identified according to local conventions. Some network-wide addressing scheme is necessary for the establishment of communication between remote processes. The process itself must be uniquely identifiable within the network. This does not of course necessarily imply that all processes in a network have a unique name. In fact the unique naming approach is both expensive and unhelpful and a hierarchical addressing scheme is to be preferred. In a hierarchical scheme processes in different hosts can have the same name. They are distinguished from each other by the host address on the network. When processes can be uniquely identified in the network they can call each other and communicate via the exchange of messages. The notion of an association will exist for the period of communication between processes. In the real-time environment in which processes operate, an association between two processes is identified by the names of the ports at each process. This is the minimum requirement for an association and we can have more than one association between two processes as well as two independent associations at a single port of a process. The only restriction is that the pair of ports at the two ends of each association uniquely identify it. Figure 7.4 illustrates this. Three processes A, B and C have associations via a number of ports. Process A multiplexes two associations with B via port a_1 and shares port a_2 for associations (a_2, b_3) with B and (a_2, c_1) with C. Each association is identified via a pair of ports, that is to say the

$$\text{association address} = (\text{port 1}, \text{port 2})$$

In a packet-switched network a message from one process to another with which it has an association carries either explicitly or implicitly the network address of the destination process and identifies the association. The structure of an address is as follows:

destination network; dest. host; dest. process; association address.

The destination host address is ambiguous in that a host can be connected to a packet-switched network at more than one point in the network. Does the address then specify the host or the network connection? As we shall see later each host is free to have a number of transport service processes through which connections are established. Should the destination host address specify also the particular transport service? Some of the solutions to these questions depend on the underlying network and how the network itself treats addresses and routes packets internally. In the above address the destination process and association addresses do not concern the network at all. Only the first two parts of the address do. In that address structure we have anticipated the need to cross network boundaries.

As well as a means of global identification of processes and the establishment of paths between them, we require that messages be exchanged on these paths without corruption or loss and that they be delivered in the same order in which they left their source. In the event of failure of the communication subnet the transport service must also provide for the processes an error recovery mechanism

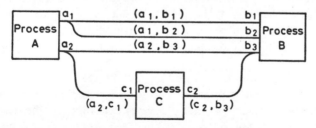

Association between processes A,B shown as (a_n, b_n)

Figure 7.4   Port associations between processes

which detects the loss or duplication of messages. As an example consider the reset of a virtual call in an X25-based network. An end-to-end protocol must be implemented to retransmit messages that have been lost due to this reset.

The transport interface provides the facility for processes to establish connections with each other and to exchange messages. We can consider the transport interface as a network-wide facility which relieves each process from the burden of managing its communication requirements. Figure 7.5(a) shows

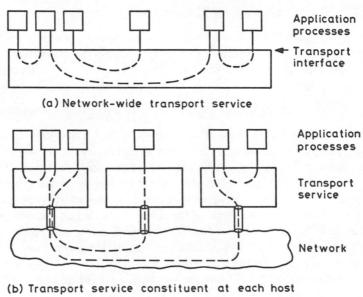

(a) Network-wide transport service

(b) Transport service constituent at each host

Figure 7.5 Transport service

the multiplexing of a number of communication paths between processes via the transport service. It is of no consequence to the processes whether their correspondent is local or remote; this is taken care of by the transport service. In Figure 7.5(b) we have split the logical structure of Figure 7.5(a) into the constituent transport services located at individual hosts. We have also shown that local communication between processes takes place through the same transport interface.

Processes exchange messages, and each complete message received implies an action by the receiving process. The transport service must not impose a restriction on the message size that processes exchange. At the destination the receiving process does not act on anything other than a complete message, it therefore does not require to be notified until such a complete message has arrived.

The Transport Interface Primitives

Now that we have outlined the requirements for association and exchange of messages between processes, we can attempt to define a hypothetical transport interface in terms of a number of primitive functions.[5]

The first requirement is for a process wishing to enter into an association or being prepared to accept an association to become known to its local transport service. To enter into an association the process actively proposes the establishment of a data transfer channel with a remote process. It does this by issuing a CONNECT to the transport service in which the address of the remote process is given and the desired service specified. The transport service will acknowledge the receipt of the CONNECT and subsequently notify the process initiating the call of the result of the call attempt. Between the acknowledgement of the CONNECT and the signal to indicate the result, control is returned to the process so that it can proceed with other tasks. When the CONNECT is serviced, an area of store is set aside which can be accessed by both transport service and process and via which the progress of the CONNECT is reported. Alternatively a message passing scheme can be used to indicate progress. Implicit in the CONNECT primitive is the establishment of a local path between process and transport service.

Processes which make themselves known to the transport service through issuing a CONNECT must call a process which is known to its remote station, otherwise the association will fail. Processes declare their willingness to accept calls by making themselves known through a LISTEN primitive. This sets up a path between the process and the transport service and indicates the readiness of the process to accept an association with a remote process. A process which has issued a LISTEN is available network-wide and will respond to an incoming call either with an ACCEPT primitive or by refusing the call with a REJECT primitive. The ACCEPT or REJECT is reflected back to the process issuing the CONNECT across its transport service interface.

A process can issue a number of LISTEN primitives and accept several calls through the network. A CANCEL primitive allows a process to withdraw previously issued LISTENs. When all of these have been cancelled, the transport service loses all knowledge of this process.

Once a CONNECT and LISTEN have been matched, and an association confirmed through an ACCEPT, messages can be exchanged between the two processes. A process indicates its readiness to receive data by issuing a RECEIVE primitive to its transport service. This implies the allocation of buffers to receive a message. The issuing process will be notified by the transport service when a complete message has been placed in the buffers and this completes the operation of the RECEIVE primitive. A RECEIVE primitive is matched by a SENT primitive from the opposite end to effect a message transfer. The SENT is issued by a process at the transport interface and points to a buffer which contains a message to be transmitted. The matching of RECEIVE and SENT can be done in a variety of ways.

One proposed method[1] is for the SENT to be stored at the location of the process which issued it, called the 'rendezvous' site and wait for a matching RECEIVE to arrive from the remote process site. The matching of RECEIVE and SENT is the responsibility of the transport protocol, and the arrival of a matching RECEIVE can be interpreted as a 'permit' by a transport service to transmit a message. Alternatively in an X25-based network, the window mechanism at level 3 can be used to control the interaction between SENT and RECEIVE at the two ends. We shall return to the use of X25 as a transmission medium interface later on in this chapter.

When a SENT or RECEIVE has been issued, the process should have the option to cancel these. In the case of SENT a CANCEL SENT can only be honoured if the total message has not been yet transmitted. This is because the transport service at the destination hands over to processes complete messages and there is no way of ensuring that the completed message has not arrived, been handed over and acted upon by the destination process. But if a CANCEL SENT is received at the transport interface before the total message is transmitted, the remainder of the message is ignored and a transport service command to purge the partially completed message at the destination is sent instead. The CANCEL RECEIVE is simpler in that, if it is issued before the complete message is handed over to the process, it can always be honoured and will result in the loss of one message. The sending process must be notified of the lack of success in completing the SENT primitive of a particular message.

The notification to the origination process that a message has been handed to its destination is a very important function of the transport service. It implies the end-to-end acknowledgement of messages by transport services. In the event of failure of the communication services the recovery will be per message. This raises the question of whether the unlimited size of a message is a practicable proposition if whole messages have to be retransmitted, or whether there should be a large, but nevertheless manageable, message size to make end-to-end recovery efficient.

A DISCONNECT primitive is used to end an association in a controlled fashion and a pair of DISCONNECTs must be exchanged, one from each end, to close the association. Before the transport service confirms the DISCONNECT, it must ensure that all outstanding messages on that association have been delivered to their destination. After a process issues a DISCONNECT it is not allowed to initiate further SENTs. Therefore a DISCONNECT is a controlled closing down of an association and follows the flow of messages arriving after the last message. A DESTROY primitive allows the process to close a call down unilaterally and will result in the loss of messages.

During the data transfer phase, the transport service undertakes to deliver messages in the order that SENTs were issued if more than a single one is outstanding. It also undertakes to recover from communication subnet failures and implement flow control between processes. For both of these functions the transport service must uniquely identify messages in a liaison, for example by the use of a numbering scheme.

Whenever flow control is employed, data flows can cease if synchronisation is lost between communicating processes. To recover from such an event we need to employ an independent control channel able to function outside the flow-controlled data channel. We can view the single path between two processes as a full duplex channel on which both data and control information flows. This channel is flow controlled and in the event of flows ceasing we need the facility to switch the flow of control information to an independent control channel. To achieve this we employ an INTERRUPT primitive whose function is the same as SENT, but the message handed over in an INTERRUPT will be transmitted outside the normal flow of messages. It can arrive at the destination before messages handed over to the transport service by previously actioned SENTs. Depending on the circumstances, an INTERRUPT message might be sent as part of the communication subnet normal flows or cause the generation of interrupts at these lower levels. For receiving interrupts, a process must allocate resources, and CONINTERRUPT is the equivalent primitive to RECEIVE in the normal data transfer channel. It declares the willingness of the process to receive interrupt messages and allocates a buffer for such messages. The resources for receiving interrupts can be withdrawn by sending a DISINTERRUPT primitive to the transport interface. It is worth mentioning that one of the requirements of processes could be to mark the position on the message stream at which the interrupt-implied action should synchronise. This is part of the protocol between processes using the transport service. Such a mark cannot be placed on messages that have already been handed to the transport service for transmission.

In the event of irrecoverable loss of synchronisation between processes, a RESET primitive forces the association path to return to an initial condition and to discard all data within the association. The outcome of a RESET can be viewed as a completely new association, where advantage has been taken of the existence of the logical path to avoid entering a new association establishment phase.

Finally, for a number of applications the concept of an association is managed by the communicating processes. This is valuable in the case where only a small number of messages has to be exchanged for the completion of a task as it is expensive in resources to set up and destroy an association through the communication subnet. We carry over the concept of a datagram to the transport service interface. A process declares its readiness to accept messages on a transport service port by sending a RECEIVE DATAGRAM primitive. Other processes can send to it single messages by the use of the SENT DATAGRAM primitive which hands over a message and the full destination process address.

SENT DATAGRAM can be considered logically as a CONNECT + SENT + DISCONNECT while RECEIVE DATAGRAM is equivalent to LISTEN + ACCEPT + RECEIVE + DISCONNECT. The implementation of the datagram service can be similar to or different from the association service depending on the communication subnet facilities.

Class	Name	Function
Association establishment and termination	CONNECT LISTEN ACCEPT REJECT CANCEL DISCONNECT DESTROY	establish association prepared to receive CONNECT association accepted association rejected revoke LISTEN control close of association uncontrolled close of association
Data transfer	SENT RECEIVE CANSENT CANRECEIVE	message for remote process prepared to receive message purge operation on SENT purge operation on RECEIVE
Synchronisation	INTERRUPT CONINTERRUPT DISINTERRUPT RESET	sent interrupt prepared to receive interrupt cancel CONINTERRUPT restart association
Datagram service	SENT DATAGRAM RECEIVE DATAGRAM	datagram to be sent prepared to receive datagram
Switch	SWITCH	change local process address

Figure 7.6 Transport interface primitives

Figure 7.6 is a table which summarises the set of primitives for the transport service interface. As well as the primitives discussed above we have added a SWITCH primitive. Its function is to inform the transport service of a change of process connecting to the transport service port. The need for such a primitive will be discussed in the next section.

Transport Protocols

The abstract description of the transport service functions in terms of a small number of primitives has evolved from the definition and implementation of transport protocols in experimental networks. Pioneer amongst these was the ARPA network host-to-host protocol.[6] Other protocols which have been implemented are the Transport Station protocols in the Cyclades and EIN networks. Experience from these has culminated in the production by the International Federation for Information Processing (IFIP) Working Group 6.1 of a 'Proposal for an international end-to-end protocol'.[4] This is the first document which attempts to separate the protocol functions from the underlying communication medium. This proposal has been input to an ISO subcommittee formed in 1978 to consider the requirements for standards in the area of distributed access and processing. This is subcommittee 16 of Technical Committee 97 (ISO/TC97/SC16) and has the title 'Open System Interconnection'. As the aim of these developments is to achieve communication between inhomogeneous systems, general agreement between manufacturers and users of computers on the functions and implementation of these services is essential. What we shall do here is to give an example of how a transport protocol can be defined for use in a packet-switched environment offering the user an X25 interface. This particular transport protocol will be one of the first to be discussed in ISO.

The X25 interface offers at present virtual call and permanent virtual circuit facilities and will by the end of the current study period of CCITT in 1980 also offer a datagram facility, see Chapter 6, Section 6.4. The virtual calls (VCs) enable users to establish connections between pairs of hosts in the network. The characteristics of these connections are that they deliver packets in the order in which they were handed to the network and without loss of data. The network can cause resets on a virtual circuit, and under these conditions packets entered in the network and acknowledged at the local interface can be lost. The restart facility can be used by the network to clear unilaterally all virtual calls and reset all permanent virtual circuits, see page 252, which can also result in loss of data. Although the public data network reliability will be high and resets, clears and restarts due to internal network failures will be minimal (for example the French Transpac network quotes that failures causing reset and restart will be less than 1 in 200 hours of operation per call) the public network cannot control local errors. Such errors causing, for example, a re-initialisation of the local link level procedures will result in a restart from the DCE end of the interface. This is rather an extreme and unnecessary action but it is nevertheless a design decision taken by the network implementers. There is also a finite possibility that link errors can remain undetected by the polynomial check sequence. The probability quoted for the loss of a 1000-bit packet is less than 10^{-10}. Most recent evidence[7] indicates that this upper bound is as high as 10^{-8}. Finally the transmission medium transports packets whose allowed maximum size is unacceptably small for messages. The transport service must overcome the shortcomings of the transmission medium and provide the facilities required at the transport interface.

In Figure 7.7 we show five associations between three processes across transport service interfaces. These are the same associations as shown in Figure 7.4. The multiplexing of a number of associations into a single port at a process is of no significance to the transport station interface. However, it does provide a unique port number for each association at the interface. Processes then can make use of this facility to suit their purposes. It can remove from each process the need to keep tables of local and remote process port numbers. To identify the association, it simply maps its data streams onto the unique transport service ports. The IFIP proposal adopts a slightly different approach, in which transport protocols identify liaisons on the basis of pairs of ports, one of the local and the other of the remote transport service, similar to the description of Figure 7.4. In Figure 7.7 the question arises as to whether the paths of the three associations between processes A and B through transport services D and E should be independent virtual calls in an X25 network, or multiplexed over a single virtual call. One should consider further whether associations between a number of processes at two hosts should all use the same virtual call.

Here we shall assume that there is a unique virtual circuit used per association. This will simplify the transport protocol design. The alternative would require further mechanisms to share the facilities of a virtual circuit and to ensure that flow control problems in one association do not adversely affect the rest. Clearly, as this choice makes for a simpler protocol, it should be preferred. Which solution is actually adopted eventually must depend on the

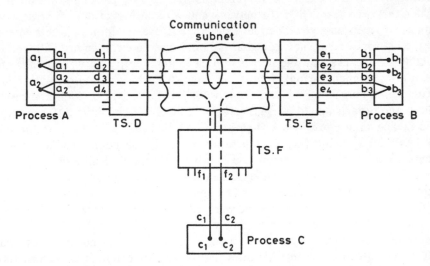

Figure 7.7   Associations using the transport service

tariff structure of X25-based networks. In packet-switched networks the primary charge to the customer is per packet and as long as this remains so the choice of individual virtual circuits per association is a sensible one. But public data networks will also levy charges on two other counts; a standard yearly charge depending on the maximum number of simultaneous virtual calls that a DTE can have and a connection charge for the duration of a virtual call. It is believed that these will be nominal charges and therefore there should be no reason to restrict the number of virtual calls. If tariffs nevertheless encourage the multiplexing of several associations on a single virtual circuit, that seems to be contrary to good design principles. This is because the procedures already provided by X25 would have to be repeated at the higher level, not for good engineering reasons, but to overcome a bad tariff structure.

7.3 A TRANSPORT PROTOCOL

The ISO subcommittee formed to study the requirements for standards in 'Open System Interconnection' considered that amongst its first areas of study would be the requirements for a transport protocol. Most urgent amongst these is the definition of a transport protocol in an X25 network. More recently CCITT has set up a rapporteur's group to look at this same requirement and to consider whether the PTTs will be offering services on their networks at this level. Clearly a standard transport protocol for X25 will be emerging soon.

We shall attempt here to anticipate such a protocol. The task is made easier as both the lower and upper interfaces in the protocol are well defined. X25 facilities define the lower interface and the primitives discussed in the last section define the upper interface. The functions to be implemented in the protocol are those which bridge the gap between the two. The description that follows must be seen as an example of how such a protocol could be defined. Although it borrows heavily from some of the concepts developed in the IFIP proposals,[4] any standard proposals developed in ISO are bound to be different in detail if not in philosophy.

Protocol Functions

The following assumptions will be made in designing the protocol. During error-free operation of X25, information packets on a virtual circuit are delivered in the same order as that in which they entered the network and without any loss. The probability that an error has remained undetected in the network is small but finite. In the event of any loss of packets or sequence, the X25 mechanisms in the network or in the host will cause a reset or clear action to be taken. The reset action will re-initialise the flows on that particular virtual circuit (VC or PVC) and packets that have been previously transmitted and acknowledged across the X25 interface can be lost. The clearing of a virtual call, which can also result from a restart across the interface, will cause the loss of the communication path and loss of data.

The transport service must recover from loss of communication and data due to clear and from loss of data due to reset. It will transmit for and deliver to the user complete messages. The boundaries of a message, which for transmission spans a number of X25 packets, will be identified by making use of the 'more data bit' in X25. The transport protocol error recovery will be per message rather than per packet.

The transport protocol will also offer a choice of the type and grade of service for the user. The type of service will either be a long-term association which we shall call *liaison* or a datagram service. The grade of service can include priority classes, extra error protection and data security by encryption.

Liaison Establishment

Processes in a distributed environment are uniquely identified in a hierarchical address space. The objects that have the ability to establish associations are the process ports and the transport service sees different ports on the same process as independent objects. The process address therefore includes the process port number.

A process CONNECT or LISTEN always identifies the local process and port in the calling process address field. The CONNECT also includes the destination process address as well as call parameters and data. The call parameters identify the grade of service for the proposed liaison. The data, if present, is handed over to the remote process.

In a distributed network of k processes with a total of m process ports, where $m \geqslant k$, there are $m(m - 1)/2$ possible full duplex liaisons. We have not counted the trivial liaison of a process port with itself. If any of these liaisons is not 'connected' it is said to be 'free'. No information exists in the network about free liaisons. The only information that exists in connection with a process port when it is not part of a liaison is where it has issued a LISTEN on a transport service and obtained a transport service port number. Multiple LISTENs can exist for a single process port. Each one is allocated a distinct transport service port. When a CONNECT is sent by another process it is matched with an existing LISTEN and a liaison is established.

A CONNECT identifies both the service and target processes and creates a block of information about the liaison at the point at which the CONNECT was issued. We shall call this information the 'liaison block'. A liaison is completed when two such blocks have been created, one at each end of the respective transport services, and are marked as active. As soon as the CONNECT is issued, a local transport service (TS) port is allocated and uniquely identifies the liaison block created. The process issuing the CONNECT is also notified of the port number. Any subsequent communication between process

Local TS port
Liaison state
Remote TS port
Local process address
Remote process address
Liaison service parameters
Send buffer size
Receive buffer size
N(S)-next send message number
N(R)- next receive message number
M(S)- maximum send message number
M(R)-maximum receive message number

Figure 7.8   Liaison block

and TS proceeds by using the TS port number. Figure 7.8 shows the possible structure and contents of a liaison block. We shall discuss the contents and significance of these fields later in this section.

As mentioned above we can consider the state of any possible liaisons as 'free' until a CONNECT is issued. This uniquely identifies the liaison with the pair of process addresses. It brings the liaison state to 'Connecting'. It will result in the despatch of a transport protocol command to the destination TS where it will be matched with a LISTEN issued by the target process, if a free one exists. We therefore have the notion of a table of process addresses at each TS which have issued a LISTEN and in which the local TS port is identified, see Figure 7.9. The data and information arriving in the CONNECT command are supplied to the process via the allocated TS port in response to the previously issued LISTEN. If the liaison is accepted, a TS command is returned to the TS which originated the CONNECT and the liaison is 'connected'. If the CONNECT fails due to target host out of service, or target process not present, or

Process address	TS port
Process name - port no.	TS port no.
— — — — — —	— — — —
— — — — — —	— — — —

Figure 7.9   TS table of processes

not prepared to accept call, the information is passed to the calling process and the liaison becomes 'free' again. When a liaison is successful, the called TS will create its own liaison block. The TS response to the 'CONNECT' in this case will supply the TS port number as well as other initialising information.

Once a liaison has been connected the data exchange can commence and is controlled by the matching of SENT and RECEIVE primitives. The X25 facilities are adequate if operating correctly to guarantee the integrity of the data exchange. The TS will monitor this and in the event of failure, will reset the X25 virtual call. The liaison can also be subject to resets or clears of its X25 virtual circuit due to local interface failures or communication subnet action. In the event of a reset of the virtual circuit, a resynchronising mechanism must establish whether messages have to be retransmitted. If the X25 call was cleared then another must be established and the liaison blocks at the two ends matched before the liaison can resynchronise and proceed. This reconnection attempt can fail if the liaison has in the meantime broken unilaterally at one end. This will result in no matching liaison block in the correct state being found. In the event of reconnection being necessary, the initiative is with the TS from which the original CONNECT was issued. Figure 7.10 shows the state transition diagram of a liaison. It shows the transitions discussed above as well as the termination of a liaison due to a process action at the TS interface, which can result from the issuing of a DISCONNECT or DESTROY primitive.

The format of the transport protocol commands for the establishment,

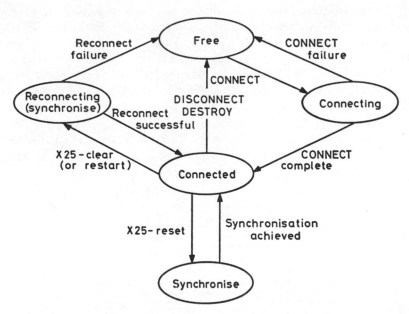

Figure 7.10   State transition diagram—liaison establishment and maintenance

resynchronisation and reconnection of a liaison reflect the information in the liaison block. A liaison initialise command sent as a result of a CONNECT will be identified as such in an operation code. The operation code identifies the local liaison state and implies the action to be performed by the receiver. In the case of a CONNECT it will search for a LISTEN issued by the destination process address on a TS port. This remote TS port number is not known to the local TS at this instant and the field can be omitted or included and set to all zeros. The latter action assumes that TS port numbers are numbered from 1 upwards. This practice was adopted by the ARPA net where each packet arriving was allocated to a TS port and port zero was allocated for servicing incoming liaison requests. The local and remote address fields uniquely identify the source and target processes. In the X25 environment, the part of the address that identifies the local and remote DTE addresses is either included in the X25 call request packet address fields, see Chapter 6, Section 6.4, or, if the X25 connection is already established, it is implied. Therefore in the liaison initialise command only the addresses beyond the DTEs are included.

The liaison service parameters, see Figure 7.8, which indicate the priority, security and the acceptable error rate for the call, will be transmitted and imply end-to-end functions. For example, if extra security is required messages can be encrypted and a per message sum check included if a very low residual error rate is requested. Priority is a little more complex: local TS priority can be given to messages of a particular liaison or use can be made of priority virtual circuits via the X25 interface. The Canadian Datapac network, for example, already offers two priority classes for virtual calls. The cost per packet is greater for high priority calls and the maximum packet size is 128 bytes against 256 bytes for low priority calls.

On the establishment of a new liaison, messages are numbered sequentially modulo n starting from zero. Therefore the next send, $N(S)$, and next receive, $N(R)$, message numbers, see Figure 7.8, are initialised to zero. The maximum receive message number, $M(R)$, indicates the number of messages, $[M(R) - N(R)]_n$ that the TS is prepared to receive on that liaison. It implies a number of RECEIVEs issued by the process. This number gives permission to the remote TS to transmit this number of messages. As RECEIVEs will probably be issued after the liaison is established and during operation their issue might be delayed, we shall assume that maximum receive message number always implies the readiness to receive one message more than the number of oustanding RECEIVEs. The matching of SENT and RECEIVE before a message is transmitted is the 'rendezvous' scheme discussed in the last section implemented via credits implied in the maximum receive message number. To allow an extra credit will increase efficiency and should have no adverse effect on flow control at this level. This is because a number of resources is allocated at the packet level of X25 in terms of packet buffers to accommodate the level 3 window size. This window will not be advanced until a RECEIVE is issued allocating a buffer for the packets to be accumulated. Therefore at liaison initialisation both the maximum receive $M(R)$ and maximum send $M(S)$ fields will be set to one.

The sent and receive buffer sizes are a matter of negotiation between the processes, but the TS must know these. They do not have to be transmitted in the liaison initialisation command.

The data handed to the TS with the CONNECT are transmitted to the target process unchanged and their function is a matter for the process-to-process protocol. They can for example in the case of a terminal connecting to an editor processor contain an identification and authorisation code.

Message Transfer and Liaison Maintenance

Once the liaison is established, two liaison blocks exist at each end of the communication path. The liaison is in the connected state, and the process addresses and TS port numbers are stored in both blocks. Figure 7.11 shows our concept of a liaison for a simple configuration with a single TS at each DTE. Processes communicate with their TS using the TS port number. The transport protocol maps each TS port number onto the appropriate X25 virtual circuit number.

As messages are handed over to the TS by the SENT primitive the maximum send message number $M(S)$ (see Figure 7.8) is checked and if $M(S) \geqslant N(S)$, the next sent message number, the message can be transmitted. It is transmitted as a complete packet sequence in X25 by use of the more data bit and the local $N(S)$ is incremented by one. There is no need to include the message number

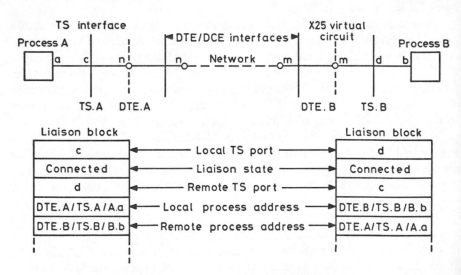

Figure 7.11   Example of connected liaison

in a TS header for message identification purposes as this can be deduced at the receiving end from the change to a new packet sequence. What must be included in a header at the beginning of each message are the following: the next receive message number $N(R)$, which confirms the receipt of all messages prior to it, and the maximum receive message number $M(R)$, which defines the number of messages that the TS is prepared to accept. It conveys to the opposite end the number of outstanding RECEIVES at the local interface. As RECEIVEs can be cancelled as well as issued by the process connecting to the TS, the $M(R)$ received by a TS might be less than the previous $M(R)$, but not less than the last $N(R)$ received. In this case it takes back authority (or credits) previously granted to transmit these messages. When this occurs, the transmission of any messages above the new $M(R)$ that has already started will cease until a new higher number $M(R)$ is received. The TS can stop the flow of any further data associated with withdrawn credits by not advancing the X25 window. Receive buffers are filled in the order in which the RECEIVEs associated with them were issued.

If a SENT is cancelled before a message transmission begins no protocol action is taken; the message is simply not transmitted. If the message was completely transmitted, then the CANCEL SENT cannot be honoured as the message could already have been handed to the destination process. When part of the message has been transmitted, a CANCEL SENT will result in a purge action being taken. To achieve this we require that a trailer be transmitted at the end of the message. This will be of constant length and should indicate to the receiver whether the message should be handed over to the process or be erased. A purged message does not need to occupy a number in the sequence of transmitted messages. At the next message transmission the $N(S)$ is not updated. Figure 7.12 shows the packet sequence of two complete messages as transmitted by X25. Messages that can fit in a single packet cannot be purged, therefore it is not essential that they carry trailer information.

In the event of an X25 virtual circuit reset the following actions are taken.

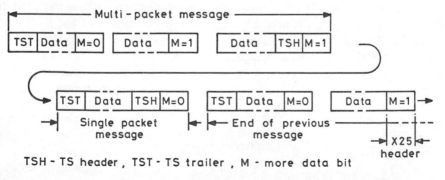

TSH - TS header , TST - TS trailer , M - more data bit

Figure 7.12   TS message transmission

Message transmission ceases, and an incomplete message, in the process of being received, is discarded. After the reset confirmations at each end, a resynchronising command is transmitted in which the next receive message number $N(R)$ and the maximum receive message number $M(R)$ are included. If $N(R)$ was previously transmitted, retransmission will commence from that message. The $M(R)$ reconfirms or updates the number of credits at each end.

When the X25 virtual call is lost as a result of a clear or restart due to local interface or network errors, the recovery action is more complex. Loss of communication can also occur locally due to remote TS failure and in some circumstances the *clear cause* field and the *diagnostic field* of the clear packet might indicate that there is no point in attempting to reconnect the liaison, as all information associated with it at the other end is lost. When reconnection seems feasible the danger still exists that the remote partner might have lost information or decided to abandon the liaison. The question also arises as to which end should attempt to re-establish the X25 channel. It seems logical that this initiative be left to the end which originally proposed the liaison, the end at which the CONNECT was issued. The other end must then start a timer as soon as communication is lost and destroy that liaison block if no reconnect is received when the timer expires. The active end of the disconnected liaison will re-establish, or attempt to re-establish, an X25 virtual call. If successful a reconnect command will be sent containing the entire liaison block information. At the receiving end this must be matched with a liaison block in the reconnecting state at the TS port referred to. As well as TS ports agreeing, the process addresses are checked and verified. The reconnection attempt will fail if any information does not match. If the address, state and port information fields agree, resynchronisation takes place so that each end can establish at which point in the liaison message stream it must start transmission.

The scheme described above will provide for all eventualities, even for the passive end of the reconnection starting a completely new liaison between the same two processes on the same TS port. In this case the new liaison block will be in the connecting state and no confusion will arise.

If, after a liaison is established, the communication path is switched to another process, the TS is notified of the change by the use of the SWITCH primitive. This passes the address of the new process to the transport service which makes the appropriate change in the local liaison block. It will also send a TS command to the remote station to update its liaison block. An example of a switch operation is where the first connection is to a logger process which will subsequently pass the connection to the process for execution of the particular task requested.

Service Parameters

The TS is in a unique position among host processes in that it has complete knowledge of the communication requirements of the overall system. It has the task of sharing the available bandwidth between a number of processes. In any system some processes will be given priority. For example, traffic from an interactive process will be given priority over traffic from a process that handles a file transfer. This is local priority and does not affect or concern the protocol and how it is managed is a matter of local implementation. The network itself might also offer X25 calls at different priority levels as mentioned earlier. Again this is a matter that can be managed by the calling end. It is nevertheless useful for the two ends of a liaison to have a standard classification of priority levels and to agree on the one to be used for the call. This will ensure that both ends of the call treat the particular liaison equally as far as priority is concerned. It would for example be pointless for a terminal handling process to operate at very high priority while the TS at the application end gives that liaison low priority.

In an earlier discussion we assumed that the TS will provide end-to-end security by keeping copies of messages until their receipt is confirmed. This provides a high grade of service which can be further enhanced by the inclusion of a sum check at the message level. When this is included, a selective retransmission scheme must be employed by the TS to request retransmission of messages whose sum check fails. This can be a simple additive sum check or a polynomial check sequence. At the other end of the scale a process might not care if some data are lost and the transport service does not need to implement the more complex end-to-end functions. These different grades of service must be provided as options at liaison establishment. For the sophisticated transport protocols implemented on large hosts there is of course no problem in implementing the more secure and complex functions. The existence of options will allow more simple devices, like intelligent terminals, to be compatible and communicate with the large hosts at the lowest level of service available; and for a number of applications where the higher grade of service is not required, it will allow resources, like message buffers, to be released more quickly.

Another optional service whose importance will increase greatly with the use of public data networks for the transmission of sensitive and confidential information is data encryption. The transport service can provide encryption on request. This will involve TS agreement on the use of ciphers and keys. Messages will be encrypted before transmission and decrypted before they are handed to the destination process. The transport service is only one of the processes in the network where encryption can be offered as a service. The variety of security requirements will require encryption at various levels.

Terminating a Liaison

We have provided two primitives for the termination of a liaison. The DISCONNECT is the orderly closing down of a liaison, while DESTROY immediately terminates the association.

The TS in response to a DISCONNECT request will despatch a DISCON-NECT TS command following the transmission of the last outstanding message. When a DISCONNECT is received from the remote TS, the liaison is terminated and the X25 call cleared. Therefore before the call can terminate, a pair of DISCONNECTs is exchanged ensuring that all messages have been correctly received. If a DISCONNECT command arrives at a TS whose local process has not yet issued one, this is passed to the process which must confirm it. After confirmation the process is not allowed to hand more messages to the TS for transmission. The TS transmits all outstanding messages followed by a DIS-CONNECT command and termination of the liaison.

When a DESTROY is issued by the process the X25 virtual call will be cleared by the TS. The X25 clear request diagnostic code field will carry an indication of the destroy action to the remote transport service. Any outstanding messages will be discarded.

When a liaison is terminated the liaison blocks which identified it at the two ends will also be destroyed.

Interrupt Facility and Reset

The interrupt facility is provided so that the process can send messages outside the sequenced flow of the liaison. We shall provide two types of interrupt and take advantage of the X25 interrupt channel in one of these.

The first interrupt type bypasses only the end-to-end message flow. The INTERRUPT primitive passes a full message to the TS. This is transmitted as such and carries a message number. The difference between this and a message handed over on a SENT is that the former is placed in front of the queue of messages awaiting transmission while the latter is placed at the back. Figure 7.13 shows what happens. The interrupt message will be transmitted immediately after the transmission of the current message is completed. In this case the interrupt message jumps the local queue, but in the X25 network it follows the sequenced flow.

We need to modify our scheme of credits to handle the allocation of interrupt buffers independently of those for normal flow. We do this by having a composite

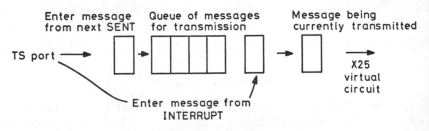

Figure 7.13   Message queue

maximum receive and sent message number field. As well as the maximum message number authorised for transmission we include the number of interrupt associated buffers: let us call them m. Therefore the number of normal messages that can be transmitted must be modified to $[M(R) - N(R) + 1 - m]_n$. We must also identify a message as interrupt and this is done in the transport service header at the start of message transmission.

This type of interrupt facility should be optional, to allow simple implementations of the TS to communicate with more complex ones. The second type of interrupt will be universally implemented and will carry only a single byte of data. This is transmitted in an X25 interrupt packet and bypasses, as well as the local TS message flow, the flow in the X25 network. Only one interrupt message at a time can be outstanding in X25. The interrupt confirmation is end-to-end and implies delivery to the destination. Thus there is no need for the TS to employ any further end-to-end protection for the interrupt which is transmitted outside the normal message numbering scheme. It does imply that the issue of a CONINTERRUPT for short interrupt messages by each process is mandatory. This can be implied in the issue of a CONNECT.

When the communicating processes lose synchronisation and flows cease, a RESET primitive is issued to resynchronise. This will result in the clearing of all local queues of messages and the sending of a reset on the X25 virtual circuit. The diagnostic code of the X25 reset will indicate to the other end that this clear resulted from a TS interface RESET. All numbers in the liaison block are reset to the initial values and the effect is to begin again as if a new liaison had started.

Datagram Service

With X25 as the transmission medium the datagram facility now defined by CCITT can be employed to carry datagrams for the transport interface user processes. The datagrams are self-contained messages. The service can operate as long as the message size does not exceed the packet size although this proviso is not essential if the X25 datagram service is defined to deliver a sequence of datagrams. The sequencing of a number of datagrams in the communication subnet is automatic if the access to and communication between datagram processes in the subnet is implemented via virtual calls as described in Chapter 6, Section 6.5.

A number of options should be offered as part of the datagram service. The user process can request delivery diagnostics if required. There are two optional facilities: the non-delivery diagnostic, which returns to the user process a message if the datagram could not be delivered, and delivery confirmation, which is returned to the user if the datagram has been successfully delivered to the destination process, and if it has not a non-delivery diagnostic is returned.

To implement the above facilities, datagrams must be uniquely identified with a reference field. If a datagram associated response has to be returned by a TS, it contains this reference field which allows the TS which originated the message to associate the response with the particular datagram. If a non-delivery diagnostic facility is implemented at the TS level it must also be offered by the communication subnet. This is to cater for the case where the remote DTE is not operational and the datagram has to be discarded by the network.

The security offered by the network for datagrams can and should be equivalent to that for packets associated with a virtual call if the datagram service is correctly designed.

7.4   PROCESSES ABOVE THE TRANSPORT SERVICE

The transport service will provide a common communications interface for all processes. It offers a number of standard functions which free the processes that use it from having to implement recovery from loss or error in the exchange of messages. Whether the standard service that emerges from the international standards bodies is like the example given in the last section or not, the functions it provides will be very similar.

The processes above the transport service will operate protocols to accomplish user tasks. The substance of these protocols will be a command structure to synchronise and execute these tasks. In contrast to the levels of protocols we discussed up to the transport level, which concerned themselves with data transmission, these processes will perform task management as their primary function. They will be defined by the users of networks to accomplish their tasks and as such are specific to these tasks. There are nevertheless a number of very important network utilities which can be defined above the transport service offering standard functions on the network. Among these are terminal handling, file transfer and remote job entry protocols. We shall in this section briefly discuss the functions of these protocols. The first of these, terminal handling, is of such importance that it will be discussed in greater detail in Chapter 8.

Terminal Protocols

Here we shall briefly discuss the requirements for terminal handling within the layered communications architecture. First we shall define a general abstract model for the communication between terminal and application.

The right-hand side of Figure 7.14 illustrates our abstract model. In the most general case, terminal and application have access to a two-dimensional data structure. The data structure consists of a number of cells which can be read or written to by both terminal and application. The application has direct access to the data structure while the human user of the terminal sees it through a display device (screen or printed page) and modifies it through a keyboard. The communication between the two is via character or symbol strings entered into the data structure. For example, the terminal operator starts entering characters into the data structure, this action is passively observed by the application until the string acquires some meaning as a command or response. The application will then take over at the appropriate instant and perform an action implied by the command. The result of the action is communicated to the user by a message entered in the data structure by the application. Instead of the application searching the build-up of user-entered characters it is normal to have a special user action which prompts the application to have a look. For example, this can be the carriage return – line feed. In our abstract model this combined operation, which is equivalent to a new line, is translated to moving the cursor from its position, say nth row, k column to the $n + 1$ row, first column. The operation of writing a character into the data structure enters the character at the existing cursor position and advances the cursor to the next column position. At any time the data structure can be erased and started afresh.

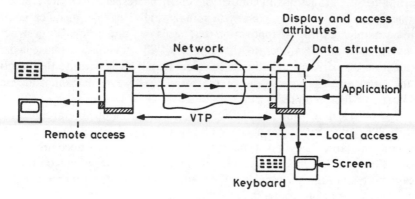

Figure 7.14   Abstract model of terminal handling

Associated with each cell of the data structure we have a display and/or access attribute. This can be modelled in terms of a second two-dimensional structure, shown in Figure 7.14. The display attribute defines the display characteristics, for example 'hide display from screen for user identifiers' or 'display in reverse video or blinking mode'. The access attributes can define areas of the data structure reserved for writing only, or reading only, for one of the correspondents, application or terminal. Finally we show at the base of the data structure a shaded area which contains non-displayable positions. These are used for special functions, such as the use of audio or visual warnings. In an alternate mode operation where after each command or message entered by either partner it is the other's turn, it can also contain information on the next turn. This completes the abstract description of interactive terminal operation. It is a model and no real system is likely to be implemented in this fashion.

To relate our model to existing terminal types it suffices to say that for teletypes the data structure is one-dimensional, and for page mode visual display units it is two-dimensional. The page mode operation can be subdivided into two further classes. The first exists where no access attributes are defined, the second where access attributes are being used for form filling. This second class of terminals are referred to as *data entry* or simply *form entry*.

Returning to Figure 7.14, when the terminal and application are connected via a network, they each have their own view of the data structure contents and thus the status of the interactive conversation. The virtual terminal protocol (VTP) must synchronise this communication. Before the remote terminal can access the application the VTP must establish by negotiation the compatibility of data structure dimensions, as well as display and access attributes. The VTP method of communication does not address the exact nature of the terminal. What it does address is a set of functions implemented in standard fashion. It will therefore enable terminal-to-application and terminal-to-terminal communication between functionally compatible entities irrespective of the type of the physical terminal. For example any terminal which has page mode capabilities can communicate with any application that needs two-dimensional data structure to operate. It can also operate through the VTP negotiation phase with an application that drives single line data structures. This is because the functions of the latter are a proper subset of the former. However, it cannot access an application which requires 'form' capability.

Figure 7.15 shows how the VTP protocol fits within our hierarchical architecture. The upper interfaces of the VTP process to the application and terminal are non-standard. They must be specifically designed to accommodate the application requirements on the one hand, and the real terminals on the other. Please note that the terminal itself is not shown at its proper place in the architecture. We shall come back to this in the next section.

File Transfer and File Access

The most important requirement in a distributed network of computers, after the ability to access computer resources from interactive terminals, is the necessity to handle files in a standard way. A file is a block of information or data which can be addressed as a whole. It can for example be the source code of a program in high level language, or the binary code after compilation. It can be a text file or a binary data set which provides run-time input for a program. Such files reside in a variety of storage media, such as magnetic or paper tapes, punched cards and discs. Operating systems provide local file management systems for creating, accessing, reading, writing and copying files.

The creation of a file gives it a unique name within the local system. For example, a tape file can be identified by the tape number and the position of the file within a number of sequential files on the tape. In the case of direct access files or discs, the file name is checked on the disc directory to find the file

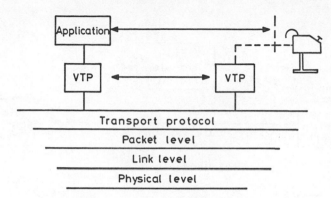

Figure 7.15 VTP in the layered architecture

position. Most systems allow a user to access parts of files called blocks or records and again the access method is device specific.

On sequential devices records can be written and read only in sequence while on random access devices, such as discs, these operations can be performed in any order. The copying of files is the operation which takes the whole file and writes it on another device. The copy must be named and copying between inhomogeneous devices will require some manipulation of the file block and record structure. Systems also use their own compression techniques to save space for the storage of files. Files that contain literal information may use different codes on different systems.

File management is performed by the local operating system according to local conventions. We need to define a network-wide file management system, to allow transfer and access of files between inhomogeneous systems in the network environment. There is one basic difference between the requirements of localised and of distributed file handling. In the former, the most common operation is file access while in the latter it is file transfer. If a whole file is to be processed it is more economic to transfer it as a whole to the point where the processing will take place. Figure 7.16(a) illustrates our concept of a file transfer in a distributed environment. In the most general case the file transfer is started at a central point which is not located at the file source or destination.[8] To manage the file transfer, three liaisons are established: two between the control point and the source and destination of the file and one between source and destination. The former carry control information associated with the file transfer, the latter carries the file itself. If the control point is collocated with one of the service processes (file source or destination) we only need a single liaison as control and data can be multiplexed on the same communication channel. This is shown in Figure 7.16(b).

For file transfer in the network environment, a network-wide convention for file identification is required. The network name is mapped by the local system

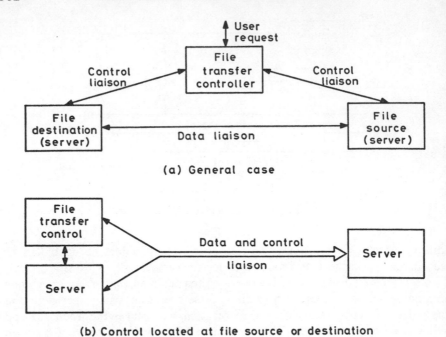

(a) General case

(b) Control located at file source or destination

Figure 7.16   File transfer protocol

into the local naming conventions, to identify the actual file. The file transfer controller must inform the systems involved whether they will act as source or destination for the file transfer and identify the files involved. It must also establish whether the transferred file will be stored in a new file or be appended to an existing one. Clearly, user authorisation and access must be verified by the controller and the participating service processes. File transfer attributes such as code-used and data compression (if applicable) must also be agreed in this phase of the protocol. The file transfer protocol may make use of a standard code such as ISO 7-bit code and a file is translated to the standard code before transmission. On some file transfers the user will require the file to be transferred without code changes, in which case the protocol will operate in a transparent mode and handle the information as a series of binary bits. Once the initial control phase is completed, the data transfer proper can begin. During the data transfer we have two levels of communication: control and data.[9] The control phase of the data transfer is between the two servers (source and destination of file) and ensures the correct operation of the protocol. It is responsible for recovery in the event of failure during the transfer.

In the transfer of long files, the ability to restart the operation at the point of failure is very important. In a homogeneous environment there is no problem, as the file structure is uniform. For example, if a file is divided into records in an identical fashion at source and destination, the file transfer can restart by the destination informing the source to restart transmission from a particular record. The uniform record structure acts as a checkpointing mechanism. Instead of defining a virtual network record structure, current proposals for file transfer protocol[8,9] actually put forward a pure checkpointing procedure during the file transfer. In the event of failure this is used to restart the file transfer.

During the data transfer phase of the protocol, checkpointing commands are transmitted by the source as part of the sequenced flow of data. These commands are sequentially numbered. When checkpointing command n is received by the file destination it associates a marker with the position in the data stream occupied by checkpoint n. A marker previously associated with the position of checkpoint $n - 1$ can be erased. The destination will inform the source of the receipt of the marker by returning a checkpoint acknowledgement. Checkpoint information is stored on a secure medium such as disc or tape. In the event of total system failure it will be used as part of a recovery mechanism to restart the file transfer from the marker associated with the last checkpoint.

Remote Job Entry Protocols

The file transfer protocol enables users to transfer files across the network. Some of these file transfers will be associated with the submission of jobs. The user will require a standard network facility to define such a job. In the most general case this will involve the transfer of files between a variety of systems in a well-defined sequence with actions defined on these files. For example, a Fortran source code file can be sent from a local to a remote system for compilation and execution. A second file residing at a different location could also be transferred to act as the data file for the job execution. The user who might have initiated the operation from a terminal would want to receive status information and a summary file containing results while the main output file is directed to a lineprinter connected to a fourth system. The total operation involves three file transfers. We shall assume that the whole operation is controlled by a job entry protocol at the system on which the job is executed. The user communicates with the job entry protocol from his terminal using a virtual terminal protocol. Figure 7.17 illustrates such a case. We also show schematically the protocols involved in the operation. We have included in the interaction between the system which executes the job and the lineprinter system a 'virtual device protocol'. This is a protocol which will establish and manage the transfer of a file onto the lineprinter. The remote job entry (RJE) process can of course be located on any system and communicate via a RJE protocol with the system that executes the job.

Before we achieve a RJE protocol of the generality of the one described in the above example we require a simpler subset which will allow the definition of a complete job as a single file, transport it for execution and return the results

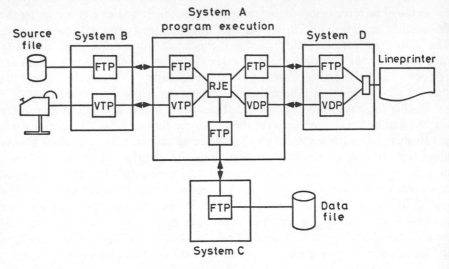

Figure 7.17   Remote job entry

to a location specified by the user. This will be the network equivalent of today's remote job entry station where the interaction is only between two systems. What we have done in our example is to separate the transfer of data in remote job entry from the control function of total task execution in the network.

As well as scheduling the series of events associated with job execution, the RJE protocol will be responsible for informing its user process of the progress of the task and its eventual completion. It must also be capable of restarting file transfers when failure has occurred in any of the systems.

7.5   DISTRIBUTED PROCESSING

In the last section we ended with the example of distributed job execution. This involved a number of protocols and their associated processes. The communication paths between processes were of two kinds. The first were paths within a single system, while the second were paths between processes on different systems. The latter require liaisons to be established across the network to carry messages between processes. Up to this point we have adopted a 'bottom up' description of our system starting from the basic communication protocols and the physical connection to the network, moving up through more sophisticated levels to the transport protocol. In a 'top down' view of our distributed system, what we have is a number of processes which must be able to establish paths between each other and to exchange information. All interactions in the system are between processes. For example, the access to a file is via processes and not directly to the stored data. The file access process acts as a monitor which ensures orderly and unambiguous access to the information it manages.

In the distributed system of processes it makes no difference whether the process being accessed is local or remote. In the latter case the hierarchy of communication protocols must be utilised to achieve controlled and correct communication. In our view of the system this is a detail of the mechanics of transport and we would like to forget it. We cannot quite do this since the transport mechanisms themselves have different characteristics of reliability and behaviour.

The example of remote job execution shown in Figure 7.17 can be redrawn to show the more simple relationship between processes, see Figure 7.18. The processes are shown as a series of boxes communicating with each other via an inter-process communication mechanism. At the top of each box we indicate the system (according to the labelling of Figure 7.17) in which the process resides. The arrows indicate standard communication protocols, and where these are between adjacent processes they imply the use of a liaison across the network. The remote job entry process has a communication path to the human user of the system at the terminal attached to system B. We see the human user as an extension of our process definition. He communicates with the RJE process according to a network standard protocol.

In Figure 7.18 we do not show the hierarchical structure of the system. Figure 7.19 illustrates the level structure for this particular task at site A where the job execution is to occur once the required source and data files have been transferred. The RJE protocol submits the job to the job stream of the machine and on completion despatches the results to site D and informs the user at site B.

Hierarchy of Processes

In a system of cooperating processes the unique classification of protocols into hierarchical levels is not possible. Each task that is executing in the system

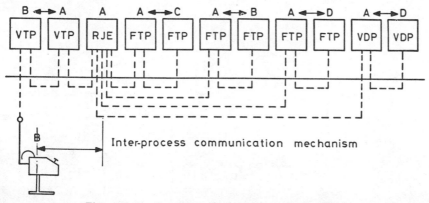

Figure 7.18   Process paths in remote job execution

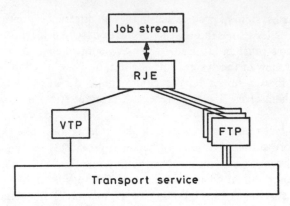

Figure 7.19   Local hierarchy at system A

creates its own hierarchy of processes. The hierarchy may be simple or complex but either way it exists only for the duration of that particular task.

The hierarchy develops naturally when a task is initiated. The task is initiated by a person entering a request at some point in the network. The request will be serviced by a process. This initial process calls a number of other processes to execute sub-tasks of the main task. It is even possible that the first process does nothing but coordinate the execution of the task by other processes and correlate their results. Processes called to execute sub-tasks might in their turn call other processes. This generates a tree-structure hierarchy as shown in Figure 7.20. This is a unique hierarchy for the execution of a specific distributed task and is different from the hierarchy of communication protocols discussed so far. At the highest level process A_1 knows only of the existence of the processes at the next level down, level B. Each process at that level has been allocated a sub-

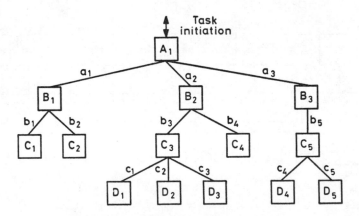

Figure 7.20   Tree-structure hierarchy

task. The division is into sub-tasks that can run independently of each other. A sub-task process, for example B_1, generates two further sub-tasks of its own and hands them to processes C_1 and C_2. When the task of C_1 is completed the results are handed over to B_1 and C_1 disappears from the hierarchy. In our example of the remote job entry, the completion of, for example, the transfer of the data file from system C to A will complete that task and the associated processes will close down. In that example the job execution cannot proceed until the complete source file arrives at A; see Figures 7.17 to 7.19. Similarly in Figure 7.20 B_1 can only report completion of its task to A_1 when both processes C_1 and C_2 have completed their task and B_1 has performed its own processing. Once this is completed B_1 also leaves the hierarchy; A_1 must still await completion of the other sub-tasks before the total task is completed. The 'top down' view of the hierarchical structure of a distributed task is in terms of a number of sub-tasks and bears little relation to the hierarchy of communication protocols. The latter caters for the point-to-point communication between two processes. In our example of Figure 7.20, if process C_1 performs a file transfer it will achieve this by employing a file transfer protocol implemented between two processes communicating with each other via a transport service which in its turn employs a number of communication protocols.

The division of the total task into a number of concurrent sub-tasks run by independent processes creates the hierarchy of Figure 7.20. This concept is very similar to the *data flow* approach to computing.[10] Data flow languages allow the programmer to define his algorithm as a series of independent actions which can proceed independently and which provide the input for another action. The example commonly used in data flow is that of the addition of two complex numbers, for example $c_1 = a_1 + ib_1$ and $c_2 = a_2 + ib_2$. The addition of the real and imaginary parts can proceed independently and the result of the additions provides the input for the function which constructs the resultant complex number. Data flow languages run on machine architectures different from the Von Neumann concept of a stored programme machine. The distributed processing problem is a data flow problem. On a macro scale the data flow cell, which performs a simple action, is replaced by the process. The internal complexity of the process is much greater but the basic principle is similar, that of a number of inputs required at process ports to complete the task and produce an output. The hierarchy of Figure 7.20 is the opposite way up to the usual representation of a data flow problem. In the latter the inputs to the problem are shown at the top of the diagram. This is equivalent to the inputs at the lowest level, level D, of Figure 7.20. The manipulation of these inputs provides outputs to be fed to the next level. These progress through the levels until they all reach the single process at the top of the diagram to complete the task. In a distributed processing problem, the structure is set up by the top process and information flows downwards. The information must reach the lowest level of processes to indicate what should be used as input. Returning to our earlier assumption that C_2 performs a file transfer, the name and attributes of the file must be passed to C_2 before it can fetch the file.

Inter-process Communication Mechanism

During the execution of a distributed task no single process has a total picture of either the processes involved or their relationship, or the state that the task has reached. As mentioned earlier the process A_1 in Figure 7.20 has knowledge only of processes at level B. In a complex task, failure of a single sub-task must not result in failure of the total task and this is particularly important if a great deal of processing associated with the task has already been completed. We have already seen that for file transfer we require a restart facility to avoid having to repeat the transfer of major parts of long files. In the more complex situation of multi-process interaction we must provide recovery mechanisms from failures and attempt to keep secure the results of completed sub-tasks. It is the function of the inter-process communication mechanism to provide this security. Figure 7.21(a) shows processes communicating via a network-wide facility. Each process is aware of its own place in the total task, i.e. its connection to the parent process which initiated it and to daughter processes initiated by it. The inter-process communication mechanism which in

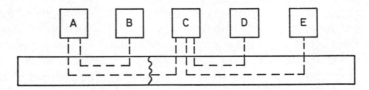

(a) Inter-process communication mechanism

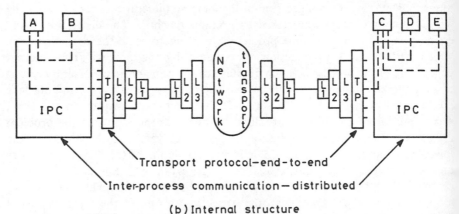

(b) Internal structure

Figure 7.21   Inter-process communication in an X25 network

the network environment must be distributed provides coordination and management of the total task. For the communication between remote processes, the inter-process communication mechanism makes use of the transport service. In the example of Figure 7.21(a), if the processes A and B are located at one system while C, D and E are at another, we shall have the internal structure shown in Figure 7.21(b) for the inter-process communication mechanism, assuming that the communication medium is an X25 network. Thus we see that above the transport service, which provides point-to-point connection between processes, we have another layer which controls interaction between a number of distributed processes. This layer has been identified by the ISO committee on 'Open system interconnection' (ISO/TC17/SC16) and has been called *session control*. It can be incorporated as part of an enhanced transport service to provide the inter-process communication facility or be implemented as an independent level. The second approach is favoured by the ISO technical working groups.

In this model the upper interface of session control provides connection ports to processes and manages sessions between pairs of local processes as well as between a local and and a remote process. In the latter case it calls on the services of the transport service to establish a path, which we earlier called a liaison, with the remote session control. Over and above the simple function of managing sessions, this level also has knowledge of services offered at its host. The intention is to define standard session control protocols for accessing these services. A call to a particular service might involve a number of sessions which will be coordinated by session control. This is the second important feature of the session control layer: that it will manage a number of distributed sessions, local or remote, for the execution of total tasks. This goal is again achieved via a protocol in which a number of distributed session control layers participate.

A further function of session control that is now under discussion at ISO is that of recovery from failure in a complex task without having to repeat completed sub-tasks. This relates to the concept of slave or daughter processes executing a number of such sub-tasks for their parent process. In the tree structure of Figure 7.20, the B level of processes are slaves to process A, B_1 is the master process for C_1 and C_2 etc. When a slave process completes its task the result is made available to the master process and secured. That is to say, if a task failure occurs it can be restarted in such a way that completed operations do not have to be repeated. For example, in the case of the remote job execution discussed earlier (see Figure 7.17) the user can be allocated a unique task identifier. If there is failure of this system A at which the job is to be executed after the data file has been transferred from system C, a restart of the task should be possible with no need for repeating that file transfer. The file should be picked up from system A. A sub-task comprises a commitment unit. The session control layer will guarantee the integrity of completed commitment units and be able to restart the task without having to repeat the processing involved in such units. It can also coordinate the total task execution during normal running of the session by allowing processes to proceed only when the required input from slave processes is available. Returning to the RJE example, the job will not be submitted to the job stream, in Figure 7.19, until both the source and data files are available.

We have outlined only some of the requirements for inter-process communication. This is an area of distributed networks where a great deal of research and development will take place in the near future. It takes the subject beyond the definition of bilateral communication protocols and moves towards definition of distributed processing systems. These will require computer operating systems which are process based and which treat local and remote process communication on an equal footing.

References

1. Walden, D. C.,
   'A system of interprocess communication in a resource sharing computer network',
   CACM, **15**, No. 4, 221 (1972).
2. Sunshine, C.A.,
   Interprocess communication protocols for computer networks,
   Ph.D. thesis, Stanford University (1975).
3. Scantlebury, R. A., and Wilkinson, P. T.,
   'The NPL data communications network',
   Proceedings of the ICCC, Stockholm, 223 (1974).
4. Cerf, V., McKenzie, A., Scantlebury, R. A., and Zimmerman, H.,
   Proposal for an international end-to-end transport protocol,
   IFIP, Working Group 6.1 (1978),
   Published also in: *Proc. Computer Network Protocols Symposium*, Liège, H5 (1978).
5 Heard, K. S., and Winsborrow, R. P. J.,
   'Functional requirements and capabilities of a portable network transport station',
   Proc. of the European Computing Congress, EUROCOMP 78, London, 215 (1978).
6. McKenzie, A. A.,
   Host/host Protocol for the ARPA Network,
   ARPA Network Information Centre, No. 8246 (1972).
7. Funk, G.,
   'Comparison of data reliability and efficiency in various standard protocols for information exchange in computer telecontrol networks',
   European Conference on Electrotechnics, EUROCON 77, 1.1.7 (1977).
8. Gien, M.,
   'A file transfer protocol',
   Proc. Computer Network Protocols Symposium, Liège, D5-1 (1978).
9. *A network independent file transfer protocol*,
   High Level Protocol Group,
   U.K. Post Office Experimental Packet Switched Network (EPSS), (1978).
10. Rumbaugh, J.,
   'A data flow multiprocessor',
   IEEE Transactions on Computers, **C-26**, No. 2, 138 (1977).

Chapter 8

Terminals in the Network

8.1 THE ROLES OF A TERMINAL

The interactive terminal is possibly the most important part of any computer network or computer system, for it is the medium through which the user communicates with the services offered to him. His view of these services is bound to be coloured by the type of terminal he is using and the way in which it aids or constrains his actions. The introduction of a network between a terminal and a computer system will place additional constraints on the user, compared with a direct connection, yet the network can offer freedom of choice between many services and so makes the ownership of a terminal potentially much more valuable. This is particularly so with a public network where all kinds of new services may appear in the future. However, some very difficult problems arise with an 'open system' where any type of terminal is required to operate with any service, due to the wide variety of terminal types that have to be supported both by the network and the attached service computers.

These problems fall into three main areas that correspond with the three major roles that the terminal has to play. This is illustrated in Figure 8.1. Firstly, the terminal serves as a peripheral device to the network and may take part in a dialogue with the user to establish calls. Secondly, the terminal performs its traditional role of acting as the intermediary in the dialogue between a remote computer system and its users. Thirdly, and from the user's point of view the most important, the terminal is a tool which helps or hinders his interaction with the outside world. These three aspects are considered in more detail below.

As a Network Peripheral

The properties required of a terminal in its role as a peripheral to a particular network depend on how it is connected to that network. With the telephone network a terminal is generally joined to a modem associated with a telephone instrument which is used to make the call in the usual manner. This has the

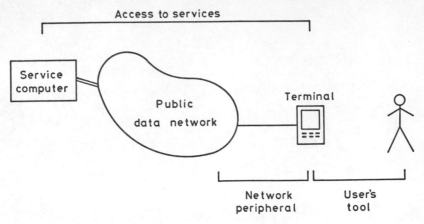

Figure 8.1   The roles of a terminal

advantage that users are familiar with the procedures involved, as well as ensuring that the telephone network signalling protocols are correctly observed.

A different arrangement is possible with new data networks where terminals can be connected directly to the data circuit terminating equipment (DCE). This allows two possibilities for the interaction needed with the network to establish calls, release calls and so forth. They are shown in the lower part of Figure 8.2. Either a special unit is provided, sometimes called a *network terminating unit* or NTU, or the signalling is done by the terminal itself.

The form to be taken by an NTU for the new public networks or, indeed, whether one is necessary at all, has not yet been established. Some of the research networks have devised their own arrangements, but there is no proposal at CCITT level that would promote uniformity between different national data networks. One view is that an NTU would incorporate similar features to the telephone instrument and would be a separate device able to establish and clear calls and provide whatever signals were necessary for the proper maintenance and operation of the network. On the other hand, there is a potential saving to be gained by incorporating the NTU within a terminal and this could well be a likely future development.

Most terminals designed for interaction with people are readily able to serve as peripherals to a network for the generation and reception of messages about call establishment and clearing. But it is important to get the interaction with the network clearly defined and separate from the dialogue with other terminals, for most users would not want to have network control messages mixed with, say, a file of text being printed from a remote computer. This suggests that, with some types of terminal, an NTU may be needed to generate and display information about the network. In practice, therefore, an NTU with perhaps a few pushbuttons and lights seems a desirable feature for a public data network.

Ideally it should be designed to pass network messages through to any associated terminal that is capable of carrying out a more sophisticated interaction, perhaps to provide a user-friendly command language.

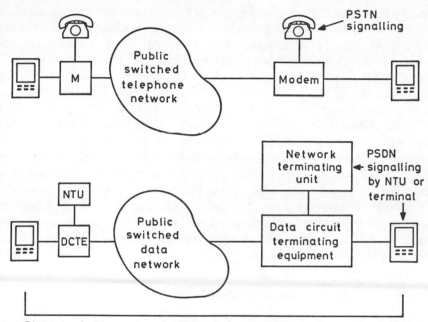

Dialogue between terminals is independent of the network

Figure 8.2   Possible forms of connection to networks

As a Computer Access Medium

The properties required of a terminal to serve as a means of communicating with a computer system are, naturally, dependent on the computer system and the kind of job that is being done. Some types of terminal may be usable for a variety of applications with greater or lesser difficulty. Others may be much less flexible, but may be particularly suitable for a certain task. There is potentially no difficulty in providing through a computer network all the traditional peripheral devices, such as tape and card readers and punches, normally associated with a large computer installation. The use of remote job entry stations is well established in private networks, and they may readily be adapted for the public network, using a dedicated connection to the parent site.

The more general purpose interactive terminals for text handling are potentially usable with a wide range of services, but again suitable protocols must be agreed. These types of terminal can be divided roughly into three categories.

Firstly, there are those terminals which present information sequentially with a minimum of structure; for example, the tickertape giving stock exchange information, or the teletype presenting messages as a sequence of characters on successive lines. The latter is often called a scroll mode terminal.

A second type of text handling terminal is the page mode terminal which handles information in the form of pages, or frames presented in succession on the screen of a visual display. This kind of terminal can build up information rapidly in an apparently random manner and this offers some advantages compared with the simpler method of display. This is because information which is not changed from page to page need not be repeated. Also, the user may interact with the information in page form in ways that are sometimes simpler than the interactions possible with a scroll mode terminal.

The third class of terminal, the data entry terminal, is an elaboration of the page mode terminal and allows areas of a screen to be reserved for special purposes. This permits interaction between the user and some parts of the information presented, while prohibiting interactions with other parts of the data structure.

Protocols for handling these various types of interactive terminal through a network are being tested in research networks and draft proposals are before some of the standards bodies. The principles behind these protocols are discussed in the later sections of this chapter.

As a Users' Tool

To serve as a tool of the user, today's terminals are generally rather inadequate; all terminals place considerable constraints on people, who usually have to adapt their normal behaviour quite remarkably to use a terminal. For example, not everyone is really keen to learn to type efficiently, so there are many one-fingered 'typists' using data terminals. Ideally, from the point of view of one person communicating with another, it should be possible to transmit and receive information as it might be exchanged, for example, between people writing on pieces of paper with pencils. Within the simple constraints of the size of paper any kind of picture or message can be indicated, of any size, in any colour, and with all kinds of emphasis, where required. Furthermore, when speech is used to help describe the picture, the information transfer is enhanced significantly, particularly when several people may interact in a conference or a committee.

It is true that terminals which transmit the movements of pencils can be associated with a speech channel, and one can send documents using scanning techniques such as facsimile or, indeed, a television camera—if the cost does not matter. But to use such techniques for interaction with a computer system is not really feasible at the present time. The truly general purpose terminal that allows users to communicate effectively with other people as well as with computer systems does not yet exist, and it may be some time away.

8.2   THE PHYSICAL TERMINAL

Physically a terminal is usually a mechanism; sometimes it is a transducer or a display. The variety is immense and, a comprehensive survey being impossible, we shall consider terminals according to their external characteristics: how they seem to their users and to the network.

The commonest terminals are general purpose units such as keyboards with printers or visual displays. We shall look first at printers and then at input devices and finally at a wider range of terminals for the human user.

Types of Printer

The earliest printers were adaptations of the teletypewriter or typewriter which printed one character at a time. Figure 8.3 shows typical mechanisms in which selection of the character to be printed is either by timing an on-the-fly

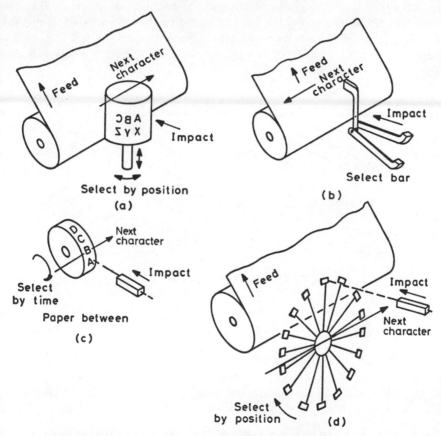

Figure 8.3   Some character-at-a-time printers

impact or selecting the position of a wheel or one of many bars. Part (a) is a teletypewriter mechanism of a similar kind to the golf-ball printer, (b) is a more traditional typewriter, (c) an on-the-fly mechanism with a single wheel and (d) the daisy-wheel which positions itself before the impact. In the typewriter, the basket of type bars is so heavy that the paper roll moves for the next character. The other mechanisms are light and themselves move to the next character position, leaving the paper-feed fixed.

From the user's viewpoint, these mechanisms match typing speeds, with a margin of speed to deal with the more copious output of a computer service. Speeds measured in tens of characters per second, together with variable 'seek' times, call for local buffering of a few characters or, if the data is handled in blocks such as packets, one such block.

Some of the recently developed character printers move so fast that the time to return at the end of the line limits their speed, whether the paper roll or the mechanism moves. So they have adopted a back-and-forward motion to minimise the repositioning, making use of storage for one line or more so that the characters of the reverse-written line can be spelt out backwards. (This method of writing is found in some ancient scripts.) Such printers, though they have a character mechanism, are like line printers in their storage requirements and their external interface.

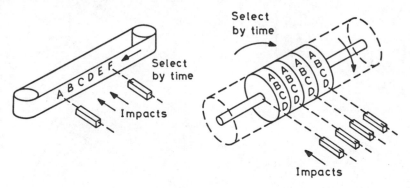

Figure 8.4   Some line-at-a-time printers

The line-at-a-time printers shown in Figure 8.4 are on-the-fly mechanisms capable of high speed and suitable for bulk output rather than interactive, single-user terminals.

All of these terminals have fairly long histories but matrix printers such as those shown in Figure 8.5 have increased in number and performance more recently, in spite of their compromise between cheapness and visual quality. They form their characters from dots, sometimes in regular array as shown, sometimes with more latitude.

The printing action can be an impact from the end of a wire, heat, electric

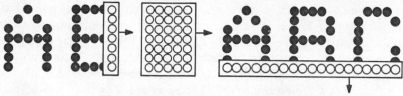

Figure 8.5   The matrix printer principle

current, burning of a metal film, electrostatic or electrochemical action or a spray of ink droplets. The scan can be horizontal or vertical so that one or many characters are formed.

Alternatively, the character can be formed by an oscillating scan of a single writing head or the completely controlled, electrically generated scan of an ink jet. The variations seem endless. Figure 8.6 shows a complete matrix used for the ISO alphabet and available in a commercial read only memory. This control aspect was expensive when matrix printing and matrix display began but is now a trivial cost.

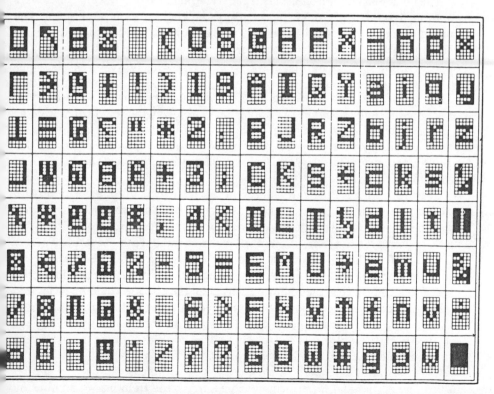

Figure 8.6   A matrix alphabet (reproduced by permission of Texas Instruments Limited)

By using a complete line of printing elements such as are shown in the third part of the Figure 8.5, the whole page is accessible and, with suitable storage, any graphic pattern can be produced. This type of printer, usually thermal or electrostatic for cheapness, can produce lines, curves and shading as well as character shapes. The loading of its two dimensional store with the graphic pattern depends on the repertoire of shapes needed. For this type of printer there are no standard languages to specify the output pattern.

Matrix printers of characters typically use a 5×7 array or a 7×9 array of dots. The former is adequate for upper case letters and the latter is more suitable for upper and lower case. The graphic quality is not very good. When the pattern is formed by an ink jet, in principle a higher degree of resolution is possible, therefore reasonable quality can be achieved. The higher resolution can be obtained from a stored pattern defined at a lower resolution, by interpolation.

Types of Display

The predominant form of display is the television tube with a scan. Characters are formed 'on-the-fly' from a repertoire of the kind shown in Figure 8.6. The same scan can be produced in colour, and colour is exploited to characterise different parts of the display. Different colours can indicate commands, responses, amendments, warnings, segments of text being processed, authorships of segments of the text and so forth.

Using the raster scan with storage for every picture element will extend its repertoire indefinitely within the limitation of resolving power. In this way, as logic and storage gets cheaper, graphics of even greater quality are produced on colour displays. As with the more versatile matrix printer, standards for writing on the store/display are lacking when we go beyond the ISO coded characters.

Erasure of lines is slightly different in its effect when compared with constantly refreshed displays that use the electron beam as a controllable pointer. These displays work by constantly converting a data structure into a display. In displays based on a store of picture elements the data structure is lost. Therefore, if one line of an intersecting pair is erased a small break appears in the other where it passed through—as though a very precise eraser had been used. The significance is the following: although the displays could be generated by identical commands and look the same, in detail they will behave differently. Consider also the interrupt given by a light pen. In the pointer-type display it can specify the part of the data structure which invoked it. In the raster display it can only indicate the x and y coordinates.

This illustrates a general problem. Although terminals can be very similar in their properties and, in principle, a mapping exists from one to another, in practice there are differences that prevent them being used freely as alternative devices by the same application software. Even when standards move forward a long way from the present day, such difficulties may remain.

At the lower end of the scale of cost are displays with a limited font of characters and not many characters per line or lines per displayed frame. These are built for a mass market. Such a mass market is the terminal which obtains its information from a television transmitter.

Teletext and Viewdata

The video signal of a TV channel occupies a high bandwith channel suitable for carrying digital data. The idea of using spare space in the TV frame to carry data was first developed by the British Broadcasting Corporation, starting from the intention to broadcast subtitles for the deaf. It soon became a general information service but, because it is a one-way broadcast channel, only information of general interest such as news, weather, sport, financial data could be accommodated. By time division multiplexing, several hundred pages of data could be sent out continuously, allowing the user to select what he wanted from an index page. The other UK television authority, ITA, separately developed a system, then the two came together to define a 'teletext' standard[1] which was based on the 625-line frame sent at 50 fields per second. (A field is one of the two interlaced patterns which make one picture frame.)

A teletext page has 24 rows of characters. The word 'row' is used to distinguish it from a television line. The row contains 40 characters except that some of the top row (or page header) is information required by the standard. Each row is sent out by a digital waveform on one television scan line. Since these lines are at the top, beyond the picture frame, they are not seen in a well-adjusted set, but are potentially visible as shimmering dots.

The television raster has 34 spare lines at the top of the picture in order to give the scan time to stabilise. They occur on two separate fields with 17 spare lines each. The first line of each field is not technically suitable so there are 16 lines per field which are potential data carriers. In the UK system, four lines: 17, 18, 330 and 331 are employed for teletext, and there are four other lines in this area which carry special analogue signals for setting picture levels. A displayed page is made up from several successive coded lines. The scheme of scan lines in the top of the raster are shown in Figure 8.7.

Using four scan lines for data enables pages full of text to be sent at four per second. The addressing scheme for the pages allows for eight magazines of 100 pages each, but if these were sent out strictly in sequence the cycle would be 200 seconds—rather a long time for the user to wait. In fact, there is no fixed cycle for pages because each carries its address. It would be possible, for example, to repeat popular frames more often and send non-interactive frames (which are stored automatically for later use) at less frequent intervals. Not all page addresses are used in practice.

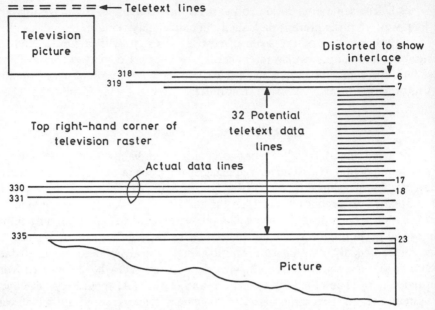

Figure 8.7   The location of teletext data lines

An unusual feature is that each row of characters is provided not only with its row address, but also with the magazine address. Therefore, though a page, once started, must be completed before starting another page of the same magazine (because page addresses are not repeated on each line), pages from several magazines could be overlaid, taking up to two seconds to send if eight were sent at once. The rows of a page need not be sent in their numbered sequence, nor need rows that carry no data be sent at all. Figure 8.8 shows the format of the page and row headers.

The time division feature can be extended further for non-interactive pages that do not need a quick response. For this purpose a so-called 'time-code' is added, but it is different from clock time (which is also in every page header) and has 'hours' from 00 to 39 and 'minutes' from 00 to 79. Potentially, therefore, any page address can be extended to send up to 3200 pages over a period measured in hours if the full range is exploited.

The code used for alphabet and numerals etc. is ISO 7-bit code, but the control functions are special ones and provide seven colours, coloured backgrounds, double height characters and flashing characters. One of the special features is a form of low-resolution picture presentation, useful for weather maps, for example. To do this, each of the 480 character positions is divided into six nearly square picture elements, so that all the possible pictures can be coded by specifying a 6-bit code for each character. Figure 8.9 shows one of these shapes. To draw a picture there is a *graphics* mode in which the alternative

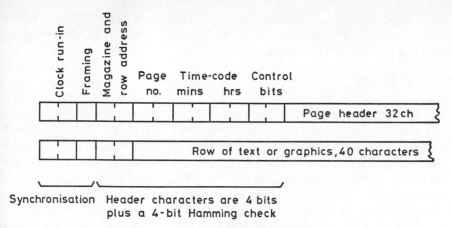

Figure 8.8   Format of teletext data lines

character code comes into play. Two forms of picture element can be used, *contiguous* in which the elements touch on all sides and *separate* in which there is a thin boundary of background colour between them. The effects are striking and make useful pictures, though of low resolution. They enable bold and large headings in unusual fonts to be written.

A different mass terminal market is expected for 'viewdata', developed by the UK Post Office. The same format for the TV display is used, so that both facilities can be added to a set at low cost. The viewdata channel, however, is a normal modem-to-modem link through the switched telephone network. The service computer chiefly provides an information service, again a 'popular' service but with almost no limitations on the extent of the stored data. The generic term for this kind of service is *viewdata* and the name for the service provided to viewdata terminals by the UK Post Office is *Prestel*.

Both services could be extended further with the aid of some local intelligence

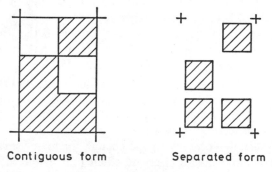

Figure 8.9   Examples of teletext graphics symbols

and storage, as the cost of these things continues to decrease. Teletext, as we have seen, could update a local store of data incrementally. Viewdata could carry out local instructions defined by programs received over the link.

Types of Input Device

The commonest input device at present is the keyboard, which is associated with a display or printer for immediate feedback to the user. The earliest and simplest terminals, starting with the teletype, moved the paper or the display upwards as new lines were written and could not go back to amend characters since each character was sent at once. This arrangement is now called a 'scroll mode terminal'. Its limitations are historical but it persists as an anachronism in many displays. The display with movable cursor allows a page to be written or corrected at any point in the display area. The movement of the cursor can be controlled by four keys for up, down, left and right, but this is a slow and tedious way to change the user's 'attention pointer'. The joystick or tracker ball moves the cursor more readily. The 'mouse' which can be moved over the desk on small wheels is a more natural way to direct the cursor.

Using a keyboard is not a skill which everybody learns. There is believed to be some resistance to learning or practising it by people who associate it with less well-paid jobs. So the more widely used skills of speech and handwriting have been the subject of intensive research as a mode of data input. Both have found practical applications.

Speech is simple and effective for a limited vocabulary. The vocabulary can be changed at each interaction and therefore the final vocabulary can be large. Speech which is bracketed by silence is unnatural. The more effective speech systems allow the chosen phrases or words to be spoken in context, without demarcation by silence. For example, a numeral 4567 might be spoken as FORFAIVSIKSEVN with one phonetic S serving for the end of six and the start of seven. This is a natural way to speak, whereas SIKS-SEVN is not. Speech systems must use natural modes of speech and allow the users a lot of variations. Speech input has been used, even in conditions of noise and stress, and it seems likely to become increasingly popular.

Handwriting can be picked up by a 'pad' on which the user writes, either with a special scriber or with a standard pen. The pen has the great advantage that it writes the customary hard copy. In order to be read, the handwriting must be heavily constrained. In practice, capital letters and numerals (and a few well-chosen extra symbols) can be read accurately with a small amount of user training. The same mechanism can capture a signature in real time (not just the two-dimensional graphic pattern) and this allows signatures to be verified with reasonable accuracy—good enough for many purposes.

The variety of input modes is greater than that of output modes and the chance of common standards which cover several terminal types seems minimal.

At best, a variety of devices could generate a data structure which has a common standard. For example, we could make a drawing with either a light pen or a mouse. The programs for these two devices would be very different. But the resultant data structure representing points, lines, coordinates, symbols etc. could be the same, so that the different terminals could be alike on the network side.

We reach tentative conclusions that standards which attempt to cover many input and output devices in one protocol are likely to run into difficulty. Standards for the data structure with which terminal devices interact are more likely to be successful. Thus a text can be prepared and edited in a multitude of ways but it is still the same data structure. Its structure varies with the use to which it will be put. For example, computer programs and natural language need different structures.

8.3 TERMINAL COMPATIBILITY AND STANDARDS

By combining various techniques for information input and output, an enormous range of terminals is possible. To make matters worse, terminal and computer system manufacturers have, for many years, endeavoured to sell terminals that, primarily, were tailored to meet particular customers' requirements. A strong selling point has always been the system designed specifically for each customer's needs; yet this approach is bound to lead to the proliferation of dissimilar systems. It would be strange if these systems were able to communicate with one another in any but a trivial way. Despite this state of affairs there are points of commonality that have led to the agreement of a few standards which have been adopted by a number of suppliers. These standards cover areas such as the keyboard layout, the interface to modems, the character sets employed, and the codes used to represent them. None of these, however, addresses the problem of how to reconcile the wide variety of existing terminals with a public data network.

To match each type of terminal individually to a network is likely to be very expensive. It is therefore desirable to classify terminals into groups that can be handled in a similar way. The ability to do this depends on the level at which the classification is made. For example, all impact printers have a mechanism to move the hammer, on receipt of an electrical signal. The power requirements for different methods of impact printing vary widely, but suitable amplifiers can be used to overcome these differences, so that all such printers can be made to operate from the same signal level from the network. This approach can be extended to embrace all printers, whether impact or otherwise, allowing the same signal level to cause a character to be printed or displayed on all types through the medium of a suitable adaptor.

This principle of adaptation can readily cover other differences between terminals so that, for example, all printers that operate on a character-at-a-time basis can be classed together, and made to appear the same as far as the network is concerned. In a similar way, all those types of terminal that handle blocks of data and print information a line at a time can be grouped together, and treated in the same way by the network.

The use of adaptors can be extended much further. With an advanced graphics terminal the various cursor positioning devices such as a light pen, a joystick or a tracker ball, can all be made to produce the same cursor positioning information, for transmission through the network. In fact, the future evolution of advanced terminals is in the direction of standardising the input–output signals and codes and the corresponding functions that the terminals perform, to enable them to interwork both with the network and with each other, at least sufficiently to allow a particular type of interaction to be carried out by all members of a given class of terminal.

An Example of Terminal Matching

To illustrate some of the principles involved in matching two terminals, we consider the example of a teletype and a typewriter that are required to be connected together.

The mechanical and electrical differences between the two devices can be considerable. The typewriter usually moves the carriage, carrying the paper against a fixed position printing head; the teletype moves the printing head along a fixed carriage. To print the same symbol on each device may well require the input of a different code. The layout of the keyboards will certainly be different, as will the correspondence between the symbols printed in the two shift positions of any particular key and, of course, the electrical interfaces to each device are also dissimilar. A teleprinter usually operates from serial start–stop characters, while a typewriter often has a parallel, character-at-a-time interface.

In as much as both devices produce printed output on paper from an electrical signal, and allow the input of text from a keyboard, they are similar. But an attempt to join them together so that they could exchange information with each other would be unsuccessful. However, it should be possible to interpose some kind of black box, so that a useful interconnection can be made. This black box would have to convert between the serial and parallel interfaces on the devices, and would also have to map the codes generated by one into the codes required by the other. Obviously, this can be entirely successful only if there is a correspondence between the symbols and keys on the two devices. Where this is not so, some compromise has to be made. For example, if one device has upper and lower case characters and the other upper case only, the latter is the only common set of symbols. The black box would therefore have to convert lower case codes to upper case equivalents.

It is interesting to note the implications of this conversion, since they have relevance to the later sections in this chapter. The device that has upper case only is able to communicate with the other device in the same manner that it operates locally, so the user sees no difference. Users of the more flexible device are still able to print in lower case, locally, so they, too, see no difference. They may be misled into assuming that their correspondents see exactly the same thing as they are typing. But, of course, interaction between the two devices is restricted to the use of the common subset of symbols, unless some more elaborate mapping procedure is adopted.

As an example, the designer of the black box could nominate a shift character. The user of the device without lower case alphabet could then use the shift character to indicate that a following character should be printed in lower case. With such an arrangement, the typist could manage to create an upper and lower case text at a remote typewriter, even if the local one had upper case capability only. Of course, the local version would look peculiar, and the process would not be acceptable in practice. But this hypothetical case is introduced to indicate that an expansion of the capability of the simpler device is possible by using strings of characters which are translated into other symbols by the intermediate black box. This idea will be elaborated when we talk about the concept of the virtual terminal.

The Impact of Terminal Differences

The evolution of terminals has been like that of most areas of technology. At first there were many ideas about how terminals should be designed. This gave rise to the conflicting types we have today. Gradually there is a survival of the fittest as the more acceptable types of terminal gain wide acceptance. With this evolution comes the need to define standards and there is the immediate dilemma of whether to standardise on the past, or look to the future. Standardisation on the past generally leads to the acceptance of two or more standards, to cover each of the major lines of past conflict. Standardising on the future requires a look ahead to the likely outcome of technology and the requirements of the customer. So far, standards relating to terminals have largely been based on the past and cover codes, keyboard layouts and interfaces.

From the user's point of view, the impact of terminal differences are in areas such as the layout of the keyboard, the key pressures required, the type style, and so on. Many of these are matters of personal choice and account for the preferences shown by people for one type of terminal or another. Others stem from the way terminal evolution has occurred. For example, the teletype keyboard associates upper case letters and numbers, because it has only upper case symbols, but with a typewriter, numbers are selected in the same shift key position as the lower case letters, for this is the normal pairing in written language. Again, there are three different standards for numeric keyboards, shown in Figure 8.10. The left one is used for pocket calculators, the middle one is for pushbutton telephones, while the third is found on card punches. One scheme is a result of counting between zero and nine, another comes from

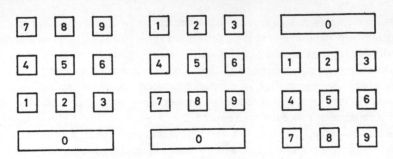

Figure 8.10   Three layouts for numeric keyboards

counting between one and ten. As the keys can be put in increasing or decreasing order, four versions are possible of which the three shown in the figure have been adopted in practice.

The existence of alternative standards can be based on historical differences in the way people model their environment, or may be much less deeply founded. But, whatever the reason, arbitrary differences are a source of error and annoyance to people, making their performance less good than it might be. On the other hand, some differences reflect a genuine need to have alternative ways of working, and so cannot be avoided.

The designer of a computer program to handle a variety of terminals is in a similar position to the designer of a black box to convert from one type of terminal to another. Apart from the interface and code matching problems, there are the differences in speeds of operation for various functions such as printing a symbol and returning a carriage. In addition, there are options such as the use of back space followed by an over strike of one character on another, to produce a symbol not in the basic repertoire of the device, and facilities such as the ability to lock the keyboard to prevent the user typing when the computer is not ready.

Options and differing facilities create problems which can be divided into two classes: those which are concerned with the handling of the device by the computer program, and those which affect its ability to represent information in a correct manner. The first of these is of importance mainly to the local user and computer system, but the second is of vital import to any other interacting party, whether it be a person at another terminal or a computer program, wishing to have messages and data presented in a satisfactory manner at another site. We shall come back to this when discussing the virtual terminal.

8.4   TERMINAL HANDLING

In the early days of computers, the input and output of information was achieved by primitive electromechanical card and tape readers and punches.

These were called peripheral devices or peripherals, and were matched to the computer by purpose-designed electronic and electromechanical circuits, which formed an integral part of the computer hardware. As computers developed, more advanced devices were connected as peripherals, and particular classes of device began to be handled in a similar manner.

It was a fairly short step to associate the specialised circuitry needed for a particular kind of peripheral with the peripheral itself so that the connection method used between the computer and the peripheral device could be standardised. This gave rise to the concept of the standard interface which is a set of connections and signals that are the same, regardless of the peripheral connected to it. Figure 8.11 illustrates these early developments. At the top, an early system is shown with separate logic tailored for each device, controlled by the central processor. At the bottom, a later arrangement has the processor controlling standard channels that connect to a variety of devices in a uniform manner.

The emergence of stand-alone peripheral devices and standard interfaces made it possible for devices designed for one computer system to interwork with

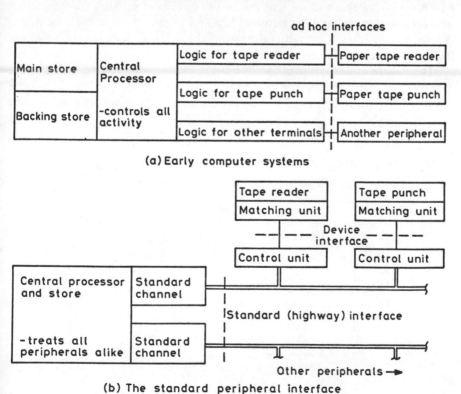

Figure 8.11   The early development of peripheral handling

another. This allowed the compatible range of computers handling a complementary range of peripheral devices to become a selling point with many manufacturers. Of course, some customers saw the advantages of using peripherals from one supplier with computers provided by another, but generally the differences in the 'standard' interfaces offered by different manufacturers were too great for this to be possible.

Within one manufacturer's range, however, the existence of the stand-alone peripheral led to the possibility of separating the peripheral and the computer, as is shown in Figure 8.12. This made possible the evolution of the private data network where a number of geographically separated peripheral devices were all connected to a common centralised computer system. It was at this stage that the name 'peripheral' began to give way to 'terminal'.

Whatever the type of terminal, it became common to connect clusters of terminals to a terminal handler which was itself connected by a leased telephone line to the main computer system. The initial justification for this was economic in that the single leased line was cheaper than separate lines from each terminal to the computer. But by basing the terminal handler on a small computer other advantages were obtained, such as the ability to edit information by interaction between the terminal and the terminal handler, so that changes could be made, if necessary, before commanding the terminal handler to forward the messages to the remote computer.

The degree of autonomy of the terminal handler gradually increased as the capability of small computers developed and in some applications it became possible for quite complex tasks to be carried out by the terminal handler with

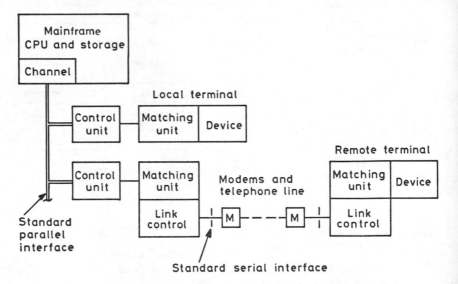

Figure 8.12   Separation of system components by standard interfaces

reference to the central computer only occasionally. Even so, the whole system of distributed terminal handlers and terminals was controlled by the main computer and most of the private networks were essentially designed to be subservient to the requirements of the central computer. In effect, a master and slave relationship existed between the computer and the network components. This is reflected in the design of the HDLC communications link protocols that have been discussed in Chapter 6.

Connecting Terminals to a Network

A network terminal does more than send and receive data. It must be able to establish and release calls, to tell the user what has happened in a case of minor network trouble and so forth. These might be the functions of a network terminating unit, such as we showed in Figure 8.2. By describing some of the functions of such a unit we can illustrate one of the features required in a network.

The example is taken from an early local network built at the UK National Physical Laboratory (NPL), which is still operating and has a population of about 200 terminals. It gives access to a dozen or so services on different minicomputers and microcomputers, via gateways to other networks and to miscellaneous services like time, teletext and viewdata.

The NTU is called a peripheral control unit in the NPL network and it has four buttons, illuminated to form four related lamp signals. The association is:

Hello button   — Ready lamp

Interrupt button — Receive lamp

ETB button   — Send lamp

Goodbye button — Call lamp

The hello and goodbye buttons initiate and release a call. When a call is initiated, the first phase is the selection of a destination, carried out if possible by the associated terminals. Communication is half duplex for terminals with an NTU, such as visual displays. More intelligent terminals have a packet interface, of course, which can multiplex many channels.

The NTU indicates, by the send and receive lamps, which of the two directions of transmission has control. The call lamp indicates that a call has been established. Any further diagnostics would have to be given by text printed or displayed, but none were found necessary. Text is used only for a few messages such as a statement that the other party has released the call.

If the user needs to obtain the channel against a continuous flow of incoming data, he presses the interrupt button. The ETB button signifies 'end of transmission block'—a way to send off a packet which has not met the other criteria for a completed packet.

There are three ways that completion of a packet is determined. Any of these is sufficient by itself. The commonest in practice is that a certain designated 'delimiter' is transmitted. Typically, delimiters are related to the format of data, for example a new line character, a space or a full stop. The second completion criterion is a time-out, when no characters have been sent for some time. The third is the maximum packet size. The button says, in effect, 'send the packet anyway— what follows is the start of a new packet'.

The NTU is a simple finite state machine. It has six states and can send seven control signals and receive and respond to seven other signals. The design of the interaction required trial and error because it is very difficult to understand the requirements without trying a system.

The control of this machine is vested in the terminal handler which is part of the packet switch. The only new feature this imposes on the local communication network is the carriage of the control signals in either direction. Any protocol needs 'control signals' which are not part of the data stream. In higher levels these are produced by defined formats and coding of fields. In the NPL local network the control signals at this lower level of interaction (user-switch and switch-user) are built into the hardware. Probably there is now a trend away from such specialised control signal channels. More and more, such functions are handled by words and phrases on the data channel, but there is always an irreducible minimum that needs hardware assistance.

The hardware took a form which subsequently influenced the design of circuit-switched networks. In the NPL network data on the lines to and from a character terminal was handled in units of an octet. With each 8-bit byte a ninth bit called the 'status bit' was associated. This enabled the byte to have one of two meanings, either a data byte or special control signal. The range of possible control signals was much larger than was needed but the penalty of one extra bit was small for a local network—particularly so because many more 'overhead' bits were necessarily sent with the octet. It is this status bit (enabling control signals and data to be mixed on a line) which now appears in synchronous, circuit switched networks[2,3] under the name '8 + 2'—eight data bits, a status bit and one further bit for framing purposes.

Control signalling at this low level is like the operation of the receiver rest and the tones of the telephone network (dialling, ringing, number busy). In principle it could be handled like a protocol over the data channel, but the limitations placed on the data channel are then irksome. A few special signals are needed in addition to the data channel, to make a satisfactory human interface in which two levels of interaction are clearly separated.

Terminal Handling in Perspective

To conclude this section on terminal handling we will review the way that the evolution of computer technology has led to the distribution of intelligence and storage amongst the geographically separated components making up today's complex computer networks. It has become common to associate intelligence and storage with simple terminals so that they may be handled remotely in a more efficient manner than their basic design would allow. For example, a group of teletypewriters, that communicate by the exchange of serial characters in start–stop mode, are connected to a terminal handler. The terminal handler exchanges characters with the teletype in the same way that a mainframe computer handles peripherals in the earlier types of computer network. The terminal handler therefore takes over the low level task of character handling and acts as an agent for the mainframe. Messages are passed between the mainframe and the terminal handler to control the latter's behaviour, according to the requirements of the applications program running in the main computer.

Two basic kinds of information flow are therefore common in handling terminals. Firstly there is the exchange of characters that occurs between a simple terminal and the intelligence that is controlling its behaviour. Secondly there is the exchange of messages that takes place between the terminal-controlling intelligence and applications programs which have overall control of terminal behaviour, and with which the user is conducting transactions. This is illustrated by Figure 8.13.

This separation of the task of terminal handling into two levels paves the way for standardisation which allows some degree of freedom in the interaction between different types of terminal. Essentially, it is the intelligence associated with the terminal that is able to disguise peculiarities of particular kinds of terminal, so that they may all appear similar to a remote system or to another type of terminal. This principle is the same whether the intelligence is associated with a cluster of terminals in the form of a terminal handler, or whether it is associated with one particular terminal in the shape of an intelligent device. This is illustrated in Figure 8.13 by the dotted line embracing the terminal and its handler. The advent of the microprocessor will accelerate the growth in

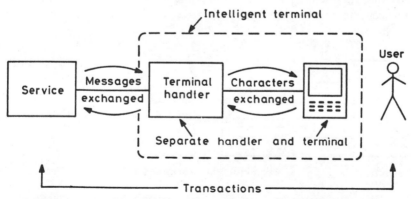

Figure 8.13   Levels of information exchange in terminal handling

intelligent terminals, so we can expect to see more and more communication between intelligent devices, and a decreasing need for networks to carry character traffic.

However, there is a considerable investment in existing systems at various stages along the path of evolution, and so various ad hoc modifications will be needed if systems are to be made to communicate in ways that are less terminal dependent. Furthermore, there seem to be some situations where a strong coupling exists between the application and the detailed way in which the terminal is required to behave; this creates problems when defining standards for communication between the higher levels of intelligence.

In discussing terminal handling therefore there are three basic considerations: firstly, the way in which the terminal handling intelligence interacts with the terminal itself; secondly, the way in which the terminal handling intelligence interacts with a remote computer or terminal handler; and, thirdly, the degree to which these two levels of interaction can be made independent. As an example we will consider the use of character echoing techniques. The connection between the terminal and the terminal handler can be either full duplex or half duplex. With a full duplex connection the terminal handler and the terminal may each independently send characters to the other, and the terminal does not display or print locally the transmitted character. With a half duplex connection, the terminal and terminal handler cannot simultaneously send each other characters, and the terminal prints locally each character as it transmits it to the terminal handler. These two cases are shown in Figure 8.14.

The half duplex arrangement has the advantage that a person using a terminal can see exactly what he has typed, as it is typed, but he does not know whether the transmitted character was corrupted on its journey to the terminal handler. With a full duplex connection, the characters are not seen as they are typed, but may be transmitted back to the terminal by the terminal handler to provide evidence that they were correctly received. Generally, this happens so quickly that the user has the illusion of using a local half duplex connection.

The scheme whereby characters are returned to a terminal to provide error

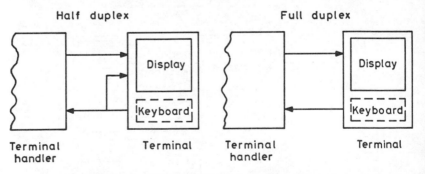

Figure 8.14   Half and full duplex terminal operation

control is known as echoing or 'echoplex', and has been quite commonly used in a variety of present-day systems, where there is no error control on the link from the terminal to the terminal handler. When a terminal operating in the half duplex mode is used with an echoing terminal handler, each character is printed in duplicate, firstly from the local echo at the terminal, and secondly from the echo from the terminal handler. This is why a full/half duplex switch is provided on terminals so they can be used with echoing and non-echoing remote systems. However, an analogous problem arises when the terminal handler itself is communicating on behalf of the terminal with a remote computer. If this remote system uses echoing, each character will also be duplicated by an echoing terminal handler and it is therefore necessary to have some method of enabling and disabling the echoing facility in the terminal handler depending on whether the remote service does or does not echo characters, as is illustrated by Figure 8.15. On the face of it, a simple initial dialogue would allow a user to set up the echoing mechanism. However, it is sometimes necessary to be able to inhibit the echoing of characters selectively. This is needed, for example, during the input of confidential information such as a password, so that it is not printed or displayed on the terminal.

It seems, therefore, that present-day systems can require a close coupling between the terminal characteristics and the behaviour of the applications programs in the service computer. However, the key to open working is to reduce this coupling to a minimum so that a service may send information to the terminal handler in the form of a file of characters, leaving the terminal handler to send them to the terminal at an appropriate rate and in whatever manner is required by each particular terminal. In this way the remote service can be made unaware of the particular type of terminal it is dealing with. We shall enlarge on this subject in connection with the virtual terminal, but first we look, in the next section, at how terminal handling has developed in public networks.

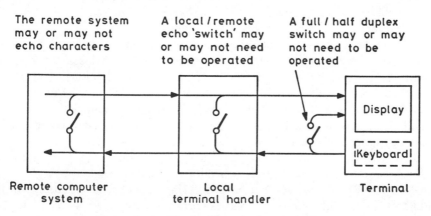

The remote system may or may not echo characters

A local / remote echo 'switch' may or may not need to be operated

A full / half duplex switch may or may not need to be operated

Display

Keyboard

Remote computer system

Local terminal handler

Terminal

Figure 8.15   The conflict of echo mechanisms

8.5   TERMINALS IN A PUBLIC NETWORK

One of the key issues to be decided by the PTTs when planning a public data network is the degree to which it should be involved in handling the terminals. One possibility would be to provide every subscriber with a data circuit terminating equipment and a network termination unit and to design the network so that a stream of information passed into one NTU was faithfully transferred to another, connected by a call through the network. Such a network is called 'transparent' and supposedly neither affects, nor is affected by, the information flowing through it.

The simplicity of the transparent network is attractive at first sight, but it fails to exploit the characteristics of the traffic which it carries, and the terminals which it connects. Furthermore, by providing no particular properties, it fails to provide any specially desirable properties to its subscribers.

If a network is not transparent the question arises of how opaque it should be. An extreme case would be to design a network to support only one kind of terminal. All the terminals connected to that network would, by definition, be able to interwork, and the network could be optimised to a high degree.

A practicable design for a network will have to be semi-transparent (perhaps translucent), supporting certain classes of terminal and handling them reasonably efficiently, while being unable to accommodate other types. The dilemma with the public network is how to support an acceptable range of terminals at an acceptably low cost for the average subscriber.

A packet switching public network is intended to handle bursts of traffic in the form of packets and is not particularly well suited to the simple terminals which exchange characters with each other. An obvious solution is to provide terminal handlers which can deal with clusters of character terminals, and interface them to the packet switching network in an effective manner. This raises the problem of whether the terminal handlers should be considered part of the public network and owned by the carrier, or external to it, and owned by the subscribers. The answer to this is not a simple one.

A future public network which connects a large number of identical terminals, for example viewdata terminals in people's homes, should, obviously, incorporate a method for handling these terminals, for the advantages of doing this efficiently on a large scale should prove beneficial to all subscribers. On the other hand, when terminals are of widely diverse types and few in number, the cost of handling them within the network could be high, and perhaps should not be shared by other subscribers.

The dividing line between what terminals are handled by terminal handlers in the network itself, and what types are handled by external ones, is a matter for debate. PTTs themselves will have differing views so the situation will be different in different countries. What is certainly required is the flexibility to have both possibilities with the public network, so that new types of terminal can be introduced, even though they are not handled by the standard arrangements for any particular network.

The PAD

The CCITT has accepted that some networks require to incorporate terminal handling facilities in order to convert information between character and packet form.[4] These facilities are provided by the PAD (packet-assembler/disassembler) which is described in draft CCITT Recommendation X3. The PAD has a similar function to the terminal handler in a typical private network, as is shown in Figure 8.16. This should be compared with Figure 8.13. The interaction between the local terminal and the PAD is covered by Recommendation X28, and the interaction between the remote terminal and the PAD by Recommendation X29. The question arises of the nature of the remote terminal covered by X29. In the CCITT nomenclature it is called a packet data terminal equipment (PDTE). But it is, in fact, assumed to be a computer system which is communicating with the PAD by an exchange of packets, through a virtual circuit defined by CCITT Recommendation X25, which was described in Chapter 6. The X29 protocol describes the rules governing the orderly exchange of these packets and the meaning of certain control packets which allow the host or subscriber computer system to instruct the PAD on ways in which the character terminals should be handled.

The terminals handled by the type of PAD described by CCITT Recommendation X3 are start–stop character terminals of the sort generally classed as teletypes, or teletype replacements in the case of visual display units. The relative simplicity of these terminals means that X28 can be fairly straightfor-

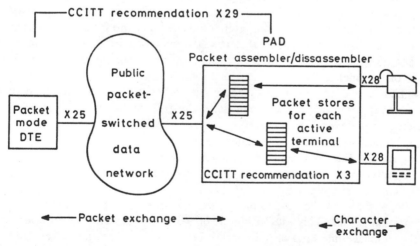

Figure 8.16   The packet assembler/disassembler

ward. It deals with the connection and disconnection of terminals, their character codes and methods of signalling and with the necessary control facilities.

The definition of the properties of the PAD is more difficult because a balance has to be drawn between the inclusion of non-essential but desirable features, and keeping the cost down to a reasonable level. The topics covered by recommendation X3 are the messages exchanged between the PAD and the users of a character terminal, the method of recovery when things go wrong, the parameters to be adopted for laying out text on the character terminal and so on.

It is clear that the role of a PAD in a public network is very similar to that of a terminal handler in a private one. The problem in the design of the PAD is to provide sufficient features to cover the majority of applications of a terminal handler used by the majority of host systems. The burden of detailed terminal handling is then removed from the hosts, as it is in a private network, but the host has to conduct a dialogue with the PAD, in the form of the X29 protocol, in order to set up the PAD at the beginning of an interaction with a particular class of terminal.

This parametric approach to handling terminals through a PAD is very attractive when the aim is to handle existing types of simple terminals. These merely have to be classified into categories such as printing units, display devices, graphics plotters, etc., possibly with a further division into groups of terminals with sufficiently similar characteristics to allow them to be handled by similar software. The initial interaction between the terminal and computer is used to establish the category and group to which a particular calling terminal belongs. This, of course, implies that a computer system must be knowledgeable about all the classes of terminal with which it may wish to interwork.

To enable existing private networks of terminals and computers to transfer to a public network without any significant changes, the PAD must incorporate a transparent mode whereby signals are passed straight through it, allowing a terminal and the associated computer to interact as if no PAD were present. It is then possible to build upon this transparent mode by incorporating in the PAD a number of extra features to relieve the computer system of some of the tasks of terminal support.

The nature of these features is the subject of continuing debate and depends on whether the intention is to minimise the task of handling a few types of simple terminal mainly for existing systems or whether a more ambitious attempt is to be made to rationalise the handling of terminals generally. Since these two aims are difficult to reconcile, it is unlikely that a precisely defined PAD specification would be possible. Different PADs may be designed for different networks and if these are later interconnected it is necessary for a computer system to discover the nature of the PAD with which it is dealing when an interaction begins. This establishment of what features can be provided by a PAD requires some kind of negotiation between the computer system and the PAD. The concept of negotiation of facilities is discussed in Section 8.9.

To be really useful the PAD functions must be standardised so that a computer system supplying services to terminals can rely upon the existence of an intermediate PAD with known properties. Furthermore, all PADs likely to be encountered by the computer system should be similar. Even so, there is still likely to be a need for considerable involvement of the computer system in the handing of terminals unless the functions of the PAD are very comprehensive.

By tacitly assuming that the PAD will correspond with a computer system using protocol X29, the arrangement of PAD and computer system is naturally unsymmetrical. The computer system is thought of as a master which is telling the PAD how to behave. It is not therefore possible for one PAD to talk to another, and hence for one start–stop terminal to talk to another through their PADs. These disadvantages may be overcome to some extent by introducing the idea of the virtual terminal. The initial proposals in CCITT for the PAD did not recognise the virtual terminal concept, but later amendments introduced the idea of symmetry, coupled with a primitive form of virtual terminal description.

CCITT Recommendation X3

When the CCITT began to consider the problem of connecting character mode terminals to a public network, there were already a number of PTT networks being planned. Telenet had adopted a parametric approach with its 'interactive terminal interface', which now has nearly 60 parameters; these are listed in Figure 8.17. Transpac too was following a similar approach, but with fewer parameters, so, when the European PTTs began to plan for Euronet, it seemed appropriate also to take the same path. In fact, the stimulus of Euronet brought about great activity by the CEPT to agree standards for its communications subnetwork and, naturally, this was accompanied by a parallel effort to have them accepted by CCITT. Accordingly, with some minor changes, they have become the present recommendations covering the PAD and its protocols.

Recommendation X3 describes and defines the facilities that must be provided by a PAD if it is to serve as an intermediary between a character terminal, called a start–stop DTE, and a packet mode DTE. The PAD performs a set of functions known as the basic mode of operation, and may also provide further facilities at the request of the users; these are called user selectable functions. The recommendation has three sections; the first describes the PAD functions, the second gives the characteristics of parameters which control these functions, while the third lists the parameters with possible values.

The basic functions that must be provided by the PAD are as follows:

assembly of characters from the terminal into packets for the PDTE,

disassembly of the data fields of packets into characters for the start–stop DTE,

setting up, interrupting, resetting and clearing of virtual calls, generation of service signals for the character terminal,

forwarding of packets when appropriate, e.g. when a buffer is full, or a time-out has expired,

transmission of characters with necessary start and stop elements to the character DTE,

recognition and interpretation of an interrupt or break signal from the start–stop terminal.

The additional functions that may be provided by a PAD allow the users to specify how they wish the assembly and disassembly of packets to be handled, and how the procedure between the PAD and the start–stop mode DTE should be managed. There are also a limited number of extra functions that may be selected to match particular features of different start–stop terminals. The

No.	Parameter	No.	Parameter
0	Connection Mode	30	Abort Output Character
1	Linefeed Insertion	31	Interrupt Process Character
2	Network Message Display	32	Automatic Disconnection
3	Echo	33	Flush Output
4	Echo Mask	34	Transmit on Timers
5	Transmit Mask	35	Idle Timer
6	Buffer Size	36	Interval Timer
7	Command Mask	37	Network Usage Display
8	Command Mask	38	Carriage Return Padding
9	Carriage Return Padding	39	Padding Options
10	Linefeed Padding	40	Insert on Break
11	Tab Padding	41	DCE-to-DTE Flow Control
12	Line Width	42	DCE X-ON Character
13	Page Length	43	DCE X-OFF Character
14	Line Folding	44	Generate Break
15	(Reserved)	45	APP on Break
16	Interrupt on Break	46	2741 Input Unlock Option
17	Break Code	47	2741 Input Unlock Timer
18	Virtual Terminal Options	48	2741 Input Lock Character
19	2741 Init. Keys State	49	2741 Output Lock Option
20	Half/Full Duplex	50	2741 Output Lock Timer
21	Real Character Code	51	2741 Output Unlock Option
22	Printer Style	52	Defer Echo Mask
23	Terminal Type	53	Break Options
24	Permanent Terminal	54	DTE-to-DCE Flow Control
25	Man/Auto Connection	55	DTE X-ON Character
26	Rate	56	DTE X-OFF Character
27	Delete Character	57	Connection Mode
28	Cancel Character	58	Command Mode Escape
29	Display Character		

Figure 8.17   Parameters of the Telenet interactive terminal interface

selection is made by setting the values of a parameter associated with each option, and it is also possible to select a standard initial profile of values by a single command. The profiles and values assigned to parameters are contained in recommendation X28, but it is convenient to bring forward this information in order to associate it with a description of the parameters. Accordingly, the additional PAD functions, numbered as in recommendation X3, together with the associated parameter values that are given in X28 are described below.

(1) PAD recall by escaping from the data transfer state, allows a character terminal to send command signals to the PAD, instead of the remote PDTE; the IA5 data link escape character DLE is used to indicate an escape sequence, which is possible if parameter 1 is set to 1; parameter 1 set to 0 inhibits the use of PAD recall.

(2) Characters may be echoed back to the terminal by setting parameter 2 to 1; it is set to 0 to inhibit echoing.

(3) Part-filled packets may be forwarded by the PAD on receipt of certain characters from the terminal. Parameter 3 is set to 0 if no character is used, to 2 if carriage return is nominated, while the value 126 requests forwarding when delete or any IA5 control character is sent by the terminal.

(4) Part-filled packets may be also forwarded after a delay controlled by an idle timer. The value of parameter 4 determines this delay in twentieths of a second, over the range from 0 to 255, to give any delay from zero to 12.75 seconds.

(5) An ancillary device control feature allows a local tape reader, or other device, to be controlled using X-ON and X-OFF signals (the DC1 and DC3 characters of International Alphabet No. 5). Parameter 5 is made 0 to inhibit this feature, and 1 to enable it.

(6) It is possible to suppress PAD service signals that, for example, inform the terminal user about the state of his call. Parameter 6 is set to 0 to suppress these signals, and 1 to allow them.

(7) The behaviour of the PAD following the receipt of a break signal sent from the terminal can be varied according to parameter 7. The PAD does nothing if this is 0; otherwise the actions are: interrupt virtual call to PDTE—1, reset the call—2 send break indication to PDTE—4, escape from data transfer state—8, and discard output for character terminal—16. These may be combined so that 21 (1 + 4 + 16) indicates discard, interrupt and indicate break. Other combinations are for further study.

(8) The contents of the data field for outstanding packets waiting to be delivered to the terminal may be discarded on receipt of a break signal, by setting parameter 8 to 1. Normal data delivery is performed if parameter 8 is made 0. The PDTE is informed when a break occurs and is expected to restore the value of parameter 8 to 1, as defined in recommendation X29.

(9) To allow time for the carriage to return on mechanical terminals, null characters may be inserted automatically by the PAD, following a carriage return command. Parameter 9 specifies the number of padding characters in the range from 0 to 7.

(10) Automatic line folding may be performed by the PAD by setting parameter 10 to indicate the line length required in the range 1 to 255 characters per line. If set to 0, no line folding is requested.

(11) The speed of operation of the character terminal may be detected automatically by a PAD and its value made available on request by a PDTE. Parameter 11 is set by the PAD according to the terminal speed; its value cannot be changed by either of the DTEs. Possible parameter values and the corresponding terminal speed in bits per second are: 0—110, 1—134.5, 2—300, 8—200, 9—100, 10—50. All but values 0, 2 and 8 are marked for further study.

(12) The flow of characters from the PAD to the character terminal may be controlled by the use of X-ON and X-OFF in a similar way to that described for option 5. This facility is selected by setting parameter 12 to 1 and inhibited by setting it to 0.

The values of the PAD parameters may be read, initialised and modified by the start–stop DTE and by the PDTE, according to procedures detailed in X28 and X29 respectively. The initialisation sequence sets the value of each parameter to what is called an *initial standard profile*. At any time thereafter, the current

Parameter	Description	Transparent profile	Simple profile
1	PAD recall	No	Yes
2	Echo	No	No
3	Data forwarding	No	Note 1
4	Idle timer	1 sec.	None
5	DTE flow ctrl.	No	Yes
6	Service signals	No	Yes
7	Action on break	Reset VC	Reset VC
8	Discard output	No	No
9	PAD after CR	No	No
10	Line folding	No	No
11	Binary speed	Note 2	Note 2
12	PAD flow ctrl.	No	Yes

Note 1. Data is forwarded on receipt of any IA5 control character or delete.

Note 2. Speeds of 110, 200 and 300 bit/s are detected.

Figure 8.18   Standard profiles for the PAD

value of a parameter is the product of an initialisation followed by any subsequent modifications by either of the associated DTEs. Two standard profiles known as *transparent* and *simple* have been agreed, and are shown in Figure 8.18. Other profiles are for further study.

The recommendation X3 described above was handled by an accelerated procedure whereby a postal ballot was conducted by CCITT. It was accepted as a draft recommendation in October 1977. However, in several places, items are left for further study so some future changes may be expected. Probably these will be confined to the addition of further options to the existing functions that may be selected by users, and possibly also to the addition of further functions or even a form of virtual terminal as mentioned in reference 15.

CCITT Recommendation X28

This recommendation defines the interface and protocols between the start–stop character mode DTE and the PAD. It comprises four sections covering the establishment of a connection, initialisation and the exchange of characters, the exchange of control information and, finally, the exchange of users' data. There is also an annex summarising the PAD commands and service signals.

Section 1 of X28 describes the connection between the terminal and the PAD; this may take several forms. The public switched telephone network and leased lines can be used in the normal manner with modems according to the V21 recommendation, and using the procedures well established in private networks for terminals calling a terminal handler. Access through a public switched data network or leased lines is also foreseen using the X20 interface and its associated procedures, as is access through a telephone network using the X20 bis interface, which is compatible with the V21 recommendation. In all cases, procedures by which the PAD can clear a call to the terminal are defined, but the possibility for a PAD to call a terminal is for further study; access to a PAD through a telex network is also in this category.

Section 2 of X28 shows that the formats for characters interchanged are similar to those commonly employed by private computer bureau services. Eight-bit characters are used, with parity ignored by the PAD on input. Even parity is adopted for PAD generated characters, which have two stop elements at 110 bit/s and a single stop element at other speeds; this allows mechanical teletypes to be handled. The PAD, however, will accept characters with only one stop element at all speeds.

Section 2 also describes the initialisation procedures using two sequence diagrams showing the events and timing of call establishment and of call clearing, together with a state transition diagram describing the overall PAD behaviour. When a connection is established, the terminal must request service by transmitting a sequence of characters (this has yet to be specified) to enable the PAD to detect the speed and code used by the terminal, so that parameter

11 can be set and an initial profile selected. When this has been done, the PAD will reply with an identification service signal at the appropriate speed, unless parameter 6—suppression of service signals—has been set to zero. The inclusion of a time-out, to ensure that the PAD clears a call if a valid service request is not promptly received from the terminal, completes the initialisation features.

The procedures for exchanging control information between PAD and terminal are the subject of Section 3 of X28. As we saw when discussing recommendation X3 the operation of the PAD is governed by a number of parameters which are set according to an initial profile, but may be changed subsequently by the terminal. Command signals are defined for use by the terminal: when selecting a standard profile, when selecting individual parameter values, when reaching the current state of the parameters and when requesting the PAD to establish and clear calls to a PDTE.

Service signals from the PAD to the terminal are provided to transmit call progress information, to acknowledge terminal commands and to transmit information about the state of the PAD itself. The terminal commands, their purpose and the PAD responses are shown in Figure 8.19.

In addition to the commands and responses given in the figure, there are a number of other messages that may originate in the PAD to report various conditions to the terminal. They are listed in Figure 8.20, which also indicates their purpose. The clearing call progress signal may be qualified in several ways

Terminal commands	Purpose	Response from PAD
STAT	Requests status of call to PDTE	FREE or ENGAGED
CLR	Requests PAD to clear down a call	CLR CONF or CLR ERR
PAR? (list)	Requests values of parameters listed	PAR (lists & values)
SET? (list & values)	Requests a change to values given & a reply	PAR (list & values)
PROF (identifier)	To give standard set of parameters	—
RESET	To reset the call to a PDTE	—
INT or INTD	To interrupt the call to a PDTE	—
SET (list & values)	Requests a change without a reply	
Selection command	To set up a call to a PDTE	—
Break signal	Out of band signal to recall command level	—

Figure 8.19 Terminal commands and PAD responses

Message	Meaning
RESET DTE	Remote DTE has reset the call
RESET ERR	Call reset due to local procedural error
RESET NC	Call reset due to network congestion
PAD	Identification service signal (further study)
ERROR	Identification of an incorrect command
COM	Call connection
CLR	Call cleared—qualified as below
-OCC	Called number engaged
-NC	Network congested
-INV	Invalid facility requested
-NA	Access barred
-ERR	Local procedural error
-RPE	Remote procedural error
-NP	Not obtainable
-DER	Called number out of order
-PAD	Cleared by PDTE

Figure 8.20   Additional messages from the PAD

as shown in the figure. Some of the coding for these is still under discussion. The remaining part of Section 3 of the X28 recommendation is devoted to the definition of the format of the various commands and responses. Generally, upper case IA5 characters are used, with parameters indicated by their number where appropriate. Separation between items is by commas and colons, so that several parameters may be referred to in a single command. This provides a fairly primitive user command language structure to allow character terminal users to instruct a PAD on how it should behave.

The fourth section of X28 covers the exchange of user's data between the PAD and the terminal. It enlarges on the conditions under which packets are forwarded to the PDTE, after a time-out or on command from the terminal, explains how flow control is accomplished using the ancillary device control commands, details the procedures for informing the terminal of a reset or break by the PDTE, and defines the method of escaping from the data transfer state. In conclusion, further explanation is also given about the use of echo, padding after carriage return, and line folding.

In summary, recommendation X28 is a fairly detailed description of the interaction between a character terminal and the PAD of a public network. To the extent that it will bring standardisation of the user interface to public networks in different countries, it is very welcome. However, some of the messages sent to users need to be improved in clarity, if ordinary people are to be catered for. There are also a number of areas left for further study, making it difficult to implement X28 in a practical design. An example is the question of a 'network user identification facility'. NUI is necessary for security, charging and network management; yet according to X28, some administrations may not provide such a feature, at least at the present stage in the development of their thinking.

CCITT Recommendation X29

This recommendation completes the trio describing the PAD and its associated protocols, by detailing the interaction between the PAD and a packet-mode DTE. Connection between these is made by a public packet-switched data network, so the interface between each of them and the intervening network conforms to recommendation X25. Recommendation X29 therefore describes the manner of using X25 to support a dialogue between the PAD and the PDTE.

Like X28, X29 has four sections and an appendix. The sections cover procedures for the exchange of PAD control information and user data, user data transfer, procedures for the use of PAD messages, and formats, and the appendix details the characteristics of virtual calls and how X25 is related to the way the PAD represents a start–stop mode DTE to a PDTE.

The dialogue between PAD and PDTE is required to establish and manage virtual calls, to allow the PDTE to read, set and modify PAD parameters, and to control the passage of user's data to and from the PDTE. This makes X29 very interesting because it represents the CCITT's view on one way to use X25.

Before the PAD concept was introduced, potential subscribers of the new public networks had to match their equipment to the X25 interface by interpreting the published specifications, prior to the existence of a working network. Now it is possible to see how CCITT itself has interpreted X25 in supporting X29, which is, effectively, an end-to-end protocol between two packet-mode DTEs. Furthermore, it requires the subscriber's PDTE to interact closely with an element of the network, namely the PAD, and to modify its operating characteristics. This is a new departure by the PTTs from previous policy. Perhaps, therefore, the items listed for further study in the preface to the X29 recommendation are specially noteworthy, they are:

The possibility of a packet-mode DTE establishing a virtual call to a non-packet-mode DTE.

The use of the permanent virtual circuit facility.

Interworking between non-packet-mode DTEs using a packet-switched data transmission service.

Interworking between DTEs with interfaces to different data transmission services.

Operation of non-packet-mode DTEs in other than start–stop mode.

Turning now to the items that are covered by X29, a matter of some significance is the way that the user data field of incoming call packets has been modified from the simple definition given in X25. This has been done to allow different types of calling subscriber, or different types of protocol, to be identified so they can be properly handled by the called PDTE. The 'call user data field' originally defined in X25 could have up to sixteen octets supplied by the calling DTE, and transmitted by the network to the called DTE. X29 defines four of these as a protocol identifier, leaving the remainder as a call data field of up to twelve octets. In the first octet of the protocol identifier, bits 8 and 7 are employed to distinguish between four classes of user:

00 —for CCITT use

01 —for national use

10 —for use by international user bodies

11 —for DTE to DTE use

The remaining six bits of the first octet are set to 000001 to indicate PAD messages relating to a start–stop terminal connection; other values of these bits are reserved for future CCITT standardisation. The remaining three octets of the identifier are reserved for future use in providing a called DTE with information about a calling DTE; meanwhile all of their bits are set to zero.

The four classes of user are not enlarged upon in X29. The implication is that further CCITT standards will be introduced, identified by the 00 indicator. No doubt the national use (01) category will be used by PTTs in developing their national networks, while the international user bodies (10) are probably intended to be organisations such as ISO.

Clearly considerable scope for future standardisation exists within the framework of the protocol identifier. In particular, it will, presumably, be possible for any pair of DTEs to agree upon the use of the fourth case (11), putting any interpretation they wish on the use of bits one to six of the first octet, and of the other three octets.

An important issue raised by the way that X29 uses the call data field of X25, is that it retrospectively restricts the use of the X25 recommendation. Section 4.2.1 of X25 states that the call user data field, of up to sixteen octets, is transferred intact from the calling DTE to the called DTE. But now, the meaning of the first four octets is defined by X29. In fact, of course, only the first two bits are usurped, so provided these are both set to 1, the remaining bits and octets from a calling DTE will be forwarded unchanged to the called DTE, and will also have no effect on any intervening networks.

A second interesting aspect of the use of X25 facilities by X29 is the way that control messages passing between the PAD and the PDTE are distinguished from messages containing user data. This is done by setting the data qualifier, or Q, bit to 1 for control messages, and to 0 for data messages. The control messages consist of a control identifier field, and a message code field, possibly followed by a parameter field. The user's data messages are called a user sequence and comprise the data streams from the PAD and PDTE. No maximum length is specified for a user sequence. However, only one control message, or user's sequence, may be contained in a complete data packet sequence of X25 i.e. all the packets of one message or sequence will be related by the more bit, M, so the end of each message is obvious.

Control messages from the PDTE to the PAD are of three kinds; the first can set and/or read parameter values; the second indicates a break condition to be passed on to the terminal, and the third is an invitation to the PAD to clear the call, after previously transmitted data has been delivered to the terminal.

Messages from the PAD to the PDTE are also of three kinds; namely, the replies to PDTE messages about parameters, the invitations to interrupt and to break passed on from the character terminals, and error messages in response to PDTE messages that are not recognised by the PAD.

Recommendation X29 implies in its Section 4.4 that all control messages for future CCITT facilities will have a control identifier field, comprising the first four bits of the first octet. (The first two bits are set to 0, to accord with the CCITT category of user defined earlier.) The next two bits are also made 0 to indicate that it is a PAD for start–stop terminals that is being controlled. The next four bits are coded to indicate the nature of the message as follows:

0010 —Set	0001 —Invitation to Clear
0100 —Read	0011 —Indication of Break
0110 —Set and Read	0101 —Error
0000 —Indication of Parameters	

As an example, a set parameter message would have a first octet set to 00000010 followed by pairs of octets, the first of each pair indicating the parameter reference number and the second its value.

Invitations to clear messages and break messages from the PDTE to the PAD need no qualifying parameters; but break messages from the PAD to the PDTE must be qualified by a reference to parameter 8 with a value of 1, in order to comply with X3 in indicating that the PAD is discarding output intended for the start–stop terminal.

Error messages in either direction are qualified by their second octet which distinguishes between a received message of less than eight bits, an unrecognised message code, an incorrect parameter field and a message with a non-integral number of octets. For the last three cases a third octet contains the message code of the message found in error.

A list of some control messages and responses is given in Figure 8.21.

In summary, X29 is a type of end-to-end protocol defined by CCITT. This shows a variety of ways of using X25 facilities, perhaps revealing by implication the intention behind some of those facilities. X29 itself contains very many areas where further standardisation is hinted at, and there are many possibilities for defining further commands and responses, within the existing framework. These could be adapted to control facilities other than the PAD described by X3.

Message from PDTE to PAD Type/Parameters	Action taken by the PAD	Message from PAD to PDTE Type/Parameters
Set/none	Reset all parameters to the initial profile	None
Set/parameter nos. and values	Set selected parameters to values given	None or error/parameter nos. in error
Set and read/none	Reset all parameters to the initial profile	/list all parameters and current values
Set and read/nos. and values	Set selected parameters to values given	/list selected parameter and current values
Read/none	None	/list all parameters and current values
Read/parameter nos. and values	None	/list selected parameter and current values
Invitation to break	Informs s/s DTE	
Invitation to clear	Clears call when data has been sent to s/s DTE	Clear/clearing cause

Figure 8.21   Some PAD control messages and responses

Some of the ideas of X29 are disappointing, for example, the use of the Q bit of X25 to differentiate between control and data messages mixes two layers of protocol. This could create difficulties in some private PDTEs that need to interact with public PADs. Again, the extensive use of bit coding to indicate parameters and their values is unfortunate because it can involve high processing overheads in the PDTE. A better choice would have been to use character and string coding based on the IA5 alphabet.

However, despite these criticisms, the X29 recommendation is an important step forward towards a standard end-to-end protocol, since it is likely to be implemented by most administrations offering a public packet switched service. Also, there seems to be sufficient room within the framework of X29 to modify it along the lines of the transport stations and network control programs developed and proved by the various research networks.

8.6   THE VIRTUAL TERMINAL

The techniques we have already described for dealing with the incompatibilities between different terminal types have been successfully applied within the private networks existing today, even when these contain a wide range of terminals and a variety of computer systems. But, invariably, the matching between these different devices has been done under the overall control and management of a single organisation. For example, the airlines set up the SITA network and the banks established the SWIFT network and in each case a separate joint company was established to build the network and set standards for the participants to observe when using the network.

With the public network, the problem of dealing with terminals and computer systems of widely different types is much more severe, simply because there is no common organisation to guide and advise on the use of standards. The magnitude of the problem is so great that it is unlikely that it can ever be solved for all users of all public networks all over the world. Indeed, this is a problem analogous to that of natural language and the telephone network, where in principle any telephone can be connected to any other, but the ability to communicate depends on whether the people at each end share a common language. By considering only groups of users who are keen to be able to communicate meaningfully with each other, there is a chance that useful standards might be agreed. The question arises then of the level at which standardisation should be attempted.

We saw earlier that the present standards for terminals are at a low level and mainly concern their mechanical and electrical properties. One approach would be to build on these existing standards and to develop higher and higher level standards covering various classes of devices and how they should be handled. This has been discussed in the context of the PAD in a public network. An alternative approach is to base the standardisation on the kind of tasks that have to be performed. This would line up with the idea of user groups operating in different areas, and could lead to standards for classes of user rather than terminal. The forward path to standardisation will include both these approaches but, whatever method is adopted, it is necessary for high level mapping between terminals to be possible, if a meaningful interaction is to occur. The *virtual terminal* concept is a step in this direction.

The Concept of the Virtual Terminal

The virtual terminal is a key concept that grew out of the work of research network projects. Like most concepts, it means different things to different people[5,6,7] and it variously can be regarded as:

(a)   a hypothetical terminal that, if it existed, would provide the facilities that a group of users require,

(b)   a generalisation of a particular class of terminals allowing it to represent all the members of that group,

(c)   a meta-terminal onto which real terminals can be mapped, and which therefore provides a translation mechanism between two terminals,

(d)   An ideal terminal with a range of desirable features that can be handled by a typical applications program.

In fact, the concept of the virtual terminal will continue to evolve, as the architecture of computer networks changes with the introduction of microprocessors. But the first ideas arose when research networks allowed service computers to be separated from terminal handlers. It seemed worthwhile to make the terminal handlers have standard properties and a uniform interface to the remote computer systems. These could then be made independent of the terminals, from which they were shielded by the terminal handlers. It was a short step then to regard the terminal handler as representing an ideal or *virtual* terminal, to be handled by the applications programs in the main computer systems, the advantage being that the applications programs could be designed independently of any particular terminal.

In essence, the virtual terminal has a set of properties, and can behave in a set of ways, which are sufficient for the requirements of a particular set of users. It has two interfaces, one with a real terminal, the other with the computer system. The interface with the terminal is tailored to suit that particular type of terminal, but the interface to the computer system is generalised in some way. The virtual terminal can be realised as a program forming part of the terminal handling intelligence, and, indeed, it is a formal description of the way that terminal handlers should behave, if they are to be compatible with each other.

In principle, the implementation of a virtual terminal in a terminal handler permits it to interact in a meaningful way with computer systems that support the virtual terminal, as illustrated by Figure 8.22. This shows how the computer

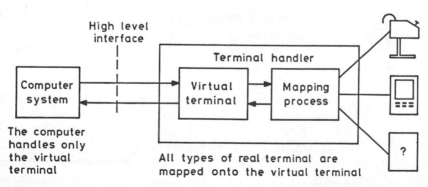

Figure 8.22   The principle of the virtual terminal

handles only the virtual terminal, while the terminal handler conducts a separate but related interaction with its real terminals, exchanging characters with them in order to map commands and data between the real terminals and the virtual terminal interface to the computer.

The interface between the computer system and the terminal handler, shown in Figure 8.22, must be a high level message exchange interface which allows a network to be interposed between the terminal handler and the computer. Depending on the nature of this interface, there are three kinds of connection that are, in principle, possible, as shown in Figure 8.23. They are terminal to

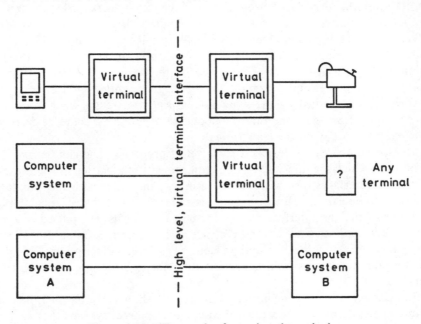

Figure 8.23 Three roles for a virtual terminal

terminal, computer to terminal and computer to computer. As we shall see later, the properties of the virtual terminal may need to be different for the three cases. But the distinction between them is not obvious and many early proposals for virtual terminals were confused about the role they were intended to play.

One of the reasons for confusion is the model commonly adopted for the virtual terminal. This is explained in terms of a set of virtual components corresponding with the component parts of a real terminal, as is illustrated in Figure 8.24. Such a model is very useful for developing the arguments about the design of the virtual terminal, for the original role in terminal-to-computer connections, but can be misleading when extended to the other two roles, particularly when designing the protocols governing the interactions on the two sides of the virtual terminal. For this reason, the model of Figure 8.25 is more

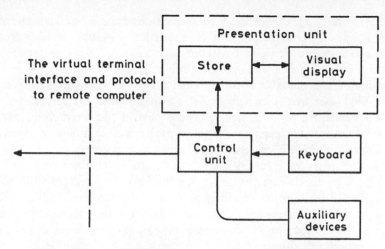

Figure 8.24 Virtual terminal model based on a real terminal

useful because it avoids the analogy with a real terminal. As the figure shows, the data structure is the primary means of communication between the terminal and the computer. Each of these changes this structure in any convenient way in order to convey information to the other, the terminal using a character protocol, the computer using a message based one. These protocols are independent except for measures that are required to prevent collisions that could modify the data structure in an ambiguous way.

For terminal-to-terminal interactions, the terminal handlers are equal partners so the virtual terminal message-based protocol must be symmetrical in

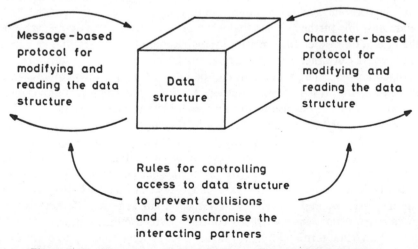

Figure 8.25 Virtual terminal model using a common data structure

some way—it must appear identical on either side of the interface between the terminal handlers. The same property is required of a virtual terminal protocol used in a connection between two computer systems. But for terminal-to-computer links an asymmetrical protocol might be acceptable.

One other factor that affects the design of the virtual terminal is the presence of a terminal user in two of the cases. To manipulate the virtual terminal requires some degree of 'intelligence' on the part of the interacting partners. Interactions between two people through the medium of terminals and a network connection can, therefore, reasonably be expected to succeed.

When the partners involved are a user with a terminal and a remote computer, the protocols covering an interaction must be more precisely defined so that they can be implemented by programs in the computer, which will act as an automaton in its dealings with the user. But the intelligence of the human user can still be relied upon to overcome difficulties, since he, at least, knows what is supposed to happen.

It is with the third possibility, the interconnection of partners that are both computer-based automata, that the problems really become severe, as we shall see later. First, however, we examine below the data structures that are appropriate for a virtual terminal.

The Virtual Terminal Data Structure

When people interact, they often appear to build a common model which encompasses their area of agreement. Sometimes this is a written document, sometimes a mental image; but the essential feature of an interaction seems to be the joint model with which they agree or disagree, and which continues to evolve until all parties are satisfied. This applies equally to a bilateral interaction or multilateral one, such as a committee meeting.

Pursuing this further we see that each person involved has a mental model of the interaction which they modify by their thought processes to take account of the remarks of other people. Agreement is the state when the information exchanged between the participants can be reconciled with their internal model of the interaction. It is unproductive here to go further along this philosophical track but it is sometimes useful to think about the way people interact, as this is common to everyone's experience. Put in the context of the virtual terminal, one might imagine a standard text structure such as an array into which messages from one computer are mapped before despatch, and from which they are transformed, as necessary, on arrival at another computer.

Because the internal data structures may vary remarkably between different computer systems, and are less well known than are the characteristics of terminals, it is more instructive to consider two terminal handlers or PADs which use a virtual terminal for the mutual interaction necessary to permit their real terminals to communicate together. In this case, a user interacting with a terminal connected to the first PAD would compose a message. This would be transformed by the PAD into the standard data structure which would then be transmitted to the second PAD. Here it would be transformed by that PAD into a form suitable for presentation on another type of terminal. This is illustrated in Figure 8.26 which shows a teletype communicating with a VDU. The figure suggests that the medium of communication is an array of C columns and L lines and that messages from each terminal are mapped into and out of this array.

The figure implies that there is a disembodied data structure located at some point between the two PADs. This is of course unrealistic and, in fact either, both or neither of the PADs may internally allocate the storage area equivalent to the standard data structure. As we shall see later the question of whether the model of the interaction is in the form of a single data structure which each side can modify, or whether it is in the form of two separate data structures which each side independently modifies, and which are kept in step by another interaction, has an important bearing on the definition of the virtual terminal. But to get ideas clear it is useful to examine further the implications of Figure 8.26 and how the two PADs might handle the terminals and their interactions.

For example, one system might employ a two-dimensional array to represent, say, the screen of a visual display and would arrange for this array to be updated as the user edits the displayed information by moving a cursor about the screen of the VDU. Each time the user signals that he was satisfied with the information

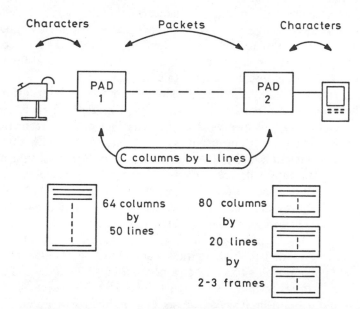

Figure 8.26   The virtual terminal between two PADs

displayed, the resulting array would be entered into a file which would eventually contain the complete record of the transactions of the user. Each instance of the array would then be a kind of window into the file of the total interactions forming one session by the user. The session file might be structured as a sequence of arrays, but this is unlikely, for any convenient mapping between the screen and the user's file would be chosen to suit the particular requirements of the computer system.

In contrast, another system might offer a line-based editor which constrains users to indicate the line and character position where changes to the data structure are required. In this case, a single line buffer could serve as a one-dimensional array, so that the window into the user's file would seem to be only one line. Even so, this might not reflect the internal system behaviour, where a two-dimensional array could still be used to ensure rapid handling of a group of adjacent lines around the line of interest to the user, although this would be unknown to the user himself.

Consider now that two PADs, each handling terminals in their own way, have to interact in such a way that the file constructed by one user at his terminal on one PAD can be read by the user at the terminal on the other and vice versa. This mapping process from one terminal to another can be made more or less difficult, depending on what is chosen as the intermediate data structure for the virtual terminal. There seem to be no very good criteria for selection and it is clear that a wide choice exists because the methods adopted for different computers are not very well in alignment with each other. Ideally, a criterion of selection is required that is independent of any particular computer system; it must therefore be based on some persuasive arguments about ways that interactions may best be done, and might also attempt to take account of the ways that people commonly communicate with each other, and the kinds of data structure that they find convenient to use.

The data structure selected for a virtual terminal must act as a transformation medium between the two parties to an interaction. In general, each party will have a file representing his own view of the behaviour of the virtual terminal, which he is manipulating in an attempt to correlate his file with that of the other party. The fact that one or both of the files may be stored in a memory or displayed on an output device does not alter the basic principles that are involved. By definition, when a file is mapped via the virtual terminal, a different file is obtained. If this were not the case, the virtual terminal would be just passing information through without modification.

The file mapping task of the virtual terminal suggests that its data structure should be closely related to a standard virtual file protocol. One of the key problems in a file protocol is recovery to a previous check-point after failure. A well-structured virtual terminal could be helpful in this respect, so it seems plausible to use a multi-dimensional array as is indicated in Figure 8.27. By analogy with accepted usage the array could comprise volumes of pages, each having lines and characters. The address of a character is therefore hierarchical in the form of volume, page, line and character position.

The question immediately arises about the size of the address field for each component of the array. The use of 8-bit fields would give 255 possible values, assuming zero is generally reserved for control purposes. This allows characters to be arranged in positions 1 to 255 along the lines which are themselves arranged in pages of from 1 to 255 lines and so on. Of course, real pages with 255 lines of 255 characters are not common although real volumes often have more than 255 pages, so the analogy with familiar usage needs to be stretched. As the file is a virtual one, the high order field structure is really not significant.

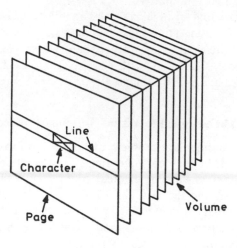

Figure 8.27   Extended data structure for a virtual terminal

In fact, each of the computer systems involved would allocate real storage in its own way to handle the file of a given size, so we are concerned here with the choice of a virtual data structure which can be mapped into the real structures used in any system, and vice versa. The choice is really quite arbitrary, but it is necessary for everyone to agree, so that ambiguity in addressing is avoided. In practice, it is unlikely that a common structure would be appropriate for all transactions, and the file transfer protocol may have to be related to the needs of a particular group of users.

8.7   THE VIRTUAL TERMINAL PROTOCOLS

Associated with the virtual terminal there are two protocols; one of these governs the interaction between the real terminal and the virtual terminal, the other covers the interaction between the virtual terminal and a remote packet terminal, which could be another virtual terminal, or an applications program in a service computer. For a long time the discussions about virtual terminal protocols confused these two different protocols.

In fact, most of the proposals have really been for protocols between the virtual terminal and the real terminal where an unsymmetrical approach has seemed most appropriate,[8,9] because the person using the terminal is able to operate in a much more sophisticated way than can the automaton represented by the computer service. The other protocol, that between two virtual terminals, could be symmetrical or unsymmetrical, depending on the degree to which this protocol reflects the other one. For it will be apparent that the interaction between the two virtual terminals can be influenced, even if somewhat indirectly, by the users at the real terminals.

If, however, the virtual terminal is seen as an interface between two computer systems, the rules for interaction must be more closely specified, because it is two automata that are interacting, rather than two people. For this reason, a symmetrical protocol is essential, with properly worked out ways for deciding which end is master and which is slave.

The Terminal to Virtual Terminal Protocol

We shall now consider the problem of how a terminal interacts with the virtual terminal, and the protocol governing this interaction. We shall call this protocol the terminal to virtual terminal protocol (TVTP). The interaction between the terminal and the virtual terminal is analogous to the interaction between the terminal and a computing system so that the discussions earlier in this chapter on the nature of terminals and the way they are connected through a network are relevant.

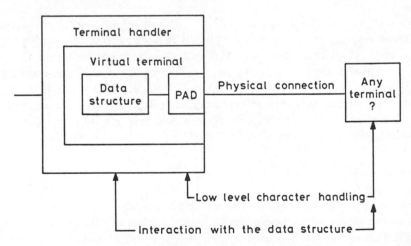

Figure 8.28   The terminal to virtual terminal protocol

In fact, the virtual terminal could very well reside in an enhanced PAD on a public network, or a terminal handler in a private one, and we can imagine it is a more sophisticated, higher level or more general description of a terminal than is implied by the CCITT recommendations, which we have already discussed in Section 8.5. We will, therefore, take as our model Figure 8.28, which shows any character terminal connected to a terminal handler. This incorporates a virtual terminal comprising a PAD associated with a virtual terminal data structure. This approach departs from the accepted definition of a PAD, but it clarifies the relationship between the PAD and the virtual terminal by suggesting that the PAD functions are only a subset of those that should be performed by a terminal handler.

The PAD needs to know precisely the characteristics of the terminal which it is handling, so the first requirement is an identification procedure. If there is a direct connection between terminal and PAD, identification is trivial, requiring only a table look-up. But with a dial-up line a more elaborate interaction may be necessary. For example, users may be required to send a known character repeatedly to allow the PAD to adjust for the transmission speed of the terminal. Similarly, any other interactions which would normally occur between the user and the remote computer to determine the way that the computer handles the terminal will have to be carried out by the PAD, for our assumption is that the remote computer is relieved by the terminal handler of all low level tasks.

Once all such preliminary interactions have been completed, a user with a terminal can begin to interact with the virtual terminal data structure, with the intention of building up a message or picture which will be sent on to the remote computer. Equally, the remote computer may modify the data structure in some way that it expects will be made apparent at the terminal. The way in which the remote computer modifies the data structure is the subject of the protocol between the virtual terminal and the computer, discussed in the next section, but it is appropriate here to consider how the modified structure is made known to the terminal. First, however, we will concentrate on input from the terminal to the data structure.

The signals from the terminal will comprise a string of characters, some printing, some non-printing and some control characters. This character string could be placed in the virtual terminal data structure as it arrives, filling up the structure line by line. There would, however, be little sense in doing this because the data structure would then be merely acting as a store, and the accumulated string would be sent on to the remote computer when the data structure was full. The whole point of having the virtual terminal is that some, at least, of the characters from the terminal affect the data structure, and do not get passed on to the remote computer system. The question arises of which characters affect the data structure and which are passed to the remote system. The answer to this question is the crux of the ongoing debate about the specification for a virtual terminal and its protocols.

We look at particular proposals for protocols later, but we will assume here that the user of the terminal interacts with the PAD to modify the data structure until he is completely satisfied, before sending it on to the remote system. One example is the use of a one-dimensional array of length equal to the line on the terminal. In this case, the terminal user edits the line using back space and overprint, or back arrow followed by retyping, with the line being despatched to the remote site only on typing carriage return. Another example is the use of an array corresponding to the screen size of a VDU. In this case, the cursor control characters are used to move the cursor around and modify the array until eventually the user is satisfied, whereupon a command to despatch the array is given. This could be explicit, in the form of a send command, or it might be implicit in that the structure is sent only when the user calls for a new array, for example by giving a form feed command.

There is a strong relationship between the size of the data structure in the virtual terminal and the amount of local editing that is provided between that data structure and the terminal. The PAD has to act as an editor within the limits set by the size of the data structure. This can be anything from a single character (the trivial case) upwards. Well-accepted units are the character, the line, the frame, the page, and a file of pages.

It follows from the discussion above that when the data structure is, for example, a line, there will be no character manipulating information passed to the remote computer. Again, when the array is two-dimensional, corresponding to a page, there will be no line manipulating information sent from the PAD to the remote data terminal. Extending the argument further, the data structure could be a file with which the user interacts, through the aid of his terminal, until he is satisfied that it is correct, before despatching it to the remote system. In this case the PAD would have to store the complete file. There would be no editing information within the file, which could therefore be parsed by a single scan, and the virtual terminal protocol would become a file transfer protocol. These limiting cases are described to indicate the principles involved, but they also indicate the wide range of possibilities to be considered when trying to adopt a standard of some kind. In practice, a single standard seems impossible. Instead, a number of standards are bound to appear, based on sizes of array which match well with particular applications.

To conclude the discussion of the input of information to the PAD we now see that it will contain two data structures and not one as might be supposed from the foregoing discussion. One of these structures holds the input string of characters from the terminal, before it is parsed and edited, the other contains the edited string which will be despatched to the remote computer. Of course, the first (unedited) data structure may be a transient one if characters are parsed as they arrive. But the second data structure must exist until the remote computer has indicated that it, too, has made a copy. This is illustrated by Figure 8.29.

Turning now to the output from the PAD to the terminal we see that the PAD will have obtained an array from the remote computer system and now has the task of transferring that array to the terminal. The procedure to be adopted is fairly straightforward. A process in the PAD has to scan the data structure and read it character by character, transferring these to the terminal. At the end of a line, the process must insert line feed and carriage return characters (or whatever else is necessary to produce the correct format on the terminal). It must also carry out any mapping operations that are requested. For example, it may have to convert a single character into a string of characters for the terminal, if it is necessary to generate a symbol by back space and overprint, as is the case with some printers.

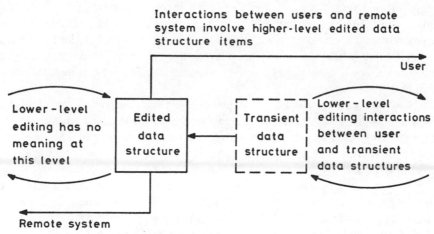

Figure 8.29   The local editing of the virtual terminal data structure

The expansion of the virtual terminal data structure into a data structure for the particular terminal may be done dynamically, so that as the characters in the array are scanned, the character or string of characters produced by the mapping function are sent to the terminal. Alternatively, the whole data structure can be scanned and expanded into a second, larger, data structure that is subsequently sent to the terminal. Again, there may be some intermediate scheme adopted by a particular designer, who might, for example, choose to scan the data structure line by line and send lines to the VDU, rather than scanning the whole array representing the screen, before sending to the terminal. In practice, the PAD is likely to use the same mechanism for delivering the data structure to the terminal, whether this has been received from the remote terminal or is the result of local modification by the user using local editing facilities.

Output of data to the terminal raises the question of whether the terminal can sensibly accommodate the structure sent to it from the remote terminal. Is the physical page size of the terminal big enough to print or display the data from the remote terminal? At first sight, it would seem that a data structure corresponding to a large page could not be reproduced on a small one. But depending on whether or not the information on the page is closely related to the dimensions of the page there is a chance that a mapping could be made onto a number of small pages which are subsequently put together by the user to reproduce a large page. This kind of thing is obviously quite possible, but it would be very difficult to agree upon a general specification which covered in general how to assemble automatically sets of small pages into large diagrams.

Where the structure is divisible into units small compared with the page size, for example, when text is being reproduced and can be divided into words, some reformatting is possible and a different layout of the text on a number of small pages may be acceptable. Again, it is difficult to write a specification for a protocol which would handle this in a standardised way, but the simple case of line folding, where long lines from a large page are reproduced by a succession of short lines on a small page, is sufficiently useful to be part of a general virtual terminal specification.

Now that we have looked at the protocol between the virtual terminal data structure and the real terminal, we can re-examine the optimum size for the data structure that was discussed above. The proposed array of 255 lines each of 255 characters is clearly large enough to accommodate input from most real terminals. Equally, it can accommodate output from a remote computer intended to drive any real terminal. If anything, it seems a little on the large size for text-handling terminals for the maximum line length found on line printers is 132 characters. On the other hand, a graphic display may well have a resolution of 1000 points across the screen, and in this case a 255-character line would be insufficient, unless some of the bits of the character code were used as additional position information. This suggests that the 255 by 255 array is a reasonable compromise capable of being used for a variety of applications, but it also suggests that a single protocol for a range of applications is likely to be inefficient, and that a range of virtual terminal protocols will be required to suit different applications.

The need for a series of virtual terminal protocols is borne out by examining the kinds of application that may have to be encompassed. Obviously, a highly interactive situation where only a few characters are exchanged at a time between the terminal user and the applications program in the remote computer does does not require large arrays to handle the messages. Neither is a large array required in the PAD during the editing of characters forming each message. In contrast, the user may be engaged in the preparation of a program by editing it locally, prior to sending it for execution remotely. In this case, the data structures for editing and exchange with the remote system may need to be much larger.

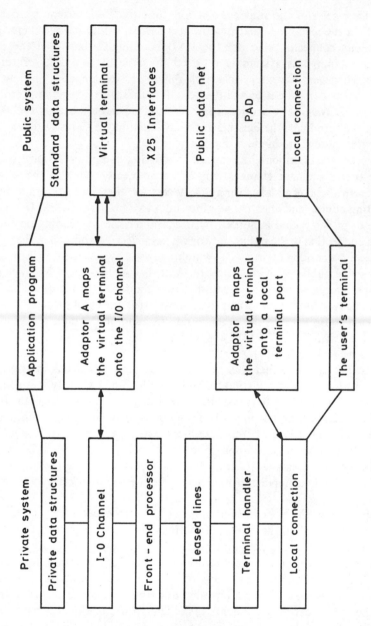

Figure 8.30 Matching between private and public systems

The System to Virtual Terminal Protocol

We have seen in the previous section that the PAD attempts to handle terminals in the same way that a computer system would handle them if they were directly connected. Because the PAD is acting on behalf of the remote computer system, this system is relieved of some of the tasks of terminal handling. However, the extent to which this is possible depends on how much editing is being carried out by the PAD, so it is difficult to design a protocol for general use between any service and any PAD. Furthermore, if the PAD is handling the terminals, the existing terminal-handling features in older designs of computer system are made redundant.

However, the enormous investment in existing computer systems makes it unlikely that significant changes can be economically made in the way they interact with their terminals. It may be necessary, therefore, to retain much of the existing equipment when connecting them to a public network. In any case, an adaptor of some kind is needed with characteristics depending on the level at which connection to the public network is achieved. To appreciate the problem more clearly, consider Figure 8.30 which shows a hypothetical private system and a possible public network structure. A cross-coupling could be made at any level, for example an adaptor A could match the I–O channel onto the virtual terminal, converting between the private data structures and those standardised for a virtual terminal. On the other hand, an adaptor B would retain more of the existing private system, at the expense of having to make the virtual terminal appear as a local terminal.

We will consider further this case of an adaptor B that has to appear as a terminal at one side and a virtual terminal at the other. Clearly it is somewhat similar to a PAD, except that instead of handling a terminal, it has to simulate a terminal. If the terminal to PAD protocol is unsymmetrical, some changes must be made to the PAD, before it can serve as an adaptor. But it would seem that the general architecture and much of the software of a PAD should be usable in the role of an adaptor for present systems. We therefore introduce the idea of the T-PAD to handle terminals and the S-PAD to interface with existing services.

In the future, the S-PAD functions could be absorbed into the mainframe of the computer, while the T-PAD functions can become part of the software of an intelligent terminal. So an interface designed now for use between the two PADs could remain of use indefinitely as a universal interface for matching terminals and computers. The purpose of this interface is, primarily, to facilitate interactions between a user at a terminal and an applications program, through which the user is carrying out some task. The nature of the task has a bearing on the size of the data structure of the virtual terminal, so it is unlikely that the PAD-to-PAD interface can be a unique one.

The involvement of a user means that the interface need not, necessarily, be symmetrical; in fact it is unlikely to be so at the task level. But at the level of the PAD-to-PAD interface, the protocol is concerned simply with the interchange of data structures and a symmetrical protocol has the advantage that the two types of PAD can be interchangeable. This permits the same protocol to serve for the three possible forms of connection shown in Figure 8.31. Firstly, the existing system of mainframe and terminal is replaced by a pair of PADs, a T-PAD handling the terminal and an S-PAD simulating the terminal at the mainframe. These two PADs communicate with each other through the medium of the intermediate network, using the PAD-to-PAD interface protocol. Secondly, two T-PADs with terminals interact, again through the PAD-to-PAD interface, to give terminal-to-terminal communication and finally two mainframes communicate through two S-PADs using the same PAD-to-PAD interface. We, therefore, concentrate on the nature of this symmetrical interface and associated protocol which we will call the *system to virtual terminal protocol* (S-VTP). This is, of course, the high level virtual terminal interface we met in Figure 8.23.

In the general case, the PAD software will be multi-threaded with many concurrent channels being simultaneously supported. But the principles underlying its operation can more easily be discussed in the context of a single channel. Later, the additional problems arising with multi-channel software can be introduced. It will be most convenient to discuss the protocol in terms of two

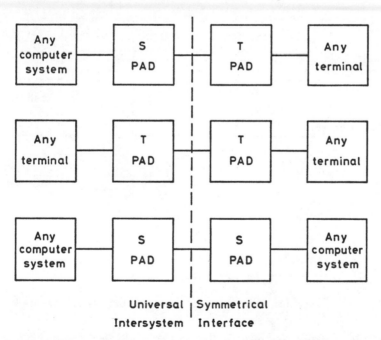

Figure 8.31   The system to virtual terminal interface

equal partners, taking the role of master or slave, as appropriate, to control the exchange between them of the virtual terminal data structure, and to ensure its integrity is maintained at each end. This is similar to the classical case of process-to-process communication, using an exchange of messages, or the equally classical case of the interaction between a pair of automata, based on state-transition diagrams and an exchange of stimuli.

As we have seen, the various cases of Figure 8.31 are not really equivalent, for the human user can intervene for terminal-to-terminal, or terminal to computer interaction, when it is obvious to him that something has gone wrong. But for computer-to-computer interaction, it is indeed two automata that are interacting and so careful thought must be given to the recovery from failures that cause deadlocks or loss of synchronism between the states of the two automata.

Some of the complexity of the S-VTP could be avoided if a precise definition

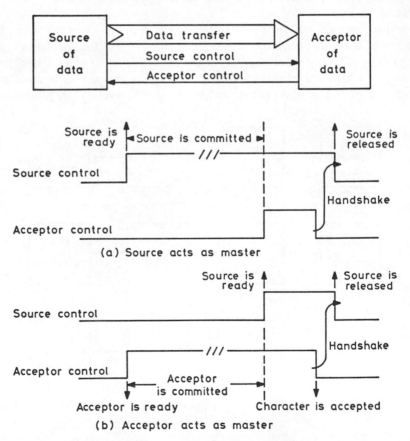

Figure 8.32   Interaction between a master and a slave

were possible, and if implementations of the protocol in different systems were exact. In fact, the protocol has to cover a range of applications, and so must contain optional features, while implementations will differ depending on the designer's interpretation, and on the constraints of the system used for the implementation. Indeed, some designs will support only a partial set of facilities, perhaps as an interim step on the way to a fuller implementation. Above all, the design of the protocol will depend on the tasks it is supporting. We therefore examine these aspects in Section 8.8 before looking at the design of the virtual terminal in Section 8.9.

The Master–Slave Relationship

In previous sections we have touched on the problem of the master–slave relationship in different systems. This problem is, perhaps, the most fundamental one arising with interactions at all levels of protocol.[10] The differing viewpoints on the part of different system designers on this topic probably account for most of the misunderstandings and arguments about protocol structures that are currently encountered. This is particularly true when the protocol is relatively complex and protagonists have lost sight of the fundamental issues.

As an example, let us consider Figure 8.32 which concerns a physical interface which connects two partners, a source of data and an acceptor of data. It is required to transfer an item of data from the source to the acceptor under the control of signals passing between them. The question arises of whether the source should inform the acceptor when it has data ready to be transferred, or whether the acceptor should tell the source when it is ready to accept a transfer. Both these possibilities lead to viable systems, and each kind of system is common in practice. Unfortunately, in one system the master is the source and in the other it is the acceptor. When a mixed system is attempted, there are either two masters, or two slaves, so an interaction is impossible. This situation has been well described in reference 11, in the context of British Standard Specification 4421.

When the two partners may both send and receive data, and are separated by a communication system so that the control of transfer of information is by an exchange of messages, which may be lost or duplicated, the situation becomes far more complex. The problems are eased by identifying which partner is the master in the initial system design, but, in general, it is necessary for each partner to be able to act as master or slave depending on the course of an interaction.

In fact, it is not always obvious which partner is the master. For example, when a terminal communicates with a network, the network is the master, because it shares its resources between all the terminals and must be able to allow or disallow a connection and to control the activity of terminals as necessary. Yet, the terminal will be the master in the sense that it will initiate a request to the network to connect it with another terminal, although the network will decide whether or not the connection is possible. Again, the calling terminal is apparently the master in relationship to the called terminal, but the called terminal may be a computer system which itself is sharing resources among several terminals and must be the master for the interaction with the calling terminal.

Evidently, the notion of a master–slave relationship is not a simple one when used in the context of a network. The difficulties arise from the fact that two or more systems with independent resource management mechanisms are trying to interact. Each appears to the others to behave in a complex and variable way. Their behaviour patterns may be deterministic in form, but variable in time, when it is simple storage that is shared. But when processing is also involved the form of their behaviour may change, so their interactions are unrepeatable.

The protocols governing the interactions in the complicated system of a public network with associated computer systems and terminals of all kinds take account of these factors, but the situation is so complex that an overall model with all levels of protocol identified seems impossible to achieve. However, two key points can be identified.

Firstly when a master communicates with a slave, the master is committed to the interaction when it sends the command to the slave. The slave may not be ready and may delay a reply indefinitely. If this happens the master is locked. It is therefore necessary to have a time-out arrangement whereby the master gives up an attempt to interact, when the interaction is no longer of significance to it.

Secondly, when two masters attempt to communicate and each requests the other to act as a slave at the same instant in time, a deadlock situation arises. It is then necessary for each to back down and try again. But the period before they try again must be different otherwise a perpetual deadlock is obtained. Either the delay before retrying has to be random, or there must be a time-out on the number of attempts to communicate, or on the time taken to establish a communication channel. Again this ensures that attempts to communicate are discontinued when the communication is no longer timely for one or other of the partners. The use of time-outs is, therefore, a fundamental aspect of protocol design. Indeed, protocols based entirely on time-outs have been described in reference 12.

8.8   TASK PERFORMANCE—THE ULTIMATE OBJECTIVE

To get the design of protocols into perspective, we will now look at the ultimate purpose of informatics systems. These, we suggest, are intended to aid people in the performance of various tasks. The tasks need have nothing to do with computing systems or computer networks, which may be, as far as the user is concerned, just tools which help or hinder him in what he is trying to achieve.

The task could be anything, but as an example we will imagine that the user wishes to buy some commodity. The task protocol might then be to determine what commodities are available, to make a selection, to place an order, to take delivery, and finally to make payment. Variations of this protocol might be to pay a deposit, ask for credit, select various options, and so on. It is clear that all of these operations can be facilitated by using a computer network, and the tasks may be seen as separate operations or a collection of operations which together make up the complete task. It is also clear that the user engaged in the task will interact with information services, manufacturers, retailers, financial services, and even delivery services. Of course, these kinds of interactions are not possible to any extent now, but as the use of public networks develops, they are the kind of thing we may expect to see become quite commonplace.

We will now consider some of the factors that are relevant to the performance of such tasks, and the design of protocols to support them. Figure 8.33 illustrates the way people interact and the data structures that they use. Interactions between people using a natural language cover a wide range of data structures where the elements involved vary from symbols and characters upwards in size almost indefinitely. The diagram shows some possible elements arranged in a table with an interest pointer to an element of particular interest to the interacting partners. As a dialogue takes place the interest pointer may move anywhere in the data structure. For example, there may be a discussion about a particular character or word, or the topic of conversation may be a book or the contents of a chapter. There are, of course, many other models that may be the basis of an interaction between people, but this diagram will suffice to bring out an approximate relationship between the size of element and the frequency of interaction and the intelligence conveyed or involved in each interaction. Generally, the smaller elements are involved in more rapid interactions and convey lower amounts of intelligence.

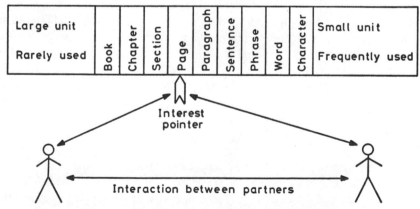

| Large unit | Book | Chapter | Section | Page | Paragraph | Sentence | Phrase | Word | Character | Small unit |
| Rarely used | | | | | | | | | | Frequently used |

Interest
pointer

Interaction between partners

Figure 8.33 People and their data structures

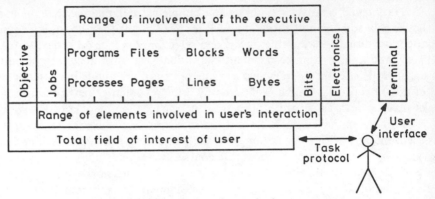

Figure 8.34　Tasks using a single computer

Consider the situation when a user employs a single computer system to carry out his tasks, as shown in Figure 8.34. The figure shows the user with an interface to a terminal through which he is manipulating the computer system in an endeavour to perform his task. The size of data interesting to the user will probably range from words up to complete tasks. The terminal is shown connected to the computer system in which the elements range from the electronic circuits of the terminal to the tasks to be performed. Above and below are shown the ranges of involvement of the executive which is controlling the behaviour of the computer, and of the user during his interactions. The diagram brings out the fact that when a user interacts with a computer system the size of the elements in the data structure he manipulates may vary widely during the course of any one interaction. There is no reason why he should not be manipulating files at one minute, and editing strings of characters at another.

The freedom to vary the scale of the interaction is reduced somewhat in a distributed system as indicated in Figure 8.35. This shows four major elements involved: the user, the task he is performing, the terminal and the service. The terminal is assumed to comprise a local physical terminal and a local intelligence which incorporates a virtual terminal. The terminal interacts with the local virtual terminal using the terminal VTP. The service supports the applications programs performing the task, and is assumed to comprise remote intelligence which is complementary to the virtual terminal and allows access to files through the medium of file access and file transfer protocols. The terminal and service interact using the system VTP.

We now look at the constraints placed on the user by reference to Figure 8.36. This shows the interactions between users and applications programs in a distributed system in more detail. The top of the figure shows a variety of terminals connected to a terminal PAD which interacts through the S-VTP with the remote system. This in turn may interact with other support services using appropriate file transfer protocols. The middle of the diagram indicates an

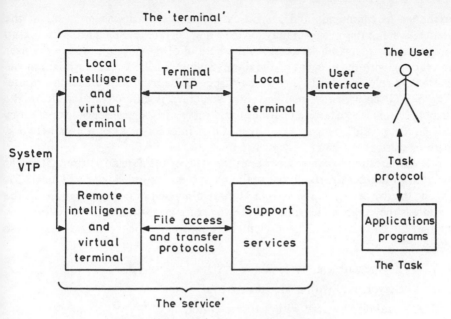

Figure 8.35   Tasks in a distributed system

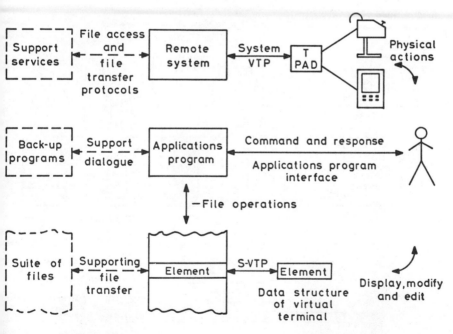

Figure 8.36   Interactions between users and applications programs

exchange of commands and responses with an applications program in the remote system; this program may, or may not, conduct a dialogue with back-up programs in supporting services. At the bottom of the diagram we see the user interacting with the element of the data structure of the virtual terminal in the T-PAD, displaying, modifying and editing the data structure as appropriate. The S-VTP ensures the modified data structure is entered into a file in the remote system where the applications program carries out appropriate operations on the file; possibly managing a suite of files in other parts of a data network, with or without the knowledge of the user.

It is interesting to conjecture about the sizes of the data structure that might be used in different parts of a distributed system, as indicated in Figure 8.37. At the top, we see again the system already discussed in previous figures. In the middle is the range of elements of data structure of possible interest to the user, and, at the bottom, the range of elements appropriate for typical devices. These are:

1. A teletype with character editor PAD.

2. A teletype used with a file editing PAD.

3. A visual display used with a frame editor.

4. A virtual terminal data structure.

5. A file transfer protocol data structure.

6. The user data structure.

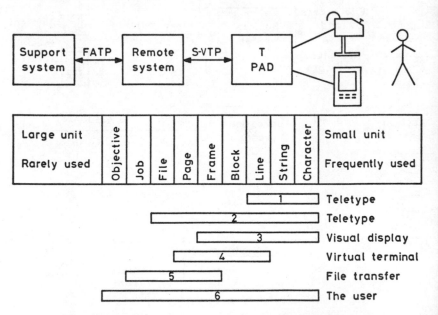

Figure 8.37   Sizes of a data structure in distributed systems

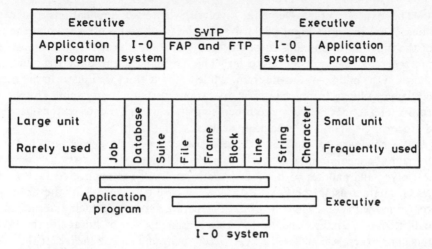

Figure 8.38 Interactions between two applications programs

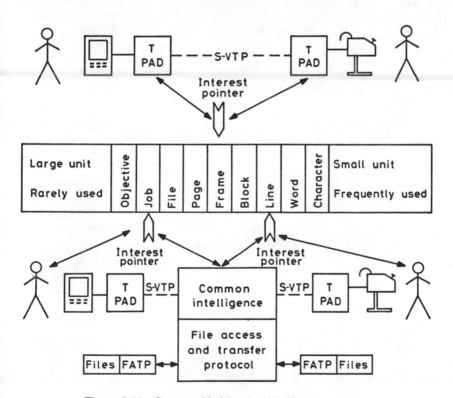

Figure 8.39 System-aided interactions between people

The data structure elements involved when two applications programs interact are shown in Figure 8.38. Again, the two systems are shown at the top of the diagram interacting through an S-VTP or perhaps through file access protocols and file transfer protocols. The elements of the data structure are shown in the middle of the diagram, while at the bottom we illustrate the range of elements likely to be of interest to various parts of the system. This figure covers interactions between two processing systems, or the interactions between a processing system and a back-up service.

We now turn to the case where a user is interacting with another user through the medium of a network. The top of Figure 8.39 shows one user with a teletype and another with a VDU, both terminals are connected to T-PADs which interact using the S-VTP. As in the case of Figure 8.33 the users are concerned with some element of data structure supporting their interaction as indicated by the interest pointer. With a reasonable size of storage in the PADs this data structure could well be restricted to around a page in size. If the users wish to interact in a data structure bigger than a page it may be necessary to adopt the scheme shown at the bottom of the figure where the two PADS are connected to some common intelligence which is able to store and manipulate files, possibly using a file access and transfer protocol with other support services. The PADs interact with the common system using the S-VTP and the two users may now be decoupled to the extent that one might be creating a file a line at

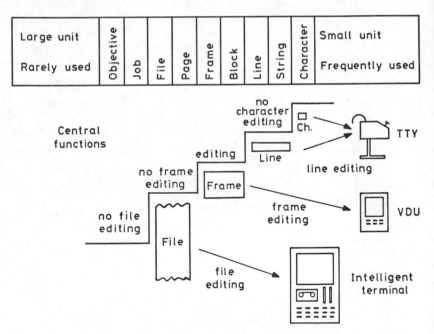

Figure 8.40   Suppression of the low level traffic by the virtual terminal

a time using a teletype, while the other may be manipulating files already created by the other user, perhaps as part of a job he is doing.

Another aspect of the virtual terminal data structure of importance in networking is illustrated by Figure 8.40 which gives the range of common data structures at the top and, below, a range of data structure sizes that might be used for a virtual terminal. At the bottom of the figure we show a file which is produced by an intelligent terminal, as a result of interactions using a frame data structure associated with a VDU. Above that we see line and character data structures associated with the teletype. To the left of the line marking the size of data structure we see that, for example, no frame editing characters appear in pages and larger data structures because all frame editing characters are suppressed by the PAD when it converts the editing dialogue between the PAD and the VDU into a frame which is part of a higher level structure. In accordance with this principle, a PAD which interacts with terminals using a line data structure will exchange characters with the terminal, but will exchange only lines at the S-VTP level. These lines will contain no editing characters which are significant at the line level.

Having seen how various kinds of interaction involve data structures of

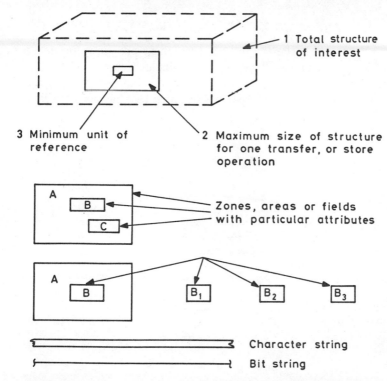

Figure 8.41   Further aspects of the virtual terminal data structure

various sizes we are in a position to consider what should be the optimum size of data structure for different levels in a distributed system. Figure 8.41 shows that there are three aspects of the data structure. Firstly, there is the total structure of interest to the interacting partners. This data structure is, in general, much larger than can be accommodated in the size of store with which they both can simultaneously interact. Secondly, there is a maximum size of data structure that can be accommodated in the user's local store and which is covered by each transfer operation from one partner to another, or indeed by a transfer from a local backing store. Thirdly, there is the minimum unit of data structure to which a reference can be made. As an example, at the file level, it may be possible to reference lines, but not characters within a line.

The ability to reference an element of the data structure smaller than that which is exchanged provides a sub-addressing facility that allows some spread in the speed of interaction dictated by the particular size of structure involved in normal transfers. Another advantage of allowing reference to a sub-structure is the need to accommodate arrays where some items stored in the array have properties which differ from those stored elsewhere. This is discussed in the next section.

8.9   THE DESIGN OF THE VIRTUAL TERMINAL

As we have seen earlier in this chapter, there are many issues, ideas and points of view regarding the handling of terminals in networks, so the evolution of this subject will obviously continue for some time to come. It is not yet possible to review the design of a virtual terminal that has been widely accepted

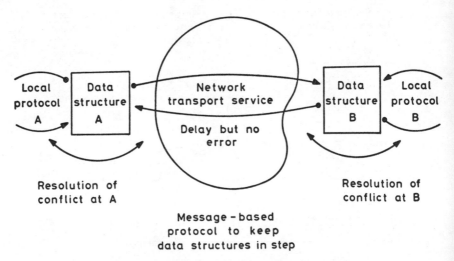

Figure 8.42   Model of virtual terminal interaction

and evaluated in a number of different networks, for no consensus view has so far appeared. However, we will briefly describe some of the principles behind the various proposals now being considered as a basis for possible future standards.

In order of increasing complexity, proposals for virtual terminals have covered the scroll mode, teletype-like, terminals, the page mode visual display terminals, and the more elaborate data entry terminals.[13,14,15] In addition, there have been proposals for a virtual device protocol that can handle other peripheral devices as well as the interactive terminal.[8]

The Architectural Model

Before a standard can emerge, there must be a general agreement on the architecture of the systems in which it is to be used. Fortunately, ideas now seem to have converged on the model shown in Figure 8.42. Two partners A and B are linked by an error-free transport service. This introduces variable delay in the passage of the messages which are intended to keep the data structures of the partners in synchronism with each other. The transport service also provides a 'telegram' facility whereby a very short message is carried with high priority, in an apparently separate channel, to allow modification of the normal message exchange mechanism.

The data structures are manipulated locally by suitable protocols, which can be message-oriented or character-oriented as required by circumstances. We assume that these local protocols, and the mechanisms necessary for resolving conflicts between local and remote access to each data structure, are entirely the responsibility of the local system. As an illustration, we might suggest that the local system could be represented by Figure 8.43, but we are not concerned with such details here, because they are in the province of the local system designer.

To define the interaction between A and B it is only necessary for us to specify the data structures and the message protocol for keeping them in step. This protocol, which is equivalent to the S-VTP we encountered in Section 8.7, will be described later. Firstly, however, we will consider the nature of the data structure itself.

The Modular Data Structure

The data structure for a virtual terminal that can represent many real terminals must be a modular, multi-level one that can provide flexibility in situations with the different interaction times likely to arise from a range of applications. The most general structure is an array of sub-arrays; these have variously been called zones, areas, fields, etc., and may be of any size from one character upwards. Usually, they will be linear or rectangular arrays, but multi-dimensional arrays might be useful for an advanced graphics application.

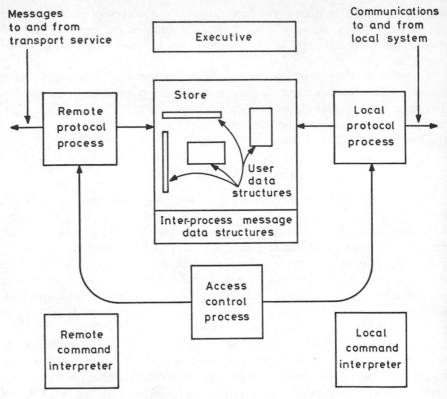

Figure 8.43   A possible model of one virtual terminal system

In general, we can suppose that any number of fields may be employed to produce any desired degree of complexity in the total data structure. (In each particular case, any appropriate constraints can afterwards be imposed. For example, the scroll mode terminal would be represented by an array of one line, if local line editing was employed, or an array of one character, if no local editing was available.) The manipulation of particular fields provides the required flexibility in response time, while the use of fields with different attributes gives the desired freedom in the presentation of information. Typical attributes are listed in Figure 8.44.

The number of attributes and the way they are described is one of the subjects for future standardisation. One cannot guess how this standardisation might proceed because the range of options is so large. For example, colour might be specified by quantizing the chrominance component of a colour video signal, or it might be done by specifying the intensities of the primary colours. Either way, the local system could interpret the information in any convenient manner, to provide differing local effects for the same received information.

Field or zone type	Definition
Protected/unmodifiable	Cannot be changed by the other partner
Numeric	Contains only numerals
Alpha	Contains only alphabetic characters
Non-displayable	Used for entry of passwords
Non-printable	Cannot be printed locally
Right justifiable	Character strings may be right justified
Left justifiable	Character strings may be left justified
Mandatory entry	Entries must be made before transmission
Selectable	Light pen or equivalent can be used
Not transmittable	For local display only
Concatenated	Follows previous field
Blinking/reverse video	Contents of field is highlighted
Scroll	Field is overwritten as a scroll
Page	Field is overwritten as a page
Top justifiable	Lines may be justified to top of field
Bottom justifiable	Lines may be justified to bottom of field
Colour	Colour of characters when displayed
Intensity	Brightness of field when displayed
Background	Colour of background of field

Figure 8.44   Some attributes proposed for virtual terminals

This is already the case with colour television, where hue, colour intensity, contrast and brightness controls allow each viewer to adjust his picture for his own requirements; seldom are two displayed pictures identical, although the transmitted signal is the same for all viewers.

The possibility of having many optional attributes makes it necessary for the two partners using a virtual terminal to negotiate which options are to be used, before a meaningful interaction can continue; this is part of the protocol governing their dialogue. But the choice of the attributes and the way they are described is really part of the data structure definition. The present approach is to assign a bit pattern in, say, an 8-bit character code to represent each attribute. This requires a precise agreement by all users on fine detail in a complex specification. A more flexible scheme is to use a string of characters to identify each attribute, perhaps making the string a mnemonic name that is obvious to people, while being also suitable for parsing by a computer. These schemes are contrasted in Figure 8.45. This shows that bit coding seems most efficient, but it requires associated software processes to operate at the bit level. Byte coding is better for processing, particularly if the codes are related to the parameters in some way, for example, by using the ISO code for the initial letter of each parameter. But string coding is most appropriate for use with future systems because it can be made redundant, unambiguous and highly mnemonic.

The further development of the virtual terminal could well be the agreement

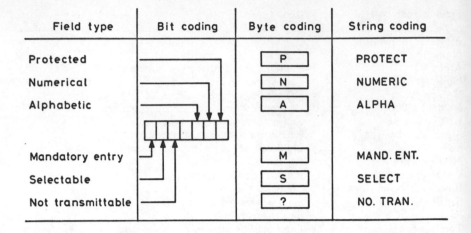

Field type	Bit coding	Byte coding	String coding
Protected		P	PROTECT
Numerical		N	NUMERIC
Alphabetic		A	ALPHA
Mandatory entry		M	MAND. ENT.
Selectable		S	SELECT
Not transmittable		?	NO. TRAN.

Figure 8.45   Coding of attributes for a data structure

of a data structure description language, possibly based on a formalised subset of natural language. This will allow translation from one natural language to another. Such a language would have to be very highly redundant to avoid ambiguities. However, this is acceptable because it is involved only in the initial stages of an interaction when two partners are negotiating with each other to define a basis for a meaningful dialogue. The longer-term evolution of a data structure definition language could well be a picture description language, suitable for use in advanced graphics applications.

An example of what might be the future trend is shown in Figure 8.46. This

1. Declare Fields
   Field := name, address, age, hobbies, user's instructions

2. Define Attributes
   Name := protected, alpha, colour—red,
                    background—green, blinking
   Age := numeric, concatenated with name
   User's instructions := non-printable, colour—blue, page
   Address := selectable, left justifiable, alphanumeric
   Hobbies := alphanumeric, mandatory entry, scroll

3. Dimension Fields
   Name := lines—1, characters—25
   Address := lines—4, characters—30
   User instructions := lines—10, characters—64
   Age := characters—3
   Hobbies := lines—2, characters—64

Figure 8.46   A hypothetical data structure description language

shows how a set of fields with various attributes might be defined in a way understandable to someone having to implement a program for an intelligent real terminal. Where this was restricted in its capability, the designer could make sensible interpretations in order to permit a worthwhile interaction to take place.

The Message Protocol

The interaction with the virtual terminal data structure is in the form of input messages which modify either the structure itself, or its contents, and output messages which report on changes to the structure or its contents. However, the messages exchanged may not completely describe the interaction, because there may be contextual information which is referred to by messages, but which is made available to the participants without using the message communication channel. We can imagine that the establishment of the contextual background is the subject of a 'higher' level protocol, that may, or may not, exist in a definable form. As an example, it could result from previous interactions through the network, but need not.

During an interaction, messages reflecting various levels of protocol will pass between the partners, for example, to set up a channel, to establish that their correspondent is the right one, and so on. We assume, however, that all such necessary low level preliminaries have been completed through the medium of suitable protocols and that we can confine the discussion to the interaction with the data structure of the virtual terminal. There are usually considered to be four active stages, or phases, to this interaction, as shown in Figure 8.47.

The initialisation, declaration or negotiation phase is required so that the data structure can be defined, by suitable control messages, either before the interaction begins, or perhaps at some intermediate stage. These control messages must allow, for example, the selection of a particular protocol, if several are available, the declaration of one or more fields, the specification of their attributes and the setting of limits on their dimensions.

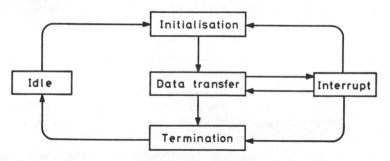

Figure 8.47   The phases of the virtual terminal

The normal or data exchange phase is the state where data messages are written into, or read from the various fields that have been defined. This state persists until the interaction is completed, until an error situation arises such as, for example, an attempt being made to write into a read only field, or until an interrupt or attention indication occurs.

The interrupt or attention phase is entered when the course of the interaction is required to be changed by command of one of the partners. This phase allows reversion to be made either to the initialisation phase, so that the interaction may be resynchronised, if necessary, by a redefinition of parameters, or to the closing or termination phase, in order to allow a premature completion of the transaction, if this is forced by one or other partner.

The termination or end phase is necesary to ensure that a clean break is made in a transaction so the various virtual terminal processes involved are returned to an idle or waiting state ready for the next interaction.

Message formats are required for signalling and controlling the transitions from one state to another, as well as for transferring data to and from the data structure. Various schemes are in use in existing networks and are mentioned below in the context of each particular phase of the virtual terminal dialogue. There seems to be general agreement on the use of a header indicating message-type and length, but, of course, there is less agreement on the contents. Early ideas used individual bits to indicate parameters, later schemes use single characters for the purpose, but, as we indicated in Figure 8.45 the use of character strings is a likely future development.

The negotiation of options is a basic requirement in higher levels of protocols and is essentially conducted by one partner assuming the role of a master and making an offer to the other, who replies with acceptance, a counter offer, or rejection. With some protocols, options are agreed one at a time; with others, a set of options can be handled in a single exchange of a command and response. In some systems, one or more standard sets or profiles can be named, as well as individual options. Most protocols also allow one partner to request information from the other about the options that are available.

There are two schemes employed for negotiation, a symmetrical one and an unsymmetrical one. With the symmetrical scheme, either side may send a declaration of the set of options, parameters or values that it desires to employ, and expects the other to reply with its own set as a counter declaration. The intersection of the two sets is the set that governs the ensuing interaction, unless either side refuses to continue with such a set.

If bit encoding is used for negotiation messages, precise agreement on the order of elements in the set is essential, because a logical 'and' operation is performed between the transmitted and received sets. But if a unique string describes each element, they may be in any order, with only those options specified included. In this case, a sorting and comparison operation determines the common set of items.

The earlier, unsymmetrical scheme employed in the ARPA Telnet protocol[16,17,18] uses four commands for option negotiation, WILL, WON'T, DO and DON'T.

—WILL indicates that the sender wishes to begin, or is already, using the indicated option.

—WON'T indicates that the sender refuses to use, or is ceasing to use the indicated option.

—DO requests the recipient to adopt the specified option.

—DON'T requests the recipient to cease performing the specified option.

These commands are used in the following way. Either party sends WILL as an indicator that it wants to use an option, while the other replies with DO or DON'T as the positive or negative responses. Similarly, either party sends DO to request an option, and the other replies with WILL as a positive, or WON'T as a negative, response.

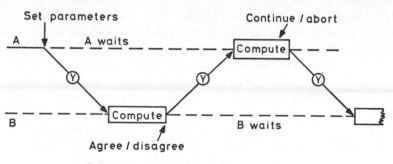

(a) Calling subscriber A is master

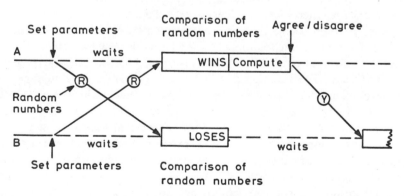

(b) Use of random numbers to resolve conflicts

Figure 8.48   The negotiation of options

Whichever scheme for negotiation is adopted there is potentially the possibility of conflict when both partners independently attempt to act as master and initiate a negotiation phase at the same time. We considered this problem in Section 8.7 and showed that the use of time-outs by each partner is essential to avoid such confrontation deadlocks. These time-outs, of course, are not part of the message protocol, but they determine the behaviour of the partners when unusual conditions have arisen, and usually result in the sending of a different message from that expected in the normal course of events. The protocol must, therefore, include such messages in its repertoire.

In practice, the lower levels of protocol will resolve an initial conflict by deciding which partner is the calling subscriber and which is the called. The designation of the calling subscriber as master at the virtual terminal level allows him to initiate the negotiation phase and so avoid a deadlock. Where there is still a need to resolve conflict, the association of a random number with each message allows priority to be given to that with the highest number. These two possibilities are shown in Figure 8.48. In case (a), A is master and sends the *set parameter* command, waiting until B replies; meanwhile B waits until A begins the interaction. In case (b), both the partners send a set parameter command, together with a random number, and then wait. Instead of receiving the reply they expect, both partners receive a set parameter command, and they compare its number with that of the command they sent. The winner waits until the loser replies with the correct response to the original command that was sent to him. Usually, a single octet is allocated as a random number field in the message header.

In the data phase, some proposed virtual terminal protocols distinguish between two modes of operation; *alternate* and *free running*. Alternate mode is a kind of half duplex interaction where a partner sends one or more messages and then waits for a reply, before sending further messages. The activities of the two partners are, therefore, interleaved with each other. Free running mode allows each partner to send messages independently of the other. This latter, it is suggested, is appropriate for applications where the messages sent and received are not directly related. While the inclusion of this mode appears to offer generality, it introduces complexity and seems of doubtful value, since some higher level of protocol has to resolve conflicts that inevitably arise.

One reason given for the inclusion of a free running mode is to cater for services that do not indicate when they have completed their turn in a dialogue with a user at a terminal. In fact, many existing systems rely on the terminal user seeing that the computer has replied, and acting accordingly, without being given a specific 'end of message' indication. In the absence of such an indication the virtual terminal apparently cannot operate in alternate mode, and so the free running mode is introduced. But this is only a palliative; the better solution is to modify the services to behave in a more satisfactory way. Even if this cannot be done, it is still possible to use an alternate mode of operation by relying on the terminal user to take over the turn by an interrupt command, as described below. The behaviour is then very similar to the way the existing system operates.

The alternate mode requires a means of deciding who begins and a method of transferring the right to send messages from one partner to the other. This necessitates a hand-over mechanism which has become known as the *my-turn, your-turn* signal. This is sent by the partner with the 'turn' to permit the other partner to send a message in reply. Clearly, the alternate mode allows one partner to monopolise the conversation by retaining the turn indefinitely. To overcome this situation, an interrupt mechanism is required to allow the inhibited partner to take control. This has been called the attention mechanism, which we describe later. The possession of the turn is decided initially by the outcome of the negotiation phase. Indeed, although it has not been proposed for present protocols, it would be possible to combine a random number field used for conflict resolution during negotiation, with the turn indication signal. The field would be set to zero for your turn, set to maximum for my turn, and set randomly for initial, probing, commands.

A second requirement in the data phase is the addressing of the items in the data structure. The simplest arrangement is to always read or write the full content of each field so that the existing contents are overwritten. With this scheme, each data message has a header with a field identifier, and is exactly the right length to fill that particular field, as it was defined in the initial phase of the interaction. A local length comparison can then be used as a validity check, if desired, so that errors in implementation can be detected.

More elaborate schemes have been proposed for some protocols, whereby various addressing features are provided so that part only of a field needs to be

Command	Effect on pointer
Next character	Move to next position (usually made implicitly on receipt of another character)
Last character	Move back one position (BS)
Next line	Move to beginning of next line (NL)
Home	Return to beginning of field
Tabulate	Move to next tabstop (HT)
Absolute	Go to coordinates given
Differential	Move by distances given
Next field	Move to next unprotected field (FF)

Figure 8.49 Some addressing commands for the virtual terminal

transmitted. These use the concept of a current position pointer in the data structure, marking where the next character is to be written or read. This pointer can be moved about the structure using addressing commands as shown in Figure 8.49.

For some of these, ISO codes are assigned but others such as differential addressing require a string giving the direction and distance to be moved, e.g. DF8C or DB4L (differential, forward or back, number of characters or lines). Possibly the use of strings for most addressing commands would ease the problem of agreeing on the coding of each command, for which universal agreement does not exist. For example, the home command is not assigned an ISO code, so a two-character string 'HO' could be appropriate.

In fact, however, complexity of addressing of the virtual terminal data structure seems scarcely appropriate at this level of protocol, where the handling of complete fields can avoid most of the detailed problems. But the home and new line commands can reduce the volume of data to be transmitted when a field is overwritten with mainly null characters and lines, as shown in Figure 8.50.

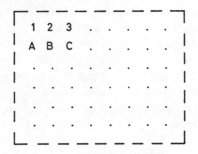

(a) Simple field overwriting requires all positions to be filled

(b) Use of 'new line' and 'home' avoids the need to send padding characters

Figure 8.50   Use of sub-zone addressing

We have described how a transaction between two partners begins with the negotiation of a common data structure and continues with an exchange of messages that relate to the data contained in the data structure, and to the way it is changed in order to convey information between the partners. The interaction can be considered synchronous in the sense that messages are sent alternately by the two partners, with the transfer of the 'turn' determined by the active partner or master. The partners act in turn as master and slave, following the initial negotiation which decides who begins the dialogue. This is illustrated at the top of Figure 8.51 where we see that the delay in the transfer of messages can be ignored because it merely alters the time taken for the transaction, and has no effect on the sequence of events.

However, at some stage, there may be a need to disturb the steady pattern of message exchange, perhaps when one partner makes a mistake, or wishes to change the rules in some way. This change is initiated by sending an interrupt signal, known in the context of the virtual terminal as an 'attention'. This makes use of the telegram feature of the transport service which supports the dialogue, as is shown in the lower part of Figure 8.51. The arrival of the telegram may

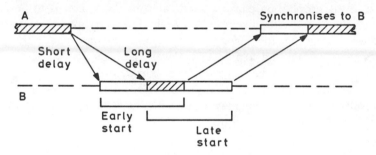

(a) Synchronous alternate message exchange

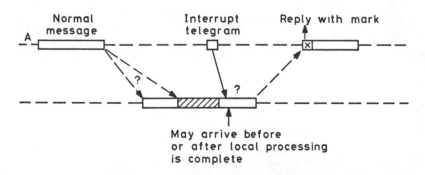

(b) Asynchronous attention telegram

Figure 8.51 Signalling in the data phase

occur at any time, relative to what is happening locally. Because the relative time of receipt might be important for subsequent events, most protocols include the idea of a 'mark' which is placed in the next message to be returned by the interrupted partner. This is also indicated in the figure.

In a sophisticated protocol, attention handling can become very complex. Some protocols provide different mechanisms for handling interrupts arising for different reasons, some employ a reply telegram to acknowledge an interrupt. A common idea is to distinguish between two different courses of action following the despatch of a telegram, and the receipt of a mark. It is argued that when one partner A issues a telegram, there will be an undetermined delay before it is received by the other B, during which time B will continue his activities, perhaps even sending messages to A, as is shown in Figure 8.52. The question arises of what to do with messages 2 and 3, following the interruption occasioned by message 1.

Many protocols include a facility by which B can qualify the mark signal (message 4) with a purge or resume indication that informs A whether to discard or process the previous messages, on the assumption that B knows the reason for the interruption. However, this seems over-complex, and a simple return to the negotiation phase, as indicated in the figure, is to be preferred, particularly as A is more likely to know why the interruption was initiated.

If we assume that the negotiation phase and the data phase are analogous to a command level and a processing level, the attention phase provides the mechanism to return to the command level. The deferment of this return, caused by the message delay in the transport service, allows processing to continue. The results of this processing may, or may not, be valuable, but it seems unlikely that this can be decided until an interaction at the command level has taken place.

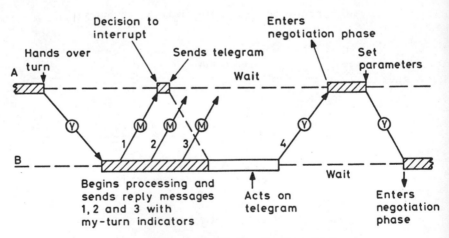

Figure 8.52   Initiating the attention phase

The most appropriate scheme might seem to be for the interrupter to store the messages received pending the subsequent command level negotiation. However, there is a good case for discarding, clearing or purging these messages in an emergency such as the congestion of the transport service, to facilitate rapid recovery. Perhaps, therefore, the simple clearing interrupt does need to be distinguished from a request for a pause, or from a request to return to the command phase, or, indeed, to the termination phase. This raises the question of whether there should be a separate termination phase to end the dialogue, or whether this should be a sub-phase of the negotiation phase, leaving only the idle, negotiation, data and attention phases as shown in Figure 8.53, which may be compared with Figure 8.47.

Our purpose in ending on this note of uncertainty is to emphasise that an ongoing debate about the design of the virtual terminal and, indeed, other high level protocols is inevitable because there is a wide variety of models that can be proposed, with numerous different features and plausible arguments for adopting one or other in particular situations. We have, therefore, tried to indicate some of the issues under discussion that seem to us to be relevant as a basis for further study of the references which we have recommended.

The Future of the Virtual Terminal

At the beginning of this chapter, we examined the roles of a terminal in a network, and identified three basic types of display, the scroll mode, the page mode and the data entry mode. The evolution of consensus thinking about the design of a virtual terminal has largely been along the lines of starting with the scroll mode model and gradually generalising it to the page and data entry models, with a view to moving forward to more advanced graphics and intelligent terminals as further generalisations at a later date.

It now seems, however, that this approach has been misleading and a better one is to consider fundamental mechanisms of data transfer and manipulation, in order to start with a general model of the interaction process, before making this specific to a particular application, type of terminal or system. There is no consensus view yet about the merits of this alternative approach so we have not been able to report on well-established ideas. However, we have tried to indicate

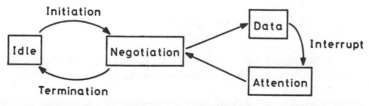

Figure 8.53   Alternative model of virtual terminal dialogue

the issues under discussion and the possible direction that further development might take.

To summarise, we can begin to see that the concept of a zone[19] or field, having uniform attributes, and capable of being addressed in its entirety or with only elementary, well-established sub-addressing commands, seems an important one. We couple with this the notion of defining any number of such fields to make up a complex data structure, with simple rules governing precedence where zones intersect. The commands to define and manipulate these zones should be strings based on a quasi-natural language which is understandable by people and redundantly coded to allow unambiguous parsing by computer, as was indicated in Figure 8.46. The data structure itself is then defined by the set of commands by which it is established. These form a data structure description language that can be 'compiled' by the virtual terminal as a program is compiled by a programming language compiler.

The protocol for interacting with the data structure should be essentially a simple one, defined without reference to any particular type of terminal. The key factor in the design should be the types of application and the response time requirements that must be catered for.

It is likely that developments along these lines will appear as the logic power of microprocessor-controlled terminals increases,[20] and their communication with each other and with databases on remote computer systems becomes message-oriented. There will be emphasis on the need to handle a range of applications, using comprehensive local editing and storage features, and the occasional transfer of files to and from other terminals.

References

1. *Broadcast Teletext Specification,*
   BBC, ITA and BREMA (September 1976).
2. 'The Nordic public data network',
   Tele, **1,** 1 (1976).
3. *CCITT Study Group VII, No. 179-182 (1978).*
   (Aspects of the Nordic Network.)
4. *CCITT provisional recommendations, X3, X25, X28 and X29 on packet-switched data transmission services,*
   International Telecommunications Union, Geneva (1978).
5. Schicker, P., and Duenki, A.,
   'The virtual terminal definition and protocol',
   ACM Comp. Comm. Review, **6,** No. 4 (October 1976).
6. Bauwens, E., and Magnee, F.,
   'Definition of the virtual terminal protocol for the Belgian University Network',
   Proc. Computer Network Protocols Symposium, Liège, D3-1, (1978).
7. Schulze, G., and Borger, J.,
   'A virtual terminal protocol based upon the communication variable concept',
   Proc. Computer Network Protocols Symposium, Liège, D2-1, (1978).

8. *Virtual device protocol,*
   CII, Siemens, ICL,
   IFIP INWG Note No. 155 (1977).
9. *Data entry virtual terminal protocol for Euronet,*
   Directorate General, Scientific & Technical Information,
   Commission of the European Communities, Luxembourg (September 1977).
10. Lauck, A.,
    'A note on network symmetry and call collision',
    ACM Comp. Comm. Review, **8**, No. 1 (January 1978).
11. Davies, D. W., and Barber, D. L. A.,
    Communications Networks for Computers,
    John Wiley and Sons, London (1973).
12. Fletcher, J. G., and Watson, R. W.,
    'Mechanisms for a reliable timer-based protocol',
    Proc. Computer Network Protocols Symposium, Liège, C5-1 (1978).
13. Zimmermann, H.,
    Proposal for a virtual terminal protocol,
    Reseau Cyclades, IRIA (1976).
14. ISO/TC97/SC16N23
    'Proposal for a standard virtual terminal protocol',
    Proc. Computer Network Protocols Symposium, Liège, H-27 (1978).
15. Jamet, B., and Monnet, M.,
    'Terminal handling protocols in a packet-switched public data network',
    Proc. Eurocomp 78, London, 601 (1978).
16. Bouknight, W. J., Grossman, G. R., and Grothe, D. M.,
    'The ARPA network terminal service—a new approach to network access',
    Proc. 3rd Data Communications Symposium, St. Petersburg, Florida, 73, (1973).
17. Davidson, J., Hathaway, W., Postel, J., Mimno, N., Thomas, R., and Walden, D.,
    'The ARPANET Telnet protocol: its purpose, principles, implementation, and
    impact on host operating system design',
    Proc. 5th Data Communication Symposium, Snowbird, Utah, 4-10 (1977).
18. Day, J. D.,
    Telnet data entry terminal option,
    Centre for Advanced Computation, University of Illinois at Urbana-Champaign,
    Technical Memorandum No. 94 (June 1977).
19. Luca, R.,
    'Zones—a solution to the problem of dynamic screen formatting in CRT-based
    networks',
    Proc. 4th Data Communications Symposium, Quebec, 1-1 (October 1975).
20. Anderson, R. H., and Gillogly, J. J.
    'The Rand intelligent terminal agent (RITA) as a network access aid',
    Proc. 1976 Nat. Computer Conf., 501 (1976).

Chapter 9

Message Authentication

9.1 THE NEED FOR DATA SECURITY AND AUTHENTICATION

Network applications will increasingly need measures to make their data secure and to ensure that messages are authentic, both as to their content and their origin. As more applications come onto networks they will be handling information which is sensitive or of great value (such as high-value funds transfer), and which must be protected against various kinds of intrusion.

Sensitive data must be protected against disclosure to an unauthorised person, fraudulent modification of messages or such tricks as deleting messages, inserting new messages, repeating old messages, one user masquerading as another or one computer service masquerading as another. Data are more vulnerable in networks than anywhere else, therefore those who are trying to misuse data are certain to look at the data network as one of their targets. Physical security is out of the question in such a widespread system as a communication network. Private networks are no more secure, because their transmission paths belong to public networks. Where these are leased circuits going by fixed paths they are easier to tap than a switched circuit or an adaptively routed packet stream.

There was much concern, starting in the early 1970s, about the supposed threat of computer systems to individual privacy. More careful investigation showed that these threats were not special to computers and that there had been real abuses in non-computer systems. The privacy debate was important because it focused attention on the dangers of concentrating data in readily accessible form, if access was not controlled and if the accuracy of the data was suspect. There has now been legislation in many countries which requires that organisations holding files of personal data should register these with a public authority. The holders of these files must ensure their accuracy, where it affects people's rights, and must safeguard the information and use it only for its lawful, licensed, purpose.

Where this information travels over networks, as it now frequently does, the laws in some countries may require a certain degree of protection to be applied.

Thus protection by cryptography, which might otherwise have been excluded because of its expense, is likely to be more widely employed in the future.

Removable storage media such as discs, tapes, cassettes, and floppy discs, may need cryptography to protect their data. These removable media are as vulnerable to illegal interference as data on a communication network. A particular case of storage is that of archives, on which it may be necessary to store personal information for many years. This information may even become more sensitive with lapse of time. For example, a criminal may have abandoned crime and the law may have decreed that his record of crime is no longer accessible even to the police. The archives which contain this data have become more sensitive.

Cryptography[1] is the technical means by which the content of messages or the traffic on a transmission path can be concealed from an 'enemy' and modification of these messages prevented. Of the various threats, cryptography can deal excellently with disclosure, modification, inserting messages and (with certain extra precautions) repeating old messages.

A current application of cryptography is the cash dispenser, one of the forms of 'electronic funds transfer' referred to in Chapter 1. For greater security, the customer identity, given by his magnetic card and personal number, is checked by a central computer which holds details of stolen cards and other reasons for withholding payment. These checks could be fraudulently overcome by an 'active line tapper' who could read the messages between terminal and computer and modify or insert messages to make any card appear valid. Cryptography is used to prevent this kind of fraud.

In this chapter we treat certain aspects of data security: the authentication of message contents and message source (terminal or person) and the construction of an 'electronic signature' which is a proof, in digital form, of the origin of a message. The methods used are related to cryptography, but their purpose is not always to conceal the message content. A signed document, for example, is only valuable if it can be read by others. We need to describe some recent developments in cryptography that have an application to message authentication.

9.2 THE DATA ENCRYPTION STANDARD

Figure 9.1 shows a typical encryption system or 'cryptosystem'. It employs two transformations which are called *encipherment* and *decipherment*. One transformation must be the inverse of the other so that the ciphertext, which is intended to be incomprehensible to the wire tapper, is restored at the destination to the original plaintext. One of the criteria for cryptosystems is that they should remain secure when the nature of the encipherment and decipherment algorithms is known. This can only be done by employing a key which enters into both processes and by devising the transformations so that, if the values of the keys

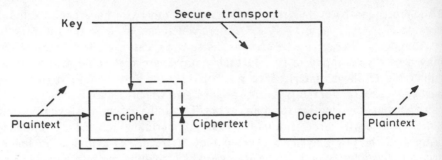

Figure 9.1   A cryptographic scheme with potential leakage paths

at the two ends are identical, the transformations are always inverse, but not otherwise. There must be a very large number of values for the key, that is, a large key space, otherwise the key could be found simply by trying all possible values to see which one turned the observed ciphertext back into a meaningful message.

The figure shows, by broken lines, some possible paths which would compromise the security of the system. Thus if the plaintext were to become 'visible' to the outside world, even in part, the system would be defeated. If the encipherment in some way 'leaked' the key into the ciphertext, the security would be lost. This might happen, for example, if the encipherment was carried out by software and the program had been tampered with to use some of the spare bits of various data formats to transmit the digits of the key, perhaps in a cipher known to the intruder. The most sensitive part of the system is the key because knowledge of it enables all ciphertext to be read and therefore the transmission of the key from one end to the other must use a secure means of transport. This sensitivity is one of the differences between the traditional cryptosystem and the *public key system* to be described later.

A modern cryptosystem must be secure, not only when the encipherment algorithm is known but also when some examples of corresponding plaintext and ciphertext have been discovered. This is a severe requirement, but it can be met.

The best published example of modern techniques is probably the *Data Encryption Standard*, known as the DES. It is actually a United States Federal Information Processing Standard, required to be used where cryptography is needed in the Government's transmission of non-classified data. The system on which it was based was developed by IBM[2] and adopted by the National Bureau of Standards for promulgation as a Federal Information Processing Standard. The specification of the algorithm is readily available[3] in complete detail. There are also standards, still partly in preparation, for the use of this algorithm.[4] It is generally accepted as a strong enough algorithm for commercial security requirements.

The DES is a *block cipher*, which means that it accepts a block of data (in this case 64 bits) and transforms it into a ciphertext block of the same length. The key is a 64-bit number, of which 8 are parity bits.

The overall scheme of a typical DES device is shown in Figure 9.2. The chip is provided with parallel input and output for one octet of data which can belong either to the plaintext, or to the ciphertext or to the key, according to the operation being carried out. The key cannot be read out. These 8-bit units are assembled in 64-bit shift registers. The key is held by an internal register which can be loaded across from the input or, in a different application, it can be loaded from the shift register that holds the output of the encipherment or decipherment process. In this way a key can be entered into the DES system encrypted by the key in use and such a key finds its correct place as the new key in the DES mechanism without ever emerging in its clear form.

The encryption mechanism contains two distinct parts shown in the schematic diagram. One of these uses the key to generate 16 different sub-keys in succession, each of these having 48 bits. They are not independent, because they are obtained by transposition of selected bits from the 56-bit key. Nevertheless, their action in the encryption algorithm makes them independent for practical purposes. The second and more complex unit carries out the encipherment by 16 logically identical steps, each step employing one of the sub-keys from the

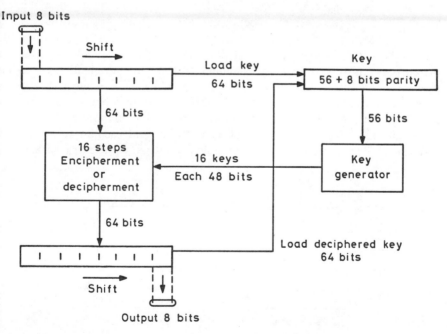

Figure 9.2   Schematic of a typical DES device

key generator. The algorithm is such that decipherment uses the same process as encipherment with the keys generated in reverse.

The existence of a data encryption standard has two valuable effects. Firstly it enables any two users of encipherment to establish a secure link with minimal effort if they have equipment conforming to the standard. Secondly it encourages the manufacture of DES devices in quantities which should bring down the price of equipment. Devices employing large-scale integration must be made in large numbers to realise their potential economy. But some reservations are needed concerning these advantages. Though the encipherment module may be cheap, the interfacing costs and the continuing cost of operating a secure cryptographic scheme must be taken into account. Concerning ease of communication, this depends on having standards for the use of the DES which, even for US Government applications, are not yet complete. These standards must cover many ways of applying the DES standard, for example to streams of characters, to encipherment over a line or to encipherment end-to-end over a switched network.

There is a danger, with block encipherment, that repetitive patterns in the plaintext will show through in the ciphertext. This is a special problem in computer-generated plaintext because of the fixed formats that are used. One way to remove this problem is to include a random or serial number in the first block and then make the encipherment of each block depend on the value of previous blocks—a method known as *chaining*. Figure 9.3 shows how this can be done. Before each plaintext block is enciphered, the contents of the previous ciphertext block are added to it by modulo 2 addition (exclusive or) in parallel over the 64 bits. The consequence of this way of using the block cipher is that the current ciphertext block is dependent on the contents of all the previous plaintext. The figure only shows the principle. If the DES input and output is done in 8-bit bytes, the registers shown can shift the data in byte-parallel fashion and the modulo 2 addition is also carried out on 8 bits in parallel.

At the receiving end the ciphertext is stored and used to transform the plaintext of the succeeding block by modulo 2 addition, so the extra 'scrambling'

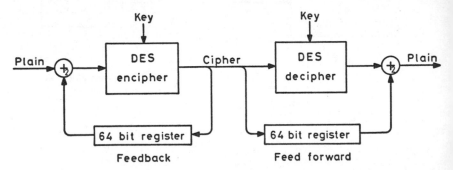

Figure 9.3   Chaining of blocks

is undone. More precisely, if we denote the ith message and cipher blocks by M_i and C_i respectively and the encipherment function by E, then:

$$C_i = E(M_i + C_{i-1}) \text{ and } M_i = E^{-1}(C_i) + C_{i-1}$$

In spite of the propagation through the ciphertext of any single change in the plaintext, errors on the line are not perpetuated. This can be understood in the following way. At the sending end, there is feedback so that changes in plaintext are perpetuated. At the receiving end there is feedforward so the effect of a change in ciphertext is felt on only two blocks, the one directly affected and the following one where the ciphertext in error is added into the generated plaintext.

We shall return later to cryptography in a new form which does not require the use of a secret key at both ends of the link. These new systems have important properties for message authentication, which will then be explained.

9.3 PERSONAL IDENTIFICATION

Authentication of messages means tracing them back to their origin and often this requires the system to identify a person who is using a terminal. In practice, the user provides his identity and the system must be able to verify or authenticate it, that is, to check that the claimed identity is authentic. An authentication system should be safe, as far as possible, against attempts to defraud it by masquerading as an individual who is allowed access to the data or is authorised to make transactions. There is no way to make an unbeatable personal identification system but we can make the task of the would-be intruder very difficult.[5]

There are three classes of personal identification depending on (a) something that a person knows, such as his password or, in banking terms, his personal identification number or PIN, (b) something which the person possesses, acting like a physical key to unlock the system, such as a plastic card with a magnetic recording on it, or (c) some personal characteristic of the individual such as his voice, handwriting or fingerprint. For greater security a combination of these authentication measures can be applied.

Identification Based on Knowledge

The earliest multi-access systems employed a password to identify or authenticate their users. It is the easiest scheme to implement because it uses no special hardware and, in its simplest form, little software. The basic problem, with most kinds of user, is their inability to remember an arbitrary number so that they write it down in an obvious place such as in a diary or even, it has been observed, on the wall over the terminal. Where discipline is possible, this can be avoided. Nevertheless, passwords of more than six or seven characters may give trouble.

It is unwise to choose passwords with an obvious mnemonic character, firstly because they may be guessed and secondly because a casual glance at the password makes it easy for the intruder to remember it, whereas an arbitrary stream of symbols is less likely to be picked up in this way. But an arbitrary string of symbols will not be remembered easily and should preferably be short, say four characters in length. In most cases this is sufficient to deter the attempt to break the system by trying all possible passwords. For those who try to do this by using a computer to run through the set of passwords, there are easy checks by the attacked system to distinguish this from normal usage, deny access and log the attempt to break the system.

An intruder who can tap the line can read the password, therefore it would seem necessary to use cryptography for full security.

One of the risks in any authentication system which is not secured by cryptography (or some related way of linking the messages of a conversation together) is that an intruder may wait until the user has logged on, then break down his connection and take over the conversation. This is a form of 'active wire tapping' which, though difficult, is not impossible. It can be inhibited by repeating the authentication at random intervals during the conversation. This would require a number of different challenges and corresponding passwords and the user would find this difficult and tedious. But suppose that the passwords consisted of miscellaneous facts from the life of the individual, such as names of friends and distant relatives, old addresses and so forth. A challenge such as 'what is Uncle Ben's profession?' could receive an instant reply from the person who invented this challenge and response but not from the intruder. This method can be made to work but it requires some ingenuity on the part of the individual. For many people, the questions and answers would tend to be stereotyped and obvious so that a determined intruder could, by research, prepare himself for most of the possibilities. Again, this is a method that can work well in disciplined situations but is probably not suitable for the general public. Since the list of challenges and responses is quickly exhausted, cryptography is still needed to combat the line tapper.

Identification by a Physical Key

To be effective, any key should have a wide range of possible values. The simplest way to carry such a key is the magnetic striped card now in common use as a credit card and for cash dispensers and so forth. The information field in the standard format agreed by banks has several tracks, some containing identification and some involved in the transaction itself. We have already mentioned the need for cryptography in cash dispenser transactions and this same feature protects the transmitted authentication number from the card.

The relative ease of copying magnetic recordings has proved to be a problem. Copying a card is known as 'skimming'. One simple technique for skimming is to place the recording over a blank magnetic stripe and raise the temperature so that the Curie point of the receiving magnetic material is reached before that of the recording to be copied. Above the Curie point the material ceases to be ferromagnetic and when it cools it carries a recording of the field to which it was subjected. If this method cannot be made to work, a simple arrangement of heads and amplifiers can be used to read and reproduce any magnetic recording of the normal kind.

To combat this forgery of cards by skimming, a number of security features have been built into the cards. One technique is to use a recording layer of the normal kind overlaying a second recording layer with high coercivity, which means that a higher magnetic field is required to change its state. Then the normal recording techniques do not affect the lower layer. The card reader in the cash dispenser, for example, applies a field to the track containing the authentication number so that any normal recording in that place would be erased. It then reads the underlying 'hard' recording where the information really lies. An inexpert 'skimmer' using single layer material would not succeed.

Although the technique for recording on these double layer materials is difficult, it is not different in nature from standard recording so the security is raised to a limited extent.

A second method employs permanent magnetic marks made in the tape during its manufacture. Normal magnetic recording material, such as gamma ferric oxide, is in the form of long thin crystals that are embedded in a kind of paint base to make the recording medium. The technique known as 'water-marking' aligns the axes of these crystals while the paint base is still wet and, by selective alignment in different parts of the tape, produces a recording which will never change. To read this recording, the crystals are magnetised by steady fields in an appropriate direction and their changing directions along the tape produce external fields, which can be read by normal heads that are suitably aligned.

In this way the plastic card used for personal identification can be given a 'unique' identity which is difficult to forge because the manufacturing technique for magnetic recording materials and for watermarking them is very difficult to acquire.

Even if forgery or copying is made to be impracticable, theft and misuse of cards cannot be prevented. Systems which use a central computer system for checking all transactions can rapidly delete a lost or stolen card from its list of acceptable cards and transfer it to a blacklist.

To reduce the risk due to lost or stolen cards, they are usually employed with a second method of authentication such as a signature or a short personal identification number.

Identification by Personal Characteristics

The personal characteristics that have been used most widely are voice, signatures, hand geometry and fingerprints. In each case the authentication device makes measurements of the individual's characteristics and from these computes indices rather like the 'features' of pattern recognition, which can be sent to the central machine for checking against a corresponding set of stored indices taken from the genuine individual. For example, a signature device might measure the number of times the pen touches and leaves the paper, the average vertical speed of the pen, the number of vertical excursions or any of dozens of similar characteristics. There is great variety of such characteristics but not all of them are uncorrelated and the trick is to find a good set of features with little cross correlation.

Signature verification depends on pen movement which cannot be deduced from the signature that can be seen on the paper. This almost completely defeats the professional forger whose skills are based on the appearance of the writing. The set of measures being used should be kept confidential because the knowledge of these would help the development of a new class of forger who would train himself to copy the measured characteristics. This has been found, in practice, to be very difficult.

Similar remarks could be applied to the other authentication methods in this class. For example, some hand geometry machines measure the opacity of webs of skin between the fingers, perhaps to avoid forgery by the use of cardboard templates. Fingerprint machines use the minutiae which are the forks, endings and gaps in the ridges on the skin. Since there are many of these in each fingerprint the measured features can depend on a selected set of minutiae.

Speech recognition systems can combat the use of a recording to impersonate the legitimate user by the challenge–response method. Thus the machine will ask for a particular set of words to be repeated by the applicant.

The feature values obtained at a series of authentication trials will vary over a small range, with a certain probability distribution. To make a decision it is necessary to determine an 'acceptance window' for each feature. In experiments to optimise performance, the window sizes can be varied. There is, in practice, no completely satisfactory set of values, as Figure 9.4 illustrates.

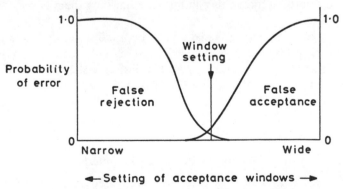

Figure 9.4   Two kinds of error in personal identification

The authentication system collects a representative set of values from the client and adjusts its window locations and sizes. It can readjust, slowly, from experience of later authentication attempts. If we widen the windows enough, we accept everybody and if we narrow them enough, we reject everybody, including the authorised users. The figure shows typical curves for the proportion of errors of two kinds. The first is the rejection of authentic persons, which happens if the thresholds are set too narrow. The second is the acceptance of impostors (or people who happen to give the wrong identifier) which happens if the thresholds are set too wide. The aim is to set the threshold so as to keep both of these errors low in number. As the figure suggests, in practice they are never both zero for any setting of the threshold. The chosen window size in the figure assumes that false rejection is the more serious error. The horizontal axis corresponds to an adjustment of all windows relative to the measured means and standard deviations.

The false rejection rate can be reduced by giving the applicant more than one chance to identify himself. In typical signature systems three attempts have been allowed and success at any attempt is regarded as a valid authentication. This procedure necessarily increases the probability of false authentication. The relative importance of the two kinds of error depends on the application. In banks, for example, the possibility of rejecting authentic users is disturbing to the bank authorities. They refer to the probability of false rejection as the 'insult ratio'. The false acceptance rate might be quite high and yet deter a would-be impostor if the consequence of rejection was a high probability of being caught.

In all these forms of on-line authentication the claimed identity of the person is assumed to be known. For example, he might use his magnetic striped card for identity and a personal number or personal characteristic for authentication. So the transaction involves only the records of one individual. It is very doubtful that any of these systems could be used as a method of identification since this would require the measures taken from the personal characteristics to characterise the individual among all the others in the population served. Though it is generally believed that fingerprints contain enough information to identify people, this is based on very careful study of good prints to extract all their features. Authentication by personal characteristics works with much less information and it serves only to check the characteristics of one, supposedly known, individual against a single stored record of previously measured features.

9.4   ONE-WAY FUNCTIONS AND THEIR APPLICATIONS

In all these authentication methods we find the need to secure the system against the wire tapper who could reproduce previously heard passwords or personal characteristics. If we now look at the central system which stores the authentication data we find a similar security problem. For example, access to the table of passwords would completely defeat the system, even if cryptography were used for the communication process. Suppose that the comparison was not made with the password itself but with the ciphertext derived from it. In this case, it would be impossible, without the key, to produce a password which would generate matching ciphertext. This idea illustrates the contribution which can be made to security by a complex transformation of the data. But since the comparison is made with ciphertext, the inversion property of a cipher system is not required. All we need is a complex transformation. Thus we are led to the idea of a 'one-way function'.

A one-way function F has the following property. Given the value of x it is relatively easy to calculate the value of the function $F(x)$ but if $y = F(x)$ is given, there is no easy way to calculate the value of x. In other words, $F^{-1}(y)$ is an extremely difficult function to compute.

Clearly, any number of corresponding values of x and $F(x)$ can be calculated and stored and they can be made into a table which enables x to be expressed as a function of y. As a method of forming the inverse this is not practicable if the range of the function is very large. For our purpose, x and y will be binary numbers of a specified length. For example, they might be 50-digit binary numbers. We are not concerned with functions of real variables and, indeed, continuous or analytic functions would tend to make numerical inversion rather easy. Rather, we are concerned with functions of a highly discontinuous and, perhaps, arbitrary kind. In our example it would be necessary to store 2^{50} numbers in order to invert the function or, for each given value of $F(x)$, a similar large number of values of x would have to be tried to see which one fitted. The notion of 'one-way' is not therefore absolute but depends on how much computation you regard as being 'impossibly large'. We say that, given the value of $F(x)$, the computation of x is *computationally infeasible* though we know that, by very lucky guessing or by choosing a value $F(x)$ which corresponds to a known x, such computation could be rendered unnecessary.

The application of one-way functions to authentication was described by R. M. Needham in the context of passwords.[6] A table of passwords held in a multi-access system is clearly highly confidential and its disclosure would defeat the system security. The idea proposed was to use a one-way function such as we have described and to store, for each password x, not the value of the password itself but the function $F(x)$. In order to check a password x, the quantity $F(x)$ is calculated and compared with the table. If it matches we accept the password.

There are no typical one-way functions but an example will show how they can be constructed. Suppose we regard the binary number x as a decimal fraction and we first calculate $\sin(x + \frac{1}{2})$. The added constant is designed to avoid the linear part of the function near $x = 0$. The values of this function have too much continuity to make them a useful one-way function, but we can take the result to 100-bit accuracy and then select alternate binary digits to give a 50-bit result. Then we can carry out the same process again, perhaps with a different function in place of the sine. We must pay attention to the most and least significant bits to ensure that they carry no useful information about the argument x. This kind of process produces the highly discontinuous functions needed for the one-way property.

There is no guarantee that the values of $F(x)$ generated from the whole range of x will be distinct. Therefore the one-way requirement reads that, for almost all values of y, there is no feasible computational method for determining *any* of the values of $F^{-1}(y)$

In the context of the password scheme, the danger of accepting the wrong password because it happens to hit the correct value of $F(x)$ is very low if 50-bit numbers are used. So the requirement of a large domain and range which is needed for the one-way property usually ensures that the range is sparsely used and the non-uniqueness of the function has no practical significance.

A One-way Function Used to Exchange a Secret Key

The special properties of the exponential function can be used to help with the task of key distribution. Both for cryptography and for authentication, established methods need a secret key held at both ends of the link. It is possible to generate this key from data transmitted in public on the link and yet keep it secret.

For this purpose the two ends agree on a base a and a large prime modulus p. All the arithmetic which follows is carried out *modulo p*. The normal rules of arithmetic can be applied, except that the result is reduced to an integer in the range 0 to $p - 1$ by subtracting a multiple of p. In this arithmetic, the function a^x is a one-way function of x. In other words, finding the logarithm of x to base a is not feasible for almost all values of x. It requires about $2p^{1/2}$ multiplications and a similar amount of storage space. But there is a method[7] which is easier unless p is chosen such that $p - 1$ has a large factor. The best choice for our purpose is that $\frac{1}{2}(p - 1)$ should itself be prime, and this is easy to arrange.

With these precautions taken, one correspondent chooses a number x and the other choses y. They keep these numbers to themselves and send to each other the values a^x and a^y. Now each can form the quantity a^{xy} by a further exponentiation. An intruder who knows only the transmitted values cannot find x or y or the value a^{xy}. The latter is the secret key that has been formed from the public communication.

9.5 MESSAGE AND USER AUTHENTICATION

A message is authentic if it has not been altered on its journey from the sender or created by an impostor. Authentication allows any alteration to be detected. In general, cryptography prevents any meaningful change to a message and therefore provides authentication.

There is an exception to the rule that cryptography prevents significant modification. Some forms of encipherment are additive—they operate by adding a pseudorandom 'key stream' to the plaintext, modulo 2. This system is transparent to changes because a change of a ciphertext bit results in a change of the corresponding plaintext bit. This could be used by an intruder to modify fields in a computer-generated format where the existing values are known with high probability. To avoid this, the start and finish of messages must be concealed.

Encipherment also acts as a user authentication because the correct key is needed to produce valid ciphertext. This validates the user if he supplies or helps to generate the key. The user's own key can be combined with a key held by the terminal to generate the communication key or used, in an interaction with a control centre, to generate a temporary *session key*. In all these cases the user's identity has been checked to the extent that he possesses the key issued to him.

But without using encipherment it is still possible to authenticate messages using what are essentially one-way functions.

Message Authentication without Secrecy

To authenticate a message we send along with it a message authenticator field which is a function of the whole message. In the same way as in cryptography, we use a secret key, since we cannot assume that the authenticating function will remain secret. In essence, the message authenticator is a one-way function of both message and key. The key cannot be calculated from a knowledge of the message and its authenticator. The size of the authenticator field is decided mainly by the threat of guessing a correct value, and it can be quite small, but the key must be big enough to prevent its discovery by searching through its entire range of values, as in cryptography.

A simple way to generate the authenticator is shown in Figure 9.5. This applies the standard kind of encipherment process to the message, then adds it repeatedly into a shift register to create the authenticator. Either normal addition or addition modulo 2 can be used here. The availability of a cheap encipherment device makes this an attractive method, although it does not use the inversion property of a cipher system. If we use an encipherment scheme such as block chaining in which the ciphertext depends on all the previous

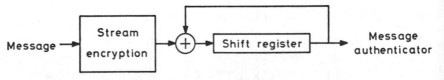

Figure 9.5   Formation of a message authenticator

message, then the authenticator can simply be the last portion of the ciphertext produced by the message. At the receiving end, the authenticator is checked by repeating the process which generated it. If the newly calculated authenticator agrees with the one received, the whole message is pronounced authentic.

An essential requirement of the authentication process is that it should not be possible to construct a message to fit a given authenticator. Generally, the secret key will prevent this. It must also not be possible to modify a message by following special rules which leave the authenticator unchanged.

In some applications, the key is provided by the terminal and the user's identity is checked by a personal identification number (PIN) which he supplies. If the PIN is of a size which fits into the message authenticator field it can be added, modulo 2, into that field, as we show in Figure 9.6. In effect, the one-way function of the message, since it is not known to an intruder, serves to encipher the PIN. If the key is known it is possible, from a valid message and its authenticator, to calculate the PIN. This feature is useful in joint networks operated by several authorities, where messages must be re-enciphered with different keys at the network boundaries.

User Authentication

We have already seen that user authentication can be obtained as a byproduct of encipherment or message authentication. This depends on the user's key or personal identification number entering into the secret key or some other part of the authentication process.

Correctness of the secret key (matching at the two ends) is a condition of successful message transport, so the system 'fails safe'. We often need a simple way to check the keys before the dialogue begins. This should be an active check, not just the exchange of standard messages, in order that each end can be sure that it is talking to a live terminal, not just receiving messages recorded from an earlier session. For example, if A and B are starting to converse on a secure communication link, A can verify that B is a live terminal by sending a random number n over the link, to have the number $n + 1$ returned by B. Then B should verify A in the same fashion. Such checks are particularly needed if

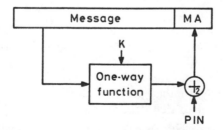

Figure 9.6   Incorporation of a personal identification number

the dialogue that follows is carried out by formal messages, such as two computers might exchange.

User authentication which is based on a key possessed by a user has to face the problem of a forged or copied key. If the cost is justified, it is possible to make a key which cannot be copied or forged, and this leaves only the possibility of a stolen key, which can be handled by good discipline in reporting theft to the centre which controls keys. The 'unforgeable' key is an active device containing a stored numerical key which cannot be read. For example it could contain a DES encipherment module which was loaded at the time of manufacture with a random key. The value of this key is not recorded outside the module. It can be constructed in such a way that an attempt to read the stored key destroys it. Such a device has a 'personality' which can be tested only by giving it numbers and noting the replies.

The physical key can be used locally, as for a door lock, or remotely, to identify the holder to a computer service, for example. We can speak of a 'lock' interrogating the key to verify its identity. On the first occasion, the identity must be determined in an independent way, in order to introduce the lock to the identity of the key. Then the lock sends a set of numbers to the key and stores the replies. Subsequently, when the key is really being used for authentication, some of these numbers are repeated, as 'challenges' to the key, and the replies are checked with the stored values. If the identification is successful, the lock can send more numbers in order to add to its list of challenges and responses.

One key can be used with many locks and one lock can respond to many keys without compromising the security of any lock or key. No investigation of such a physical key can extract its stored key if the cryptosystem it contains is effective. But if all the challenges and responses for a given lock are overheard, the key's action can be simulated. From that point, the bogus key must take over all future authentication sessions if it is not to be discovered by its new responses. Using a large number of responses and creating new ones on each occasion makes it reasonably secure but it may be more practicable to use encipherment, with the terminal's key, to protect these exchanges from observation. In the case of local access such as a door lock, an optical fibre coupling would be one way to prevent the dialogue being overheard.

The Problem of Disputes

The authentication of messages which we have just described depends on both parties to the communication possessing the same key and keeping it secret from any possible intruders. One can then be certain that no message has been produced or altered by another party. This is also true of messages where cryptography has been used that depends on both sender and receiver knowing an otherwise secret key. There is, however, one drawback. Security depends on the existence of trust between sender and receiver. Such trust does exist among groups which commonly work together—among banks or airlines, for instance; but, in the future, networks will be used by the whole community and authenticated messages may have to be passed between people who have not previously communicated with each other.

Where trust between the two ends cannot be relied upon we could have the following problem. The sender S may send a message to the receiver R and then S may deny that the message has been sent. To give an illustration, imagine that R is a stockbroker and he receives instructions from S to buy certain shares. The shares turn out badly. Then S could claim not to have sent the message. When R presents the authenticated message to prove that S originated it, S could claim that it was forged by R, since R knows the key. Thus we can have disputes either if R did forge a message or if S alleges, without truth, that he did so. Such a dispute cannot be resolved because the authentication mechanism, using a key which both parties know, gives them an equal control over the message path. We therefore have to look for a different kind of authentication process in which such disputes can be resolved. Such a method has been found as a byproduct of the 'public key cryptosystem' which we shall now describe.

9.6 THE PUBLIC-KEY CRYPTOSYSTEM AND ITS USE FOR AUTHENTICATION

We shall first describe the public key cryptosystem in general terms by means of a block diagram and then show how it can be used to provide a kind of authentication which enables disputes between the sender and receiver about the sending of a message to be resolved. The system relies (like cryptography) on a rather special class of functions so that, by itself, the block diagram of such a system does not show convincingly that a practical version could be made. Therefore we describe, later, one particular form of public key system that has been proposed. Diffie and Hellman described the principle of the public key system in reference 8.

The block diagram of Figure 9.7 shows the public key system in general terms. The plaintext is enciphered by the sender and the inverse transformation at the receiving end deciphers it again to plaintext. This can be compared with Figure 9.1 for the traditional cryptosystem. The difference in the public key system is that the keys used in the encipherment and decipherment algorithms are different. Whether the algorithms used at the two ends are the same is not important. In fact, working examples of public key systems have been produced in which the encipherment and decipherment algorithms are identical in one case and entirely different in another. The essence of the method is that the keys are different.

Clearly the two keys must be related and in the diagram they are shown as being derived by a known algorithm from a common starting key. In some cases the starting point will be the secret key and, from this, by a known calculation,

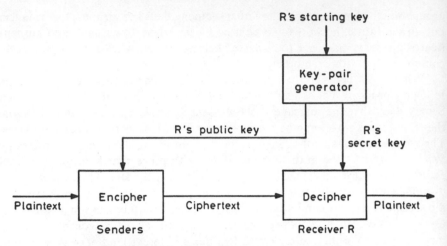

Figure 9.7 The public key cryptosystem

the public key will be derived. As we shall see later, a key may comprise more than one number. The process of calculating the keys is carried out by the receiver of the messages, who keeps to himself the key that he will use—the secret key. He sends to the sender of messages the other key which can be called the 'public key' because there is no risk in making it widely known. Because it is widely known, anyone can generate a ciphertext and send this to the receiver who owns the public key. For a two-way conversation, each party provides the other with his public key.

As in other forms of cryptography, the algorithms used are public knowledge and this includes the method of generating the keys.

Inspection of Figure 9.7 shows some of the characteristics which the various functions must have. The most important is that the encipherment and decipherment functions are inverses when provided with a correctly related pair of public and secret keys. It is also clear that the public key must be a one-way function of the secret key, otherwise an intruder could deduce the starting key and hence the secret key. Similarly, even when the public key is known, the ciphertext must be a one-way function of the plaintext, which is quite different from encipherment in the traditional, secret key system. However, this one-way function has a kind of 'trapdoor' in that knowledge of the secret key would enable it to be inverted. Since the functions shown in the figure are one-way functions, the size of the blocks of data which they encipher or the keys which they generate must be large enough to defeat inversion by trial and error or by large-scale storage. These are not very different from the requirements for normal cryptosystems. As shown, the system is basically a block cipher system, rather like the data encryption standard.

The virtue of the public key system is that the encipherment key is public.

There is no longer the difficult problem of secret distribution of the keys. This could be of great value where secure conversations are needed between computers and terminals on a casual basis—the so-called 'open network'.

Authentication by Public Key Cryptosystem

In order to adapt a public key system for authentication we have to assume another property of the functions. Clearly it would be convenient if the ciphertext block occupied the same number of bits as the plaintext. In the example we shall describe later this is indeed so. There are, however, cases where the ciphertext is longer and we have to exclude these from our consideration as possible authentication schemes. Assuming now that the encipherment algorithm maps the possible values of the plaintext into an equal number of possible values of ciphertext, then the decipherment function produces the inverse mapping. We could treat the text by these two transformations in the opposite order and still come back to plaintext. This arrangement is shown in Figure 9.8. Since the secret key is still the one which enters the 'decipher' algorithm we see that it is now the sender who transforms the plaintext in secret while the receiver can transform it back to plaintext by means of the public key. If one receiver can do this, so can any other which knows the public key. Therefore we can no longer regard the transformed text as a cipher. This is not a mechanism for security against wire tapping but a method to ensure the integrity and authenticate the origin of messages. The first box in Figure 9.8 is labelled 'decipher' where the quotation marks indicate that, while it is the same function as that used in Figure 9.7, it is now serving a different purpose. The 'encipher' process now restores the original text.

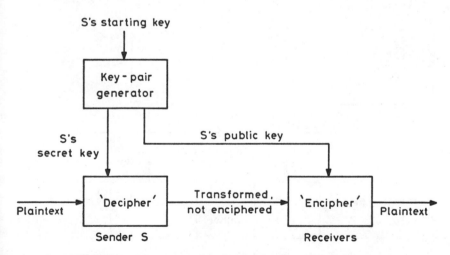

Figure 9.8   Message authentication by the public key system

The purpose of this change of functions is to give a means by which the receivers of any of these transformed messages can, with the aid of the public key, prove to themselves and others that they came from the sender S. This must be true because they have been transformed by means of the secret key which only S knows. The same process which restores the original text serves to verify that the text came from S, assuming we can be sure that the public key we used was that of a particular sender.

The particular property of the method of authentication shown in Figure 9.8 is that disputes can be resolved. The receiver cannot construct a bogus message with the sender's signature so it is pointless for the sender to accuse him of doing so. The receiver can go to a third party such as a judge in a law dispute and present the value of the public key, which is common knowledge, together with the transformed message he received and the plaintext which it gave (which anyone can check). Thus the content of the message and the identity of the sender are established. We only need to be sure that the public keys we use are authentic.

If we need a way both to authenticate messages and also to encipher them with the aid of a public key, this can be done by using the two methods we have described in cascade. This is shown in Figure 9.9 by taking the cipher process for receiver R and surrounding it by the authentication process for sender S. Such a scheme is a link between one sender and one receiver, each of which can be certain of the other's identity if he knows that he is using the other's public key. Thus the sender knows that only the intended receiver can read the message and the receiver knows that it came from the apparent sender.

There is a technical problem in the practical application of the cascaded

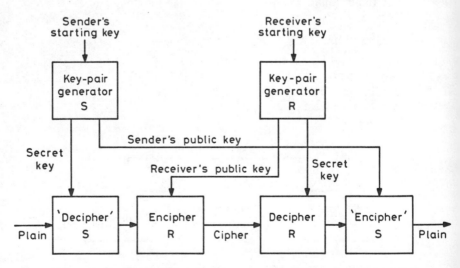

Figure 9.9   Public key authentication and cryptography combined

system of Figure 9.9. In the public key system most suited to authentication, the size of the block over which the transformations are made varies with the secret key chosen. We need a way to avoid re-blocking the message when it passes between the crypto and authentication parts of the system, which use different keys. A solution was proposed by Kohnfelder,[9] which makes use of the alternative way in which the two subsystems can be nested. We chose the sequence of operations shown in the figure so that 'the judge' could compare the input and the output of the 'Encipher' S operation, using the public key of the supposed sender.

In the Kohnfelder scheme, if the block sizes do not fit, because those of the S subsystem are greater than those of the R subsystem, we reverse the order of applying the two transformations at both ends of the line and this solves the problem of block sizes. The new problem is to decide how the judge is to verify the authentication transformation and link it with the plaintext without having to know the decipherment key. He can compare the input and output of the 'Encipher' S operation, as before, and this verifies the origin of the message, but it is in cipher form at this stage. The essential link with the plaintext is made as follows. The receiver shows the plaintext message to the judge and provides his public key (which the judge can verify). The judge enciphers the message and compares it with the output of the 'Encipher' S operation. If they match, the given plaintext corresponds to the ciphertext that has been authenticated.

In these ways, public key systems give us a function which has been called an 'electronic signature'. It is, we hope, an unforgeable signature and, in particular, the receiver of a message, though he can check the signature, is not able to reproduce it or attach it to any other message. We now have to demonstrate an actual set of transformations having the properties required, without which the public key cryptosystem would just have been an interesting idea.

The Public Key Cryptosystem of Rivest, Shamir and Adleman

The first published, practical, public key system was described by Rivest and his co-workers in reference 10. It depends on number theoretic properties and on the degree of difficulty of certain calculations with large numbers. It is easier to describe this system in two stages, beginning with a similar system which has inverse algorithms for encipherment and decipherment, but is not suitable for public key operation. We can then show how to elaborate this to produce the working system.

We have already remarked that all the functions of the arithmetic of natural numbers can be applied equally to the residues of numbers modulo some prime p. The numbers in question comprise the finite set $0, 1, ..., p - 1$. They can be combined by addition, subtraction and multiplication, using ordinary rules of arithmetic and reducing the result to a number in the range by adding or subtracting multiples of p. The advantage of using a prime is that division is always possible—division is closed in this set of numbers. The congruence $ax = 1$ has a solution for x in modulo p arithmetic, which is the (unique) inverse of a.

For example, in modulo 7 arithmetic let us look for the inverse of 3. The seven multiples of 3 are 3, 6, 2, 5, 1, 4 and 0. They are all different so one of them must be unity. Since it is the fifth of the series, the inverse of 3 is 5. There is a simple and efficient algorithm for finding the inverse.

We now describe the system in its simplified but insecure form. Encipherment and decipherment are carried out using modulo p arithmetic so both the plaintext and ciphertext consist of numbers in the range 0 to $p - 1$ inclusive. The prime p must be a large number, to give large encipherment blocks, if we are to have the one-way property. Let us call the plaintext message M and the ciphertext which it generates C. The prime modulus p is part of the public key. Encipherment can be expressed very simply by the expression $C = M^s$ in which the exponent s is also part of the public key.

We need to examine this transformation for three requirements. The first is that each value of M generates a different value of C. With a prime modulus this is always the case so we have a transformation suitable for use as a cipher. The second requirement is that the transformation can be carried out with reasonable ease and an amount of computation which is not excessive. Here, the biggest difficulty is the multiple length arithmetic involved since p is necessarily a large number. Each multiplication, consequently, employs a number of machine instructions. Raising the number M to a power s is not a very big problem. We can form M^2, M^4, M^8 and so forth by repeated squaring and then multiply the powers we need, selecting them by inspecting the binary form of s. So the number of multiplications required is only of the order log s.

The third requirement is that we have a one-way function even when the value of s is given. The simple system breaks down in this respect. The inverse or decipherment function is of the form $M = C^t$ where the exponent t must be chosen such that $M^{st} = M$ for all values of M. Fermat's theorem states that $a^{p-1} = 1$. The value of t is therefore a solution of the congruence $st = 1$, modulo $p - 1$.

This simplified scheme cannot function as a public key system because t is so easily deduced from s, but it could be used as a cryptosystem of the traditional kind in which both s and t are kept secret. This utilises the difficulty of inverting the exponential function in modulo p arithmetic which we noted earlier. So we have a secret key system, but not yet the public key system for which we were looking.

The method employed by Rivest, Shamir and Adleman to make a more secure system was to give up the prime modulus and employ instead the product of two large primes. Thus we use as modulus for the arithmetic $r = p\,q$ where p and q are large primes. The method depends on the computational difficulty of finding the factors p and q when only r is known. The number r belongs to the public key because the arithmetic is carried out with this modulus but the receiver of the message does not reveal the values of p and q which he used to derive it. The primes are chosen so that $p - 1$ and $q - 1$ have large factors, in order to defeat the method of inverting the exponential function described in reference 7.

Encipherment and decipherment in the Rivest system take the same form as we described above, namely, raising the plaintext to the power s for encipherment and raising the ciphertext to the power t for decipherment. But the calculation of t is no longer feasible if p and q are not known.

The difficulty of factorising a composite number with large factors is known from the intensive efforts to do so over many years. Nevertheless the existence of this cryptosystem has given impetus to find new methods of factorisation and there can be no guarantee that the system will necessarily remain secure.

We have mentioned already that the encipherment and decipherment processes are not too heavy in computation. To ensure that the encipherment process is bi-unique s must be relatively prime to $p - 1$ and $q - 1$. That is, s must have no common factors with these two numbers. It is not difficult to find suitable primes and a value for s.

To find the value of t, which is the secret key of the decipherment function, we need to know the values of p and q, then the calculation is simple. First we find the quantity x which is the least common multiple of $p - 1$ and $q - 1$, then we solve the congruence $st = 1$ in modulo x arithmetic.

To illustrate the method we give a trivial example in which the composite number r is 55. No example with small numbers can illustrate the strength of the method. Any speculations about the ease of cracking it should be tested against the very large numbers which are used in practice. For our simple example, $p = 5$ and $q = 11$ and therefore $x = 20$.

A suitable value for the key s used in encipherment is 3. The function $y = x^3$, modulo 55 in enumerated in full in Figure 9.10(a). The inverse function is obtained from $st = 1$, modulo 20, giving $t = 7$. The function $y = x^7$ is shown in Figure 9.10(b) and is easily seen to be the inverse of the encipherment function.

In this trivial case the values of p and q are revealed by regularities in the tables. For example, whenever the message is a multiple of 5 or 11, so is the ciphertext. In the real application of the method, p and q are large and the chance of finding such a regularity is no greater than that of finding p or q by searching. A more serious form of attack is to iterate the encipherment function until an identity is found. Starting with the ciphertext value 4, for example, we obtain by repeated encipherment the values 4, 9, 14, 49, 4. The last value before the starting value is reached, 49, is the plaintext value. But this attack can be prevented[11] with certain precautions in the choice of the primes. Even more complex atacks are proposed,[12] and the security of the system remains an open question.

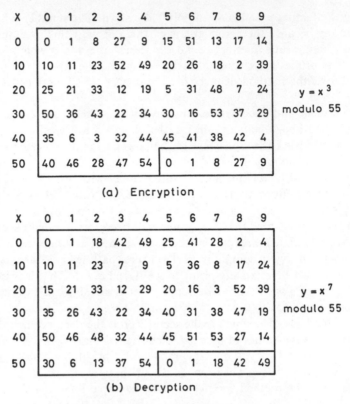

Figure 9.10 Illustrative example of the Rivest system

If no other weakness appears, the strength of the method seems to depend on the difficulty of factorising large numbers. If the factors are about 100 decimal digits long the best known factorisation method occupies of the order of 10^9 years of computer time. Encipherment or decipherment take only a second or two per block, but this is not fast enough for some purposes. Special hardware would be need to put the method into general cryptographic use.

For use as an electronic signature, however, a few seconds of time is acceptable. It is not necessary to transform the whole of a long message by the public key system. By using a one-way function that is easier to compute, the whole message can be represented in one message block. This authentication block, together with identifiers such as a title and date, is subjected by the sender to the public key transformation. Then the evidence for authenticity is the message itself (which could be enciphered with the receiver's key) the authentication block and its transform with the sender's key. The problem of block lengths does not arise because the two transformations are applied to different data.

9.7 AUTHENTICATION FOR OPEN NETWORKS

In the public key system, impersonation is still possible by persuading one party to a conversation to accept as valid a false public key. Thus A believes he is talking to B but he is actually using a public key generated by an intruder and made to seem as though it came from B. In any open system where people need to communicate without complex preparations there must be a reliable source of public keys. The simplest scheme we could devise is widespread publication of a printed book; but this does not suit the need to change keys and particularly to renounce a key which a forged signature shows to have been compromised. For these requirements there seems to be no escape from having a central authority handling public keys. This authority has been called by Needham and Schroeder[13] an *authentication server*. It is obviously convenient if we can obtain these keys from the server in a reliable manner through the communication network itself.

Using the public key system this is not difficult. The authentication server would have its own public key which would be very widely published and changes to this key would be so widely published that deception would be difficult. Anyone wanting to find the public key of a person, authority or company would then obtain this from the authentication server which would have the latest value and would enforce a stop on any compromised keys. The information from the server would be authenticated using the server's public key.

Needham and Schroeder point out that, once such a service has been established, it is no more difficult to provide authentication using methods of a traditional kind. These, it will be remembered, require that the sender and receiver employ a common key which only they know. For this purpose, the authentication server distributes, on demand, a randomly chosen 'session key' used for authentication purposes in just one session of communication. A scheme of distribution is illustrated in Figure 9.11. In this figure, AS is the authentication server and we suppose that A initiates a conversation with B, who is also known to the server. Both A and B have keys called KA and KB respectively, which they use for communication with AS. These, in effect, establish their identity as far as AS is concerned.

At the beginning of the interaction A sets up a communication with AS using the key KA. In the figure this is shown as the large cylinder protecting this communication from the outside world. Within this secure channel the authentication server supplies to A the randomly chosen session key KS. It also sends to A an encrypted message destined for B which is enciphered with the key KB which is unknown to A. Inside this message are the value of KS and the identifier of the originator A. A receives these data on the secure channel and passes them directly to B who can decipher them with the aid of the key KB. Now both parties to the future conversation are provided with a session key and then can be sure that this came from the authentication server. But notice that,

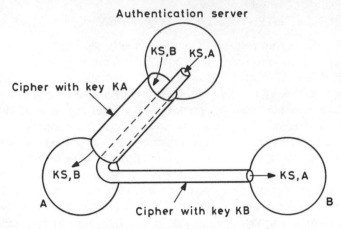

Figure 9.11   The operation of an authentication server

although there can be no dispute about the value of KS, the authentication method which is brought into operation with this key is of the traditional kind and is therefore open to the threat of dispute which we discussed earlier.

In order to provide a true electronic signature without using a public key cryptosystem, Needham and Schroeder propose that the authentication server should encipher the authenticator with its own, secret key. In this scheme, the sender A computes an authenticator and sends it to AS to be enciphered. This transaction is secured using the key KA. The identity of A is incorporated with the enciphered authenticator, to show it came from him and eliminate the possibility that the receiver B might have obtained it from AS. This cipher block is passed on to B with the message. Receiver B, or a judge in a dispute, can ask AS to decipher the authenticator and then check it with his own computed value.

The authentication server for public key systems holds only public information. It merely has to protect this information from unauthorised changes. The authentication server for single key systems has to hold secret keys for each of its users, which is an onerous task.

It is perhaps too early to make a mature judgement about the importance of public key cryptosystems. Let us assume that completely satisfactory and practicable systems can be demonstrated. Then their value for avoiding the problems of key distribution in networks is not conclusive. In a rapidly changing situation, public keys will be distributed via the network and the organisation needed to distribute them could equally well distribute session keys. It seems likely that any effective public key system will have a considerable computational load for encipherment and decipherment. Cryptography by secret keys might be preferred. We have seen that a session key can, in principle, be generated using the exponential function from a public exchange of messages. The importance of public key systems may therefore lie in their ability to provide an electronic signature which is even more secure than signatures on documents.

Because the keys used in electronic signatures would have to change, in order to remain secure, a registry of keys seems to be necessary and this registry would increase in size as more users were introduced and changed their keys. This problem could be overcome by attaching a certificate to each signature soon after it was received. For this, the authentication server would examine the evidence for a signature (using its registry of public keys) and then link to the signature a certificate, with its own, signed authentication, which would remain valid after the public key used in the signature had lapsed. The only need for long-term records would then be the public keys of the authentication servers, including their past values, to check old certificates.

It seems that a system of authentication depends on some degree of trust, in this case the public trust of the authentication server which provides up-to-date public keys and certifies the correctness of signatures.

References

1. Kahn, D.,
   The codebreakers,
   Weidenfeld and Nicolson, London (1966); also Macmillan, New York (1967).
2. Feistel, H., Notz, W. A., and Smith, J. L.,
   'Some cryptographic techniques for machine to machine data communications',
   Proc. IEEE, **63**, 1545 (November 1975).
3. *Data encryption standard,*
   FIPS publication 46,
   National Bureau of Standards (January 1977).
4. *Telecommunications: Compatibility requirements for use of the data encryption standard,*
   Proposed Federal Standard 1026,
   Federal Telecommunications Standards Committee (December 1978).
5. *Guidelines on evaluation of techniques for automated personal identification,*
   FIPS publication 48,
   National Bureau of Standards (April 1977).
6. Wilkes, M.V:,
   Time sharing computers,
   American Elsevier, New York, 1975.
7. Pohlig, S. C., and Hellman, M. E.,
   'An improved algorithm for computing logarithms over GF(p) and its cryptological significance',
   IEEE Trans. Inf. Theory, **IT-24**, 106 (January 1978).
8. Diffie, W., and Hellman, M. E.,
   'New directions in cryptography',
   IEEE Trans. Inf. Theory, **IT-22**, 644 (November 1976).
9. Kohnfelder, L. M.,
   'On the signature reblocking problem in public-key cryptosystems',
   Comm. ACM, **21**, 179 (February 1978).

10. Rivest, R. L., Shamir, A., and Adleman, L.,
    'A method for obtaining digital signatures and public key cryptosystems',
    Comm. ACM, **21**, 120 (February 1978).
11. Rivest, R. L.,
    'Remarks on a proposed cryptanalytic attack on the MIT public-key cryptosystem',
    Cryptologia, **2**, 62 (January 1978).
12. Herlestam, T.,
    'Critical remarks on some public-key cryptosystems',
    BIT (Nordisk Tidskrift för Informationsbehandling), **18**, 493 (1978).
13. Needham, R. M., and Schroeder, M. D.,
    'Using encryption for authentication in large networks of computers',
    Comm. ACM, **21**, 993 (1978).

Chapter 10

Network Optimisation

10.1 PROBLEMS AND METHODS

When the system design of a network has been completed we have available a set of 'components' such as switching nodes, transmission lines, concentrators and multiplexers with known performance ratings. There may also be design constraints such as that a concentrator can handle a certain number of terminals and no more. We are accustomed to thinking that, at this stage, the design is complete but for the network operator this is not true. He must find the best way to lay out these components to meet the traffic requirements, usually the cheapest solution that meets a certain performance criterion (delay, throughput or reliability, for example). This second stage of design can be described as 'network optimisation'.

The problem is of such complexity that there is no hope of solving it in a general form and so scores of different approaches to sub-problems have been proposed, tested and published. The literature is vast. Probably the reason for the great attention to optimisation problems is their intellectual challenge and the interesting mathematics and heuristics employed. Compared with some other important problems of network design such as formalisation of protocols and the study of flow control, optimisation has probably had more than its share of attention. Nevertheless, it would be wrong to ignore it because the potential saving in large networks by the correct placing of nodes, choice of topology and so forth can be considerable.

To attempt a comprehensive treatment of network optimisation would require the space of several volumes. Therefore we have been selective and describe a sample of the methods and approaches which the reader will find in more detail elsewhere. The emphasis is on the variety of methods rather than wide coverage and much of the theory is taken for granted. Hopefully this will guide some readers towards a fuller study of the subject. The references are as selective as the material itself but they can be used to start out on comprehensive reading.

The General Problem

Network optimisation problems are *geographic* because it is the size and spread of a network that mostly determines its cost and performance. Consequently, the basic data for an optimisation problem are the locations of the terminals. By terminal we mean, as usual, anything which the network serves, from a simple character terminal to a multi-access computer. These terminal locations will be shown on a map. Because their characteristics may vary enormously the next most important data is contained in the *traffic requirement matrix*. This matrix gives the amount of traffic which the network is expected to pass from each terminal point to all the others. The unit might be packets or octets—whichever best represents the load on the network. It might also be necessary to segregate traffic by priority or by message size if there is no easy way to give a single measure of traffic.

Traffic varies throughout the day and differs according to the day of the week. In most cases the network is designed for the heaviest traffic load. To avoid ambiguity from statistical fluctuations the conventional rule is to consider the average traffic in the busiest hour of the busiest day. In a few cases there is a 'tidal flow' where the busy hour is different for different parts of the network or different directions of flow. In the telephone network this can assume some importance but experience with computer networks has hardly reached this level of detail.

With the statement of traffic requirements only a very small part of the problem has been defined yet already we have complications sufficient to make even the smallest optimisation problem difficult. For a tractable problem we usually have to employ the most extreme simplifying assumptions and just ignore most of the detail. To give an example, terminal locations may be replaced by locating multiplexers or other access points on an ad hoc basis. The traffic requirement matrix is sometimes replaced by uniform traffic between each pair of access points in the hope that network design is not too sensitive to details of the matrix, as seems to be the case. But in order to illustrate the full complexity of optimisation problems let us continue to state the general problem in some detail and then make simplifying assumptions when we describe the approaches to optimisation.

The next set of data concerns the set of components from which the network is to be built such as the nodes, concentrators and multiplexers and perhaps a satellite with its ground stations. For each of these we have a performance limit and a cost. There may, for example, be a choice of switching nodes, each with its cost and packet handling performance limit. In a similar way, the available transmission lines are specified by cost and performance.

For all these components there are topological constraints. Thus a multiplexer or concentrator may be able to accommodate a number of terminals up to a certain limit and a switching node may be able to interconnect with lines up to a certain limit, perhaps depending on their capacities. The basic problem of network optimisation can be stated as the placing and interconnection of these components. Moving inwards from the terminals, concentrators and multiplexers will be connected, then main switching nodes and then the communication lines will be chosen and joined between the nodes.

The criteria for a successful solution of the problem can be expressed either by the need to optimise a variable or by a requirement which the design must meet. Thus it is not possible to ask for a network which minimises both cost and average packet delay. Either we must establish a *figure of merit* which produces a tradeoff between these parameters or we must treat one as a requirement and the other as the subject for optimisation. So we could ask for a minimum cost network with an average delay better than 0.1 s or we could ask for a minimum delay network with annual cost less than a given quantity. It is often useful to present a curve relating optimum solutions with varying cost or delay requirement.

The main parameters are cost, throughput, delay and reliability. Cost is often the optimising parameter and is the only one for which a single figure for the entire network is sufficient.

The throughput of a network is related to its traffic requirement matrix. Sometimes the throughput is not a given quantity, but is to be maximised. Then we introduce a multiplier to scale the requirement matrix and maximise the multiplier. In this way the total traffic becomes a meaningful parameter and the traffic matrix indicates how it is spread between the terminals.

Delay can be expressed as a mean transit delay for all traffic but in most cases the spread of delay is also important. It is often sufficient to calculate probability distributions of delay and check that these are acceptable while treating average delay as the principal criterion for the optimisation work. In the same way, priority classes and their effect on delay are usually treated as a separate problem.

Reliability strictly means the availability of the network service to all its users. The rate of breakdown of lines and nodes and their mean time to repair are the details, but the *availability*, measured as the percentage of time for which a terminal has service, is the parameter used in optimisation work. The reliability requirement can often be shown to be nearly equivalent to a requirement for a certain *connectivity*. This is a topological constraint we shall discuss later on. Detailed probability calculations come into the picture in those networks where failure is a major concern, such as military networks.

Optimisation in Practice

Even if it was possible to solve very general optimisation ·problems this ability would rarely be needed. In all practical cases there are other important constraints which reduce the size of the problem. Let us consider private and public networks separately.

In private networks it is very unlikely that sites will be chosen for network units that are outside the property of the organisation. It is probable that the size of the traffic will largely determine where the main switching nodes are to be located; the problem that remains is one of interconnection, choosing the topology and perhaps the sizing of the bandwidth of transmission lines. Optimisation can be important when the network is first established, but after the requirements have changed the replacing of nodes or lines is done without major changes to the whole network, so the new optimisation problems are relatively small.

One artificial factor in private networks is the way in which the tariffs for communication lines operate. It is artificial only in that tariffs do not reflect the true costs so the resulting choice of lines does not minimise the cost to the public network that provides them.

Optimisation in a public communication network is heavily constrained by the existing equipment and the access points into the transmission lines. Unlike the private network designer, the engineer who is planning a new facility in a public network knows the real cost and is likely, for example, to place major switching nodes at the points where carrier systems meet. This designer also has to think ahead to a greater extent than the private network designer because the planning for installing transmission facilities is closer to a ten-year than a one-year timescale. It usually works on the principle that spare plant must be provided for a reasonable expectation of network expansion. Minimising the cost of spare plant can be more important to the economics of a public network than calculations based on present-day traffic.

For all these reasons, practical optimisation problems can look very different from those treated in the literature. Organisations which do this optimisation work have an armoury of preferred techniques with the software to implement them, but each client's problem has some special constraints which require changes to the standard programs.

Approaches to Optimisation

The ideal would be to employ rigorous mathematical methods and derive exact optima. Even where the mathematical problem can be formulated and solved in principle this is sometimes an unnecessarily heavy approach. The techniques that are used can be described under three headings, combinatorial, analytic and heuristic.

Combinatorial methods deal with finite sets and manipulate relations between them. The prime example in networks is the topology. The nodes and their connecting lines form a *graph* and there is an extensive body of graph theory which can help to manipulate and measure characteristics of such structures.

The complexity of combinatorial problems comes from their size and the large number of possibilities that need to be considered, for example a network of 30 nodes has 435 possible locations for a line between two of these nodes and therefore, including a lot of trivial cases, it has 2^{435} possible patterns of lines. Examining topology by trying all the possibilities is unproductive. Very often the problem requires heuristic methods, that is to say a 'trial and error' method of solution.

Allocating flows to lines in order to optimise the total carrying capacity of a network is an example of a problem which has an analytic solution. Some of the analytic approaches to network optimisation use very severe approximations such as those needed to reduce non-linear to linear problems. It can often be shown that the approximations affect the outcome very little. This can be demonstrated by using exact calculation for a few cases to see how close the approximate methods are. Taking a certain risk, the designer then proceeds with the approximate solutions expecting them to be near the truth.

Whether the problem is basically analytic or combinatorial the best methods in network optimisation are often heuristic. The program may, for example, generate topologies with improved properties using 'reasonable' rules instead of an algorithm which can be shown to converge to an optimum. Solutions of flow problems may be improved in many steps without any certainty about the result. Random changes are introduced to ensure that possibilities are explored widely enough so that one of the 'best solutions' is probably near the optimum. Typically, the starting point for these heuristic approaches is chosen by random methods and a number of such starting points is tried so that the results can be compared. The best one is chosen.

In the following sections these three approaches to network optimisation will be illustrated.

10.2   THE GRAPH MODEL OF A NETWORK

A graph consists of a set of nodes and lines connected in such a way that both ends of each line are joined to nodes. Figure 10.1 illustrates a graph

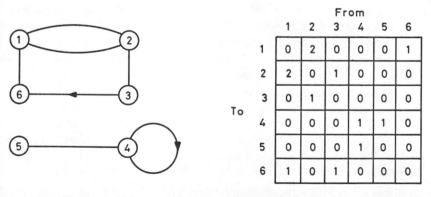

Figure 10.1   A graph and its adjacency matrix

together with its adjacency matrix which we shall describe shortly. The relationship between nodes and lines is not a symmetric one because a line joins two nodes whereas a node can be joined to any number of lines, including the possibility that it connects to no lines at all. The number of lines joined to a node is called the *degree* of that node.

Graphs are mathematical constructions for which there is an extensive theory, for example in the books of C. Berge[1] and F. Harary.[2] We shall describe a graph as consisting of a set of nodes connected by undirected lines. Graph theory begins with a set of 'points' or 'vertices' and first considers directed lines or *arcs* which join them. The undirected lines of our networks are represented by two arcs, one in each direction and the arc or arcs which join one vertex to another are jointly described as an *edge*. The terms vertex and edge are found in the literature of graph theory applied to networks.

We often meet the concept of a 'route' through a network by which packets can pass from node to node. Such a set of lines (edges) is called a *chain*. A chain which comes back to its starting node is called a *cycle*. When we study the connectivity of a network this will be related to the number of chains which join two nodes and have no other nodes in common.

Figure 10.1 shows a number of features that we would not expect to find in actual communication networks. One of these is the directed line from node 3 to node 6. This could be a unidirectional communication line but in practical networks full duplex lines are almost the rule and if one direction of transmission fails the other must shut down because the link procedure cannot continue. Therefore our attention will be restricted to undirected graphs. The figure shows two lines joining the same pair of nodes and this is a possible network feature, but not all network theories and optimisation algorithms allow it. The graph shown in the figure is disconnected, which means that one part of it (nodes 4 and 5) has no line joining to the other part. When we are considering how to measure connectivity the concept of a disconnected graph is used but the graph which represents the whole, undamaged network is always connected. In a connected graph every pair of nodes has a chain which joins them together.

The way that node 4 is connected to itself by a line has no relevance to communication networks so this feature is usually forbidden.

The essentials of the graph can be expressed by stating which node pairs are directly connected by a line. A matrix of integers known as the *adjacency matrix* shows the number of lines from each node to all the others. In the absence of loops such as that connecting node 4 to itself the diagonal elements are zero. In the absence of directed lines the matrix is symmetric about its main diagonal. In the absence of multiple connections such as those between nodes 1 and 2 all the matrix values are 0 or 1.

If A is the adjacency matrix a matrix multiplication yields a square matrix A^2 of similar size which has a useful meaning. Each element of this matrix shows how many chains of two lines lead from one node to another. Chains of three lines are represented by A^3 and so forth. The chains, which consist of a sequence of connected lines, can fold back on themselves so the results are not generally useful but, if a good matrix multiplication programme is available, this can be a quick way to discover whether the matrix is connected. If there are p nodes in the graph, the matrix

$$1 + A + A^2 + \cdots + A^{p-1}$$

has no zero elements if the graph is connected. This is because any pair of nodes in a connected graph must have a chain of $p - 1$ lines or less joining them. The series can be terminated earlier if no new non-zero elements are being created. Its length is then one greater than the diameter of the largest connected part of the graph.

Labelling Algorithm for a Connected Graph

Testing connectivity from the adjacency matrix is only convenient if the graph is specified by such a matrix. For very large and sparsely connected graphs the structure of the graph can be described by a list structure with pointers for the connection between each node and its connected lines. To test that such a graph is connected it is easier to use a *labelling algorithm* and since this is a good illustration of labelling algorithms, which are widely used in connection with graphs and networks, we shall describe it here.

The aim is to search the graph in such a way that all the nodes connected to the starting node will be visited at least once. We have to associate with the data structure additional items called 'labels' to indicate the current state of the algorithm. The method of searching employed can be described as 'depth-first tree searching'. Figure 10.2 illustrates the method and shows that each line is

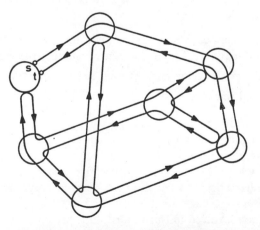

Figure 10.2 Searching a connected graph

traversed twice in opposite directions during the search procedure. An arbitrary start point s is chosen. The paths which are used can clearly be seen to constitute a tree traversed twice over. The 'twigs' of the tree are represented by the traverse folding back on itself. The procedure has two distinct states, 'searching' in the forward direction and 'backtracking' when it has reached a twig.

To formalise this procedure we have to explain how the graph is labelled. In this case, we need to label only the lines that have been used. It might be convenient to label the nodes visited, but these are implied by the labelled lines. The lines may be labelled in one of two ways: used only once (if the traverse has passed over in one direction) or used twice, after which they cannot be used again. These are distinct labels.

The rules for the algorithm determine which exit line to use when we arrive at a node along a certain entry line. The information available for the decision is the labelling of the exit lines. The rules depend on whether the traverse enters the node on a line which it is using for the first time (this is the searching phase) or whether it enters the node on a line that has already been used in the opposite direction (this is the backtracking phase).

For the *searching* phase, when the node is entered on a line being used for the first time, there are two rules:

(1) If there are other lines connected to this node, none of which (except the entry line) is labelled, the traverse can leave on any line except the entry line and continue searching. In the unusual case that only the entry line joins this node, the traverse must return the way it came, and this starts the backtracking phase.

(2) If one or more of the lines connected to this node, other than the entry line, is labelled, the traverse should leave on the entry line and start backtracking.

In the *backtracking* phase the node is entered on a line that cannot be used again and there are three rules:

(1) If any of the lines connected to the node has not yet been labelled the traverse should leave on such a line, thus resuming the searching phase.

(2) Otherwise, if there is a line not yet used twice it must leave on this line.

(3) Otherwise, if all lines have been used twice, the algorithm ends.

The effect of the algorithm (though we shall not prove it here) is that case (2) of the backtracking rule only applies when all the lines but one have been used twice so there is a unique line on which the traverse must exit. The traverse ends at the point where it started. It can be proved that all nodes connected to the starting node have been visited. For a connected graph, all nodes will have been visited.

The computation involved in this algorithm is proportional to the size of the graph measured by its numbers of lines. Using the adjacency matrix requires a number of operations proportional to the diameter of the matrix and the square of the number of nodes. Clearly the labelling algorithm is more economical for large graphs.

The Connectivity and Cohesion of a Graph

Connectivity is a measure of the degree to which a graph will resist disconnection when nodes are removed. For example, in Figure 10.3 the removal of nodes 1 and 4 produces a disconnected graph but removal of fewer nodes cannot. This is expressed as a connectivity of 2. The symbol κ is used for connectivity.

If, on the other hand, we consider the removal of lines, we see that three lines have to be removed to disconnect this graph. For example, the three lines which attach node 2 could be removed. To distinguish this measure from connectivity it is called *cohesion* and is represented by the symbol λ.

A set of nodes, the deletion of which will disconnect the network, is called a *node cutset* and a set of lines is a *line cutset*. So we have the definitions:

The *connectivity* of a graph is the minimum size of node cutset.

The *cohesion* of a graph is the minimum size of line cutset.

Figure 10.3 illustrates a third quantity δ which is the minimum degree of the graph. The *degree* of any node is the number of lines which join it. Evidently the cohesion of a graph must be less than its minimum degree because a node which has this degree could be disconnected by the removal of δ lines. In fact it can be shown that:

$$\kappa \leqslant \lambda \leqslant \delta$$

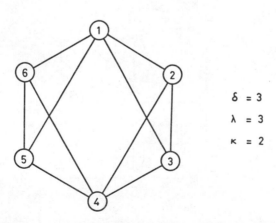

$$\delta = 3$$
$$\lambda = 3$$
$$\kappa = 2$$

Figure 10.3   Illustration of connectivity and minimum degree

The proof that connectivity is less than or equal to cohesion is straightforward. Consider a cutset of λ lines and, for each line, choose a node at one end of it. The resulting set of nodes is a node cutset because removing the nodes makes the corresponding lines ineffective. Now the nodes may be λ in number or less because some of the nodes selected may coincide. Therefore a node cutset exists with at most λ nodes. The connectivity cannot be greater than this value.

It is possible to define a third kind of connectivity based on a mixed cutset containing lines and nodes. It is easy to show that the minimum size of mixed cutset is equal to the connectivity. Mixed cutsets do not generate a new measure of connectivity.

The fact that connectivity is less than or equal to cohesion implies that, in

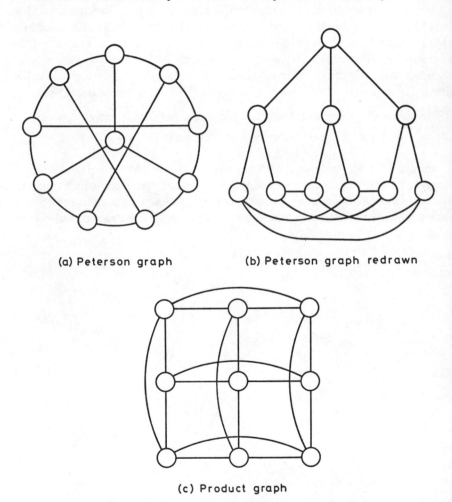

(a) Peterson graph　　　(b) Peterson graph redrawn

(c) Product graph

Figure 10.4　Examples of regular graphs

general, a network is more vulnerable to loss of nodes than to loss of lines. The reason is that the loss of any node puts out of action at least one line and often more. The stratagem which is described in Figure 2.9 on page 54 helps to preserve connectivity after the loss of a node. A network which is protected in this way would require a new definition of its 'effective' connectivity. Without this stratagem it would be wise to regard connectivity, rather than the cohesion, as the best simple measure of a network's resilience to damage. We return later to the calculation of network reliability and availability.

Synthesis of Network Topologies

One approach to the construction of network topologies with desirable properties is to synthesise graphs by a mathematical construction. Figures 10.4 and 10.5 show examples of graphs constructed in this way. Typically these graphs have a certain regularity. The 'view' from each node is the same.

Figure 10.4(a) is the Peterson graph with 10 nodes, 15 lines and connectivity 3. The degree of each node is 3 so the connectivity is as great as it could be. Such a graph is said to have optimal connectivity. This is the same graph that we used in Figure 2.10 to connect subnodes and make a node of greater reliability, but it is drawn differently. There is another sense in which the Peterson graph is optimal and it relates to the *diameter* of the graph, the greatest distance between any pair of nodes, measured in 'hops' from nodes to adjacent nodes. If we start from any node and construct a tree of adjacent nodes, as in part (b) of the figure, because of the degree 3 there will be 3 nodes on the second level. For the same reason, each of the three second-level nodes will be connected to at most 2 nodes at the third level. This gives a total of at most 10 nodes if we count the starting node and all those that can be reached from it in 2 hops. Therefore, with degree 3, if we require a graph of diameter 2 the graph cannot contain more than 10 nodes. The Peterson graph achieves this maximum.

Part (c) of the figure is constructed as a product of two graphs. The graphs which have been multiplied are simple triangular graphs. When graphs A and B are multiplied, any node pair a_i and b_j gives rise to a node p_{ij} in the product. Adjacent nodes a_x and a_y in A give rise to a multiplicity of adjacent node pairs in P, namely p_{xk} and p_{yk} for all elements b_k in graph B. Similar adjacent pairs in the product derive from each adjacency in graphs A and B. Thus the product graphs are heavily connected. By multiplying fully connected graphs, it is possible to generate graphs with optimal connectivity. With this kind of multiplication the connectivity of the product graph is the sum of the connectivities of its components. It is an interesting exercise to construct the complement of the product graph in the figure by starting with the 9 nodes and linking those pairs which are not adjacent in the product graph. This is, in fact, another kind of product graph but it is not guaranteed even to be connected. In this case it happens to be 4-connected.

Figure 10.5 shows two more such examples. The one in part (a) has connectivity 4. The outer lines of this graph form a *Hamiltonian cycle*, that is, a cycle which connects all the nodes. The inner lines also form a Hamiltonian cycle which has no links in common with the first one. Any two nodes can be connected in opposite directions round one of the cycles and in opposite directions round the other, making 4 line-disjoint paths; so graphs of this kind must have a cohesion of 4. It does not follow that their connectivity is 4 though the case shown in our figure has this property.

In part (b) of the figure an even cycle of nodes has been connected across its diameters. This always generates a graph of connectivity 3. A similar graph with 8 nodes retains the diameter 2 (which has been a property of each example) but with 10 nodes if we need diameter 2 in a 3-connected graph we must go to the Peterson graph which has no Hamiltonian cycle.

Synthetic graphs like these are of great theoretical interest and they may become important in the construction of switches from identical components. Circuit switches already use regular arrays of components and this may become a feature of switching generally if the economics of manufacture moves that way. It is rarely possible to use synthetic graphs for geographically spread networks because the cost of the lines is a large factor in optimisation and these costs take different values depending on the geography.

Calculation of Cohesion and Connectivity

The connectivity of a small network may be obvious by inspection. When a network is large it can be difficult to estimate connectivity with certainty. In optimisation programs it is essential to have an algorithm for determining the connectivity of a graph. For many nodes this is a heavy computational task.

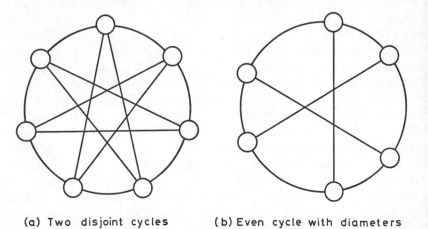

(a) Two disjoint cycles   (b) Even cycle with diameters

Figure 10.5   Further examples of regular graphs

The measurement of cohesion and connectivity was made much easier to understand and to carry out computationally by the discovery of a link between this theory and the calculation of flow in a network. Figure 10.6 shows a network and identifies two nodes, a source s and a terminal t. If this was a network of pipes, each with a given maximum capacity, we might ask 'what is the maximum flow the network can sustain from s to t?' This 'single commodity' flow problem is neatly solved by the Ford–Fulkerson algorithm.[3] Briefly described, this algorithm augments the flow in stages until no more can be carried. To augment the flow it must find a chain from s to t on which there is still spare capacity. It does this by systematically searching from s as though seeking a way through a maze in which each pipe carrying maximum flow in the desired direction is effectively blocked. As it searches, accessible nodes are labelled by the maximum flow augmentation to which they are accessible from s. If the search reaches t an augmentation is possible.

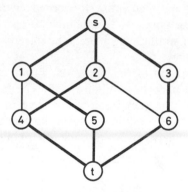

Figure 10.6   Example of s–t flow

This labelling algorithm continues its search–augment procedure until the search fails to reach t. It follows, from the method used, that there is a set of pipes separating s from t which are all at maximum flow in the s–t direction, in fact a cutset. From this it can be deduced that the maximum s–t flow equals the minimum capacity of an s–t cutset.

To apply these ideas to cohesion it is only necessary to think of the graph as having *unit* capacity for each line. Then the maximum s–t flow equals the cohesion, which is the number of lines in the minimum s–t cutset. Also, because each flow has unit value, if the cohesion is λ there must be exactly λ line-disjoint chains from s to t along which such flows could pass to carry the maximum s–t flow. In the figure three such chains are shown for an s–t cohesion of 3. Since in this case the chains are also node-disjoint the s–t connectivity is also 3.

This useful parallel between flow and connectivity calculations gives another result, known as Whitney's theorem,[4] which states that for connectivity n each pair of nodes, such as s and t, is connected by at least n node-disjoint chains.

There are many similar theorems which relate the size of cutsets with the number of independent chains.

Although the calculation of connectivity for a pair of nodes is tractable, even for large networks, the number of such calculations mounts very rapidly. Normally for large networks we are dealing with relatively 'sparse' situations, such as looking for three-connectivity in a 100-node network. We do not want to make a connectivity calculation for all 4950 pairs of nodes. There is an elegant method due to Kleitman[5] which reduces this problem.

The Kleitman Connectivity Test

When the connectivity of a large graph has to be measured it is usually done to ensure that the connectivity is at least some value which we shall denote x. Kleitman's method does not determine connectivity but provides a test that the connectivity reaches the specified value. It proceeds by iteration, taking out one node at a time from the graph and reducing the test from connectivity x to $x - 1$, $x - 2$ and so forth until the problem to be solved is whether the remaining graph is connected at all.

Let us examine one step in this iteration. From the graph we identify a single node such as the node N in Figure 10.7. The large shape in the figure represents the whole of the remaining graph. We are trying to answer the question whether the whole graph has at least the connectivity x. The first step is to test the connectivity between N and each other node in the graph. Suppose, therefore, that A and B are two of these nodes. Then the test has to show that

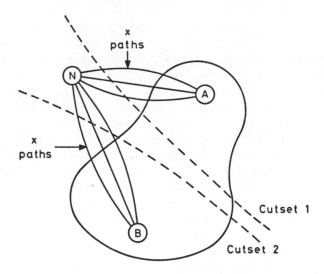

Figure 10.7   The Kleitman connectivity test

between N and A there are at least x node-disjoint chains. In the same way, there must be at least x node-disjoint chains between N and B.

Now consider what remains to be proved. For each pair of nodes A and B in the part of the graph not containing N we must show that there is no node cutset which divides A and B and has less than x elements. Consider the two locations for the cutset shown in the figure. The cutset 1 is impossible because it intersects the x chains already established between N and A so it will have at least x elements. Similarly, cutset 2 is impossible for it also will have at least x elements. A cutset which is relevant to the problem must therefore include the node N. It would follow, if such a cutset existed with less than x elements, that less than $x - 1$ of these were in the graph which remains when N is deleted. We now know the nature of the remaining task. It is simply to prove that the graph with N deleted has a connectivity of at least $x - 1$. We have therefore reduced the magnitude of the problem.

The procedure continues by selecting from the remaining graph a further node and testing that it is connected to every node of the remainder with a connectivity of $x - 1$. Repeating the previous argument we find that the remaining task is to prove a connectivity of $x - 2$ in the graph with the two nodes deleted.

Proceeding in this way, after having selected $x - 1$ nodes and eliminated them in the way described, we have reduced the problem to the simple question 'is the remaining graph connected?'. This can easily be tested, for example by the labelling algorithm given earlier.

The number of pairwise connectivity tests at the first stage in a 100-node graph is 99. At the second stage it is 98 and at the third stage 97. These 294 tests would suffice to prove that the graph was at least 4-connected if we further test that the remaining graph of 97 nodes is connected. For larger networks or for smaller connectivities the advantage of Kleitman's method over the full pairwise testing is even greater.

10.3   NETWORK RELIABILITY AND AVAILABILITY

The advantage of mesh-connected data networks compared with star networks, loops or trees is the improved availability in the presence of occasional line failures. Node failures are important and for this reason we suggested earlier that connectivity, which concerns nodes and lines, is the significant measure rather than cohesion which considers only lines. Nevertheless, for simplicity, we shall consider only line failure. The extension to both line and node failures adds complexity but does not introduce new principles.

The simplest assumption is that each line fails and is repaired independently of all the others so that its performance can be measured by a single parameter p which is the probability that it is out of operation. We wish to express the availability performance of the whole network as a function of p and the topology. The performance could be measured in many different ways. For example it could express the fraction of time for which a pair of nodes is connected, averaged over all node-pairs. The importance of not disconnecting *any* node from the network suggests a more stringent definition which states that the network failure rate f is the probability that any node on the network is disconnected.

In principle the calculation is very simple but, as in many calculations associated with topology, the simple methods become time consuming for larger networks. Figure 10.8 explains the straightforward method of calculation.

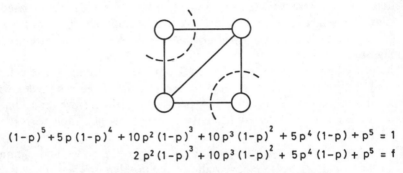

$$(1-p)^5 + 5p(1-p)^4 + 10p^2(1-p)^3 + 10p^3(1-p)^2 + 5p^4(1-p) + p^5 = 1$$

$$2p^2(1-p)^3 + 10p^3(1-p)^2 + 5p^4(1-p) + p^5 = f$$

Figure 10.8   Exact calculation of failure probability

When we are considering only line failures a network with m lines can be in any one of 2 states depending on whether each line has failed or not. The probability associated with one of these states depends on how many lines have failed, since we are assuming the same failure probability for each line. The top equation in the figure shows a binomial expansion in which the probabilities of all the different failed states are summed to unity. The first term is the probability of no line failure. There are 5 ways in which one line can fail and this gives the coefficient 5 in the second term. There are 10 ways in which two lines can fail and so forth.

To determine the probability of network failure by disconnection it is necessary to count how many of these failed states result in a disconnected network. The lower equation is the expression for f, the probability of network failure. Disconnection requires at least 2 lines to fail so the first non-zero term is the one in p^2. For the coefficient of this term, we count how many of the 10 pairs of line failures would result in a disconnected network and there are 2 of these, indicated by the broken lines on the graph. This gives the coefficient 2. Since all cases of 3, 4 or 5 line failures will result in network disconnections the coefficients of these terms are the same as those given when all the failed states were included in the top equation. In this way the failure probability f can be calculated as a polynomial in p by enumerating all the node cutsets.

Disconnection between a Pair of Nodes

An alternative calculation of network reliability is to determine the possibility of failure associated with a pair of nodes s and t. This is the probability $f(s,t)$ that there will be no path between them. Figure 10.9 gives an example. In the network joining s and t there is no possibility of disconnection by a single line failure so the failure probabilities have no term in p. The term in p^2 has a coefficient which equals the number of different cutsets of two lines which divide s and t. These are shown in the figure by broken lines. They are 6 in number and they lead to the approximate value of $f(s,t)$ shown in the figure. The multiplier due to the probability of unfailed lines is not included because terms in higher powers of p have not been included. For the typical line failure probabilities of today's networks it is often sufficient to use only the first term of this series. There would be a risk of significant error if the number of failure states with 3 lines broken was very much higher—for example some ladder networks might have this property.

For the example in Figure 10.9 it is just as easy to determine the first term in the series for f, the failure probablity of the whole network. There are four further cutsets of two lines which would result in network disconnections—specifically those which isolate the nodes marked x in the figure. With these included, the coefficient of the first term in the expansion increases to 10 in the formula for f.

These approximate expressions for failure probabilities are valid for small values of p. Their integer coefficients may be large in large networks but it is still most important to discover which power of p appears in the first non-zero term. This number is given by the size of the smallest line cutset—in other words the cohesion.

Exact Calculation for Large Networks

For these small networks it was possible to determine the number of minimum size cutsets by inspection. With 3-connected and 4-connected networks this can be difficult. Furthermore with large networks there is a need for exact calculation of the polynomial in p.[6]

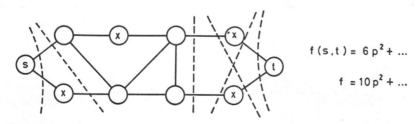

$$f(s,t) = 6p^2 + \ldots$$

$$f = 10p^2 + \ldots$$

Figure 10.9   Enumeration of cutsets

Lines which are connected in series or parallel can be combined and the failure probabilities determined for the combination. Let us call a two-terminal network which can be built up in this way a *branch*. To do this calculation we must recognise the possibility of three distinct states in such a branch.

The first or unfailed state, denoted 0, may have failed lines within it but it has no disconnected parts and it continues to connect the two terminals.

The second state, denoted 1, has the two terminals disconnected from each other by failures, but all the internal nodes of the branch continue to have access to one of the terminals. This is a significant state because a 'repair' is possible if the break is paralleled by a good connection.

The third state, denoted 2, has a disconnected set of nodes within it. These cannot be reached from either terminal so the network containing the branch is disconnected, whatever other paths there may be. In this state it does not matter whether the two terminals of the branch are connected together or not.

Figure 10.10 shows how the states of two branches connected in series or parallel determine the state of the combined branch. Note that the presence of any disconnected component, shown by state 2, results in an overall state 2 because the disconnection counts as a network failure. With a series connection, state 1 in both component branches leaves the middle node disconnected, hence the combined system is in state 2.

Probabilities can be associated with each of these states and using the state tables the probabilities for the three states of the combined branch are obtained.

For a simple line with failure probability p, state 2 is impossible and state 1 has probability p. From such lines the more complex branches are built up. With the aid of this transformation, complex networks can be reduced to simple ones but the process stops when there are no series or parallel branches in the remaining network. Further progress uses the technique of 'expansion' about a single branch.

In the expansion process a single branch is chosen and the probability calculation is then divided into three separate cases, following the consequences of this branch being in each of its three states. For state 2 no further calculation is necessary because the network has failed. For state 1 the branch can be

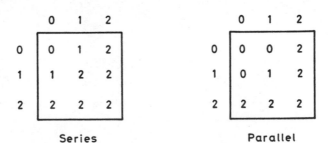

Figure 10.10   Resultant state of series or parallel combination

removed from the network and the remainder of the network should continue its series–parallel reduction. For state 0 the two terminals of the branch are firmly connected. These two nodes of the graph can be made identical and, with any luck, the series–parallel reduction can continue.

Success in reduction depends on a good choice of the branch around which to reduce the network. In a complex network more than one stage of reduction will be needed and each stage doubles the amount of computation still to be carried out.

Figure 10.11 shows an example, using series–parallel reduction, which requires a single expansion to complete the analysis.

From the original network shown in Figure 10.11(a), series–parallel reduction leads to the network in Figure 10.11(b). For example, the lines 1–2 and 1–8 are in series and reduce to a branch 2–8 for which the state probabilities can be calculated. This is paralleled by the line 2–8 and the resultant branch is in series with the line 7–8. Next the parallel connection with 2–7 and the series combination with 2–3 are calculated. The result is a branch 3–7 which represents all the part of the network containing nodes 1, 2 and 8. This is shown by the wavy line in Figure 10.11(b). In a similar way, nodes 4 and 6 are connected by a branch representing the effect of the triangular networks 4–5–6. For both of these branches the probabilities of states 0, 1 and 2 can be calculated.

We have now reduced the network to that shown in Figure 10.11(b) and no further series–parallel reduction can be made. We need an expansion. We choose (arbitrarily) to expand about the branch marked A, thus dividing the calculation into three cases, according to the state of A, with known probabilities. For state 2 of the branch A, the network is always in state 2. For state 1, we can replace the network by the first term shown in Figure 10.11(c), because nodes 3 and 7 are disconnected. This network yields to series–parallel reduction giving its own

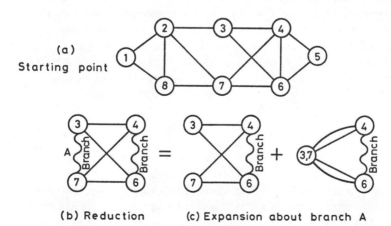

(a)
Starting point

(b) Reduction   (c) Expansion about branch A

Figure 10.11   Series–parallel reduction and expansion

set of state probabilities. For state 0 we know that nodes 3 and 7 are connected and therefore we show them in the second term in Figure 10.11(c) as identical, yielding another reducible network. The calculation is completed by multiplying the state probabilities of the two terms in Figure 10.11(c) by the known probabilities of these terms, derived from states 1 and 0 of the A branch. The component probabilities of the three states are added, not forgetting the probability of state 2 of branch A.

10.4   OPTIMISATION OF LINE CAPACITY AND FLOW

If we are allowed to assume that the topology of the network is fixed then the optimisation problems concern the choice of line capacity for each line and the allocation of flows to the lines. In practice, the flows of traffic are the result of the way the network's routing method works. Flow optimisation usually treats the network as a whole so it can obtain better optima than normal routing would give, being based on a full knowledge of the traffic requirement and the whole flow pattern.

The data which are fixed in order to define the problem, in addition to network topology, are the traffic requirement matrix and some relationship between capacity and line cost. Then we can look at the problem in one of two ways. We can keep the total cost D constant and minimise the average delay T or we can set a limit on average delay and minimise total cost. It usually seems that these two approaches give similar results.

Defined in this way, the optimisation problem requires both flows and capacities to be design variables, for which the values must be discovered which give minimum D or T. This proves to be difficult and it is best approached by looking first at two sub-problems, namely the capacity assignment problem with fixed flows and the flow assignment problem with fixed capacities. In the following sections we shall describe the two sub-problems and then the combined capacity and flow assignment problem. The intention is to describe the method without attempting mathematical completeness or proof. References are given to the original papers and to surveys which describe these methods in full detail.

We shall find that the three problems require different mathematical methods. The capacity assignment problem for communication networks was first treated in detail by Kleinrock[7] who made many approximations in order to obtain an explicit analytic solution. This is the so-called 'square root' capacity assignment which is described below.

The flow assignment problem is solved by approaching the optimum in a number of steps. At first, a feasible flow is obtained and this is progressively modified to become nearer the optimum. This can be shown to approach a true, global optimum and this 'flow deviation method' is computationally efficient.

The full optimisation problem of capacity and flow assignment uses a combination of two methods. Unlike optimisation for flow alone, the capacity and flow assignment problem has a very large number of local optima so the method employed is to choose many patterns of starting flow at random and find the local optimum, taking the best of these as representative of a true global optimum. This is a heuristic method with no guarantee of optimality, but it works adequately in practice.

The three problems are treated in detail by Kleinrock[8] and there is a further summary by Gerla and Kleinrock[9] leading on to a comparison of methods for topological design.

The Capacity Assignment Problem

Increased line capacity reduces the average network delay but costs money and this is the root of the optimisation problem. For each line we have a relationship between the cost of a line and its capacity C measured in bits per second. Cost depends also on line length. In practice this is not a continuous relationship because the designer is faced with a choice from a finite set of line capacities each with its own cost. For convenience the relationship is usually expressed as a continuous one. Furthermore, the 'classic' work on this subject assumes a linear relationship between cost and capacity. It has been shown[8] that a range of power law cost functions give very closely similar results.

In this problem we are given, for each channel i, a flow λ_i and we make the assumption that the network delay calculation depends only on these total channel flows. The channel i has a capacity C_i and an associated cost $d_i C_i$. The d_i are given and the C_i are to be found.

The channel is one direction of a line, so a line is made up from two channels. Clearly the flows of packets in the two directions can be different yet, in practice, the capacities are equal in both directions of a line. This constraint is not explicitly taken into account in the theory, which treats channels as though they were independent. Artificially we can use a symmetric traffic requirement matrix and route the flows so that the opposing channels of each line have the same flows. This is a 'symmetric flow'.

The calculation of average packet delay T requires the solution of a complex queueing system. The approach used is to make very considerable simplifying assumptions in order to achieve a simple formula for T. The first stage of this approximation is to associate a queue with each outgoing link from a node, that is to say with the input to each line. Associated with this ith line there will be an average queuing delay (waiting plus service time) denoted T_i.

Even before we look at the queuing problem and further simplify it, we can obtain a general result connecting T with the individual average queuing delays. This is a form of Little's result. Let γ be the total network traffic, namely the number of packets per second entering (and therefore leaving) the whole network. Then if T is the average packet delay the number of packets contained in the network is on average γT. The number of packets contained in each queue is similarly $\lambda_i T_i$ and therefore, summing over all the channels in the network,

$$\gamma T = \sum_{i=1}^{b} \lambda_i T_i$$

If we now examine a single queue we find that the service time is proportional to packet length and we can introduce the parameter μ to represent average length. The queue receives arrivals from any other of the lines attached to the node, possibly including packets newly arrived in the network. These streams of packets are the output of other queues and have a complex distribution of arrival intervals. The solution of the exact problem is exceedingly difficult so Kleinrock took the bold step of approximating the queue as an M/M/1 system. This means that he assumed Poisson arrivals at a rate λ_i per second and exponential service times with a mean μ^{-1} seconds. It is difficult to justify such broad assumptions except by saying that they work and are known to produce reasonably accurate results. Quite complex models of node behaviour have been tested by simulation and shown to give mean delays close to those predicted by the simplified queuing theory. The well-known result for the average delay of this simple queue is

$$T_i = 1/(\mu C_i - \lambda_i)$$

Substituting this formula in the equation for T produces the average delay, which we need to minimise, as a function of capacities which are variables in the following form

$$T = \sum_{i=1}^{b} \frac{\lambda_i}{\gamma} \left[\frac{1}{\mu C_i - \lambda_i} \right]$$

In this equation two significant contributions have been ignored, the processing time for the packet in the node and the propagation delay. We have also ignored the traffic in acknowledgements and other non-productive packets. These factors can be included in a more accurate formulation.

The calculation of the minimum for T and the corresponding values of capacity is done by Lagrange's method of undetermined multipliers and it gives equations which have a simple interpretation. We first note that a certain minimum capacity is needed for each channel to carry the given traffic. This capacity is λ_i/μ. If only this minimum capacity was provided the queues would become infinite. This represents the point of saturation so the real question is by how much the minimum capacity should be exceeded.

It is also possible to calculate the cost of providing this minimum capacity on all lines, and unless the available money exceeds this value there will be no useful solution. The capacity assignment which results from the equation is

$$C_i = \frac{\lambda_i}{\mu} + k\sqrt{\lambda_i d_i}$$

In this equation, the first term represents the minimum capacity to carry the traffic and the second term is proportional to the square root of the flow. The constant k is proportional to the money which is left over after the bare capacities have been paid for. What the equation states is that the excess capacity (above the bare minimum) should be proportional to the square root of the flow in the line. A symmetric flow gives equal capacities to each of the two channels of a line. Having made this 'square root capacity assignment' the delay which results proves to be inversely proportional to the money which remains after the bare capacity has been paid for.

Thus the capacity assignment problem yields an explicit analytic solution after we have made a number of broad assumptions to simplify the problem.

The Flow or Routing Assignment Problem

The second of the two sub-problems assumes that the capacities of the lines in the network are given and an optimum flow pattern must be found. Now the traffic requirement matrix becomes important and we are concerned with exploring all the possible flow patterns which are consistent with this matrix. Cost is no longer significant because this was related to the line capacities which are now fixed. We use the same expression as before for the individual channel delays T_i but now it is the individual flows λ_i which are variable.

First we must describe the flow pattern and the constraints which it satisfies. The flow in each channel, λ_i, comprises packets with a variety of sources and destinations. Since the traffic requirement shows what traffic must pass from each source s to each terminal t, we have to find a flow pattern, throughout the whole network, for each of the (s,t) types of packet. Therefore for each channel we need the individual flows $f(s,t,i)$ and the sum of these over all s and t in the network is the total channel flow λ_i. We call this three-dimensional array of f values a 'flow' and denote it $\mathbf{f}$. Note that the variables s and t range over all nodes and the variable i ranges over all channels in the network. All the f values are non-negative.

The flow $\mathbf{f}$ satisfies two kinds of constraint. One is due to the requirement matrix and the other due to the capacities. Equations can be written for each node giving the conservation of each class of packets. For each node there is an equation for each value of s and t which equates to zero the net inflow derived from the incoming and outgoing packets of each line, together with packets coming into the network or leaving the network at that node. These are linear constraints.

For each direction of each line there is a capacity constraint. Since the delays increase without bound as flows approach the line capacity it turns out that these inequalities are unnecessary. The mere fact that a weighted average of the T is being minimised ensures that the capacity constraints will be obeyed.

If we are given two flows $\mathbf{f}_1$ and $\mathbf{f}_2$ which satisfy the various constraints a third flow can be calculated which also satisfies the constraints, namely

$$\alpha f_1 + (1 - \alpha)f_2 \quad \text{where} \quad 0 \leqslant \alpha \leqslant 1$$

Geometrically, this new flow lies on the line segment joining the two given flows. The feasible flows therefore form a convex set and we might consider what the *extreme* flows of this set could be.

Suppose we associate with each channel in the network a positive *weight* and for each (s,t) flow we find a path which minimises the sum of the weights. This is a well-known routing problem with many methods of solution.[10] A minimum weight routing would place all the (s,t) flow on this best path. For the flow as a whole in our network we can define a minimum weight routing as one in which each (s,t) flow takes the best path for a particular assignment of weights. Although the weights can vary continuously there will be a finite number of such flows. They are a sub-class of the unbifurcated or fixed routing flows in which each (s,t) commodity goes by a single path.

It can be proved that the extremes of the feasible flows are the flows which correspond to some minimum weight routing.

The method we shall outline for minimising T in this flow space is known as the 'flow deviation' method.[11] This starts with a feasible flow, finds, from local derivatives, the best direction for a flow deviation to reduce T and then finds the amount of deviation which gives the smallest T. The process is then repeated until the change at each step is sufficiently small that it is near enough to the optimum. It can be shown that this problem has no local optima so the one found is a true global optimum. Figure 10.12 illustrates the method, but a two-dimensional plot of the space of feasible flows is, of course, oversimplified. The polygon represents the constraints on the flow. The vertices are the extreme flows, each corresponding to a minimum weight routing.

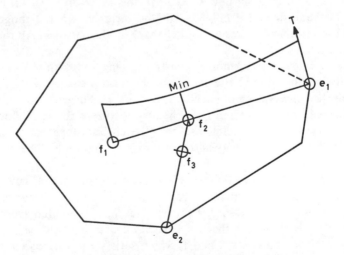

Figure 10.12   Schematic of the flow deviation algorithm

The key to the deviation method is the way in which the 'direction' of flow deviation is found. This is done by associating with each channel a quantity

$$\frac{\partial T}{\partial \lambda_i} = \frac{\mu C_i}{\gamma(\mu C_i - \lambda_i)^2}$$

which can be described as its 'weight'. This represents the effect on mean total delay of a small change in the flow in the channel. It is, in effect, its 'resistance' to a flow addition. Then we find one of the extreme flows which obeys minimum weight routing for this selection of weights. This flow deviation is denoted e in what follows. In the figure, f_1 is the starting flow and e_1 the flow deviation derived from it. The amount of deviation is still undecided so the next step is to examine all the flows on the line segment:

$$\alpha f_1 + (1 - \alpha)e_1 \quad \text{where} \quad 0 \leqslant \alpha \leqslant 1$$

The flow on this line which minimises T is the best value that can be obtained in one stage of flow deviation. f_2 is the result of the first cycle of the algorithm. The partial derivatives of T with respect to channel flows are recalculated from the new starting point and a second flow deviation is made. The process continues until the change in T is small enough that no further improvement is expected.

A symmetric flow will remain symmetric because the weights are equal for the two channels of a line. This requires a symmetric requirement matrix.

There remains the problem of finding a feasible flow with which to start the process. Because of the requirement matrix conditions and the capacity constraints this may not be easy. The method recommended is to use the weights which the flow deviation method would give for zero flows and thus produce a minimum weight flow. If this satisfies the capacity constraints, by pure luck we have a feasible flow. If not, the flow requirement matrix is proportionately reduced so that no individual flow exceeds the capacity of the line. This is a feasible flow, but too small to solve the problem for the actual requirement matrix. Next, the flow deviation algorithm is applied to minimise T with the reduced traffic requirement matrix. Now the requirement matrix multiplier is adjusted again to give the highest flow within the capacity constraints.

This succession of flow deviation and total flow adjustment will produce a feasible flow with the correct requirement matrix if there is such a flow, otherwise the attempt must be abandoned. The detailed algorithms and the criterion for giving up the quest for a feasible flow are given in references 8 and 9.

The flow deviation method gives the optimum flow and, in a sense, this is also a routing assignment because the quantity of (s,t) flow in each line is determined. It does not follow that such a routing method could be achieved in any practical algorithm because routing is normally based on local knowledge. Flow deviaton produces a solution based on an overall view of the network. Nevertheless, there is a routing method due to Gallager[12] which uses the same principle for changing flow assignments using a separate calculation at each node. Gallager's method has not been tried in practice but, if conditions remain constant for long enough, it should arrive at a global optimum.

Flow Assignment with Fixed Routing

The result of applying the flow deviation method is to produce an optimum flow pattern in which the flow from a particular source to a particular destination is in general divided among many paths. This is the kind of routing described in Chapter 3 as *bifurcated*. If the flow from source s to destination t could be routed independently of all the other flows it would take a minimum weight path with a certain weighting and this would be a single path, not a bifurcated one. The reason for bifurcation in the optimum routing given by the flow deviation algorithm is that all the flows interact.

If the network is large the number of (s,t) flows to be routed is large and the effect on other flows of rerouting just one (s,t) flow should be small. We might expect that the optimum flow pattern would approximate to a non-bifurcated, that is to say fixed-routing, flow. It is found in practice that a flow pattern with fixed routing can be found which is very close to the true optimum.

This method of routing, though less than optimal, is easier to compute. The conditions for applying it are usually described as 'a large and balanced network'. 'Large' is a vague term, but the method has been applied successfully to a 20-node network. 'Balanced' refers to the traffic requirement matrix and means that the elements of this matrix are not widely different in magnitude. Reference 8 gives a more quantitative expression of the condition 'large and balanced'. For such networks, the method of calculation is again to start from a feasible flow and improve it (reducing T) until no further significant improvement is possible. At each stage, a weight is associated with each channel using the same partial derivative as in the regular flow deviation method. Each (s,t) flow is then rerouted along the minimum weight path if this change produces a feasible flow and also reduces T. When all the (s,t) flows that can be relocated have been, there is a new flow pattern for which the weight associated with each channel is recalculated and the rerouting of flows begins again. The process terminates when no individual flows can be rerouted.

The Capacity and Flow Assignment Problem

In the earlier sections we have described the minimisation of T by choosing capacities with a given flow and by choosing the flow with given capacities. In the first of these problems there was a cost constraint in which the cost of each link was proportional to its capacity. We treated these as sub-problems leading to the solution of the capacity and flow assignment problem. This can be expressed as the minimisation of $T(\mathbf{f},\mathbf{C})$. The bold letters for flow and capacity signify that these each represent many variables.

Since the capacity assignment problem has been solved explicitly we can substitute the values of capacities giving minimum T into this expression which then becomes a function of flow alone $T(\mathbf{f})$ and we have, apparently, a problem of the same form as the flow assignment problem. One difference is that the additional constraint is no longer a capacity constraint but a cost constraint. The effect is very similar. If flows increase so that the capacities they require can only just be afforded within the cost constraint, the average packet delay T will increase. So the cost constraint is the same kind of 'penalty function' as the capacity constraint was for the flow assignment problem. In this problem also the feasible flows form a convex set.

There is, however, a very important difference between this problem and the earlier flow optimisation which had a global optimum that could be found by any reasonable step-by-step optimisation method. In this new problem, if the standard flow deviation method is applied, the change of flow pattern is complete, that is to say, the local optimum is entirely the flow deviation, which is one of the extremes of the feasible flows. We therefore have a situation very much like the case of fixed routing described in the previous section. Each time that flow deviation is applied the change will be from one fixed routing to another until a decrease of T is no longer possible.

A further consequence of the properties of $T(\mathbf{f})$ is that the optimum found by flow deviation is only a local optimum. A *heuristic* approach is needed to obtain a reasonably good solution of the problem.

Figure 10.13 attempts to illustrate the new situation. Successive flows and their corresponding T values are illustrated by the points 1, 2, 3. In the flow plane these are extreme values. They yield a minimum, but there may be other

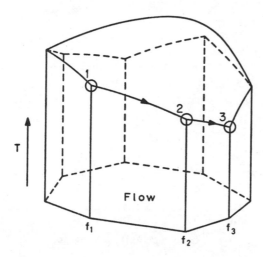

Figure 10.13   Capacity and flow assignment

local minima. In fact, there are very large numbers of minimum-weight flows which give local minima. The figure cannot adequately show the multi-dimensional picture.

The heuristic method is to explore as large a part of the space as is practicable in the hope of finding a local minimum which is reasonably close to the optimum. The technique proposed is as follows. First, a random set of weights is associated with the channels of the network and the minimum-weight flow is determined. If the cost of carrying this flow is less than the money available, the flow is feasible and the flow deviation method is applied by calculating the partial derivatives as the new weights, rerouting, testing for feasibility and so forth. In this way a local optimum is found. On the other hand, if the flow obtained from the random weights is not feasible, it is abandoned and another set of random weights is tried. The process is repeated until a sufficient number of suboptimal T values is obtained and the smallest of these, together with its flow and capacity assignments, is taken as the best available solution. With a large number of trials, it would be reasonable to expect that the result is close to the true optimum. Flow deviation is found to be a practical method for flow and capacity assignment.

Concave Branch Elimination

We have described how the flow deviation method is applied to the capacity and flow assignment problem when the cost of a line is proportional to its capacity. In this method, the flows are routed with weights which represent the incremental delay due to increasing flow in each channel. If the flow in a channel becomes small the capacity is also small and the incremental cost of adding

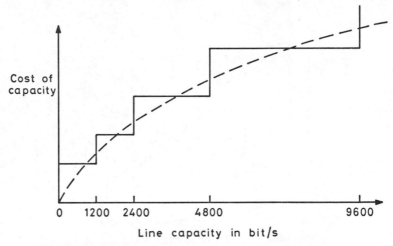

Figure 10.14   Concave approximation to cost–capacity function

extra flow begins to increase. The effect of this is to decrease the flow still further. Channels which get into this condition tend to have flow components taken away from them during the iteration of the algorithm. A channel with zero flow has an infinite weight and will not be used again. Assuming that we work with a symmetric traffic requirement matrix and with symmetric flows, the two channels of a line will reach zero flow together. For practical purposes, parh lines are eliminated.

This suggests a method of topological design[13] in which, starting with a rather well-connected network, the flow deviation method is applied and when the best solution has been obtained only the lines with non-zero flow are retained. These lines form the chosen topology.

The same property of eliminating lines is experienced whenever cost is a concave function of the capacity of a line. In the real world there is a finite set of line capacities and costs giving a stepped curve such as the one shown in Figure 10.14. By replacing this, for the analysis, by a concave function the capacity and flow assignment method can be applied to eliminate lines from a rather full topology. This is known as the 'concave branch elimination' method for topology design. A comparison with other methods[9] shows that it produces reasonable optima but, according to the cost–capacity function assumed, it produces very different topologies. The connectivity requirement will stop the concave branch elimination before too many lines are removed. For practical purposes the tendency of this method to give an unexpectedly wide range of topologies has been considered a disadvantage and the heuristic methods now to be described are generally favoured.

10.5 TOPOLOGY OPTIMISATION

Methods for topology optimisation are essentially heuristic methods for discovering a good topology. In principle, topology is related to capacity assignment because the absence of a direct link between two nodes can be interpreted as a line with zero capacity in each direction. This is how concave branch elimination works. Many of the successful heuristics for topology optimisation explore a large number of topologies, testing each topology in two ways. Firstly, it must meet the criterion for connectivity. Secondly, it must allow for a flow and capacity assignment which gives a high throughput, a small average delay or a small line cost, whichever of these variables is being used for minimisation. Some of the topology optimisation methods set an upper limit on the average delay and then, for each candidate topology, increase the flow until this delay is reached, recording both the flow achieved and the cost for that topology. The results can be plotted as a scatter diagram in a plot of throughput against line cost so that the network operators can make a choice of how much they wish to pay or what throughput they need.

In order to make the throughput into a variable, a traffic requirement is chosen which is representative of the traffic expected in the network and the flow parameter is used as a multiplier for all the elements in the matrix. Earlier investigations[14] explored the topology by a method designed to avoid changes to connectivity as far as possible.

Branch Exchange

A topology created by some random process is unlikely to be satisfactory and will probably not meet the connectivity criterion. When we have a topology which does meet the criterion we would like to make local changes to improve its performance and choose these in a way which is least likely to upset the connectivity. The connectivity is a property of the whole network and the most we are able to do is to choose nodes with a sufficient number of lines joined to them (degree) and make changes to the network which do not disturb the degree of any node. This is the essence of branch exchange.

Two lines or branches in the network are chosen which connect four separate nodes and they are replaced by two different lines, still connecting the four nodes in pairs. Figure 10.15 shows an example in which the nodes labelled A, B, C, D are affected and their initial connection A–B, C–D is altered by branch exchange to A–C, B–D. This is an example of a local change which will alter the performance. If it improves it the change can be adopted and then a new set of nodes and lines is chosen for testing out another branch exchange.

Figure 10.16 shows the way in which network topologies can be explored and a set of local optima collected.

The first stage of the procedure employs random numbers to generate a topology and thus ensures that a wide range of initial topologies will be tested. For example, different numbers can be associated with each node and then, by starting with the smallest numbered node and joining to the next smallest, lines can be introduced one by one. Lines are introduced so as always to join the nodes which have lowest degree. In this way, the degrees of all the nodes become 1 before nodes of degree 2 will occur. In an attempt to generate a topology with

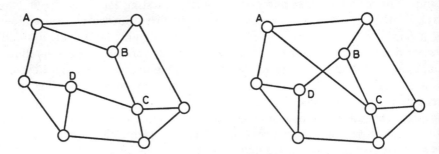

Figure 10.15   Example of branch exchange

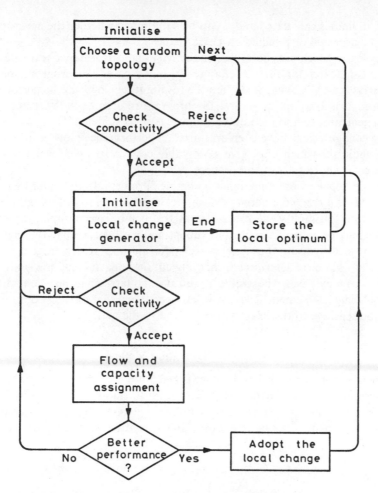

Figure 10.16   Heuristic method for topology optimisation

connectivity *n*, lines can be accumulated until the degree of all the nodes is at least *n*.

Degree *n* at all nodes is necessary for connectivity *n* but not sufficient. The next step is to test the connectivity and either accept or reject the candidate topology. Accepted topologies go forward to the heuristic optimisation procedure. This consists of local changes which can be generated systematically, for example by branch exchange. After each local change the connectivity is again tested and the change will be rejected if the connectivity test fails.

The main part of the procedure takes the candidate topology and goes through a flow and capacity assignment, then (following the strategy suggested above) traffic is increased until the delay criterion becomes critical. At this point the cost of lines is calculated and it can be determined whether the new topology should be accepted or rejected on performance grounds.

Topologies which pass both the connectivity and performance tests are taken back as candidates for further change. In many cases the program for local changes is eventually exhausted, then the resultant topology and its performance are stored as a local optimum and the program returns to the starting configuration generator to find the new candidate. After a sufficient time, when many starting configurations have been optimised, a performance plot for all the local optima indicates which ones give acceptable cost and traffic-level values and these are the end results of the process.

Clearly, topology optimisation is a complex problem. In the inner loop of the figure we find a complete network design calculation. Many investigators have been obliged to simplify the procedure at this point. For example, the routing of traffic may be done by simple and suboptimal methods. Capacity assignment can be avoided by using the same capacity for all links at this stage and, when the topology has been determined, carrying out the capacity and flow assignment proper. In many cases, the traffic requirement matrix has been chosen with equal off-diagonal elements because it has been found that topology optimisation is not too sensitive to the exact nature of the traffic matrix.

The Cutset Saturation Method

It will be remembered that a cutset is a set of nodes and lines which, if they are removed from the network, will disconnect it. Suppose that the traffic in a network is gradually increased until it can carry no more. Because of the routing or flow assignment which is employed, flows are diverted to alternative routes

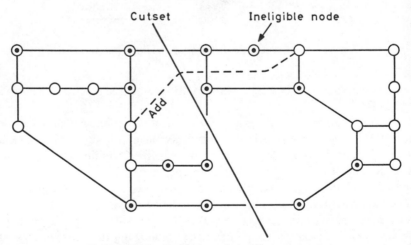

Figure 10.17   Operation of the distance 2 rule

until a cutset of nearly saturated lines appears in the network and, at this point, there are individual flows which cannot be increased without excessive delay. The cutset now revealed is a weakness of the topology and it can be helped by a new line joining a pair of nodes, one on each side of the cutset.

Clearly, the routing or flow assignment algorithm is critical to the cutset method. The flow deviation algorithm is used because it gives a true optimum flow. Saturated links are inconvenient so the flow is increased until the network shows a cutset of highly utilised lines. Utilisation in the region of 80–90 per cent is a suitable figure. Enumerating the lines in order of decreasing utilisation, starting with the highest, will indicate the component lines of the cutset.

We now have to make a choice of the line which is to be added across the cutset. If the lowest cost line is chosen this will usually join nodes that were already adjacent to the cutset. In practice, this is found to shift the cutset slightly without greatly improving the network's performance. An ad hoc criterion called 'distance 2' has been found to work better. This requires the two nodes joined by the new line to be at least two hops away from the nodes adjacent to the cutset. Figure 10.17 shows an example with the set of nodes which may be joined to relieve a particular cutset. The distance between the newly connected nodes was thus at least five hops before the new line (shown broken) was introduced.

As we have described it, the cutset saturation method will augment a sparse topology but must quickly terminate because it increases both cost and performance. Optimum topologies are more likely to be discovered if lines can also be deleted. For example, suppose that there is a given traffic requirement for the network. Lines can be added by the cutset saturation method until the throughput exceeds the requirement, then a poorly used line or lines removed until the requirement is no longer met. Each line deletion must be tested against the connectivity constraint. A recent discussion of topological optimisation for large networks[15] describes the criterion, based on cost and utilisation, for the choice of lines to remove. A comparison shows that the cutset saturation method gives consistently better solutions.

A network designer can usually make modifications to network topology that are more consistently optimal than those given by any simple program. For this reason, a powerful combination is the use of a cutset saturation technique with occasional interventions by a designer to make changes which are apparent to his intuition.

10.6 HIERARCHICAL AND MIXED-MEDIA NETWORKS

The published work on network optimisation mainly deals with networks of uniform structure such as a mesh or tree. Large networks, as we have seen in Chapter 3, can be made more economically in a hierarchical structure where each level of the hierarchy is designed as a network with its own topological rules. The principal economic reasons for hierarchical networks are that they allow traffic to be concentrated on main routes where economies of scale can be exploited and that they reduce the number of hops so that transit delay is reduced and less switching capacity is employed. These reasons for building hierarchical networks imply that the topological constraints are very important and that routing rules are an essential feature of their design.

Mixed-media networks have the same motivation. They can use different switching, multiplexing and concentration techniques at different levels of the hierarchy and different transmission media which are appropriate to the concentration and statistics of traffic. For example, at a high level in a hierarchy, according to the routing method employed, the traffic may be either more or less fluctuating than elsewhere, so the type of switching and concentration can be chosen accordingly.

Figure 10.18 shows an example of a mixed-media network designed with particular topological constraints. The locations shown are based roughly on large cities of the USA. Its terrestrial network is two-connected and at five of its nodes there are satellite ground stations which, with the satellite itself, form the high level network.

The diameter of the terrestrial network is 7 but when the satellite connections are added each node is within three hops of any other. This is because no node is distant more than one hop from a satellite ground station. At worst, a terrestrial – satellite – terrestrial route will reach the destination in three hops.

To take account of the possibility of terrestrial line failures or outage of ground stations, there is in this network a useful alternative routing property that each node has a second route to a different ground station with at most two hops. Perhaps the biggest factor in this network's availability is the possibility

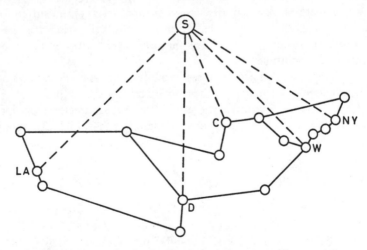

Figure 10.18　Topological features of a two-media network

of failure of the satellite repeater, but without failure statistics for all the network components we cannot go further in an analysis of availability.

The routing rules in such a network will depend on how the satellite system is employed. This in turn will be influenced by whether the chief requirement is good throughput or reduced transit delay. With an ALOHA-type satellite system, for example, the MASTER philosophy might be employed in which retransmission after collision is always through the surface network, but this will make poor use of the surface network under light load and all packets will then suffer the satellite delay. If routing by minimum delay is employed a light load will use the terrestrial network. The satellite system will take the overflow after transit delay builds up. There is perhaps a strong case for priority classes in networks of this kind where the lower cost of satellite transmission for long distances is counterbalanced by increased transit delay.

If a network design has topological constraints as strong as the one we have described (distance 1 to ground stations and an alternative ground station no greater than distance 2) then the available topologies are very restricted and it seems likely that a reasonably good topology can be arrived at by trial and error. A critical element of cost will be the number of satellite ground stations. The best balancing of this cost against the greater line cost for fewer stations can be obtained by designing networks with a smaller and greater number of stations.

Optimisation of Hierarchical and Mixed-media Networks

There is not yet a large literature on optimisation of these more complex networks, but the paper by Boorstyn and Frank[15] contains a useful discussion. We would like to reduce the total problem to sub-problems that we can manage, such as the optimisation of the individual networks at each level of the hierarchical system. This can be done if all the points of contact between these levels are previously specified.

For example, consider a hierarchical network comprising a 'backbone network' which has mesh topology and local distribution networks which have a tree topology. Very often the location of the backbone nodes is almost fixed by the way that the terminals are clustered. Towns and conurbations tend to dictate the way in which nodes are placed to pick up the traffic economically. If we can fix these nodes the design of the backbone network becomes a problem we have already studied and the design of the access tree networks is like the design of the early kind of computer centred network. The location of the node within its service area can be treated as part of the local optimisation problem if its effect on the cost of the backbone network is small.

Given that the availability, throughput and transit time problems are mainly associated with the backbone network, then the main way in which these two separate optimisation problems interact is the need to make a choice of the number and location of nodes—the points where the two networks meet. Clearly, adding an extra node will cost money and how much depends in a complex way on the backbone network design. To simplify the problem we can introduce a marginal cost per node and then forget the backbone network and treat the optimisation problem for the access networks, minimising the total cost of lines and concentrators and treating the node merely as a standard incremental cost.

This kind of problem has been treated in the operational research literature as the 'warehouse' problem. The nodes represent factories, the concentrators represent warehouses and the terminals represent customers. As we would expect, the methods of solution are heuristic.

Figure 10.19 shows another kind of mixed-media network which results in the same optimisation problem as the one we have just described. The design of the Satellite Business Systems network presented this kind of optimisation problem. Here, the nodes of the 'backbone' network are satellite ground stations, the satellite cost is fixed and the local distribution networks have the tree structure we have been discussing. If the clustering is fairly obvious, as in the figure, the problem resolves into a number of separate tree network designs. But since the cost of the ground station is important, designs with different numbers of ground stations must be compared. In the work done on the Satellite Business Systems network each possibility from two stations to a station at each terminal was separately optimised. There proved in this case to be a broad optimum which gave considerable flexibility in choosing how many stations should be employed.

Heuristic methods for the clustering problem have been proposed[16] for use when the terminal locations do not naturally form clusters. The technique is to join the closest pairs of terminals into clusters and represent each cluster as it is formed by its centre of mass and the associated number of terminals this represents.

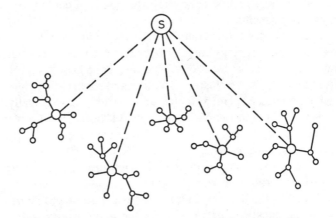

Figure 10.19   Satellite system with local access networks

Having begun by associating single terminals to form clusters, the algorithm continues to associate the closest units, whether they are terminals or clusters, until each cluster reaches its maximum size and can no longer be merged with other terminals or clusters. It may be necessary to introduce an arbitrary rule to prevent the joining of clusters which are too far apart, otherwise the remaining undersized clusters would eventually join at great distances.

The location of the node within a cluster is usually a matter of choosing one of the terminal sites as the concentrator location. Since the centre of mass of the cluster is known, it is sufficient to investigate the nearby terminal sites and determine which gives the lowest line costs.

An alternative form of local network has its terminals joined either to a concentrator or to the main node. There is a limit on terminals per concentrator and terminals per node. For this problem the clustering method is used first to form concentrator groupings and then to form the groupings of concentrators and loose terminals which are associated with nodes. Each terminal must also be examined to see if it would be more economically connected directly to the node. A suitable series of operations for these tree networks is (1) form clusters for concentrators, (2) form clusters for nodes, (3) locate concentrators and nodes, (4) reconsider allocations of terminals and (5) adjust concentrator and node locations.

There are many variations of this type of optimisation. For example, in some designs the terminals are joined by multi-drop lines with a limit to the number of terminals per line and then the multi-drop lines connect to controllers with a limit on the number of lines per controller. These applications are discussed in the paper by McGregor and Shen[16] which also gives references to the literature on the 'access facility location problem'.

One of the sub-problems in this kind of optimisation is to allocate terminals to a set of concentrators when the number of terminals per concentrator is limited. This is illustrated in Figure 10.20. The calculations described here are performed with a matrix giving the distances between all the terminals and all the concentrators but it is easier to see what it means in practice by looking at an actual terminal layout. Here, the terminals are shown by small circles and the concentrators are labelled 1–4. In this example, there can be no more than four terminals per concentrator.

The first stage of the algorithm is to examine each terminal in turn and associate it with the nearest concentrator. When the nearest concentrator has its full complement of terminals the terminal being examined is left, for the moment, unattached. Let us suppose that the sequence in which the terminals in the figure were examined has been such that terminals A and B are still unconnected. The full lines in the figure show the first association that has been made of all the other terminals to concentrators.

At the next stage we consider each of the unattached terminals in turn and look at the possibilities for attaching them. In the case of terminal A the first

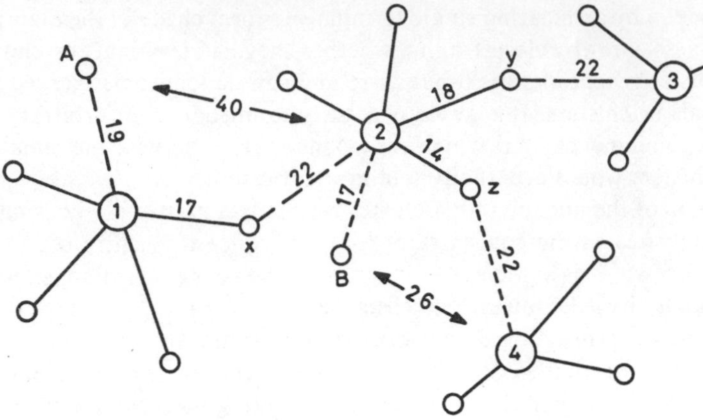

Figure 10.20   Terminal allocation to concentrators

option is to connect it to the nearest concentrator, number 1, for which the line cost (proportional in this case to distance) is 19. As a consequence, one of the existing terminals of concentrator 1 must be 'bumped' and each is considered in turn. The one with the least cost proves to be terminal x and this is connected to concentrator 2, its next nearest concentrator at a net cost of $22 - 17$, the difference of the new line cost and the saving on the line relinquished. Concentrator 2 now has a problem and, of all the terminals which it might bump, y and z prove to be the cheapest. They incur costs of $22 - 18$ and $22 - 14$ respectively. Clearly y will be preferred. Now we have the net cost of this option which is $19 - 17 + 22 - 18 + 22 = 28$. In the complete algorithm this is compared with all the other possibilities, not just the obvious ones which we have selected. For example, one of these is to connect A directly to concentrator 2 which, with the consequent bumping of y to concentrator 3 produces a total cost of 44.

Having dealt with terminal A the next unattached terminal B is treated and for this there are two possibilities, connection to concentrator 2 and bumping of z with a net cost of $17 - 14 + 22$ and direct connection of terminal B to concentrator 4 which has a greater net cost of 26. Proceeding in this way, all the unattached terminals are connected. The consideration of all the possibilities of bumping and reconnection, not only those which are obvious in the figure, produces many more possibilities but the final result is known to be optimal.

The approaches to mixed media and hierarchical networks which we have described are the result of separating the problems of each level. At best the cost of other levels are reflected in the optimisation in a very approximate way, such as a cost per node. For the simplest examples, such as the satellite network with local access trees, there is a reliable approach in which the optimisation is repeated for each choice of number of stations. The more general optimisation methods do not seem to extend easily to mixed media.

One of the more comprehensive investigations of these networks has been by Maruyama who was able to extend to mixed media a capacity assignment method[17] which allowed for discrete values of link capacity. He elaborated his methods successively to deal with packets in different priority classes and to handle capacity and flow assignment. Applied to mixed-media networks,[18] these calculations were made with a given topology. The networks treated have a satellite 'backbone' and a terrestrial part which can either be connected or a set of local networks. The satellite channels are dedicated to each link, with no contention, but Maruyama believes that once a delay model is available it could take multi-access satellite systems into account. As it is described, the existence of two communication media is represented by using a different set of link capacity options.

In order to approach the topology problem, the 'capacity priority flow assignment' algorithm was run with interaction by the user to delete or add lines, using as a guide the poorly utilised links (delete) or flows with a high average path length (add). The user was able to apply the kind of topological constraint we discussed in connection with Figure 10.18. In this way a 20-node network was optimised with five different kinds of connectivity requirement, three of them with a satellite portion. For many practical problems this man–machine method could be effective, while the problem of devising algorithms or heuristics to optimise mixed-media networks unaided remains a challenge to network designers. The same author has shown[19] how to apply more complex topological constraints in the interest of network reliability, retaining the ability for human interaction during the optimisation.

References

1. Berge, C.,
   The theory of graphs and its applications,
   Wiley, New York (1962).
2. Harary, F.,
   Graph theory,
   Addison Wesley, Reading, Mass. (1969).
3. Ford, F. R. and Fulkerson, D. R.,
   Flows in networks,
   Princeton University Press, Princeton, N.J. (1962).
4. Whitney, H.,
   'Congruent graphs and the connectivity of graphs',
   Amer. J. Maths., **54**, 150 (1932).
5. Kleitman, D. J.,
   'Methods for investigating connectivity of large graphs',
   IEEE Trans. Circuit Theory, **CT-16**, 232 (1969).
6. Rosenthal, A.,
   'Computing the reliability of complex networks',
   SIAM Journ. of Applied Maths., **32**, 384 (1977).

7. Kleinrock, L.,
   Communication nets, stochastic message flow and delay,
   McGraw-Hill, New York (1964), and Dover, New York (1972).
8. Kleinrock, L.,
   Queuing systems, Volume 2: Computer applications, Wiley, New York (1976).
9. Gerla, M., and Kleinrock, L.,
   'On the topological design of distributed computer networks',
   IEEE Trans. on Communications, **COM-25**, 48 (Jan. 1977).
10. Floyd, R.,
    'Algorithm 97, Shortest path',
    Comm. ACM, **5**, 345 (1962).
11. Fratta, L., Gerla, M., and Kleinrock, L.,
    'The flow deviation method: an approach to store and forward communication network design',
    Networks, **3**, 97 (1973).
12. Gallager, R. G.,
    'A minimum delay routing algorithm using distributed computation',
    IEEE Trans. on Communications, **COM-25**, 73 (Jan. 1977).
13. Yaged, B.,
    'Minimum cost routing for static network models',
    Networks, **1**, 139 (1971).
14. Frank, H., Frisch, I. T., and Chou, W.,
    'Topological considerations in the design of the ARPA network',
    AFIPS Conf. Proceedings, **36**, 581 (May 1970).
15. Boorstyn, R. R., and Frank, H.,
    'Large scale network topological optimisaiton',
    IEEE Trans. on Communications, **COM-25**, 29 (Jan. 1977).
16. McGregor, P. V., and Shen, D.,
    'Network design: An algorithm for the access facility location problem',
    IEEE Trans. on Communications, **COM-25**, 61 (Jan. 1977).
17. Maruyama, K., and Tang, D. T.,
    'Discrete link capacity assignment in communication networks',
    Proceedings of ICCC, Toronto, 92 (Aug. 1976).
18. Maruyama, K.,
    'An optimisation algorithm for mixed media communication networks',
    Conf. Proceedings, Eurocomp 78, On-line (May 1978).
19. Maruyama, K.,
    'Designing reliable packet-switched communication networks',
    Proc. ICCC, Kyoto, (Sept. 1978).

Glossary

Adaptive Routing

A routing scheme for packets or messages in which the behaviour adapts to network changes such as line failures or variation of the traffic pattern. Various adaptive methods have been proposed, including isolated, distributed, centralised and delta routing (q.v.).

ALOHA

An experimental network operated by the University of Hawaii using packet broadcast techniques, the first of this kind.

Alphabet

An agreed set of characters used to represent data. The best-known standard alphabet is International Alphabet No. 5 (IA5) or CCITT or ISO 7-bit code.

Alternate Mode

This is a mode of using a virtual terminal by which each of two interacting systems or users has access to its data structure in turn. The associated protocols include facilities to allow the orderly transfer of control from one user to the other. This is in contrast to free running mode (q.v.).

Anisochronous Signal

A signal which is not related to any clock and in which transitions could occur at any instant.

ARPA

The Defence Advanced Research Projects Agency of the USA funds research in many fields. Its network project began in 1969 and produced one of the first large-scale packet-switched networks usually known as ARPANET. The switching nodes or IMPs (interface message processors) were augmented in 1970 by terminal IMPs or TIPs which connected simple terminals to the subnet.

This ARPA project promoted the development of network protocols beginning with the host–host protocol. Later developments were packet radio, the satellite IMP, packet voice and secure communication by cryptography. From the design of ARPANET, a public service (Telenet) and a military network (Autodin II) were derived.

Attention

In the context of the virtual terminal, the attention or interrupt facility allows a user operating in alternate mode (q.v.) to regain access to the virtual terminal data structure when it is under the control of a remote computer. The receipt of an attention signal is acknowledged by a mark (q.v.).

Authentication of Messages

Addition of a check field to a block of data so that any change to the data will be detected. A secret key enters into the calculation and is known to the intended receiver of the data. In a different form of authentication, the whole block is transformed and this can be a public key cryptosystem (q.v.).

Authentication of Users

Verification that the user at the terminal corresponds to his claimed identity. Authentication of a distant computer service may also be needed to prevent tricks of 'masquerading'.

Availability

The time for which a service is ready and fit for use, measured as a fraction of the scheduled time. It is one way to specify the effect of system faults for the user but there are other factors such as the distribution or mean duration of periods of failure.

Backwards Learning

A method of routing in which nodes learn the topology of the network by observing the packets passing through, noting their source and the distance they have travelled.

Baud

The unit of signalling speed. It is the number of signal elements per second. Since a signal element can represent more than one bit, baud rate is not the same as bits per second.

Block Chaining

A method of linking together a sequence of blocks for transmission with block encryption. The purpose is to hinder cryptanalysis based on the statistics of individual blocks.

Block Encryption

Encryption of a block of data or text as a unit. Successive blocks are transformed independently but dependency may then be introduced by block chaining.

Branch

In graph theory, all that directly links two vertices is a branch. It can therefore be directed or undirected but in most discussion of networks the undirected (two-way) branch is meant. A less usual meaning is to denote a two-terminal part of a network that is being treated as a single entity, for example in calculations of availability.

Buffer

A store, usually associated with a peripheral device or communication line, which accommodates differences or variation of data rate.

Byte

A small group of bits of data which is handled as a unit. In many cases it is an 8-bit byte and this is also called an octet.

Byte Multiplexing

In this form of time division multiplexing the bytes from different subchannels follow one another in successive time slots.

Capacity

An abbreviation of 'channel capacity' which is the rate at which data are carried on the channel, measured in bit/s.

CCITT

The initials of the name in French of the International Telegraph and Telephone Consultative Committee.. At CCITT, representatives of telecommunications authorities, operators of public networks and other interested bodies meet to agree those standards which are needed for international interworking of telecommunication services. The recommendations which result are published in the reports of the plenary meetings which take place at intervals of four years. There is a speeded-up procedure for deciding recommendations between plenaries. Data transmission over the telephone network is the subject of the V series recommendations and public data networks are the subject of the X series.

CCITT together with CCIR (radio) form the International Telecommunications Union which is responsible to the United Nations.

The results of the 1976 plenary are recorded in the 'Orange Book' published by the ITU, Geneva, 1977. It contains the agreed recommendations and also the set of 'questions' which form the agendas for the various study groups in the next period.

Centralised Adaptive Routing

A method of routing in which a network routing centre dictates routing decisions, based on information supplied to it by each node.

Channel

A path along which signals carrying data can be sent. Unless otherwise stated the term implies one-way communication whereas the word 'circuit' implies two-way communication.

Cipher

A form of cryptography depending only on the sequence of characters or bits. On the other hand, in a cryptographic *code*, meaningful words or phrases are the units that are encoded.

Ciphertext

Text or data which has been transformed by encipherment.

Circuit Switching

Switching as performed in the telephone network where communication is along a circuit established, for the purpose, from one subscriber to another, the circuit being held for the duration of the call. The alternatives are message switching and packet switching.

Closed User Group

Members of a closed user group cannot receive calls from outside the group. Usually they can make calls only to each other but in the 'closed user group with outgoing access', calls to subscribers outside the group are allowed.

Cohesion

The cohesion of a connected network is the least number of lines which must be removed to separate the network into disconnected parts.

Combined Station

The station used in balanced HDLC procedures. A combined station generates commands and interprets responses received as a result. It also interprets commands received and generates responses.

Concentrator

A concentrator accepts traffic from a number of lines and places it on a common line. In the other direction it distributes traffic from the common line. There is not usually sufficient capacity in the common line to carry all the traffic that could be offered, hence a risk of congestion.

Congestion

The condition of a communication network beyond the limit of the traffic which it can readily handle, where there is a reduced quality of service and the network must restrict incoming traffic in order to remain effective.

Connectivity

The least number of nodes or lines which must be removed to separate the network into disconnected parts. This may be compared with cohesion, where only the removal of lines is considered.

Contention

A competition between parts of a system for use of a common resource. Examples are: contention for store access, contention of terminals for a port into a computer and contention for use of a radio channel.

Control Character

The alphabets used in communication may reserve certain characters for functional purposes rather than carrying data or text. These control characters may, for example, delimit or separate messages.

Control Signal

A signal within a communication network which is part of its control system. Examples are the messages which set up calls in a circuit-switched network and the internal flow control signals in a packet-switched network.

Cryptography

The technique of concealing the content of a message by means of a secret transformation which should be reversible only by the intended recipient(s).

Cutset

A set of elements of a connected graph (nodes, lines or both) which, when removed from the graph, separates it into disconnected parts. Cutsets are used to measure cohesion and connectivity (q.v.).

Data

Information expressed in a formalised way (usually in digital form) for processing, storage or transmission. The word 'information' is best reserved for the significance which the data have for people.

Data Circuit Terminating Equipment (DCE)

Term used to describe the postal administration's equipment at the end of a circuit and located on the customer's premises. The other side of the DCE connects to the data terminal equipment using a standard interface. An example is a modem on the telephone network using the V24 interface.

Data Encryption Standard (DES)

An algorithm defined for Civil Government applications of cryptography in USA. It is a 'Federal Information Processing Standard' and its definition is FIPS Publication 46.

Datagram

A packet which is transported by a network independently of other packets. A datagram service handles packets separately as compared with a virtual call service in which a call must first be established.

Data Rate

The rate at which a channel carries data, measured in bits per second (bit/s), known also as 'data signalling rate'. If there are restrictions on the pattern of bits, the information capacity of the channel could be less than the data rate.

Data Terminal Equipment (DTE)

The user's equipment which is joined to a data communication network. It might be anything from a simple terminal to a big computer system.

Degree

In the application of graph theory to networks, the degree of a node is the number of lines which connect to it.

Delay Vector

Associated with one node of a packet-switched network, the delay vector has as its elements the estimated transit times of packets starting there and destined for other nodes in the network. Nodes may send copies of their delay vector to their neighbours as part of an adaptive routing scheme.

Delta Modulation

A method of representing an analogue signal (generally a speech or video waveform) in which the 'one' bits represent increments of the signal. The increment's direction and size may vary according to the previous pattern of bits.

Delta Routing

A method of routing in which a central routing controller receives information from nodes and issues routing instructions, but leaves a degree of discretion to individual nodes.

Demand Multiplexing

A form of time division multiplexing in which the allocation of time to subchannels is made according to their need to carry data. A subchannel with no data to carry is given no time slot. Another name is 'dynamic multiplexing'.

Directory Routing

A way of routing packets or messages which uses a directory or routing table at each node which states, for each destination, the preferred outgoing line. The directory might also show a second preference.

Distributed Adaptive Routing

A method of routing in which the decisions are made on the basis of exchange of information between the nodes of a network.

Duplex Circuit

A circuit used for transmission in both directions at the same time. It may be called 'full duplex' to distinguish it from half duplex (q.v.).

Dynamic Multiplexing

See 'demand multiplexing'.

European Informatics Network (EIN)

A European project to facilitate research into networks and promote agreement on standards. Its first task was to construct a packet-switched subnet and this became operational in 1976. The five centres on the network are in London, Paris, Zurich, Milan and Ispra and there are also 'secondary centres' which join in the research on network protocols. The transport protocol of the EIN is the basis of the one adopted by IFIP Working Group 6.1.

Fixed Routing

A method of routing in which the behaviour is predetermined, taking no account of changes in traffic or of network component outages.

Flag

In 'high level data link control' (HDLC) procedure the sequence of eight bits (01111110) employed to determine the opening and closing of a frame.

Flooding

A packet routing method in which each node replicates incoming packets and sends copies to its neighbours, thus ensuring that the actual destination is reached quickly and with certainty, though with considerable use of transmission capacity.

Flow Control

The control of data flow to prevent overspill of queues or buffers or loss of data because the intended receiver is unable to accept it.

Four Wire Circuit

A telephone circuit carries voice signals both ways. In the local network this is achieved over two wires because the waveforms travelling each way can be distinguished. In the trunk network, where amplifiers are needed and multiplexing is used, it is necessary to separate the two directions of transmission physically. This is called a four wire circuit because, in its primitive form, it uses a pair of wires for each direction.

Frame

In time division multiplexing a frame is one complete cycle of events. The frame usually comprises a sequence of time slots, one for each subchannel, with some extra bits for framing, alarms and so forth. The word is also used for the transmission block used in the 'high level data link control' (HDLC) procedure.

Framing

The method, in time division multiplexing, by which individual frames are recognised so that the slots can be identified correctly.

Free Running Mode

This mode of using a virtual terminal allows two associated systems or users to have access to the data structures simultaneously. The possibility that conflict between them may cause difficulties must be taken account of by the users. This problem is avoided in alternate mode (q.v.).

Frequency Division Multiplexing

In this form of multiplexing for analogue signals each subchannel is shifted in frequency by modulation with a particular carrier so that it fits into its own section of the spectrum. The combined signals can be transmitted as a wide band signal and then separated by filtering and demodulation.

Gateway

The junction of two networks. It may look to each network like one of its own nodes; on the other hand a special purpose junction node may be specified.

Half Duplex Operation

The use of a circuit only in one direction at a time. The alternative word 'simplex' is best avoided because it is used in two different senses.

Handshaking

When each signal or operation across an interface is followed by a signal or operation in the other direction this is described as handshaking. Both sides of the interface can then control the rate of operation. Timing is easy but there is a risk of faulty operation causing a 'staredown' in which each side is waiting for the other.

Heuristic

A procedure which uses trial and error or random searching and therefore cannot be certain of its results. In contrast an algorithm is expected always to arrive at a correct or optimal result.

Hierarchical Network

A network in which the lines and nodes can be regarded as belonging to various levels. Each level has its own, characteristic connection pattern. For example the lowest level may be star-connected whereas higher levels are mesh-connected and the highest fully-connected. Terminals are generally connected at the lowest or near lowest levels.

High Level Data Link Control (HDLC) Procedure

A set of protocols defined by ISO for carrying data over a link with error and flow control. Versions of HDLC are also being developed for multi-point lines. In spite of its name HDLC is not a 'high level protocol'.

High Level Data Link Control (HDLC) Station

A process located at one end of the link which sends and receives HDLC frames in accordance with the HDLC procedures.

High Level Protocol

A protocol to allow network users to carry out functions at a higher level than merely transporting streams or blocks of data.

Host Computer

A computer attached to a communication network, usually but not exclusively to provide a network service.

Hot Potato Routing

Packet routing which sends a packet out from a node as soon as possible even though this may mean a poor choice of outgoing line when the preferred choices are not available.

IMP

An 'interface message processor', which is the name given to the switching node of the ARPA network.

Intelligent Terminal

A terminal containing a microprocessor and therefore able to emulate other terminals, validate data, implement protocols and so forth.

Interface

A boundary between two parts of a system across which the interaction is fully defined. The definition might include a type of connector, signal levels, impedances and timing, the allowable sequences of signals or messages and their meanings. By analogy we speak also of a software interface.

International Federation for Information Processing (IFIP)

A federation of professional and technical societies concerned with information processing. One society is admitted from each participating nation. IFIP has established a number of technical committees and these have formed working groups. The technical committee for data communication is TC 6 and was formed in 1971. Among its working groups is WG 6.1 which is also known as the International Network Working Group (q.v.). Working group WG 6.3 deals with human–computer communications.

International Network Working Group (INWG)

INWG was formed in 1972 to be a forum for discussion of network standards and protocols. In 1973 it was adopted as working group 1 of IFIP TC 6 with the title 'International Packet Switching for Computer Sharing'. It has about 100 members organised into four study groups. This working group distributes 'INWG Notes' to exchange ideas on protocols, on interworking and on network research generally.

Isarithmic Control

The control of flow in a packet-switched network in such a way that the total number of packets in transit is held below a certain limit.

Isolated Adaptive Routing

A method of routing in which the decisions are made solely on the basis of information available in each node.

Key

A parameter used in an encipherment process so that a very large number of different encipherments is available by choice of the key. In most encryption schemes the keys are kept secret since they allow the data or text to be read. This is not true of the public key cryptosystem (q.v.) where only the decipherment key is secret.

Leased Circuit

A telecommunication circuit hired by the user for his exclusive use. The circuit is ready for immediate use, without switching. It may be point-to-point or multipoint.

Liaison

A virtual connection (like a virtual circuit) which can be set up between two transport stations. A concept used in the end-to-end transport protocol defined by INWG.

Line Folding

This is necessary when a text message has a line longer than the maximum allowed by a printer. The excess characters are printed on the next line by generating a local new line signal. The appearance of the message is marred, but its sense is preserved.

Lock-up

An unwanted state of a system from which it cannot escape, such as a 'deadly embrace' in the claiming of common resources.

Logical Channel Number

The packet interface defined in CCITT recommendation X25 allows many virtual calls (or permanent virtual circuits) to use the interface together. Each virtual circuit is identified locally by its logical channel number.

Mark

In the context of the virtual terminal, a mark is a signal inserted into an output data stream by the virtual terminal, to acknowledge that an attention (q.v.) or interrupt input signal has been received.

Message

A block of text (or, by extension of the meaning, a block of data) which the user of a communication network wishes to have transported as a whole.

Message Switching

A method of operating a communication network in which messages are moved from node to node. The message switch at a node must be capable of storing a message but need not necessarily wait for the whole message to be received before starting the onward transmission.

Minimum Weight Routing

Each line in a network has a 'weight' associated with it. The route chosen is the one which minimises the sum of the weights of the lines it uses. For example, if the weights chosen are the transit delays associated with lines, we have minimum delay routing.

Modem

The device which (1) accepts a digital waveform and from it forms a signal suitable for transmission over an analogue channel such as a telephone circuit and (2) receives the analogue signal from a distant modem and converts it back to a digital form. The word is a contraction of 'modulator demodulator'.

Modulo 2 Addition

Binary addition without carries, such that $1 + 1 = 0$. Also known as the logical operation 'exclusive OR'.

Multi-access

The ability of a computer system to serve more than one user at the same time.

Multidrop Line

See 'multi-point line'.

Multiplexer

Equipment which takes a number of communication channels and combines the signals into one common channel (of greater data rate or bandwidth) for transmission. At the far end, a 'demultiplexer' extracts each of the original signals to separate the channels again.

Multi-point Line

A circuit which is connected by branching points to several terminals distributed along its length. Also known as a multi-drop line or way wire.

Negative Acknowledgement (NAK)

A control signal which reports that a data block with errors has been received. In a line control procedure this signal usually causes the block to be retransmitted.

Negotiation

When a connection is established between the virtual terminals in different systems, an initial dialogue is needed to establish the parameters that each will use during the transaction. This is known as the negotiation phase.

Network Termination Unit (NTU)

A network termination unit is an equipment forming part of a network. Typically it has a keyboard, to select (dial) calls, and lamps or a display to indicate call progress signals.

Node

A point in a network which is a junction of lines. The word is often used to refer to a switching centre in a packet-switched network.

Octet

A byte containing 8 bits.

One-way Function

A function which it is reasonably easy to calculate but for which the inverse is so difficult to compute that, for all practical purposes, it cannot be done.

Packet

A block of data handled by a network in a well-defined format including a header and having a maximum size of data field. Consequently, a message may have to be carried as several packets.

Packet Assembler and Disassembler (PAD)

That part of a packet-switched network which performs the conversion between packets and a character stream suitable for a simple terminal.

Packet Interleaving

A form of multiplexing in which packets from various subchannels are interleaved on the line. The X25 interface is an example.

Packet Radio

Packet switching in which the transmission paths are radio links and a transmitted packet may be picked up by more than one station. May be used with mobile stations.

Parity

The property of being odd or even. The parity count of a binary sequence is the parity of the number of ones it contains. This is also the sum, modulo 2, of the bits in the sequence.

Permanent Virtual Circuit

A virtual circuit which is established for a period by agreement between the two subscribers and the communication network operator. It is the equivalent, for a packet network, of a leased circuit.

Plaintext

In the context of cryptography, messages in their normal, readable form are called plaintext.

Polling

Inviting a station to transmit data. When several stations are connected to one circuit, polling from the centre is used to ensure an orderly flow of data to the centre.

Primary Group

The multiplexing of a large number of channels (for example telephone channels) is carried out by stages. The basic signals are first multiplexed into a primary group then a set of primary groups is multiplexed, and so forth. In the frequency division multiplexing of 4 kHz speech channels the primary group contains 12 channels and occupies 48 kHz. The primary group of PCM channels contains either 24 or 30 speech channels and uses approximately 1.5 or 2.0 Mbit/s of channel capacity, respectively.

Primary Station

In HDLC the primary station controls the operation of the link level procedure by generating commands and interpreting responses. Unbalanced classes of procedure are defined in terms of one primary controlling one or more secondary stations.

Private Wire

See 'leased circuit'.

Protocol

A strictly defined procedure for interaction across an interface or through a communication facility.

Public Key Cryptosystem

A method of cryptography which uses two matching keys. One is kept secret and held by the receiver of data. The other can be made public so that anyone can send data securely to the holder of the secret key.

Pulse Code Modulation (PCM)

Representation of an analogue signal by sampling at a regular rate and converting each sample to a binary number. Applied to telephony the sampling rate is 8000 per second.

Qualifier (or Qualifying Bit)

A one-bit field which modifies the use of another field. For example, a qualifier attached to a data byte may characterise it as either user data or a control signal.

Queue

A store or buffer for discrete items such as messages or packets which has the 'first in – first out' property.

Real-time

A real-time computer interacts with external events and must respond fast enough to meet the timing requirements of the whole system or application.

Regenerator

A regenerator takes a digital signal that has been distorted by transmission and produces a new signal with the correct shape, timing and amplitude of pulses restored.

Remote Job Entry (RJE)

Submission of a batch computing task to a distant computer via a data link or network. The job is entered at an 'RJE terminal'.

Response Time

The time between the last key depression by an operator and the receipt of the first character of the response. In a communication network the time is measured between completion of message input and the start of message output at the destination.

Routing Table

A table associated with a message or packet switch which states, for each destination, the preferred outgoing link. Also known as a directory. See also 'directory routing'.

Secondary Station

A secondary station in HDLC is directed by the primary station to perform actions associated with the HDLC procedure. It interprets commands received from the primary station and generates responses to these commands.

Selection

The process of indicating the number of the terminal being called. In the telephone network this is dialling. The signal 'ready to select' is an invitation to select the destination of the call.

Signal

The physical process used to carry information, which might be a voltage or current waveform, a pulse of light or a radio signal, for example. The word is also used to mean a short message as in 'control signal'.

Simplex Circuit

May mean either (1) a circuit used in one direction only or (2) a circuit used in either direction but not at the same time. It is perhaps better not to use the term but to use the word 'channel' for meaning (1) and 'half-duplex' for meaning (2).

Sink Tree

For a given destination (sink) the paths taken by packets sent to it from all points of the network form a tree when fixed routing tables are used. This is the sink tree.

SITA High Level Network

The Société Internationale de Télécommunications Aéronautiques operates a worldwide message network serving more than 150 airlines. Their high level network began operation in 1968 and offers a combination of packet and message switching. Conversational traffic (type A) requires transit times less than one second and is handled by packet switching. Message traffic (type B) is held in magnetic storage and can be retrieved later or, if the terminal is inaccessible, held for delivery when this becomes possible.

Slotted ALOHA

A packet broadcast system like ALOHA (q.v.) in which packets are timed to arrive at the centre in regular time slots, synchronised for all stations.

Space Division Switching

A method for switching circuits in which each connection through the switch takes a physically separate path.

Start–stop Envelope

A form of digital signal which is anisochronous and comprises a short group of signal elements, fixed in number and length. For example, 11 elements at 300 elements per second is a common format. The envelope can begin whenever the line is clear of the previous envelope and the timing starts with the first signal element, the start element. The following elements carry the information and the envelope concludes with a stop element or elements.

Store-and-Forward

The handling of messages or packets in a network by accepting them completely into storage before sending them forward to the next switch.

Stream Encryption

Encryption of a data stream (such as a stream of characters) with no hold-up of data in the system. Thus a single character can pass through the encryption, transmission and decryption processes without waiting for other characters. The encryption may depend on previous data in the stream.

Subnetwork (or Subnet)

The communication subsystem of a computer network. A public data communication service could function as the subnet.

Symmetric Flow

A flow pattern with a symmetric traffic matrix and, on each line of the network, an (s,t) flow component equal and opposite to the (t,s) flow component for each pair s,t of terminal points. Thus the overall flow is symmetric and so also is the routing of each flow component.

Synchronous Network

A network in which all the communication lines are synchronised to a common clock.

Teletext

The transmission of coded digital information as part of a television signal, which can be decoded and displayed as text and graphics on a special domestic receiver has become known as teletext. The teletext service provided by the British Broadcasting Corporation is called CEEFAX and that of the Independent Television Authority, ORACLE.

Telex Network

A switched public network with teleprinters as its terminals.

Terminal Handler

A part of a data communication network which serves simple, character stream terminals. It has other names such as terminal processor, terminal interface processor (TIP) in the ARPA network and packet assembler and disassembler (PAD) in public packet networks.

Time Division Multiplexing (TDM)

A multiplexing method in which time on the channel is allocated in turn to different subchannels. The allocation may be regular in a fixed cycle or frame, or it may be varied according to the needs of the subchannels.

Time Division Switching

A switching method for time division multiplexed channels. Data enters a switching stage in one time slot and emerges in another. For the switching of PCM channels, the time slots each contain one coded sample, such as 8 bits.

Time-out

In carrying out an agreed procedure, one party may have to take special action if it gets no response from the other within a specified time. This is an example of a time-out. The event on which the 'clock' is started must be specified, the length of time, the event(s) which will stop the clock and the action if the time expires.

Time-sharing

The sharing of a resource between several users by giving each of them access (a time slot) in succession. It usually refers to processor time-sharing.

Topology of Networks

The layout of the nodes (switches, concentrators) and lines of a network. The strict meaning refers to their pattern of connection but the word is used to include distance and geography.

Trace Packet

A special kind of packet which functions as a normal packet but because its 'trace bit' is set, causes a report to be sent to the network control centre for each switch it passes through.

Traffic Requirement Matrix

A matrix of which the (i,j) element denotes the amount of traffic originated at node i and destined for node j. The unit of traffic could be packets per second or calls per minute, depending on the type of network.

Transparency

A transmission path is said to be transparent to some property of the data stream if it passes it through unchanged. The word should be qualified by the property in question, for example 'bit sequence transparency'.

Transport Protocol

The basic level of protocol which is concerned with the transport of messages. The software which carried out this protocol was called a transport station in the Cyclades network and the term has been widely adopted.

Viewdata

The use of equipment based on teletext (q.v.) techniques to access databases through the telephone network, has been given the generic name of viewdata.

Virtual Call

A virtual circuit which is set up by a subscriber when required and released when no longer required.

Virtual Circuit

A facility in a packet-switched communication network in which packets passing between a pair of terminals are kept in sequence. Since this is a property of a circuit the two terminals are said to be connected by a virtual circuit. It can be a permanent virtual circuit or a virtual call.

Virtual Terminal

A conceptual terminal which is defined as a standard for the purpose of uniform handling of a variety of actual terminals. The virtual terminal may contain parameters to help it to match the real terminal. The mapping or conversion between the virtual terminal and a real one is possibly carried out in the terminal handler.

V-series Recommendations of CCITT

Recommendations for data transmission using the telephone network. Many of the recommendations deal with modems. The best known is V24 which lists the interchange circuits between a modem and its data terminal equipment.

X-series Recommendations of CCITT

Recommendations for new data networks. Examples are X1 on 'classes of service' and several definitions of DTE/DCE interfaces: X20 for start–stop terminals, X21 for synchronous terminals in circuit mode and X25 for packet mode terminals.

Index

Page number of glossary entries are in italic.